BRITISH PARTY POLI

BRITISH PARTY POLITICS, 1852–1886

ANGUS HAWKINS

First published in Great Britain 1998 by
MACMILLAN PRESS LTD
Houndmills, Basingstoke, Hampshire RG21 6XS and London
Companies and representatives throughout the world

A catalogue record for this book is available from the British Library.

ISBN 0–333–57080–4 hardcover
ISBN 0–333–57081–2 paperback

 First published in the United States of America 1998 by
ST. MARTIN'S PRESS, INC.,
Scholarly and Reference Division,
175 Fifth Avenue, New York, N.Y. 10010

ISBN 0–312–17537–X

Library of Congress Cataloging-in-Publication Data
Hawkins, Angus.
British party politics, 1852–1886 / Angus Hawkins.
p. cm. — (British history in perspective)
Includes bibliographical references (p.   ) and index.
ISBN 0–312–17537–X (cloth)
1. Great Britain—Politics and government—1837–1901.
2. Political parties—Great Britain—History—19th century.
I. Title. II. Series.
DA560.H338 1997
320.941—dc21   97–9963
                                                         CIP

This book is printed on paper suitable for recycling and made from fully managed and
sustained forest sources.

10   9   8   7   6   5   4   3   2   1
07   06   05   04   03   02   01   00   99   98

Printed in Hong Kong

CONTENTS

Contents

For Emma and Kate

ACKNOWLEDGEMENTS

In writing a survey text a large number of debts of various kinds are incurred which can only be inadequately, but no less gratefully, acknowledged. The comments of Michael Bentley, Tom Buchanan, Terry Jenkins, Bruce Kinzer, John Powell, John Prest, and the unfailingly supportive editorship of Jeremy Black were invaluable. My heavy debt to the scholarship of others is indicated in the notes. The unstinting efforts of Linda Cox saw the typescript through to completion. Valery Rose and Jocelyn Stockley expertly guided it through the press. My colleagues at Oxford and family enabled this project to be finished when much else demanded my time. I hope they find what follows worthy of their valued friendship and unfailing support.

INTRODUCTION

Between 1852 and 1886 the structure of British politics changed profoundly. Parliamentary government gave way to a modern party system. In the 1850s parliament stood as the prestigious centrepiece of British politics. Governments were made and unmade in the House of Commons. Parliament largely determined the national political agenda, instructed the nation on the great issues of the day, and provided the authoritative setting for party leaders to proclaim their policies. In the mid-1860s the liberal commentator James FitzJames Stephen described the House of Commons as 'the only real depository of all political power'.[1] Sovereignty, the absolute source of constitutional authority, rested in Westminster. Parliamentary sovereignty legitimised executive (cabinet) power. Walter Bagehot, in his celebrated study *The English Constitution* published in 1867, observed that the cabinet governed subject to the endorsement of the Commons. The 'efficient secret' of the English Constitution, according to Bagehot, was the nearly complete fusion of the executive and legislative powers in a government subject to parliament.[2] In this way Westminster was generally seen to check the dangers of both despotism – an arbitrary executive – and democracy – a wayward populace. Parliament's relations with the constituencies, extra-parliamentary organisations, electors and the nation beyond were loose, sporadic, and often informal. Parliamentary elections and the rituals of constituency contests were more a function of local dynamics and provincial allegiances than national imperatives. It was within Westminster that the selection of governments, the scrutiny of official policy and the definition of the national need occurred.

This was part of the Whig achievement of the years after 1830. For the 36-year period between 1830 and 1866 Whigs were in power, alone or in coalition, for all but just under nine years. They saw themselves as the natural party of government. They wished for the increasingly diverse and complex social interests being advanced by economic and intellectual progress to be balanced and integrated, the rule of law preserved, liberties safeguarded, and social order, protecting property and wealth, to be maintained. Central to these aspirations stood Westminster as the authoritative arena of national politics. It was in parliament that political ills were cured, remedial reforms were passed, the wisdom of the nation was expressed and governments were chosen. All this required parliamentary parties sufficiently cohesive to withstand the Royal prerogative (the Crown's ability to choose the government), yet sufficiently fluid to ensure that the Commons, not the electorate, was sovereign. It was these constitutional assumptions that framed the party politics of the 1850s. They formed the foundation of mid-Victorian parliamentary government.

Between 1867 and 1884 the structure of parliamentary government was dismantled and the sufficiency of parliament challenged. By 1886 the contrasting assumptions and values of a modern party system were supplanting the axioms of Whig parliamentary government. Parties themselves, rather than parliament, now exercised that sovereignty which legitimised government authority. Governments were becoming the product of electoral mandate, with parties themselves possessing increasing autonomy. The power of choosing who should hold office was passing from the Commons directly to the electorate as organised by mass national parties. As William Gladstone, Liberal leader and four times premier, declared momentously in a speech at Greenwich in January 1874: 'That authority which was in 1868 amply confided by the nation to the Liberal party and its leaders . . . can in no way be so legitimately and effectually restored as by an appeal to the people.'[3] The following year it was recognised that 'the floor of the House [of Commons] has ceased to be the exclusive, or even the most effective, standing-point from which to address the true rulers of the country'.[4] The necessary

Protestant nation, but she was no longer largely an Anglican one. Yet what was even more striking, particularly in urban areas, was the increasing number of those who did not attend religious services at all. As far as can be judged from the 1851 religious census roughly 40% of the population of England and Wales attended a religious service on Sunday. Such statistics deeply shocked contemporary educated opinion. In London only 25% of the population regularly attended religious services, while a higher than average number attended church or chapel in rural areas. By the 1880s institutional religion was a diminishing force in many people's lives. The growth of religious pluralism and the advance of secularism began transforming religion from being a collective social force into a private matter of individual faith and conviction.

By the 1870s and 1880s traditional communities were finding themselves under growing economic and social pressure. Old ties of affiliation and obligation were being eroded. The historic vocabulary of estates, degrees, orders and ranks was becoming out-dated. Notions of social status, as much as being dependent upon region or religion, were becoming increasingly defined in terms of class. By 1900 the subtly nuanced hierarchical graduations of pre-industrial society were giving way to class distinctions, reinforced at work, in the growing prestige of the professions, in schooling, housing, pronunciation, and through recreation. Rural radicalism and working-class activism fleshed out new social forces. Communities of faith or locality were becoming subsumed by affiliations of class. In the 1860s religion provided much of the force behind popular political activity. Public affairs were defined in the language of moral debate. By the 1890s religion was giving way to class as a major impetus to popular activism.

The social, technological, and economic transformations experienced by Victorian society accompanied the constitutional transition from mid-Victorian parliamentary government to the modern party system. The conception of the state became broader as the relationship of parliament to a more complex political nation was redefined. The scope of government was enlarged and the function of political parties expanded. In 1867 Bagehot declared that 'the whole life of English politics is in the action and reaction between the ministry and the parliament'.[6] By the 1880s it was clear that the life of British politics occupied a wider and more varied terrain. The nature of that structural transition is a major theme in what follows. None the less, against this theme of profound change, it is helpful to note two important and consistent features of Victorian politics. First, the importance, to all parties, of the past as a source of legitimacy in the present. Secondly, the degree to which parties with widely differing aims embraced constitutional strategies.

The idiom of Victorian politics was rooted in memories of earlier political struggles. Contemporary debate was steeped in a pervasive sense of history, all parties carrying with them the legitimacy of a revered past; albeit that these partisan pasts were as distinctive as the contemporary aims they served. Evocations of Magna Carta, the Petition of Right of 1628, social mythologies based upon clashes between Anglo-Saxons and Normans, or references to Oliver Cromwell, John Milton, or the Whig champions of the 1688 Glorious Revolution gave a vivid potency to Victorian political rhetoric. Victorian Whigs presented themselves as the trustees of the Glorious Revolution which had tamed arbitrary kingship. Under Benjamin Disraeli in the 1870s Conservatives talked of protecting the authentic and ancient institutions of Britain against cosmopolitan Whiggism; while Victorian radicals called for the recovery of the ancient freedoms and liberties of the people, which had been usurped by a foreign aristocracy after 1066. The past gave force and meaning to present struggles. The Victorian sensibility was profoundly shaped by past myths. It was, therefore, entirely appropriate that the brand new Palace of Westminster, completed in the 1850s, was a stylistic revival of an earlier Gothic age.

Constitutionalism was also part of the idiom of Victorian politics. Conservatives, Liberals, radicals, and others articulated their aspirations through the language of legal entitlements bestowed by parliament. The franchise, parliamentary sovereignty, and the nature of political representation – the relationship between Westminster and the political nation – framed their aims and policies. Republican calls for the abolition of the monarchy, demands for a socialist redistribution of wealth, and the challenge women's rights made to an exclusively male conception of the political community were marginalised. Advocates of violent revolution remained, from 1852 to 1886, at the periphery of mainstream politics; violent revolution most commonly during this period being associated with the emergence of the nationalist Fenian movement during the 1860s in Ireland. The constitutional tradition, however, focused debate on who comprised the legitimate political nation? Who was within and who outside the pale of the constitution? Historical empathy requires that what Victorian politicians themselves took seriously later historians should also take seriously.

What follows, therefore, is an attempt to reassert the importance of understanding the constitutional context of Victorian politics. Chapters 1 and 8 can be read as complementary essays on the changing structure of party politics between 1852 and 1886. Between these constitutional essays stands a narrative of party politics during this period comprising Chapters 2 to 7. Not that one would wish to revive an arid legalistic analysis of constitutional mechanisms. But an appreciation of the *structures* of political life and the *function* of the electorate or of parliamentary parties is doubly necessary. First, in order to help historical understanding of the period. Secondly, because it was how Victorian politicians themselves understood the context of their actions.

The shift towards a more democratic party system and the gradual abandonment of parliamentary government was not greeted with unanimous celebration. In 1896 the historian W. H. Lecky declared that 'it does not appear to me that the world has ever seen a better constitution than England enjoyed between the Reform Bill of 1832 and the Reform Bill of 1867'.[7] Nevertheless, by the 1880s there was emerging a recognisably modern national political framework: the basis of what would be a much-vaunted British party system. It gave an increasing majority of adult men and (after 1918) women a direct formal voice in national politics. Party organisation promised strong and stable government, defined by principle or programme, based upon electoral supremacy. It suggested that parliament reflected, rather than defined, political concerns. It determined the form of those democratic precepts which were to frame political debate in Britain throughout the twentieth century. Popular sovereignty, as defined by national political parties, replaced the sufficiency of parliament as the bedrock of constitutional thought.

1

PARLIAMENTARY GOVERNMENT

The triumph of the Reform Act of 1832 consists not so much in the recognition of certain abstract principles, or in the readjustment of the franchise, as in the fact that for a quarter of a century Parliamentary Government has been established in this country with greater purity and efficiency than it ever possessed before; that during this period innumerable measures of unequalled public importance have been adopted in rapid succession by the legislature; and that while discord has shaken, and despotism subdued, almost every other nation in Europe, the people of England have never been more heartily attached to their institutions, or more happily at peace amongst themselves.

This eulogy appeared in the Whig *Edinburgh Review* of July 1858.[1] It complemented the confident declaration made the same year by Lord Grey, son of the premier who passed the 1832 Reform Act, 'that Great Britain stands distinguished among the nations of the earth for the prosperity it has enjoyed, and for the social progress it has made during the time it has been under a Parliamentary Government'.[2] Grey felt obliged to exclude Ireland from this sanguine state of affairs. But it remained, for him, self-evident that by the 1850s England, Wales and Scotland were enjoying a social stability, economic prosperity and political harmony to be envied by the rest of the world.

There was good reason for patriotic satisfaction. The middle decades of the nineteenth century saw England, carried along by the momentum of industrialisation, becoming the 'workshop of the world'. Industrial investment was at a peak. Business profits were rising and total national production was growing. A buoyant mood of celebration infused the Great Exhibition, displaying Britain's technical and industrial achievements, held at the Crystal Palace in 1851. Scotland too was drawing benefits from the empire and an economic boom. Unlike France in 1789 and 1830, and most of Europe in 1848, Britain had not been traumatised by revolution. Since 1745, it was claimed, peaceful adaptation and reform had pre-empted violent political upheaval; though here again Ireland had to be carefully excluded from the picture.

Historians debate the variety of reasons why Britain avoided revolution during the nineteenth century. But most mid-Victorian Englishmen saw it as a simple proof of the virtue and resilience of their constitution. Parliamentary government checked the evils of tyranny and mob rule, secured the rule of law, safeguarded liberty and provided government with authority. It located true liberty at the precise point of balance between arbitrary government and anarchy. In the words of the *Edinburgh Review* 'parliamentary government includes all that is most essential to the mechanism of the State and to the maintenance of freedom'.[3] There were defects, of course, but unhampered by a written constitution the system was self-regulatory and sufficiently flexible as to be able to reform itself, as for example in 1832. Parliament was ensconced, by the early 1850s, in Sir Charles Barry's splendid new Gothic Revival Palace of Westminster; its Victoria Tower, upon its completion in 1858, being the tallest secular building in the world. The Lords first met in Barry's new chamber in 1847. The Commons met in their new lower chamber in 1852. In this setting Britain's parliamentary government stood as a venerated model of sophisticated, historically evolved, statecraft. The British political genius for peaceful and well-ordered progress was embodied in the prestige of parliament. As one modern historian has remarked: 'The British constitution is unwritten, but not unbuilt.'[4]

The Nature of Parliamentary Government

In his 1858 essay *Parliamentary Government Considered with Reference to Reform*, Lord Grey provided a succinct definition of the mid-Victorian constitution. The distinguishing characteristic of parliamentary government was that the former executive power of the Crown now belonged to ministers, as members of the cabinet, responsible to parliament. The cabinet was answerable most importantly to the House of Commons, whose proceedings the government had to be able generally to guide. So it was parliament that, in practice, provided an administration with the authority to govern, even though by convention ministers remained servants of the Crown, appointed by the monarch. Grey outlined the advantages of this system. The close interaction of executive and legislature promoted the integration of the different powers of the state. The confrontation and possible deadlock inherent in a system based upon a distinct 'separation of powers', often advocated by writers on the constitution in the eighteenth century, was avoided. Bagehot saw 'the efficient secret' of the British constitution in the nearly complete fusion of executive and legislative powers, with the cabinet, answerable to parliament as the connecting link. The cabinet had to submit to both Houses the measures it wished adopted. So parliament controlled the executive without directly interfering in it. All the cabinet's actions were open to censure in parliament, where the executive was called upon to defend its conduct. This meant, Grey concluded, that 'parliament, and especially the House of Commons, had become not only the authority which virtually decides the contest for power among different candidates for it, but also the arena in which the contest is mainly carried on'. In short, the essence of parliamentary government was that it was to Westminster that government was accountable and within Westminster that governments were selected.

Bagehot, in his own famous subsequent study of parliamentary government, confirmed Grey's argument that the single most important duty of the Commons was the election of the executive. The Commons represented the true interests of the nation and expressed the matured opinion of the people. It provided

11

instruction and example. It initiated, discussed and passed legislation. The responsibility of parliament to educate and uplift public debate, from the splendid and imposing setting of the new Palace of Westminster, moreover, was seen as more important than the requirement to pass legislation. But all these aspects of Commons activity were, as Bagehot declared, subordinate to its elective function.

The fate of governments between 1835 and 1867 illustrates the point. The resignation of Sir Robert Peel's Conservative ministry in 1835 followed six Commons defeats in six weeks. The fall of the subsequent Whig government, led by Lord Melbourne, in 1841 was occasioned by a Commons vote of want of confidence. Peel's second ministry, in the aftermath of the Corn Law crisis, ended upon a Commons defeat on an Irish coercion bill in June 1846. Lord John Russell's Whig government was ejected from office in February 1852 by a majority of hostile Commons votes. Later that same year a Conservative government resigned over a Commons budget defeat. The political embarrassments of the Crimean War produced a crushing Commons defeat and resignation for Lord Aberdeen's coalition in January 1855. The ministry that followed, led by Lord Palmerston, was brought down in February 1858 by an adverse Commons vote over the Orsini crisis. Lord Derby's second Conservative administration resigned following defeat on a Commons motion of confidence in June 1859. Liberal government was then ended in June 1866 when an Adullamite parliamentary reform amendment placed the ministry in a Commons minority.

The practical moral was clear, governments were made and unmade in the House of Commons. Cabinets could no longer, as in the eighteenth century, rely upon the monarch and the Crown's ability, through patronage, to return a favourable House of Commons. Party was a necessary safeguard against exactly such a corrupting reliance on the prerogative. In Bagehot's words, 'the House of Commons lives in a state of potential choice; at any moment it can choose a ruler and dismiss a ruler. And therefore party is inherent in it, is bone of its bone, and breath of its breath.'[5] Yet, at the same time, preserving parliamentary sovereignty demanded the exclusion of any executive authority derived from two powerful rival sources, not only the monarchy, but also the people. If parliamentary parties were not to some extent fluid then only a dissolution could prompt a change of ministry, the selection of a government becoming simply a matter of direct electoral mandate. Political associations had to be stable enough to fulfil the needs of ministerial existence, yet loose enough to leave open the possibilities of a ministerial defeat without a dissolution. Without parties of some cohesion the prerogative would rule. Without parties experiencing some instability the people would rule.

Again the history of parliaments between 1841 and 1868 illustrates the point. The parliament of 1841, the product of a Conservative electoral triumph, brought down a Conservative government in 1846. The parliament of 1847 brought down a Whig administration in 1852. The parliament of 1852 engaged in the downfall of a Conservative government and the Aberdeen coalition. The parliament of 1857, conventionally seen as the result of a personal electoral victory for Palmerston, threw Palmerston out of power in 1858. The parliament of 1859 forced a Conservative government to resign and the parliament of 1865, following Liberal electoral success, brought down a Liberal government in 1866. Each of the six parliaments elected between 1841 and 1868 brought down at least one ministry, if not two, before its dissolution. Again, the practical moral was clear, governments were not directly assured of power by electoral success. This was the work of parties of a kind intrinsic to parliamentary government, safeguarding the sovereignty of Westminster; what Bagehot dramatically described as 'the incessant tyranny of parliament'. Parties in mid-Victorian parliaments made and unmade governments, scrutinised policy, debated legislation and defined the national political agenda. Yet they were flexible associations born of voluntary subordination not unconditional obedience. Enforcing party uniformity too strongly only drove away men of talent: 'a party could not be disciplined like a regiment'.[6] As the Conservative leader Lord Derby described them in 1854, parliamentary parties were made up of those 'who are in the habit of acting together'.[7] Precisely what was absent was those modern requirements for party government adopted by the late nineteenth century, such as centralised party bureaucracies and extensive constituency organisation enlisting a mass membership. What did cohere parliamentary parties of the 1850s as voluntary associations of like-minded colleagues, was a social setting, constitutional understanding, and a deference intrinsic to the mid-Victorian political world.

The political, intellectual, literary, and fashionable elites of mid-Victorian society were at once predominantly based in London and intimately interrelated. Indeed, in the drawing rooms of the great hostesses, at dinner parties and in the clubs around Pall Mall, these elites merged to form, as the novelist Anthony Trollope described it in *Phineas Redux* (1874), 'a single special set that dominates all other sets in our English world'. Other contemporaries referred to the 'upper ten thousand'. Politicians, churchmen, academics, authors, and other shapers of high culture inhabited the same social circles. The intellectual unity of mid-Victorian culture complemented this social intimacy. This cultural unity was represented by the heyday, between the 1850s and 1880s, of that 'higher journalism' contained in general periodical reviews such as the *Quarterly Review, Cornhill Magazine, Edinburgh Review, Fraser's Magazine, Westminster Review*, and *Saturday Review*. Here politics, literature, theology, mathematics, biography, history, contemporary fiction, the classics, science and philosophy, were all addressed as of immediate interest to the sophisticated, intelligent, general reader.

The vast majority of MPs, through membership of Clubs such as the Carlton, Reform, Brooks's, Travellers, or the Athenaeum, attendance at large parties given by Lady Palmerston or Lady Waldegrave, and invitations to dinner parties given during the recess, inhabited a closely-knit social and intellectual world reinforcing political ties and shared opinions. In 1859 *The Times* described parliament as 'the first Club in the world'. The Commons was, as Palmerston stated to his fellow MPs in 1852, above all, 'an assembly of gentlemen'. In 1861 Lord Stanley noted it was 'curious to see how entirely the House regards itself as a club'. Similarly, the radical journalist E. M. Whitty observed of the Commons in 1852: 'The House is a great theatre, with its green-room as well as its stage. It is a great club, all in all, in itself and to itself, with its own heroes, its own way of thought, and its own way of talk.'[8] Reputations made outside Westminster were no guarantee of success within the Commons. Parliament functioned as an intimate specialised community with its own conventions, expectations, requirements, preoccupations, tastes and peculiarities.

Easy and informal social familiarity and the centrality of Westminster to the orbit of this governing elite obviated the need for formal organisational ties. The radical MP Sir John Trelawny observed in 1860: 'It is one main element in House of Commons life that opinions undergo a vast deal of preliminary discussion in the form of mere conversation between small knots of 2 or more. Few would believe, without experience, the number of speeches made in this manner.'[9] Thus asperities were softened, flawed arguments refuted and opinions modified. Acting together in parliament was a habit and conviction which emerged naturally out of a wider social association. The fact that the great hostesses of the London season, such as Lady Palmerston, Lady Salisbury, Lady Waldegrave and Lady Clarendon, were the wives of prominent politicians reinforced the point. This was what Benjamin Disraeli in his novel *Endymion* (1880) described as 'the fierce competition of inexhaustible private entertainments'. Election to parliament brought with it access to the metropolitan community of leading mid-Victorian minds. A man could gain, Bagehot observed, far more social standing by entering parliament than he could gain in any other way. In his novel *Can You Forgive Her?* (1865) Trollope declared it 'the highest and most legitimate pride of an Englishman to have the letters MP written after his name. No selection from the alphabet . . . confers so fair an honour.' This was an intimate world into which even provincial middle-class radicals, such as John Bright, found themselves drawn. Gladstone noticed how 'the fervour of radical neophytes . . . cooled down under the influence of a prolonged sojourn in the parliamentary atmosphere'.[10]

The Whig ideal of parliamentary parties based upon voluntary subordination, rather than unconditional obedience, was dependent upon a wider social intimacy operating through Clubland, the London 'season', and invitations to shooting parties and fishing expeditions in the country. The vast majority of MPs were products of the leading public schools, Eton, Harrow, Winchester, Westminster, and Rugby, at which friendships and acquaintances were forged, strengthened by rites of passage through Oxford and Cambridge Universities. In parliaments between 1832 and 1867, moreover, over one-third of MPs were, on average, members of aristocratic families. Over 70 per cent of MPs in the parliament of 1841–7 were descendants of peers, baronets or gentry families.[11] The aristocratic mores of this world reinforced deferential attitudes and instincts. Title and birth remained an invaluable asset to political ambition. These mores also complemented a particular ideal of independence that underlay the understanding of parties as voluntary associations. An MP should not be the powerless pawn of party, but a consenting participant in common action. A secure income and status, independent of political reward, it was argued, safeguarded personal integrity. Judgement became the product of conscience and principle, untainted by self-interested gain. MPs received no salary and bore the cost of election largely themselves. In this way, it was claimed, MPs could rise above narrow sectional interest, in recognition of the broader national need. Declarations of independence were often made in mid-Victorian hustings speeches. What such statements conveyed was not criticism of party in principle, but the conviction that party allegiance could not be assumed, bought, or coerced.

Party cohesion was, therefore, also dependent upon personal loyalty to the party leader: a sense of personal loyalty, often reinforced by social attentions, that Lord Palmerston, for example, successfully exploited during the 1850s and 1860s. This had to be so, given the limited formal organisational resources available to a party leader in keeping his parliamentary supporters together. In 1853 Lord Stanley noted that MPs for commercial boroughs, middle-class Liberals, were the most conscientious attenders of divisions, followed by government ministers and then members of the Irish Brigade. Country gentlemen, as a group, were rarely in the chamber after dinner, except for critical divisions. While in opposition Disraeli complained of the difficulty of getting his backbenchers to attend to business during the hunting season.[12]

By the 1850s a 'whipper-in', or 'Whip' as he was gradually becoming known (appointed Patronage Secretary of the Treasury), operated with usually two assistants (normally appointed as Junior Lords of the Treasury). From 1832, and particularly after 1841, MPs functioning as Whips increasingly acted as tellers in important divisions, replacing individual ministers with a direct departmental interest in the vote. Getting government business through the division lobbies became the responsibility of the ministerial Whips and by the 1850s they were serving as tellers in 60–70 per cent of Commons divisions. Yet communication between the Whips and the party leader, though crucial and constant, was discreet, leaving the Whips as a powerful, yet shadowy, presence in events. Barry saw no need to allocate rooms to the Whips in his design for the new Palace of Westminster as they had no official status. Whips were, Gladstone observed, 'the medium everybody knows, but nobody names'.[13] The radically-minded William White, doorkeeper of the House of Commons, referred to the 'mysterious arts and powerful incantations' of the Whips.[14]

Chosen for their social amiability and acknowledged integrity, as much as for their political talent, long-serving Whips, such as Sir William Jolliffe for the Conservatives and W. G. Hayter and Henry Brand for the Liberals, had not only the lobby, tea-room and smoking-room of Westminster, but also the Clubs and the houses of the great society hostesses as their natural habitat. Notes to MPs from the Whips were studiedly solicitous, in contrast to modern curt summonses, made not in the name of the party but for 'the welfare of the country'. This had to be so given that there were very few sanctions that the Whips could impose on wayward MPs. Unlike their modern counterparts, mid-Victorian Whips could only persuade or cajole their charges, not drive them. MPs owed their seats to local standing and their own financial resources, not to the endorsement of a central party bureaucracy. Whips worked hard to ensure a good attendance at the beginning of each session. The patient and persistent persuasion of individual MPs to attend important divisions during the remainder of the session, required official circulars to be supplemented by private letters and continual private conversations. The effectiveness of the Whips, therefore, was crucially dependent upon their individual character and reputation, as well as their personal credibility in claiming to represent the party leaders' wishes. The dispersal of patronage, honours, and appointments when in office was one of the resources they could use to persuade the reluctant. But great care had to be taken not to affront or alienate the recalcitrant. Thus was fleshed out a Whig ideal of parties as virtuous and free associations of MPs, fulfilling their essential function within the framework of parliamentary government. The essential nature of parliamentary leadership was the careful building of coalitions and the diligent preservation of alliances.

The House of Lords was not a silent partner in this parliamentary process. Two prime ministers of the 1850s, Lords Derby and Aberdeen, governed from the Upper House. Moreover, certain cabinet positions, such as the Foreign Secretaryship, were more often than not held by members of the House of Lords. Lord Clarendon in 1853–8, 1865–6, and 1868–70, Lord Granville in 1870–4 and 1880–5, Lord Malmesbury in 1852 and 1858–9, Lord Russell in 1861–5, Lord Derby in 1874–8 and Lord Salisbury in 1878–80 and 1885–6 all held the Foreign Secretaryship. The aristocratic mores of mid-Victorian political culture inevitably gave peers a considerable influence over events. Formally, the Lords possessed the constitutional authority to block, amend, or reject legislation coming up from the Commons. Yet, clearly it was in the Commons that the fate of governments was decided. The ability of the Lords to block legislation championed by the Commons and apparently supported by a body of popular opinion was seriously checked during the 1831–2 reform crisis, when William IV was required by the government to threaten the creation of a large number of peers in order to secure passage of a reform bill. Thereafter, parliamentary leaders assiduously sought to avoid confrontations between the Upper and Lower Houses; a contest of authority which ultimately, it was felt, the Lords would lose.

Party feeling in the Lords was less intense than in the Commons. After 1846 Conservative and Peelite peers found it easier to act together than their bitterly divided colleagues in the Commons. Attendance was more lax in the Lords than the Lower House. About 70 of the 635 temporal peers who sat in the Lords between 1846 and 1865 were active debaters conscientious in their attendance. By contrast, according to Lord Stanley, son of the Conservative leader Lord Derby, in the early 1850s about half of the Commons were regular attenders contributing to debate.[15] Exceptions in the Lords occurred when, as with the debate about life peerages in 1856, the Lords' own privileges became the question at issue or during set-piece debates following the Royal Address. At other times the challenge facing Conservative and Whig–Liberal Whips in the Upper House was as much ensuring attendance as securing allegiance. This was particularly true at the end of sessions when a large body of legislation, delayed in Commons debate, came up to the Lords, with peers given scant time to discuss it. This legislative log jam dogged the Lords during the 1850s and throughout the following decades.

After 1852 Derby was fortunate in having the judicious Lord Colville as Conservative Whip in the Lords. Colville possessed good sense, considerable knowledge and much tact. Similarly, Lord Bessborough effectively served Lord Lansdowne, the courteous Whig leader in the Lords until 1855. Thereafter, Bessborough worked closely with Lansdowne's Whig–Liberal successor Lord Granville. Colville and Bessborough headed a structure of party discipline similar to that operating in the Commons, centred on the Conservative Carlton Club and the Club favoured by Whig–Liberal peers, Brooks's. Their Lordships, moreover, enjoyed a facility unavailable in the Commons, that of voting by proxy, as well as the system of pairing used in both Houses. Yet it was also significant that Derby, while prime minister and enjoying a Lords majority in 1858, was anxious to avoid a dangerous confrontation between Lords and Commons over the admission of Jews to parliament. He devoted considerable energies to securing a compromise settlement between the two Houses. It was clear that the Commons, seen to embody legitimate national opinion, held the power to make and unmake governments. When attempting to put together a Conservative government in 1851, Derby, despite the bulk of his experienced colleagues being in the Lords, was clear that at least eight members of the cabinet should be in the Commons. Failure to secure even six credible ministers from the Commons destroyed his hopes of forming a ministry. Commons opinion was what mattered most.

Some historians have seen in the 1850s the 'disintegration of parties', the 'decay of parties', 'political chaos', executive weakness and a decline into 'the natural incoherence of politics'.[16] The period 1846 to 1867, it is argued, after the emergence of a coherent Commons two-party alignment between 1832 and 1846, suffered chronic party instability, eventually remedied by the hardy resilience of parties after 1867. Yet such a view must be rejected on a number of grounds. Mid-Victorian parliamentary parties were not nearly so fragmented or chaotic as such a view suggests; albeit that the flux in non-Conservative party connection between 1855 and 1859 assumed at times a particularly acute form. Analyses of Commons division-lobby voting shows, by and large, a steady clustering of party support, though both parties tended to fray along their progressive fringes. Most frequently it was the radicals who broke away from Whig and Liberal colleagues, while the Conservative party, in particular, remained a largely cohesive body, returning loyal Commons votes at critical divisions throughout the 1850s and 1860s.[17] This was a more remarkable achievement given the long years of opposition which the Conservatives experienced during this period and the difficulty of getting many Conservative backbenchers to attend to more mundane Commons business.

Mid-Victorian parties only appear disorganised if subjected to the inappropriate and rigid demands of late nineteenth-century standards. They did not employ centralised bureaucracies, extensive constituency organisation and mass membership, and did not generate the expectation that MPs should vote and speak as a bloc, thus demanding unconditional obedience in pursuit of ideological unanimity. Such expectations belong to the 1900s not the 1850s. It is true that in the parliament of 1852–7 twenty-five

Commons amendments to ministerial legislation were carried against the government Whips. In the parliament of 1859–65 twenty-seven such amendments were passed. But by the parliament of 1874–80 only one amendment to government legislation was carried against the ministerial Whips.[18] Yet to dub mid-nineteenth-century parties 'immature' is the anachronistic condescension of posterity.

Placed in their appropriate constitutional context, what we see during the 1850s and 1860s are the healthy workings of loosely affiliated parties in Westminster of a kind intrinsic to Whig parliamentary government. They were largely cohesive – though not rigid – associations of like-minded MPs, based upon voluntary subordination, recognising a degree of independence, making and unmaking governments. As common as straight party voting in divisions, in the mid-Victorian period, was the phenomenon of the bulk of both parties joining together in opposition to the extreme wings of either the Conservative or Liberal parties. Most frequently this occurred when radicals found themselves opposed by the vast majority of MPs.[19] Throughout the period 1832 to 1867 both the Conservative and Whig/Liberal leaderships would often combine to put down either Ultra Tory or radical Commons proposals; moderate men coming together to subdue dangerous extremism.

Yet such behaviour was not inconsistent with a belief in fluid party allegiances that, upon critical occasions, could be galvanised in order to determine who should hold office. It is true that at times during the 1850s, because of the rivalry between Russell and Palmerston, radical independence, and Peelite aversion to Palmerston, the party connection among non-Conservatives became particularly unstable. Most noticeably this occurred in 1858 when many Whigs and Liberals feared collective action was becoming impossible. But this was an episode of extreme uncertainty within a party system that assumed a degree of fluidity. Party alignment was never rigid. Between 1861 and 1863 the constitutional authority Sir Thomas Erskine May, a future clerk to the House of Commons, in his *Constitutional History of England since the Accession of George III*, in three volumes, provided a panegyric on the theme of party.

We acknowledge, with gratitude, that we owe to party most of our rights and liberties. We recognise in the fierce contentions of our ancestors, the conflict of great principles, and the final triumph of freedom. We glory in the eloquence and noble sentiment which the rivalry of contending statesmen has inspired. We admire the courage with which power has been resisted; and the manly resolution and persistence by which popular rights have been established. We observe that, while the undue influence of the crown has been restrained, democracy has been also held in check.[20]

By steering the constitution between the Charybdis of the prerogative and the multi-headed Scylla of the populace, fluid parties in Westminster were the essential guardians of parliamentary sovereignty.

This helps us to understand important aspects of mid-Victorian elections: in particular, the number of constituencies which were uncontested. In the 1847 general election 368, over 55%, of a total of 658 Commons seats were uncontested. In the 1857 election 328 seats were uncontested, while in 1859 a total of 379, or 58%, of all Commons seats remained uncontested.[21] Clearly general elections were *not* a simple plebiscitary verdict directly passed on the current executive by the political nation. Such judgement was passed in parliament, not on the hustings. The Commons was a deliberative assembly, not a gathering of delegates. At no general election between 1835 and 1867 did more than a thousand candidates stand for election to the 658 seats in the Commons. Elections were less the occasion for the people to pass judgement on the government, than the opportunity for the wide variety of interests comprising the political community to be represented. Because of this, Grey argued in 1858, the anomalies and irregularities in the composition of constituencies and possession of the vote should not be erased in the name of democratic uniformity. MPs should owe their seats to various kinds of influence, not just to the collective choice of large bodies of electors. It was important, Grey maintained, that unpopular as well as popular opinions be heard within the House. The Commons, possessing a near fusion of executive and legislative power, had within it the potential for tyranny. If the Commons became merely the creature of a direct popular will it would become simply a channel for the democratic tyranny of the majority, unpopular or minority views being ignored or persecuted. It was crucial, Grey felt, for the status of the Commons as a sovereign deliberative assembly that anomalies in the representative system be preserved.

Parliament's relations with the constituencies and the electorate, therefore, were loose, sporadic and informal; largely a function of local influence and energies. After 1832, for example, a number of Conservative Associations were established in the country. But they were primarily the result of local initiatives. As Robert Stewart has observed, after surveying the growth of Conservative constituency organisations prior to 1867:

> To be elected a mid-nineteenth century candidate nearly always needed some money of his own and the backing of influential men in the constituency. He was not, as the modern candidate is, *primarily* the representative of a potential government. In those circumstances the Conservative Associations were mostly a gloss on the structure of politics. They did not provide a link between the parliamentary party and the electorate. They did not, like modern parties, carry the element of government into the constituencies. Despite their existence, party, as an institution, remained a parliamentary creature.[22]

Electoral politics remained essentially a matter of local allegiances, particularly in those older constituencies that had existed before 1832. Electoral contests were symbolised in traditional, often idiosyncratic, local emblems of colours, clubs and flowers which varied widely throughout the different regions of the country. This infused the elements of carnival and ceremony, involving both electors and unenfranchised, which comprised the robust noisy rituals of voter registration, nomination hustings and canvassing, culminating in the public polling of votes and the chairing of the successful candidate. Public meetings, private dinners, treating and toasting, bands and processions, as well as incidents involving beer and brawls, accompanied the addresses, posters and hand bills conveying the platform of individual candidates with their differing emblems of flags, colours, flowers and banners. Rituals, both mock and official, often embraced intense local rivalries enlisting non-electors in boisterous public demonstrations. These were often activities from which it was prudent for the candidates to distance themselves. 'The brisk election day . . . and its humours', the writer George Meredith observed in his political novel of the 1850s *Beauchamp's Career*, 'are those of the badly-managed Christmas pantomime without a columbine – old tricks no graces.'[23]

Party identities in the constituencies had no fixed form, but were usually the product of long-standing local affiliations. Indeed, the strength of local feeling and pride fuelled a strong suspicion of centrally imposed party organisation. Electors voted for men as much as parties. In the election of 1857, for example, roughly one in five electors in English constituencies with two votes split their votes between different parties. For general elections between 1832 and 1867 an average of 14 per cent of electors of this kind in English constituencies split their votes between two parties.[24] This warns us against reading a direct causal relation between party activity in the constituencies, suspicious of outside control, and party dynamics in parliament. The 1832 Reform Act did bring to some constituencies more disciplined partisan voting than had existed before. This was aided by the very frequency of general elections during the 1830s, in 1832, 1835, 1837, and again in 1841. But the purpose of parties in the constituencies was to win local elections; no more and no less than this. This was the boisterous, often shady world inhabited by local party agents, returning officers, neighbourhood committees and political clubs. Where contests regularly occurred party organisation could be expected to be active and disciplined. In *Beauchamp's Career* Meredith memorably describes a lively contested election in which the radical candidate canvasses from door to door, 'like a cross between a postman delivering a bill and a beggar craving alms', where 'patiently he attempts the extraction of the vote, as little boys pick periwinkles with a pin'.[25]

It would be a mistake, however, to see party organisation in some parts of the country as automatically leading to increasingly disciplined parties in parliament. The relation between the electorate and the Commons was much more complex than such an anachronistic reading allows. Rather, in the Whig view, constituency and Commons operated as two distinct, if both important, levels of political activity, with local organisational necessities not directly constraining national political possibilities. During the 1850s and 1860s this perspective did become increasingly difficult to sustain. A burgeoning provincial press with an intense interest in parliamentary affairs, the gradual growth of constituency organisation, and the presence of militant pressure groups with specific aims and demands, put mounting pressure on such Whiggish distinctions. Within the constituencies themselves partisan affiliation became tighter. Nevertheless, the status of parliament as an autonomous assembly argues against reading an easy or direct causal connection between partisan intensity on the hustings and party alignment in Westminster.

The Whig view of the constitution was established as conventional wisdom after 1830. By the 1850s and 1860s Grey and Bagehot used it as orthodoxy. But it had been Edmund Burke in the 1770s, as the publicist of the Rockinghamite Whigs, who originally argued for the virtue and legitimacy of parliamentary parties as the basis of both government and opposition. When bad men combined, the good must associate. In this way MPs, voluntarily acting together in good faith upon shared ideals, could constrain a potentially arbitrary prerogative. At the same time, the Commons, through calm deliberation, became the forum, raised above popular and volatile clamour, in which true national interests were discerned. Burke's doctrine became the basis upon which Whigs acted as a party during the long years of opposition from 1783 to 1830. Isolated from power, yet surviving in a brilliant intellectual milieu, located in the salons of Lords Holland and Lansdowne, the Whigs refined a constitutional doctrine containing the principles of parliamentary government. The early editors of the *Edinburgh Review*, Francis Jeffrey, Francis Horner and Sydney Smith, as well as Henry Brougham, reissuing lines learnt at the feet of Dugald Stewart at Edinburgh

University, promulgated the doctrine publicly prior to 1830. Party reinforced the natural authority of an enlightened aristocracy and the operation of legitimate influence. Thus the popular will was channelled through a hierarchical social order into the calm and rational deliberation of parties in parliament. In the pages of the *Edinburgh Review* in 1810, Jeffrey observed that the Whigs stood between two 'violent and pernicious factions – the courtiers, who are almost for arbitrary powers – and the democrats who are almost for revolution and republicanism'.[26]

During the 1820s there emerged a moderate, commercially-oriented liberalism influencing Tory ministers, such as Canning, and a few Whigs. This liberalism ascribed to government a narrowed range of technical tasks, allowing for increased economic opportunity and improvement. It defined a 'public opinion' outside Westminster legitimising policy, and looked to the economy, liberated from constraints, as the engine of progress. During the 1820s the term 'middle class' also began to enter the political vocabulary. But it did not denote a particular social group primarily distinguished by its material and economic circumstances. Rather, it emerged as a political term describing the responsible and moderate portion of society which stood free of both the aristocracy and the ultra-radical populism of the lower orders. An independent self-sufficiency, standing apart from traditional influence, the state, and demagogic extremism, characterised middle-class attitudes. Liberal Tory ministers such as Canning proposed more efficient government, allowing middle-class 'public opinion' opportunity and security. Abuses of patronage, economy, and finance were to be removed. At the same time, Canning opposed the ceding of executive authority to parliament. A constitutional conservatism framed economic and social liberalism. This posed a threat to most Whigs and challenged their oligarchic views centred on parliament and legislative reform. But in 1827 Canning, prime minister for barely five months and only 56 years of age, died. Between 1828 and 1830 the Tory hegemony collapsed. After 1830, with the Whigs dominating office and power, what had formerly been opposition Whig doctrine became orthodoxy. From 1830 to 1868 the Whigs commanded the heights of political power.

With the possession of office Whiggism reasserted itself and emphasised parliament as the authoritative arena of national politics. From Westminster issued political solutions to national problems in the form of large-scale legislation; the catalogue of Whig reforms of the 1830s affirming the point. Prior to 1830, beyond certain areas such as finance, it was not seen to be the job of government to promote legislation. After 1830, the Whigs established the idea that it was an important part of government to pass wide-ranging legislation. Whig governments during the 1830s established firm control of parliamentary procedure and legislation. Added to the purely executive function of the government, the initiatives for changes in the law, and legislative proposals passed from individual MPs to the cabinet. Alighting on this change in 1836, the Whig grandee Lord Holland observed that his 'grandfather in 1755 or 1756 was nearly impeached for saying he was to *manage* the Commons – and we are assailed with invective and menace because we do not *command* them'.[27] The formal segregation in the parliamentary schedule of government business from private members' business forcefully proscribed the legislative initiative of individual MPs. By the 1840s the government controlled the business schedule of the Commons. At the same time, particularly after 1838, the doctrine of collective ministerial responsibility became established. This required all members of the government to support the measures introduced to parliament by the ministry to which they belonged. The doctrine of ministerial collective responsibility also assisted the government in its control of parliamentary business.[28]

Through this control patrician Whig traditions were upheld, it was claimed, by a responsible and disinterested aristocracy in office, aloof from provincial or sectional perspectives, acting through parliament to promote the collective welfare of the nation. Whigs were reform's protagonists of the practicable. In response to social, economic, and intellectual change the interests of differing classes should be harmonised. At the same time, the rule of law, the bedrock of civilised order, was upheld. The firm, fair rule of law advanced the morality and prosperity of the intelligence of the nation through the guarantee of liberties and the encouragement of responsible and moral citizenship. In religion Whigs favoured a broad, undogmatic Anglican creed. In politics they saw their duty as integrating, through progressive parliamentary legislation, the increasingly diverse interests of the nation. Thus progress was safeguarded by political reforms from the centre. Traditional forms of localism became synonymous with narrow self-interest, corruption, and bigotry. The reforms Whigs introduced during the 1830s, including the Reform Act, were designed to prove that parliament could provide responsible, disinterested, and progressive aristocratic leadership; those with genuine grievances being domesticated and kept away from dangerous demagogues and radicalism. In 1831 Russell insisted that it was the intention of reform to strengthen, not eradicate, legitimate aristocratic influence.[29]

> Wherever the aristocracy reside, receiving large incomes, performing important duties, relieving the poor by charity, and evincing private worth and public virtue, it is not in human nature that they should not possess a great influence upon public opinion, and have an equal weight in selecting persons to serve their country in parliament.

The legitimate influence of rank and wealth, or deference as Bagehot called it, reinforced, through compliance rather than coercion, the status of the landed as the natural leaders of the community. Reforms to parliament, the Church, financial institutions, Ireland, the economy, local government and empire during the 1830s showed aristocrats in Westminster keeping the nation in order. The perceived greater respectability of aristocratic morals and behaviour after the 1830s, in contrast to the laxness of Regency upper-class morality, enhanced the claim to responsibility.

Whig remedial reforms after 1830 helped to establish a secure status for parliament as the embodiment of the nation's intelligence, as opposed to an unchecked prerogative or an unstable and bigoted popular will. 'The House of Commons of the present day', Bagehot affirmed in 1859, 'coincides nearly – or sufficiently nearly – in habitual judgement with the fairly intelligent and reasonably educated part of the community. . . . Most people wish to see embodied in parliament the *true judgement* of the nation.'[30] In 1858 the *Edinburgh Review* phrased it thus: those governing the nation had to be 'sufficiently independent in their judgement to originate or adopt a progressive system of polity, [and] sufficiently independent in their position to resist the exactions of the sovereign or the people, when these are at variance with the permanent interests of the State'.[31] The Commons stood as the essential mediator, through legislative reform, of that spectrum of interests constituting the political community. The purpose of government was the continual adjustment and re-balancing of those interests being constantly transformed by the force of social and economic progress. It was in this spirit that the Whig-educated Lord Derby, in 1853, expressed his conviction that 'real political power was not to be had in England: at best you could only a little advance or retard the progress of an inevitable movement'.[32] Prudent oversight was to be applied to the onward advance of property and intelligence. The strength of parliamentary government, it was argued, was that it showed itself sufficiently flexible to provide judicious adjustment, while being sufficiently resilient as to withstand dangerous or impetuous change.

That the doctrine of parliamentary government enjoyed an ascendancy by the 1850s was demonstrated by Grey and Bagehot among others. It embraced not just avowed Whigs, but also those self-designated Liberals who formed the bulk of non-Conservative MPs. In the 1852 parliament, which brought down Lord Derby's short-lived Conservative government, 33% of MPs called themselves Liberals; a designation not widely used prior to 1846, but by the early 1850s an increasingly popular alternative to the older labels Whig and Reformer. In the parliament of 1852, 47% of MPs called themselves Conservatives, 6% Radicals or Radical Reformers, 2% Repealers, and just over 6% styled themselves Whigs.[33] That some MPs described themselves as Liberals rather than Whigs was indicative of the family circles from which they felt excluded as much as betraying distinctive opinions. An intense clannishness, partly political and partly familial, bound leading Whigs together. It also revealed generational differences as younger MPs took up the Liberal label. But Liberals shared with the Whigs a commitment to the axioms of parliamentary government. They subscribed to notions of liberty secured through responsible and moderate progress, legislative reform harmonising differing social interests. A common commitment to Free Trade also helped bind them together. Yet differences of degree existed within Liberal opinion over the franchise, the ballot, and those religious questions, such as the Maynooth Grant, touching on Protestant–Catholic relations. None the less, a confident sense of being the natural party of government complemented an easy contempt for Conservatives, shorn of Peelite talent, and a fear of radical recklessness. Firm economy and Free Trade supporting rational, disinterested government, underpinned a collective rectitude that suggested a shared Whig–Liberal purpose. It also encouraged Liberals to look to Whigs for leadership. Even advanced Liberals, Russell noted in November 1852, would 'give their practical support to men less extreme and more judicious'.[34] By the 1850s, Whiggism embodied a tradition of administrative experience providing safe hands for progressive aspirations.

The Critics of Parliamentary Government: Peel and the Court

But Whig doctrine did not monopolise early Victorian constitutional debate. Different views, deeply antagonistic to Whig axioms, were pronounced by those attached to older notions of executive government or by others committed to radical change. Sir Robert Peel, as leader of the Conservative party from 1834 to 1846, attempted to preserve important aspects of earlier executive government. Peel had served his political apprenticeship under Lord Liverpool prior to 1827. He rejected the Whig notion of an executive subservient to parliament, with little resources to pursue a view of the national need different from that of the majority of the Commons. On becoming prime minister for a second time, in 1841, though enjoying the nominal support of a Conservative majority of MPs, Peel made his views clear to his backbenchers. He would not, he declared, 'hold office by a servile tenure which would compel me to be the instrument of carrying other men's opinions into effect. . . . I tell everyone who hears me, that he confers on me no personal obligation in having placed me in this office.'[35] The message to those sitting behind him was clear.

Peel's views harked back to the official doctrine of Tory administrations prior to 1830. Citing the defence of property and the inspiring nature of tradition, this Tory doctrine emphasised order and the independent resources of executive authority. Peel's views also evoked liberal Canningite notions of an intelligent, moderate 'public opinion' outside parliament as the true sentiment of the nation. Cabinet decision was not the product of parliamentary dictate. These views underscored the authority of ministers of the Crown as the monarch's chosen ministers. This was the context for the Duke of Wellington's remark, as victor of Waterloo and premier from 1828 to 1830, that he knew nothing of Whig and Tory principles; only that the country must be governed and order maintained. Sound administration was a fact, principles hazy abstractions. Peel never accepted the tenet, central to parliamentary government, that party opinion in parliament constituted the legitimate source of executive authority.

During the 1830s Peel provided the inspiration for a reconstituted Conservatism. What he gave the Conservatives, however, was not a party doctrine but an executive ethic. This ethic was codified in his published electoral address of 1834, the Tamworth Manifesto. The Manifesto was addressed to that 'great and intelligent class of society . . . which is much less interested in the contentions of party, than in the maintenance of order and the course of good government'.[36] The word Conservative never appeared in the Manifesto. A strong executive upholding order Peel saw as the essential need in the turbulent years after 1832. This need for strong government required 'public spirited men to give all reasonable aid to the government of the day not from interested motives, but because they were "ministers of the crown" who want it'. The usurping of many of the functions of 'Executive Government' by the Commons was the 'great public evil' to be prevented and feared.[37]

Peel played little part in the formal organisation of the Conservative party during the 1830s. He supplied an executive ethic around which others, notably the Conservative agent F. R. Bonham, assembled a party structure. It was therefore fitting that Peel's position as Conservative leader was confirmed by the actions of William IV in the autumn of 1834, rather than by Conservative backbench opinion. By asking Peel to form a government in December 1834, upon the Duke of Wellington's advice, the King effectively installed Peel as Conservative party leader; despite deep Conservative bitterness at Peel's apostasy over Catholic Emancipation in 1829. It is also significant that Peel resigned as prime minister in 1835, not because he was in a minority in the Commons, so he claimed, but because to retain office without some certainty of carrying measures would weaken an already vulnerable executive power. Finally, it is no accident that Peel, in 1839, was the last prime minister to request an overt sign of confidence from the monarch as a precondition to taking office.

The election of 1841 was a great party triumph for an anti-party view of government. After 1841 Conservative backbenchers found that a victory for Peelism meant scant regard for their religious, economic, or social sensibilities, while increasingly Peel found the demands of party obligation incompatible with his own elevated view of the national interest. Thus the violent Conservative schism of 1846 was about much more than Free Trade and repeal of the Corn Laws. At its root it was about the mutual obligations of party government and the source of constitutional authority. As Disraeli observed in December 1845, Peel 'is so vain, that he wants to figure in history as the settler of all the great questions, but a parliamentary constitution is not favourable to such ambitions; things must be done by parties, not by persons using parties as tools'. The basis of Disraeli's famous and damaging attacks upon Peel during 1846 was that it was unbecoming in a politician to decry party who had risen by party, 'for it is only by maintaining the independence of party that you can maintain the integrity of public men, and the power and influence of parliament itself'.[38] Disraeli later defied anyone to find a specific commitment to Protectionism as such in his speeches. This was the Protectionists using the Whig constitutional stick to beat their erstwhile leader. Sir Fitz-Roy Kelly, Peel's Solicitor General during 1845–6, recalled with bitterness that 'Peel's contempt for his party was very apparent to those who were in office with him. Taking it as a matter of course that the party would follow him, go where he might.'[39] The anguished outcry of the Tory *Quarterly Review*, in September 1846, was that a minister owed at least equal gratitude and fidelity to his party as to his sovereign, for the former was the earlier and greater benefactor. That same month Peel wrote to a confidant: 'I will take care too not again to burn my fingers by organising a party. There is too much truth in the saying, "the head of a party must be directed by the tail . . .". As heads see and tails are blind, I think heads are the better judges as to the course to be taken.'[40] Peel's disdain for Peelite party organisation after 1846 was entirely consistent. He looked to maintain an Olympian aloofness from party combinations. The Duke of Wellington's military analogy was that the Peelites were officers without men, while the Conservatives were men without officers.

The most important ally for Peel's view of executive authority by the late 1840s was Prince Albert. In August 1847 Peel assured Prince Albert that 'the quiet good sense of the people of this country will be a powerful instrument on which an Executive Government may rely for neutralising the mischievous energies of the House of Commons'.[41] Clearly, after 1846, Peel was looking to step forward as the personification of executive expertise emancipated from the restrictions of party support. Prince Albert, for his part, was happy to contemplate the Court reinstated as a senior partner in the formulation of public policy: 'Nowhere does the constitution demand an indifference on the part of the sovereign to the march of political events, and nowhere would such indifference be more condemned and justly despised than in England'.[42] In conversation Prince Albert continually quoted Peel. He constantly conveyed to ministers, without hesitation, what were presented as the Queen's wishes. In December 1851 the Court engineered Palmerston's dismissal as

Foreign Secretary and a year later, in December 1852, helped to bring about Prince Albert's ambition of creating a moderate coalition government. Such behaviour was quite sufficient to strike terror into Whig hearts. Lord Stanley noticed how the Peelites themselves seemed to see parliament 'as an encumbrance, no longer wanted now we have a free press, unsuited to the time and a drag on popular legislation'.[43]

Peel's accidental death in 1850 unexpectedly closed any possibility of preserving older traditions of executive government. After 1850 the Whig vision of party and parliamentary government gained ascendancy. The Conservatives were led by a peer, the 14th Earl of Derby, schooled in the Whig tradition, whose view of policy, disdain for the press, and suspicion of popular prejudices were framed within the axioms of parliamentary government. Derby served his political apprenticeship in Lord Lansdowne's Whig salon at Bowood House in the 1820s. Aristocratic power in parliament was what mattered. Derby neither understood nor cared for the press. On principle he repudiated the claim of any journal to represent his views. Or else Derby believed the compromise of one's opinions or the giving of offence to friends was unavoidable. He had no liking for meeting or speaking to large popular audiences, beyond what his sense of social duty demanded. Power operated within the walls of Westminster and stood upon the strength of legitimate influence in the constituencies. In 1841 Derby told parliament that English landlords, whether Whig or Tory, should derive satisfaction from the fact that their tenants usually felt a desire to comply with their landlord's wishes at elections. The operation of deference in the constituencies protected the sovereignty of parties in parliament. Derby had seen Peel's dismissal of party as dangerous, Peel '*must* be *a* leader in spite of himself'. For his own part, Derby stated in 1849 that 'I have nothing at heart but the support of the views which I entertain in public affairs and as a means to that end, the maintenance of union and *party*.'[44]

After their leader's death the Peelites themselves also came to extol the virtues of executive authority standing upon party support in parliament. Even in the late 1840s many Peelites were deeply frustrated by Peel's refusal to act as party leader.

Through the pages of the *Quarterly Review* in 1856 Gladstone decried the disorganisation of parties as an impairment to the strength of the executive. Yet, while accepting the constitutional desirability of parties in parliament, Gladstone retained a Peelite contempt for the bulk of the Commons. Most MPs were 'stupid, incompetent, mere dandies or coxcombs'. Whig placemen were 'decrepit, crotchety and to a man slaves of routine', while the failure of quality in the Conservative leadership was 'undeniable and egregious'.[45] None the less, even senior Peelites like Sir James Graham, were pronouncing by 1859 that if parliamentary government were to be maintained it must rest upon the basis of party, however poor the materials available. In a transmuted form Peelism, within Westminster, became part of the administrative ingredient of a broader liberal movement. Outside parliament it helped to shape the ethic of a professionalised civil service within Whitehall. Between 1848 and 1869 the number of civil servants increased by 52 per cent and by 1870 nomination had given way, by and large, to entry by competitive examination. This expanded, more meritocratic, civil service became deeply imbued with Peelite axioms of duty and executive efficiency. But within Westminster, by the 1850s, Conservatives and Peelites, as well as Whigs, endorsed the function of parties within the constitutional framework of parliamentary government.

The Critics of Parliamentary Government: Radical Traditions

Radicals also used language deliberately subversive of Whig constitutional doctrine. Radicalism embraced a wide-ranging body of individuals and groups who called for extensive reform in a variety of not always compatible ways. What radical traditions did offer was a rhetoric articulating interests and defining purposes deeply antagonistic to Whig perspectives. Indeed, by the 1850s what radicals of all shades shared, despite their differences, was contempt for comfortable and elitist Whig precepts. Whig assertions of sympathy for popular grievances smacked of condescension. Radicals saw complacency in the

Whigs' self-confident claim to disinterested, economic and efficient government. The belief that a restricted and varied franchise could produce a sovereign assembly, embodying the real interests of the whole community rather than the selfish concerns of a narrow section, deeply offended radical minds. It was this antipathy that encouraged Disraeli's speculations during the 1850s on an improbable Conservative–radical alliance. In 1850 Disraeli thought 'the radicals would be glad to have us in (Bright said as much) since they would then be relieved from their present irksome position, as involuntary and unthanked supporters of a [Whig] ministry which they disliked'.[46] Radical contempt for the Whigs, meanwhile, was reciprocated in the second Lord Grey's judgement that no public men were 'more base, more detestable, more at variance with all taste, decency, as well as all morality, truth and honour' than prominent radicals. There was not one, Grey suggested, 'with whom you would trust yourself in the dark'.[47]

A confluence of traditions flowed into the radical repudiation of Whig principles. Its main current was an historic populist tradition based on notions of the Norman Yoke, Magna Carta as a foundational bill of rights, and the struggle for ancient freedoms and liberties; rhetoric which echoed the political struggles of the seventeenth century. The language of the Authorised Bible, Bunyan and Milton inspired a sense of moral and intellectual independence creating a populist culture, most firmly embedded in Nonconformist communities, strongly corrosive of oligarchic Whig assumptions. 'Old Corruption' embodied the immorality of aristocratic privilege. Accompanying the ferment of the French Revolution Dr Richard Price had asserted the right of the people to choose who governed them; governors to be held accountable by the governed, the people being able to select the form of government they wished. Burke dubbed Price's pronouncements 'an unheard of bill of rights'. The secular radical retort to Burke came from Thomas Paine in his *Rights of Man* of 1791. Paine's writing enjoyed a wide circulation, particularly among the lower classes, mobilising opinion and popularising the doctrine of natural and inalienable rights. The prime minister William Pitt described the 'rights of man' as 'a monstrous doctrine' laying the ground for a whole system of insurrection. During the prolonged titanic struggle with France and Napoleon which followed, Burke's warnings and Pitt's policies held sway. Loyalism triumphed over radicalism, though Paine's ideas remained a residual memory in radical circles.

The philosopher Jeremy Bentham and his Utilitarian philosophy offered up additional secular intellectual weaponry with which to prise apart Whig doctrine. Through his *Fragment on Government* (1776), the *Plan of Parliamentary Reform* published in 1827, and his *Constitutional Code*, which appeared in 1830, Bentham applied his principle of utility to government; its object becoming the promotion of the greatest happiness of the greatest number. Rejecting the theory of natural rights, Bentham argued for a tight identity of interest between government and governed. The key to this was a universal suffrage; frequent, possibly annual, elections; the ballot, and freedom of information. From this would emerge a Utilitarian democracy ensuring a direct identity of interest between nation and government.

The publicist of Utilitarian ideas, James Mill, built upon Bentham's critique. Rejecting the Aristotelian typology of monarchy, aristocracy, and democracy, Mill also rejected traditional arguments for the benefits of a balanced or mixed constitution, whereby merging types of government secured the benefits of each, while purging them of their attendant defects. Burke's notion of 'virtual representation' (by which the unenfranchised were represented by those with the vote) was also rejected on the grounds that only each individual could testify to his own interests. The Utilitarian psychological model required universal suffrage supported by education. Democracy was only dangerous if languishing amid ignorance. The Whig response to Utilitarian argument was voiced by the historian and MP T. B. Macaulay in the *Edinburgh Review* during 1829. Benthamites, he declared, embraced abstraction in defiance of experience; rigid theorising obscuring empirical reality. 'The fiction of philosophers' Bagehot was later to label Benthamism. Moreover, Whigs maintained that universal suffrage, by giving a poor majority power over a rich minority, was a doctrine of plunder. Nevertheless, in its political form of Philosophic Radicalism

37

during the 1830s, Utilitarianism gave a keen intellectual edge to radical thrusts at Whig constitutionalism.

The rise of Chartism and the Anti-Corn Law League, in the late 1830s, gave renewed momentum to populist radical rhetoric. As a focus for popular radical sentiment, the 'People's Charter' was based upon a belief in self-government by direct representation. After 1832 the term 'working class' entered radical vocabulary giving expression to the sense of political exclusion felt by those beneath the middle class. The vote was not a privilege or a duty, but a 'right', born of a worker's claim to the fruit of his own labour. It was inherited landed property that defiled the natural justice of God's creation. The six-point Charter drawn up in 1838, portrayed as the Magna Carta of the lower classes, demanded annual parliaments, universal manhood suffrage, the abolition of property qualifications for MPs, the ballot, equal electoral districts, and salaries for MPs. By 1839 Chartist advocates of physical force, such as Feargus O'Connor, were organising mass meetings, which often degenerated into violent riots. Bitter strikes occurred in 1842 as a Chartist petition, bearing 3 million names, was presented to parliament; to be rejected by 287 to 59 Commons votes. In early 1848 serious Chartist rioting again broke out in Glasgow, Manchester, and other cities, as another huge petition, allegedly containing 5 million signatures, was prepared for parliament. Yet the London convention of April 1848 marked the demise of Chartist agitation. The petition was ridiculed in parliament. Regional rifts, lack of a strong sense of national solidarity, and conflict between advocates of physical force and those committed to moral persuasion fractured Chartist support. The motto of London Chartists, 'Unity is Strength', assumed a pathetic irony.

The Anti-Corn Law League provided a rallying point for middle-class radicalism that attacked the selfish protectionist instincts of landowners. But while the language of class was on occasion used by League leaders, it was the populist idiom which provided a potent rhetoric with which to decry the moral corruption and irresponsibility of the upper classes. Some League publicists even talked of the ancient freedoms of a Saxon people being repressed by a Norman caste; language echoing the clashes of the seventeenth century and the struggle against 'feudal' privilege. The League leader Richard Cobden denounced the English state as 'a thing of monopolies, and Church-craft, and sinecures, armorial hocus-pocus, primogeniture and pageantry!' Peel's repeal of the Corn Laws in 1846 brought the League victory. Bright declared repeal to be Holy Writ put into an Act of parliament. Cobden, together with John Bright, proposed a moral radicalism that saw free trade as not only a basis for domestic prosperity, but also a pacific internationalism – tenets of what became known as the 'Manchester School' of radicalism. Traditional foreign policy was expressed through an implicitly bellicose vocabulary of national interest, balance of power and spheres of influence. This, Cobden maintained, was simply the external expression and preoccupation of a privileged elite, safeguarding their own interests and diverting popular attention away from real domestic grievances. Nationalism was an outdated and foolish superstition. As Bright dubbed it, traditional foreign policy was a system of out-door relief for an aristocratic clique.

By the 1840s and 1850s the rise of militant Nonconformity gave another powerful extra-parliamentary dimension to radical activity. The Liberation Society, calling for the disestablishment of the Church of England, led by Edward Miall through his journalistic mouthpiece the *Nonconformist*, and the United Kingdom Alliance, committed to temperance, expressed an increasingly militant moral condemnation of existing values. What they shared with other radicals was a deep disgust for the patrician nature of Whiggism. The differing strands of thought, religious belief, and social background embraced within the populist radical movement found common cause in a well-established critique of aristocratic exclusiveness.

For radicals sovereignty resided not in parliament, but with the people. Radical MPs saw themselves as delegates with a direct responsibility to their constituents. Many, such as Sir John Trelawny, MP for Tavistock, gave annual accounts or verbal reports to their constituents explaining their Commons votes during the previous session. Such behaviour highlighted radical disdain for Whig ideals of elevated independence. Radical lan-

39

guage projected popular grievances and aspirations less as issuing from a class, than as the legitimate demands of 'the people'. This continuity with historical populist traditions was an appeal to all those excluded by unmerited privilege and aristocratic monopoly. As Cobden complained to Bright in 1849: 'we are a servile, aristocracy-loving, lord-ridden people'.[48] The broad, rather than specifically class-based, nature of the populist critique allowed radicalism to encompass differing social groups, religious associations, and political alignments. It was 'the people' who were dispossessed of their God-given rights and self-respect by Whig condescension and patronage. This focused radical animus on the elevated sovereignty of parliament and suggested issues such as the ballot and franchise extension as those most likely to elicit common action; precisely because they struck at the Whiggish root of oligarchic corruption.

Many historians have seen a break in radical activity after 1848, as working-class Chartism was smothered by industrial paternalism and middle-class indifference. During the 1850s radical activism, they suggest, went into decline. But such perspectives ignore the continuity of rhetoric, evident in populist attacks on oligarchy, which informed radical language of the mid-Victorian period. Long-standing demands for popular government, public accountability, and civic virtue, pressed by radical reformers of the 1780s and Chartists in the 1830s, continued to play a part in the popular Liberalism of the 1860s. For their part, Whigs only heard two notes struck in radical oratory, pathos and fury.

Radical disunity gave Whigs some safeguard against plunder. Clever and crotchety radical MPs were prone to adventurous isolation in parliament, the pursuit of their individual causes preventing them from enjoying easy cooperation. At the same time certain elements of radical thought actually complemented aspects of Whig principle. Radicals too, by the 1850s, were to some extent enmeshed within the framework of Whig constitutionalism. First, most radicals recognised parliament as the authoritative arena of national politics. They aimed their strategies at settlements achieved through Westminster and celebrated the 1832 Reform Act for establishing constitutional sovereignty in the Commons. They saw their causes leading to a parliamentary resolution. The Poor Law Amendment Act of 1834, the Municipal Reform Act of 1835, and the 1839 Rural Police Act were pieces of reform legislation certain radicals believed to have been secured by their exertions both outside and within Westminster. The Anti-Corn Law League and the Chartists campaigned for political solutions delivered by parliament. Testimony to the prestige of parliament, even within radical circles, was provided by the increased petitioning of Westminster that continued during the 1850s and 1860s. This reached a peak during 1868–72 when a total of 101,573 petitions were presented to parliament, representing an annual total of over 3 million signatures. The security of progress, liberty, and rights was a matter of political reform. This opened up the possibility, in favourable circumstances, of radicalism being domesticated. Secondly, shared faith in the law as a possible means of achieving just settlement strengthened the possibility of collaboration. Whigs were deeply sceptical of abstract natural rights, arguing that rights only had meaning and legitimacy within a legislative and legal context. Rights were the creation of law. Radical recognition of the importance and necessity of securing rights through the judiciary and magistracy also suggested common ground. A shared commitment to the rule of law offered further possibilities of conciliation.

After 1848 radicalism assumed more constitutionalist forms. Physical force Chartism quickly faded in the disheartening aftermath of the Kennington Common meeting of April 1848. Chartist activists either turned away from politics, concentrated their energies on local issues, or looked to more moderate radicals in parliament to realise their aspirations. In 1848 the rapidly-ageing radical Joseph Hume told the Commons that he would not 'ever refuse to property its just weight, or deny to noblemen and men of superior merit that just influence which they ought to possess, and which he hoped they always would possess'.[49] The triumph of Free Trade in 1846 and the relative prosperity of the 1850s dulled the edge of radical invective. In 1858 the National Charter Association finally dissolved itself, having failed to revive the Chartist mass platform. Chartism had continued in the early 1850s as a viable political presence in London, while withering in the provinces. But by 1858 even metropolitan Chartism had given way to alternative constitutionalist modes of radical activism.

The tone of social relations softened. A sense of crisis eased and the political atmosphere became less frenzied. Evangelicalism became less doom-laden and apocalyptic: a shift in religious thinking, characterised by the historian Boyd Hilton as a change of emphasis upon atonement to greater stress on the redemptive power of the incarnation, which produced during the 1850s more ameliorative social and economic attitudes. Having reached fever pitch during 1850–1 popular anti-Catholicism cooled during the 1850s, until during the 1860s the threats of Tractarianism and ritualism once again stirred up anti-Papal fervour. Class vocabulary receded in radical rhetoric, giving way to an older discourse emphasising the grievances of the people, as part of the progressive movement of humanity, against aristo-cratic exclusivity. Radical MPs carried forward the historic populist cry for greater control over a corrupt, self-interested and oligarchic executive. It was aristocratic morality that en-feebled governments.

But it was from within Westminster that radicals increasingly sought to establish greater popular control of government. This focused attention on a domestic agenda of government economy, disestablishment of the Anglican Church, and parliamentary and administrative reform. It was also to highlight the impor-tance of events abroad, the Crimean War, the Italian Risorgi-mento and the American Civil War, as causes during the 1850s and 1860s around which radicals could gather and mobilise. To that extent radicalism was domesticated. Tellingly, the veteran campaigner Cobden advised Bright in 1859 that it would be wiser to 'rely on your House of Commons influence' and to be more shy of the stump. 'Your greatest power is in the House.' Cobden continued, 'I have an opinion that if you intend to follow politics and not eschew office, you must in future be more exclusively a House of Commons man.'[50] During the Crimean War the patriotic and Russophobic strands in much popular radical sentiment, especially in London, emphasised Palmerston's appeal and Bright's isolation. None the less, radicalism survived within Westminster as a populist solvent of Whiggish precepts.

In 1852 approximately 55 MPs (30 self-declared Radicals or Radical Reformers and roughly 25 MPs describing themselves as Liberals) regularly voted in Commons divisions against the Whigs. This diverse group included veteran Philosophic Radicals such as John Roebuck and other survivors from the 1830s; independent Liberals such as George Hadfield (MP for Sheffield), Thomas Headlam (MP for Newcastle upon Tyne), and Peter Locke King (MP for East Surrey); as well as Manchester School free traders such as Richard Cobden (MP for the West Riding of Yorkshire) and John Bright (MP for Manchester).[51] These radical MPs looked to control public expenditure, widen the suffrage, redistribute parliamentary seats, introduce the ballot, and slacken the ties between church and state. They represented constituencies, whether the large newer boroughs of Lancashire, Yorkshire, and London, or older, smaller constituencies in Devon, Cornwall, or along the Welsh border, in which resentment of aristocratic patronage was strong and organised. Opposition to the Whigs' propensity to centralise and a strong desire for economy (Whigs being distrusted as fiscally lax) helped to galvanise local support. These MPs provided a channel for extra-parliamentary pressure; particularly from organised Nonconformity. Anglican radicals, such as Thomas Duncombe (MP for Finsbury), Roebuck, and most importantly, Sir William Clay (MP for Tower Hamlets) and Sir John Trelawny, acted as spokesmen for the Liberation Society. They also maintained crucial links with parts of the metropolitan press, such as the *Daily News* and the *Weekly Dispatch*, and carried on communication with those members of the chastened Chartist leadership who were prepared to support radicals such as Roebuck and Duncombe in parliament.

In December 1852 a few radicals were given appointments in Aberdeen's coalition government. This was as much due to Peelite pressure as a result of Whig wishes to draw in broad parliamentary support. The Philosophic Radical William Molesworth (MP for Southwark) entered the cabinet as First Commissioner of Works. Charles Villiers (MP for Wolverhampton), brother of Lord Clarendon and a free trade campaigner, became Judge Advocate General. Ralph Bernal Osborne (MP for Middlesex) became Secretary to the Admiralty. These appointments suggested the benefits of constitutionalist strategies; a presence in executive power – although radical MPs were not to be easily disarmed or House-trained. In December 1852 Cobden and Bright made it clear to Aberdeen that any support for his coalition government from the Manchester School would require a commitment to the ballot and the abolition of the newspaper stamp duty.

Summary

On the continent of Europe, during the eighteenth century, a theory of the state was constructed based upon the citizen endowed with 'natural rights'. The French philosopher Jean-Jacques Rousseau, for example, in his *Social Contract* of 1762, celebrated liberty and the rights of man; citizens being rendered unfree by absolute or arbitrary institutions. But in Britain during the eighteenth century the mainstream of political theory followed a distinctly different course. Natural law was an acceptable legal fiction, but was not to be translated into the political sphere as natural rights. The franchise, for example, was not an inalienable right, but a public duty extended to respectable and responsible men. Edmund Burke, more than John Locke or Thomas Paine, proved a seminal theorist. Rather than citizens endowed with natural rights, it was subjects existing under the authority of parliament that formed the foundation of English political theory. By the 1830s this thinking upheld the primacy of parliament; the sufficiency of parliament's own authority. What was constitutional was what parliament did. There were no rights, freedoms, or privileges beyond those bestowed by parliament. Sovereignty resided in parliament, where governments were chosen, where the national interest emerged from party debate, where instruction and edification were provided for the rest of the nation, and where legislation was enacted. The prestige of parliament was paramount. The sufficiency of parliament's authority provided autonomy. Governments were no longer chosen through the prerogative or to be selected by the populace. Fluid party alignments within Westminster determined who governed.

This was the essence of Victorian parliamentary government. After 1830, Whig governments brought forward reform legislation showing parliament safeguarding progress, the rule of law, and prosperity. The 1832 Reform Act, it was claimed, secured political tranquillity, calm and balance. The large-scale parliamentary legislation that followed upheld the view of Westminster as bringing efficiency, rationality and expertise to national problems. Reform after 1830 was, therefore, also about centralisation. Localism became synonymous with corruption and inefficiency. Parochial government was condemned, the power of parish vestries eroded and localities were deprived of authority by poor law reform. As the historic administrative structures of traditional local communities were dissolved, so power shifted to the centre. Increasingly, talent and ambition focused on centralised power in Westminster, rather than on local authority and status. In his *Autobiography*, novelist and failed parliamentary candidate Anthony Trollope described a seat in the Commons as 'the highest object of ambition to every educated Englishman'. Royal Commissions and landmark legislation seemed to reinforce the authority and sufficiency of parliament to provide enlightened and benign government. By the 1850s the precepts of Whig constitutionalism, upholding parliamentary government, were orthodoxy. Older executive traditions associated with Robert Peel and Prince Albert were fading. Conservatives, Peelites, Whigs and Liberals saw themselves acting within the political structure described by Bagehot, Lord Grey, and Erskine May.

Radicalism after 1848, as noted above, assumed more constitutionalist forms. Violent class rhetoric became more muted, giving way to older populist expressions of radical grievances. Yet the Peelite executive tradition and radical populism continued to challenge, in different ways, Whig belief in the autonomy of parliament. Whigs saw constituency politics as a necessary activity separate from the dynamics of Westminster politics. Public opinion was expressed in the Commons. Democratic pressures were contained by compliance, rather than coercion, through the operation of deference. Peel had disparaged such notions. He authorised executive action by invoking a moderate and responsible public opinion existing in the country distinct from Commons opinion. The notion of respectability, embodying ideas of character and property, became central to political discussion; respectability being aligned with definitions of responsible political intelligence. Radicals saw popular opinion, articulated through an extended franchise, as a direct control on Commons opinion. MPs were delegates, authorised to carry out the wishes of their constituents. After 1852, the legitimate relation between parliament and the nation formed a central theme in the public debate and private thoughts of British politicians.

2

MID-VICTORIAN PARTIES, 1852–9

If the Whig constitution of parliamentary government framed party politics during the 1850s, two powerful factors shaped party dynamics within Westminster. First, there were the moderate policies and strategic intentions of Derby's Conservative party; the single largest and most cohesive body of votes in parliament. Secondly, there was the shifting and ill-defined nature of non-Conservative, namely Peelite, Whig, Liberal, and radical, alignment. After formally relinquishing protectionism in 1852, Derby sought to establish the Conservatives as the representatives of moderate progress and responsible centrism; a party fit for government responding to the need for genuine reform as opposed to reckless innovation. Caution and non-commitment in opposition, as well as statements and legislation delivered while in office during 1858–9 and 1866–8, were intended to affirm Conservative claims to the guardianship of enlightened and safe progress. The bigoted backwater image of Protectionism was deliberately shed. The Whigs were to be deprived of their exclusive claim to the natural and disinterested leadership of responsible opinion. For example, Derby deliberately distanced himself from the fervent anti-Catholic elements within his party. He believed the vehemently anti-Catholic National Club was 'a mischievous body whose extreme pretensions and views must not be encouraged'.[1] In tactical terms this constantly kept open the prospect of merger with penitent

Peelites, disillusioned Whigs, Irish Catholics or, in 1866, anxious Adullamites. By 1852 about 30 former Peelite MPs, approximately one-third of their total number, had rejoined the Conservatives, including members of the 1852 Derby ministry such as Sir Fitz-Roy Kelly, Sir Frederick Thesiger, and Sir John Pakington.

Derby's single greatest difficulty during the 1850s and 1860s was that, despite having a unified party, at no time did he enjoy a clear majority of Commons votes. In 1852, 306 MPs declared themselves Conservatives (a further 4 MPs calling themselves Protectionists and 2 Tories), constituting roughly 48 per cent of the Commons.[2] The non-Conservative majority of the Commons was slim and unstable. This recommended a Conservative opposition strategy of watchful inaction designed to embarrass and incapacitate those groupings arrayed against them. Opposition non-commitment was not a confession of doctrinal bankruptcy. Rather, it sprang from Derby's firm conviction that, in attempting to act together, non-Conservatives would discover their deep-seated differences. Without the Conservatives providing a reactionary foil, those differences, he believed, would appear all the more forcefully. It should be noted that when, in January 1855, March 1857, and February 1858, non-Conservative governments suffered major defeats it was as a result of hostile *radical*, not *Conservative*, Commons motions.

It is also important to place Derby's opposition strategy of watchful inaction, awaiting the internal fracture of government support, in its proper context. Not only was it a product of Derby's strategic acumen. It also reflected the general role of the opposition within the context of parliamentary government. The belief that a parliamentary opposition should persistently contest all government measures again belongs to a later period; a notion rooted in the party system that arose after the 1880s, rather than the mid-Victorian system described by Grey, Erskine May, and Bagehot. As noted in the previous chapter, it was not unusual for the opposition to combine with moderate government supporters to defeat extreme, often radical, proposals. During the late 1830s, Peel frequently adopted such a course, enabling him, as Ian Newbould has shown, to 'govern from opposition'.[3] It was rare for the opposition to move motions of 'no confidence' in the government. This was done only in August 1841 and June 1859 during the decades immediately prior to 1867. Opposition amendments to the Royal Address, which opened the session and laid out the government's legislative programme, were unusual; being reserved for moments when the cabinet's authority was all but shattered. In times of war, as in 1854–6, patriotism and the accusation of factionalism were powerful inhibitors of any opposition urge blatantly to undermine the government. Attacks on the capability of individual ministers, during discussion of particular measures, were more common. The control party Whips had over MPs when in opposition was weaker than when office provided patronage, honours, and appointments to help cement Commons support. Derby's vigilant inactivity while in opposition, therefore, was not idiosyncratic. What made the strategy the more striking in Derby's case was that he led a party that experienced opposition for so long.

Meanwhile, competing claims to the parliamentary leadership of non-Conservative opinion created a constant jostling for pre-eminence among leading Whigs, Peelites, Liberals, and radicals. The fluidity inherent within the parliamentary system of 1832 to 1867 assumed an extreme form. This contest focused on the rivalry between Lord John Russell and Lord Palmerston. In December 1851 Palmerston had been driven into resigning from the Foreign Secretaryship in Russell's Whig–Liberal government. Two months later, in 'a tit for tat', Palmerston assisted in bringing Russell's ministry down. Throughout the 1850s both men manoeuvred around each other in pursuit of the prize of a consolidated Liberal leadership. Russell represented Whig rectitude through his association with the reform measures of the 1830s. He consciously portrayed himself as part of a tradition going back to Charles James Fox, and always kept a small bust of Fox before him on his writing desk. By 1852, however, Russell's authority was much eroded, his judgement widely questioned, and his Whig clannishness much criticised. Palmerston, the Foreign Office expert, was 'intensely the Englishman, above party, and always talking, or seeming which is as good, to talk from the national cue'.[4] Rather than the sober European tradition of foreign policy maintained by Castlereagh, Wellington and Aberdeen, Palmerston espoused the flamboyant, insular tradition of Canning. Around the two wrestling titans of Russell and Palmerston others adjusted themselves for position and opportunity.

In 1855, sixty-three actual or past cabinet ministers (sufficient for over four cabinets), the great majority non-Conservative, took part in parliamentary debate. There existed little distinction in being distinguished. The difficulty of obtaining strong government, Prince Albert observed, was not in the paucity of men, but in the oversupply of Rt Honourable gentlemen. A surfeit of talent and ambition inevitably complicated relations, intensified asperities, and fostered instability. Non-Conservatives were 'over-charged with an excess of official men, and the way stopped up against expectants, which led to subdivision, jealousy and intrigue'.[5] Fifteen or so Irish MPs, nicknamed the Pope's Brass Band though officially called the Irish Brigade, sought reform of landlord–tenant law and redress for Irish agrarian grievances. But their pledge, not always observed, to 'independent opposition' to any administration was deliberately intended further to unsettle party alignment. The fact that Derby's short-lived minority Conservative ministry, from February to December 1852, was most notable for surrendering the commitment to protectionism opened up further options.

The Aberdeen Coalition, 1852–5

The formation of Lord Aberdeen's coalition government (containing Peelites, Whigs, and one radical cabinet member) in December 1852 represented one attempt at an official alignment of non-Conservative opinion. The strains within the coalition, however, were from the start powerful and debilitating. Under the elderly Peelite Aberdeen, despite their small parliamentary numbers, Peel's erstwhile followers claimed the 'lion's share' of government office.[6] The Duke of Argyll, a talented 29-year-old Scottish peer with a deep, sonorous voice, long red hair loose over his shoulders, and an arrogant self-regard, took the Privy Seal. The ambitious Duke of Newcastle, who had privately hoped to form a purely Peelite ministry with himself eventually as leader, took War and Colonies. While Sir James Graham, a senior Peelite in the Commons whose cold manner repelled familiarity and whose administrative talent demanded respect, took the Admiralty. The talented William Gladstone became Chancellor of the Exchequer and the socially accomplished Sidney Herbert, a ready speaker though bitter in his invective, Secretary for War. Sir John Young, Edward Cardwell, and Lord Bruce took junior posts. The Peelites themselves saw this as a just reflection of their own administrative expertise. Their camaraderie stood on the pious cult of a dead leader and a self-adulatory sense of innate superiority.

Many Whigs, however, saw the Peelites' claim to office as proof of their collective conceit. 'They are a *Sect*-entre nous *Prigs*', Joseph Parkes declared, 'there is a snobbism that runs from their deceased head all down thro' his tail'.[7] Among the junior Whigs at the Reform Club in particular it rankled. Russell's membership of the coalition cabinet, initially as Foreign Secretary, was only secured by a pledge to reform and Aberdeen's indication that in time he would stand down as premier to make way for Russell. Palmerston's presence, in the unaccustomed role of Home Secretary, added to frontbench strains. None of five or six ministers in the cabinet were 'likely to acknowledge the superiority or defer to the opinions of any other . . . every one of these five or six considering himself abler and more important than their premier'.[8] Aberdeen being in the Lords exacerbated these difficulties. They ensured that the coalition enjoyed no solid or stable backbench support. Rather, it survived on transitory goodwill and grudging forbearance.

As Chancellor of the Exchequer Gladstone shored up the Aberdeen coalition in April 1853 in a characteristically Peelite manner. His ambitious and large-scale free trade budget embodied administrative expertise in action and established both the office of Chancellor and national finance as central to executive politics. Tactically, it trumped the colourful Benjamin Disraeli, who in 1852, as Derby's Chancellor of the Exchequer, had attempted a political coup with his own free trade Conservative budget. Personally, it established Gladstone as the most prominent of Peel's younger disciples. The 1853 budget, delivered in an impassioned speech of epic proportions, displaying a powerful technical mastery, was Peelism writ large. It reduced or abolished a range of indirect taxes or duties. At the same time it extended the income tax until 1860, increasing the number paying income tax and so broadening its social base. This financial policy Gladstone saw as the most effective means of establishing 'right relations' within society. It became 'the social contract of the mid-Victorian State' and defined the framework of national finances for the rest of the century.[9]

Yet, despite Gladstone's success, it was to be parliamentary reform and war that were to dominate and eventually overwhelm the Aberdeen coalition. As prime minister in the late 1840s Russell had revived the question of reform, publicly revoking his former commitment to the finality of the 1832 settlement. Around the need for further reform Russell had tried to consolidate Whig and Liberal opinion. He signally failed. Even members of his own cabinet between 1848 and 1852, as well as backbenchers, saw it as a personal indulgence rather than a potent rallying cry. His even more impulsive response to the ecclesiastical titles issue, and the publication of his Durham letter in 1850, did further damage to his reputation. Upon the Pope announcing the re-establishment of the Catholic hierarchy in England in November 1850, Russell wrote an open letter to the Bishop of Durham denouncing Papal aggression and the 'mummeries of superstition'. Russell's judgement and integrity came under serious question. His parliamentary reform bill of 1852 was stillborn.

In February 1853 Russell became Minister without Portfolio, succeeded at the Foreign Office by the able Whig lover of gossip Lord Clarendon. Anxious to return to the premiership, throughout 1853 a restless Russell indicated his deepening dissatisfaction with his position. In October 1853, reasserting his status as the Whigs' living link with 1832, Russell again pushed forward the reform question. While Aberdeen acquiesced, forming a cabinet committee in November, Palmerston seized the opportunity for sabotage. Enlisting Lansdowne's support, Palmerston declared his refusal 'to be dragged through the dirt by John Russell'.[10] In particular, Palmerston denounced the disenfranchisement of small boroughs proposed in Russell's scheme; Palmerston himself sitting for Tiverton, and Lansdowne being the proprietor of Calne. In a dexterous move in mid-December 1853 Palmerston resigned from the cabinet, combining his objections to further reform, the real reason for his going, with well-publicised misgivings about the government's foreign policy. But failing to bring Lansdowne with him, two weeks later Palmerston agreed to rejoin the cabinet, presenting this as proof of his indispensability and emphasising Russell's isolation. In the following months, intriguing busily and playing fast and loose, Palmerston smothered Russell's reform plan, an act in which he enlisted varied Whig and some Peelite support. In the Lords the Whig peers Grey, Beaumont, and Clanricarde attacked the government for bringing forward a needless reform measure. In April 1854, after the outbreak of the Crimean War, a tearful Russell was finally forced publicly to withdraw his reform bill from the consideration of the Commons.

From the opposition benches the Conservatives impassively watched the government advertise its internal dissensions. In January 1853 Derby declared it 'difficult to imagine how a government can go on formed of such discordant materials as that which Aberdeen has brought together'.[11] At a party meeting in January 1854 he declared the coalition represented a confusion, rather than a fusion, of principles. Disraeli saw only disappointment and resentment among the Whigs at the preponderance of Peelites in office, distrust among the radicals, and hostility in the Irish Brigade. Derby's intention was clear: 'Wait, don't attack ministers, that will only bind them together. If left alone they must fall to pieces by their own disunion.' This was 'killing [the coalition] with kindness'. When, in the Commons, Disraeli lampooned the Whigs as subservient to the Peelites, and the radicals as the tools of both, it was 'a most skilful and ingenious rubbing up of old sores'.[12]

The onset of the Crimean War in 1854, with Britain and France supporting Turkey against Russian expansion, put further pressure on the coalition. Military disappointments and scandalous reports of mismanagement fell heavily on a ministry supposedly packed with administrative expertise. The luckless Duke of Newcastle, as Secretary for War, was inevitably the focus of criticism. Despite being in favour at Court he was discredited. Aberdeen was also seen as wavering and ineffective. Graham's talents were 'neutralised by his reputation for inconsistency'; his temperament being regarded as a compound of rashness and cowardice.[13] Despite recognition of his administrative talents, Gladstone, because of his want of tact, high-handed manner and the verbose obscurity of his reasoning, was widely distrusted. Clarendon lacked debating power, while the third Lord Grey, the rogue elephant of the Whig herd, rampaged around the Lords.

By the winter of 1854–5 prominent parliamentarians were positioning themselves for a post-coalition administration, against a volatile background of growing popular attacks on the corruption and inadequacy of aristocratic government. Populist critiques provided radicals and others with ready explanations for the Aberdeen coalition's failure, calling for meritocratic efficiency in place of nepotism and oligarchic incompetence. While the opening up of the civil service to entrance by competitive examination, as proposed by the Northcote–Trevelyan Report in 1853, pointed the way to reform, widespread frustration threatened broader assaults on the governing capability of the nation's elite. Armed with W. H. Russell's graphic reports from the Crimea of appalling ineptitude, *The Times* led the cry for urgent change.

By January 1855, as popular awareness of the disease, hunger, and fatigue decimating British troops grew, the outrage against official incapacity intensified. Popular patriotic radicalism, particularly in London and including the National Charter Association, was generally aggressively supportive of a more efficient prosecution of the war. In the Commons, on 26 January 1855, a censure motion on the government proposed by the patriotic radical MP John Roebuck overwhelmingly passed. The announcement of the vote in the Commons, 305 opposition votes to 148 government votes, was met with a slight incredulous laugh, one side of the House astonished, the other stunned and mortified. This ended, with ignominy and in sudden collapse, the Aberdeen coalition's existence. Who now could the nation look to for effective leadership?

During the last months of the coalition Russell tried to distance himself from government policy, but only confirmed a reputation for waywardness. He became regarded as worn out in body and mind. Shortly before Roebuck's motion, in 'a dexterous leap out of a sinking boat', Russell resigned from the ministry, allowing his supporters to bring down the cabinet of which he had just been a member.[14] From the Home Office Palmerston had, with greater success, managed in the eyes of many outside the ministry to dissociate himself from the coalition's inept management of the war. On the opposition benches Conservatives, following Derby's strategy of masterly inactivity, continued to allow the government to amplify their own divisions.

Want of attack from without allowed mutiny to ravage the coalition camp. Intense and complex negotiations immediately followed the coalition's fall. Derby was commissioned by the Queen with the formation of a government. He led the largest and most unified body of votes in parliament. But without accessions of strength from other groups the Conservatives lacked a Commons majority. Palmerston agreed to serve in a Derby ministry, but attached conditions, such as the Whig Lord Clarendon being retained at the Foreign Office. Once the Peelites Gladstone and Herbert, and predictably Clarendon, refused to join Derby, the Conservative leader surrendered his commission. But Derby kept his options open for a second attempt once the impossibility of any alternative government being formed had been proved. The Conservative Whip made known to Disraeli the great relief felt by many of his backbenchers at the narrow escape from a junction with Gladstone. Such a union, Disraeli was told, would be a source not of strength, but of weakness.

Derby, like Russell, did not believe Palmerston to be a prospective prime minister. Disraeli thought Palmerston suffered from age, infirmity, and an overrated reputation. Lord Lansdowne, the elderly Whig patriarch, declined the Queen's invitation to form a government. Russell tried next to form a ministry, but also failed as leading Whigs ostracised him. Then, despite Queen Victoria's extreme reluctance, and to Derby and Russell's surprise, Palmerston managed to form an administration. Under his premiership Palmerston elicited Whig, Liberal, some radical and, for the first few weeks at least, general Peelite support. Russell was passed the poisoned chalice of appointment as plenipotentiary to Vienna, where he quickly became mired in the complexities of negotiating a Crimean peace.

Palmerston's first ministry, 1855–8

In retrospect Palmerston's accession to power, amid the snowstorms and bitter cold of February 1855, acquired a gloss of inevitability. In the midst of a mismanaged war Palmerston was the man called upon by the country to provide decisive and effective leadership. Palmerston was, indeed, popular in the country. By late January *The Times*, as well as the *Morning Post* and *Morning Advertiser*, were calling for a Palmerston government. While the *Daily News* defended Russell, as the only real Liberal leader, the *Morning Chronicle* lamented the downfall of Aberdeen, and the *Morning Herald* declared for Derby. But within the walls of Westminster, where it mattered most, Palmerston's claim to the premiership was far from certain. Disraeli saw Palmerston as 'really an imposter, utterly exhausted . . . and now an old painted Pantaloon . . . [but] he is a name which the country resolves to associate with energy, wisdom and eloquence'.[15] The Whig Lord Clarendon observed: 'extravagant expectations are raised of the good [Palmerston] is to do and the great acts he is to perform, all of which will only lead to disappointment and mortification'. The shrewd and well-informed diarist Charles Greville, Clerk to the Privy Council, recorded on 19 February 1855: 'Palmerston has no authority [in the Commons], the House is in complete confusion and disorganisation, and, except for the Derbyites, who are still numerous and act together in opposition, in hopes of getting into power, nobody owns any allegiance or even any party ties, or seems to care for any person or any thing'.[16]

Under the pressure of the premiership it was anticipated that Palmerston's health and strength would fail. The hatred of the Manchester School radicals for Palmerston was even stronger than that felt at Court, and many Whigs were likely to revert to Russell. As he was over 70 years of age and suffering from gout, Palmerston's health was a constant subject of political speculation; the supposition being he could not remain active for long. This consideration alone led many to see his prominence as inevitably only temporary. His parliamentary support was unstable; his success being largely the result of Whig exasperation at Russell's fickleness, Derby's underestimation of Palmerston's potential, and Peelite distaste for the exotic and untrustworthy Disraeli. Within a month Gladstone and Herbert, to the delight of a number of Whigs, resigned from Palmerston's cabinet. The Peelites Lord Canning and the Duke of Argyll stayed on in Palmerston's ministry. The hard-working Whigs Sir Charles Wood, Sir George Grey and Sir George Cornewall Lewis compensated for the lost talents of the departing Peelites. In July 1855 Russell, in a bitter and jaundiced mood, also resigned from the government and began fomenting discontent within ministerial ranks. 'The House of Commons', Russell privately declared, 'is as unstable as water. But the people have great qualities and they may in time cease to bow before the idols, and resume their ancient love of truth.'[17]

It was the turn of events in the Crimea, the capture of Kerch in June and the fall of Sebastopol in September 1855, that kept Palmerston in power. For the moment, Palmerston seemed to shed his years and appear a 'babe of grace'.[18] Yet, aware of Palmerston's still precarious position, Derby returned to an opposition strategy of masterly inactivity prepared, through 'armed neutrality', passively to await the inevitable fracture of Palmerstonian support. It was better that Palmerston be brought down in due course by erstwhile friends than by Conservative attack. Particularly as Palmerston himself, though old, was an obvious and desirable recruit to Conservative ranks should Whig and Liberal connection shatter. Difficulties and government embarrassment over the Crimean peace negotiations at Vienna during the summer of 1855 had brought Derby's hopes close to realisation. In November 1855 Disraeli agreed with Derby that 'silence and inertia are our wisest course'. That same month the progressive Conservative Lord Stanley, son of Lord Derby the Conservative leader, declined an invitation to join Palmerston's cabinet as Colonial Secretary. Apart from considerations of filial duty, Stanley believed such a secession would be a move from the stronger to the weaker side; Disraeli, Gladstone and Bright all being in strong opposition to the government and Russell's hostility rendering Palmerston's claim to Whig support uncertain. Leading Conservatives were happy to bide their time. In the circumstances Palmerston had no choice but to play to his proven strengths.

During 1855 and 1856 Palmerston defined a national policy that pointed to the primacy of foreign affairs. Palmerston promised forthrightly to defend British interests abroad. This, he declared, ensured national prosperity, light taxation, and safeguarded British freedoms and stability. It also gave Britain 'moral force' abroad as the guardian of liberal progress providing 'a bright example' to others. The popular pursuit of national interest and progressive improvement overseas, therefore, was presented as the key to secure freedoms, social harmony, cheap government, and economic prosperity at home. Palmerston's combining of patriotism, Russophobia, and support for constitutionalism abroad accommodated radical populist sentiment, helping to defuse extra-parliamentary demands for the overhaul of aristocratic government. This emphasis was, therefore, not merely a reflection of Palmerston's Foreign Office expertise or the inevitable priorities of a wartime government. It was a perspective of the national need sustained beyond the Treaty of Paris ending the Crimean War in March 1856. Nor was it entirely a simple reflection of Palmerston's liberal Tory apprenticeship as an administrator prior to 1830, though he certainly had no temperamental disposition toward proactive legislation. Most importantly, it reflected Palmerston's parliamentary vulnerability on domestic issues. Foreign affairs, the radical MP

John Bright complained, were 'elevated as the chief, if not the sole department of national politics and interest'.[19] During the 1830s and 1840s Whigs, Liberals, and radicals had primarily defined their purposes in terms of domestic issues requiring large-scale legislative reform. Russell's threat to Palmerston was that he still personified precisely that virtuous probity which had propelled such aims. The expectation during 1856 of a liberal movement led by Russell prompted thoughtful Conservatives such as Stanley and Sir John Pakington to take up social, particularly educational, reform. Russell's rectitude exposed the soft underbelly of Palmerstonian rhetoric.

Within Palmerston's Commons support, from Whigs, Liberals, and radicals, there existed no ready agreement on domestic reform, as debates on religion, education, administrative reform and law reform during the sessions of 1855 and 1856 showed. Yet the precepts of foreign policy, injected with Palmerston's distinctive and energetic jauntiness, did secure a Commons majority. Therein lay the ultimate constraints on Palmerston's presentation of national policy. During 1856 it sustained him in power. The appointment of *The Times* editorial writer Robert Lowe (MP for Kidderminster) as Paymaster General in August 1855 helped to take the steam out of the Administrative Reform Association's call for the dismantling of aristocratic, and therefore inefficient, government. This was despite Lowe joining a cabinet amply manned by members of the peerage. At the same time, the establishment of the Civil Service Commission in 1855, assessing the suitability of appointees; the economic orthodoxy, evident intelligence, and calm capability of Sir George Cornewall Lewis as Chancellor of the Exchequer; likewise Sir George Grey's quiet proficiency as Home Secretary, the increasing use of Royal Commissions to investigate social and administrative problems, and the attempt to introduce life peerages in 1856, suggested that those in power could respond to the call for more efficient and economical government. Ecclesiastical appointments, recommended by the prime minister's son-in-law Lord Shaftesbury, also appeased low church and Nonconformist sections of support. In 1856 Archibald Tait was appointed bishop of London, while in the following year the evangelical Robert

Bickersteth was named bishop of Ripon. Little interested in religious matters himself, Palmerston sought to make denominational differences as politically imperceptible as possible.

None the less, in May 1856 it was the fall of the fortress at Kars in the Crimea, a foreign policy question on which he stood on strong ground, that Palmerston portrayed as a question of confidence. After haranguing supporters at a private meeting, Palmerston secured a great Commons success. Once again the Crimean campaign carried Palmerston through. Meanwhile, he shelved a local dues bill in select committee, laid aside the question of the purchase of military commissions, postponed law reform, and let a public health bill run into the sand. Yet the priorities of Palmerstonian policy could only defer not resolve fractious domestic concerns. These survived as the potential solvent of Palmerston's parliamentary support. In April 1856 Graham observed that 'the government goes on because there is no organised opposition prepared and able to take its place, and the government receives a sufficiency of independent support, because all feel that the business of the country must be carried on'.[20]

Those who resign from governments often become their bitterest enemies. In 1855 both Russell and Gladstone left Palmerston's cabinet. By late 1856 both were working assiduously to destroy it. When parliament met in February 1857 hostile groups marshalled themselves for an all-out assault on the government. 'The war cloud under which they had cowered having drifted by', Russell, Gladstone, Graham and Disraeli 'raised their heads, like Milton's fallen angels, from the oblivious pool, to plot anew for the recovery of all that the last two years had cost them'.[21] Russell, just returned from a trip to the continent, was known to be looking for an issue with which to embarrass Palmerston's cabinet. In the Lords the third Lord Grey, a renegade Whig with impeccable credentials, looked to attack the ministry over the outbreak of hostilities with Persia; the government attempting to end Persian encroachment into Afghanistan, which was a buffer state to British India. Lord Aberdeen, as leader of the Peelites, also clearly indicated his impatience with Palmerston's policies.

In the Commons Gladstone, panting for office, prepared a comprehensive financial assault focusing on Cornewall Lewis and the Chancellor's handling of the income tax. Aberdeen once commented that Gladstone should be kept in office, 'give him plenty to do, else he is sure to do mischief'.[22] Intense frustration at being denied office gave Gladstone's attacks on Cornewall Lewis a violent acerbic edge. In the Commons Gladstone spoke with peculiar vehemence, like a man under personal provocation. By contrast, the stolid Cornewall Lewis spoke without animation and with the demeanour of a clerk reading accounts. Other Peelites, such as Sir James Graham, supported Gladstone. But they did not share Gladstone's strategic intention that the discrediting of government fiscal policy be associated with the Conservatives as a basis for reconciliation, the schism of 1846 thereby being healed. Derby and Disraeli, meanwhile, gave careful encouragement to Gladstone, always prepared to welcome possible accessions of strength, but also keenly aware that Gladstone was extremely unpopular within Conservative ranks. Possible junction with Gladstone always raised the prospect of mutiny within the Conservative camp.

In the event, on 13 February 1857, Cornewall Lewis delivered a budget which skilfully pre-empted Peelite–Conservative attack. The Chancellor dropped income tax to the fixed rate originally introduced by Peel and proposed a gradual reduction of tea and sugar duties. Disraeli's own financial resolutions, attacking the Chancellor's policy, were resoundingly defeated. The cabinet viewed this victory as 'the benefit of a junction between the haters of Gladstone and the haters of Disraeli'.[23] With the wind promptly taken out of their sails, both Gladstone and Disraeli were becalmed for the remainder of the session.

Six days later, on 19 February 1857, Russell unveiled the real threat to the government. By supporting the radical Locke King's motion for an identical £10 suffrage in both county and borough constituencies, Russell successfully resuscitated the issue of parliamentary reform. The great bulk of Whig, Liberal and radical votes fell in behind Russell. Locke King's motion was only defeated because the front bench rump of Palmerstonian votes was joined by the mass of Conservative

MPs. A debate on the Maynooth Grant which immediately followed revealed further deep divisions within government support. The message for Palmerston's cabinet was simple and clear. On a progressive domestic issue such as parliamentary reform Russell's authority still surpassed that of Palmerston.

The radical Cobden tabled a Commons motion criticising the government for a high-handed policy in China. In response to a technical insult to the British flag the government's representatives had resorted to armed force, which had culminated in the bombardment of a defenceless Canton. Russell, radicals, Peelites and Conservatives all quickly swung their support behind Cobden's motion. During subsequent debate the radical Thomas Milner Gibson observed that Palmerston had abandoned the Liberal watchword of 'Peace, Retrenchment and Reform' for 'Bombardment of Canton and no Reform'. Disraeli characterised the government's policy as 'No Reform! New Taxes! Canton blazing! Persia invaded!' Palmerston, ill with cold and gout, spoke poorly in reply. On 3 March Cobden's motion of censure passed, supported by Russellite Whigs and Liberals, radicals, Peelites and Conservatives. Palmerston quickly decided to dissolve parliament and call an election. Never, Lowe observed in the *Edinburgh Review*, was 'so much faction crowded into so small a space of time'.[24]

The general election of 1857 has been conventionally portrayed by historians as a triumphant plebiscite in support of Palmerston. But as we have seen, it was not in the nature of mid-Victorian elections to pass plebiscitary judgements on incumbent administrations. Where national issues infiltrated constituency contests they were shaped by local circumstances. This was no less true of the 1857 election than of other mid-Victorian general elections. Moreover, the number of candidates standing for election in 1857 was the lowest of any general election since 1832. The number of uncontested constituencies was the highest, with the exception of 1847, of any election since the Reform Act. Frontbench candidates did present an orthodox Palmerstonian platform. At Tiverton Palmerston declined to enter into detailed pledges or hold out distinct promises with regard to domestic reform. But in Ireland and Wales religious questions were prominent. Scottish constituencies displayed a wide range of differing concerns. In English constituencies such as Leicester and Aylesbury religion also tended to dominate the hustings. In Devon and Cornwall Liberals gained nine seats through the exertions of the Liberation Society. Indeed, in England generally the Society secured the election of a number of advanced Liberals. While many Whig and Liberal candidates expressed a very general support for Palmerston, one specific issue did become more prominent in English constituencies as the election progressed, namely parliamentary reform.

On 19 March 1857 in the City of London Russell spoke of the necessity for reform and promotion of the cause of progress. Thereafter a significant number of Whig, Liberal, and radical candidates picked up on Russell's cue. A number of leading radicals were defeated and lost their seats, including Richard Cobden, John Bright, Thomas Milner Gibson, A. H. Layard, and Edward Miall. But in Sheffield, Bolton, Stoke, Carlisle, Stockport, Greenwich, and Bristol, anti-Palmerston candidates were returned. By the end of the election an infuriated Palmerston suspected that the Ryder Street Committee, who were helping to sponsor government candidates, were 'trying to pack the parliament with ballot men willing and unwilling'. This 'bit of treachery' he saw as an indication that some Liberals were anticipating 'a radical parliament with John Russell as its head'.[25] The Conservatives found their Commons numbers reduced to about 260 MPs. But Derby and Disraeli consoled themselves with two thoughts: first, that the Conservatives were more compact and united than before; secondly, that with reform now a live issue the government's ranks were even more deeply divided than prior to the election. The Peelites did fare badly. Sidney Herbert feared they were now nearly extinct. It was clear they must look to a merger. But while Gladstone favoured rejoining the Conservatives, Graham and Aberdeen looked to Russell as their best prospect. Gladstone directed his energies into Homeric study and impassioned, idiosyncratic denouncements of divorce law reform. In truth, the 1857 election did little to clarify the nebulous alignment of non-Conservative opinion.

Meeting the new parliament in May 1857, Palmerston's cabinet were well aware of the dangerous undercurrents lying just below the surface of seeming electoral success. As one Whig source observed: 'the immediate victory is Palmerston's, the second is the Liberal party's, and the third will be Lord John's'. Though, to the casual observer, there appeared a large and firm Palmerstonian majority, the US ambassador George Dallas noted that informed sources said 'wait a little'. In due course the force for reform 'will have fermented, found its way to the top, and be prepared and able to shake the smooth surface of the ministerial cauldron. . . . The power "to wait" is a great one'.[26] News of the outbreak of the Indian Mutiny, which reached London in June, temporarily deferred consideration of domestic reform. In the face of popular outrage generated by reports of native atrocities Palmerston, to the alarm of many, maintained a calm optimism. Then in September 1857, as two years previously, news of military victories, the recapture of Delhi and the first relief of Lucknow, momentarily defused mounting domestic criticism. Palmerston immediately pushed forward the issue of administrative reform in India. As Lord Granville, government leader in the Lords, noted; 'one of Palmerston's motives is to do something great which will distinguish his premiership and another to have something that will act as a damper to [parliamentary] reform'.[27] Nevertheless, by the beginning of 1858 hostile parliamentary opinion was once again steeling itself for an assault on Palmerston's ministry.

In December 1857 Palmerston incited popular anger by the extraordinary appointment of the scandal-ridden Lord Clanricarde as Lord Privy Seal. Three years earlier Clanricarde had been implicated in accusations of child abuse, sexual immorality, and association with individuals charged with murder. Widespread indignation hardened the opposition's resolve. While preparing legislation dissolving the East India Company, Palmerston also found himself forced to draw up a parliamentary reform bill. In the hope of eliciting Conservative support against more extensive demands, the cabinet drafted a moderate reform measure preserving the existing borough suffrage, lowering the county suffrage to £20, and offering special franchises to particular professions such as lawyers, physicians, and clergymen. Disfranchisement was narrowly limited to a number of small boroughs. No parliamentary schedule accompanied the scheme, moreover, and while India might further defer consideration of reform Palmerston could be expected to be compliant. Meanwhile Russell, in high spirits, was known to be organising the demand for immediate substantial reform; the significant disfranchisement of small or venial constituencies being the mark of a genuine measure. Then in January 1858 a foreign crisis, the attempted assassination of the French Emperor Louis Napoleon by conspirators (led by Felice Orsini) based in England and carrying British passports, added to the government's difficulties. Lord Clarendon, as Foreign Secretary, feared that French outrage would forge an anti-British alliance in Europe, led by France and Russia. His conciliatory response to public French attacks on British asylum laws ignited domestic opposition anger at a government apparently amending British law in response to Gallic threats. Again, seeking Conservative support, Palmerston drew up a Conspiracy to Murder bill, increasing penalties for proven conspirators, which he hoped would be the diplomatic maximum and political minimum that need be done. The Orsini crisis, Clanricarde scandal, reform and India, however, provided plentiful ammunition with which to demolish Palmerston's Commons support.

Russell and Roebuck led an immediate parliamentary onslaught on the government over the Orsini issue in early February 1858. Only Conservative support secured the first reading of Palmerston's Conspiracy to Murder bill. A week later Conservatives *en masse* attacked the government's India bill. A motion made by the radical Milner Gibson, on 19 February, criticising Clarendon for not responding to a despatch from the French Foreign Minister decrying British rights of asylum, brought radicals, Russellites, Peelites, and Conservatives together. Driven to an open display of anger, waving his fist at radical Members, an increasingly erratic Palmerston denounced the motley forces arrayed against him. Milner Gibson's motion was subsequently carried by 234 to 215 votes, the government being put in a Commons minority of 19. Russell led nearly 90

Whig, Liberal, and radical votes into the opposition lobby alongside the Conservatives. A burst of cheering broke out in the chamber when the result of the division was announced. Disraeli looked triumphant. Graham, in raptures, seized the hand of John Bright, recently returned in a by-election as MP for Birmingham, as if he had met with a great deliverance. The next day Palmerston decided to resign. His decision, however, should not be readily accepted as dutiful compliance with the verdict of what Palmerston insisted was a chance defeat. Resigning over the Orsini affair was preferable to more debilitating defeats over reform or India. Part of Palmerston's intention in resigning was to embarrass the combination of parties arrayed against him (Lady Palmerston hinted at such), and the Orsini question had the greatest potential for causing just such dismay. The Queen immediately sent for Derby, who, after informing his monarch of the difficulties he would face, agreed to form a Conservative ministry.

Derby's Conservative Government, 1858–9

Lord Derby saw the opportunity, while holding office, to establish the Conservatives as a party of moderation and responsible reform. This amounted to more than those unavoidable concessions demanded by minority status. It was the complement to Derby's strategy of inactivity and non-commitment while in opposition. Once in power Conservatives should, as Derby formulated it, advocate progress: judicious changes meeting the increased demands of society, improving the old system and adapting institutions to altered purposes. There could be no greater mistake, he informed the Lords, than supposing that a Conservative ministry necessarily meant a stationary ministry. After some hesitation Gladstone, as advised by Graham and Herbert, declined joining Derby's cabinet, but confirmed a presumption of favourable support. Once again, expressions of profound relief came from certain sections of the Conservative back benches at deliverance from a union with Gladstone. The Duke of Newcastle and Lord Grey also declined the invitation to join Derby's front bench. The new premier's hope of broadening his support through official accessions was frustrated. The cabinet was drawn from solely Conservative resources.

None the less, Derby's policy was to put even greater pressure on a fragmented opposition. Though not possessing a Commons majority, Derby's cabinet headed a relatively cohesive Conservative party facing divided Whig, Liberal, Peelite, and radical forces increasingly prey to internal acrimony. Throughout his 1858–9 ministry Derby consistently sought to exploit the rivalry between Russell and Palmerston, to encourage the possibility of disillusioned Whigs moving towards a centrist coalition, to emphasise the divergence within Peelite intent, and to frustrate the radicals' need for a clear polarisation of parliamentary opinion. Meanwhile, assisted in the Lords by his Whip Lord Colville, Derby re-established the traditional Conservative majority dismantled by the party split of 1846. From 1858 onwards Derby could presume a Conservative ascendancy in the Upper House.

By March 1858 the diplomatic quarrels with France were resolved. A concerted opposition attack in both Houses on Derby's Indian policy in May 1858, focusing on Lord Ellenborough, his President of the Board of Control, fell apart with devastating effect on Whig and Liberal morale. Palmerston's influence was further diminished. Edward Cardwell had proposed the opposition motion in the Commons, Lord Shaftesbury a similar one in the Lords, at the behest of Palmerston and Granville. With the covert help of Russell and Milner Gibson the ministry's Indian government legislation was steered around dangerous shoals. The cabinet's pilot, Lord Stanley, first as Colonial Secretary then as Ellenborough's successor, skilfully navigated the Conservative measure through to the royal assent.

In July 1858 a private measure allowing practising Jews to become Members of the Commons was passed; the single most important piece of legislation from the 1850s signalling greater religious liberty. Disraeli's 1858 budget reinstated Gladstone's 1853 settlement. Property qualifications for MPs were abolished; a Chartist demand from the 1840s. A conciliatory reform of church rates was proposed. Acts conferring self-governing status on British Columbia, extending municipal government, and facilitating drainage of the Thames were passed. Concessions were made to Catholics. A contract was negotiated for a direct mail service between Ireland and America, expected to create a commercial boom in Galway. Catholic chaplains in the army were given permanent rank and salary. Easier access to prisons and workhouses was allowed to Catholic priests, and the government let it be known it was considering the reform of Irish landlord and tenant law. Meanwhile in foreign affairs Derby's Foreign Secretary, Lord Malmesbury, pursued a sober *via media*. Anglo-American tensions over Central America were soothed. The 1858 session provided ample substantiation of Derby's moderate rhetoric. As the session drew to a close the radical Trelawny saw Derby as 'Palmerston redivivus'. The 'Whig hacks must be frantic. Why, good God! the country may learn, if this goes on, to forget the value of Whig government!'[28]

While 1858 was an encouraging year for the Conservatives it only brought further disarray to a demoralised opposition. By the recess Palmerston seemed a spent political force, old, ill and with a rapidly diminishing influence. The collapse of his popularity after his removal from office was striking. Gladstone noted that the former premier was even hooted at by crowds in Hyde Park. The events of February 1858, Gladstone observed to his brother, released Liberals from the discreditable position of supporting 'the worst government of our time'.[29] Over dinner tables Whigs were eloquent about the miserable condition of the party – a situation for which Palmerston was blamed. Cornewall Lewis thought the Liberal party extinct. Grey observed that men such as the Duke of Bedford and himself were far nearer Derby in their political opinions than they were to the likes of radicals such as Milner Gibson. By August 1858 the opposition seemed without form and void. The broken fragments of the Whig party, Graham observed, were shattered. 'The old stagers have known each other too long and too well; and they dislike each other too much.'[30] Sidney Herbert saw only chaos on the opposition benches. Trelawny was dismayed by 'the devices of certain ex-ministers. When Lord John and Palmerston happen to concur, Graham and Gladstone seem to stand aside or oppose them. When Graham and Lord John concur, then, Palmerston adroitly moves to defeat them. No Liberal government seems possible while this system goes on.' By July 1858 the India bill had become 'merely the stage on which a fencing match or triangular duel is taking place between the great party leaders opposed to the ministry'.[31]

That parliamentary reform remained an unresolved issue offered the opposition some hope of recovery. Derby was committed to introducing a reform bill in 1859 which, if suitably meagre, might provide Whigs, Liberals, and radicals with a rallying cry. During the autumn of 1858 an increasingly confident Russell, the more prominent as Palmerston's stature dramatically waned, busily sounded out Peelite, Whig, and radical opinion. Certain that the Conservatives would have a difficult, if not impossible, game to play on reform, Russell awaited the government's plan, ready to pronounce it inadequate and propose a genuine liberal measure in its place. Time spent with Lord Stanley, following an invitation to the ancestral seat at Woburn in September 1858, convinced Russell that the Conservatives would themselves be unable to agree on reform.

During the winter a restless Gladstone, despite having declined a second invitation to join Derby's cabinet in May 1858, accepted charge of a diplomatic mission to negotiate a constitutional settlement for the Ionian Islands. Gladstone's Homeric interests made the offer particularly attractive. Peelite colleagues such as Graham and Edward Cardwell understood his acceptance as preparing for Gladstone's subsequent merger with the Conservatives. Thinking Gladstone's mission a curious one, Russell suspected it also provided a pretext, while abroad, to be absent from awkward parliamentary debate on reform. Certainly, during the winter of 1858–9, Gladstone felt reform to be 'an unattractive subject'.[32]

Meanwhile, from October 1858 to January 1859, John Bright, exploiting the expanded railway system, undertook an extensive public speaking campaign, visiting Birmingham, Manchester, and Glasgow, outlining radical expectations of reform. The speeches reasserted Bright as the foremost radical voice in parliament, an authority intended to put Milner Gibson and Roebuck in their place. Transcribed by forty to fifty reporters crowded around the platform, the speeches were directed, through the growing popular provincial press, to a national public as much as to the immediate audience. The detailed recommendations Bright made at Bradford in January 1859 seemed to some, apprehensive of extensive demands, relatively moderate; a £10 poor relief borough suffrage and a £10 rental value suffrage for the counties, protected by the ballot and accompanied by a schedule of disfranchisement. Redistribution, not the franchise, as Bright had learnt from Cobden, was presented as the heart of the reform issue; the 'very pith and marrow' of reform. Bright's proposed redistribution was extensive. But it was the violent language Bright used in his speeches, in particular his attacks on the House of Lords, that excited alarm and fears of class warfare. As always, privilege not property was Bright's target.

Away from the platform, Bright claimed he was being misrepresented and talked of a Granville government with Russell as leader of the Commons. This suggested that, once the threat of radical change was seen to be real, Bright might in private prove amenable. In characteristically Whiggish manner Russell deplored not so much the substance of Bright's speeches as the manner in which he delivered them directly to popular audiences outside parliament. Certainly by January 1859 the Whigs Clarendon and Grey, the former Peelite Duke of Argyll and former minister Cornewall Lewis, were drafting reform schemes they hoped would be reassuringly moderate; no more than was sufficient to elicit radical support, while substantial enough to trump any Conservative proposals. The radical Roebuck was also privately dissociating himself from Bright's demands and encouraging cross-party discussion.

Derby's challenge in 1859 was to design a reform bill extensive enough to capture some Whig and Peelite support, while preserving Conservative unity. Disregarding Disraeli's initial lack of enthusiasm for reform, the premier achieved his aim with greater success than many had anticipated. A cabinet committee, chaired by Derby, from which particularly recalcitrant ministers such as Spencer Walpole, Lord Hardwicke, and J. W. Henley were excluded, drafted a measure for England and Wales. It betrayed the influence of progressive ministerial minds such as Lord Stanley and the Commons Chief Whip Sir William Jolliffe. At the cost of two resignations in February 1859, from Walpole and Henley, the cabinet finally agreed to a measure based on equalising the county and borough franchise; the county franchise to be lowered to the existing £10 household borough franchise. This was precisely the principle endorsed by Russell and Locke King in 1857, which when proposed again by Locke King in June 1858 had received widespread Whig, Liberal, and radical support. It carried with it nearly a decade of radical advocacy, since Locke King's proposal was first passed in the Commons in 1850, as a significant curtailment of vested landed power in the county constituencies. At the same time, Derby attached clauses confining borough freeholders to borough votes and stripping some of them of their existing county suffrage, and a redistribution scheme helping to mitigate the radical effects of an identity of suffrage. While these latter aspects of the measure, he hoped, would allay Ultra Tory fears, Derby anticipated his main franchise reform securing acceptance of the Conservative bill as a broad, comprehensive and final settlement.

Italy saved politicians from an exclusive preoccupation with reform during the 1858 recess. A broad sympathy for liberal Italian nationalism existed within English political circles and the Kingdom of Piedmont Sardinia was seen as a possible champion of such aspirations. Italian nationalists wished to overthrow the Vienna settlement of 1815 and drive the Austrians out of Lombardy and Venetia. A deep-rooted anti-Catholicism and contempt for the temporal power enjoyed by Pope Pius IX, dislike of Austrian repression in Lombardy and Venetia, and loathing for the corruption endemic in the Kingdom of the Two Sicilies, fostered English sympathies. After visiting prisons in Naples, capital of the Kingdom of the Two Sicilies, in 1850, Gladstone and subsequently Russell had fiercely denounced Neapolitan barbarity. But such sympathies were counterbalanced by a deep suspicion of Emperor Louis Napoleon, distrust of expansionist French ambitions in the peninsula, and anxiety that a disruption of the balance of power in Europe would forge a hostile Franco-Russian alliance exploiting Austrian weaknesses. When, in November 1858, Palmerston visited Louis Napoleon at Compiègne an anti-French outcry was prompted at home which emphasised Palmerston's fall from grace. In 1858 the immediate British fear was that French intrigue was inciting Piedmont and its prime minister, Count Cavour, to contemplate intemperate acts of aggression against Austria, threatening a dangerous European war, with Piedmont the gullible pawn of French ambition. This fear created a broad consensus among Conservatives, Whigs and Liberals. Napoleonic aggrandisement and Austrian humiliation, with dangerous consequences beyond desirable local reforms, without striking at the real root of evil repression in the Papal States and the Kingdom of the Two Sicilies, would be too high a price to pay for Italian liberty. A wish for vigilant non-intervention prevailed.

Lord Malmesbury, as Foreign Secretary, shaped his policy to this domestic consensus. The question remained, however, as circumstances developed, how opposition leaders such as Russell, with a record of decrying the illiberality of the Papal States, and others such as Gladstone, as a prominent critic of political repression in Naples, would act. Palmerston shared the wish not to see Austria crippled as a European power. In the event of war, Palmerston agreed with Granville that Britain's only course was neutrality. The radical John Bright's fear, as international tensions mounted into the New Year, was that Italy might cast reform in the shade. The Liberal Edward Ellice feared the revival of a Palmerston ministry should war break out. The Conservative minister Edward Bulwer Lytton wrote to Gladstone in the Ionian Islands: 'Affairs as to war . . . may suddenly lift up Palmerston into a power no one dreamed he could have again.' But Graham agreed 'in "Fudge" as the right answer to Palmerston's divine mission as the minister of England in the event of war'.[33]

Conservative Defeat and Liberal Union

1859 should have been and nearly was Russell's year. The agenda seemed ideal, reform the main business, with Italy a supplementary issue. By January 1859 Russell was poised to achieve that which had eluded him ten years before: the forging of a progressive alliance, embracing Peelites, Whigs, Liberals and radicals, fired with rectitude for a decisive measure of domestic reform. The climax of high political activity, between the death of Peel in 1850 and the death of Palmerston in 1865, came in the months between January and June 1859. For success Russell required the Conservative party, while providing a reactionary foil, to fracture over reform. He needed radicals such as Bright, Milner Gibson and Roebuck to endorse his leadership. Finally, he required Palmerston's demise to continue; the waning of his rival's influence leaving his own star shining the more brightly.

In the event, between January and June 1859, Conservative concession, radical reticence and Palmerston's patience decisively destroyed Russell's hopes. On 28 February 1859 Disraeli presented to the Commons a Conservative reform bill more moderate than most had expected, endorsed by the whole cabinet, less Walpole and Henley. It was a measure, *The Times* declared, all reasonable men ought to concur in supporting. This was an important endorsement for the broad nature of the government's bill. The 130 MPs threatened with disfranchisement under Bright's proposed scheme were delighted with the reprieve. The Whigs remained silent and the Palmerstonians still and impenetrable. Russell could not attack the government's measure without appearing dangerously radical. As an alternative, during March, Russell brought forward on the second reading a narrower motion attacking the clause transferring borough freeholders' voting rights from the county to the urban seat. This pre-empted a general discussion of the broad merits of the bill. Moreover, it focused debate on an issue capable of pulling together opposition opinion, including Palmerston and the radicals, otherwise implacably divided over other aspects of the measure. One Conservative minister dismissed the motion as 'a rope of sand'.[34] But early in the morning of 1 April 1859 Russell's motion was carried by 330 to 291 votes, a majority of 39. At a cabinet meeting later in the day the government decided to call an election.

Russell's victory, however, was less than complete. Forced to throw a narrow, rather than broad, assault on the Conservative bill, his ascendancy over the reform issue was not authoritatively established. Palmerston, for one, denied that his support for Russell's motion was intended as a vote of censure requiring the withdrawal of the government's bill. Palmerston supported Russell's motion in a manner that helped scuttle its author's ambitions. The Whig Lord Clarendon favoured a dissolution rather than the Conservatives resigning and an extreme reform bill being brought in by their successors. The radical Roebuck, meanwhile, indicated his willingness to countenance the Conservatives continuing with a modified version of their bill.

Then, as preparations for the hustings were begun during April, dramatic events in Europe thrust forward the question of Italy. Contrary to general expectation, on 19 April Austria, rather than French-backed Piedmont, initiated hostilities. Austrian nerves, stretched beyond their limit by French and Piedmontese bellicosity, snapped. In a speech at the Mansion House on 25 April Derby quickly abused Austria for opening hostilities, but restated the government's intention to maintain a strict, though armed, neutrality. However, the false assumption that Piedmont would be the aggressor did, in retrospect, expose government policy to criticism. Russell immediately decried official neutrality as a sham, concealing Conservative sympathy for Austria and opposition to reform in Italy. It was now clear, Russell argued, that Austria was the villain, obstinately suppressing Italian freedom. A panic collapse on the London Stock Exchange heightened the sense of crisis.

The elections of May 1859 increased the government's strength, the Conservative Chief Whip tallying a total of 306 Conservative MPs. It was to prove the best electoral result the Conservatives achieved at any time between the Corn Law crisis of 1846 and their triumph of 1874. The Conservatives' greatest successes were in their natural electoral base: the rural communities of the English counties and those small English boroughs under the sway of landed patrons. Of the 117 English boroughs won by the Conservatives, 86 had less than 1,000 voters, a further 23 boroughs returning Conservatives having 1,000–2,000 voters. Only 8 Conservative victories were in populous English borough constituencies with over 2,000 voters.[35] A further 8 seats gained in Ireland vindicated the modest legislative concessions Derby's cabinet had given to Catholics. In 1852, 42 Conservative Irish MPs faced a majority of 63 Irish Liberal MPs. Overlooking religious antipathies, in private Disraeli declared: 'Ireland is agricultural, aristocratic and religious: therefore Ireland ought to be Tory'.[36] By 1859 a majority of 57 Conservative Irish MPs sat opposite 48 Liberal Irish MPs. But the Conservatives still lacked an absolute Commons majority. On the other side of the House sat 349 non-Conservative MPs of various kinds, although it was still not clear precisely how that body of opinion would be aligned and under whom they would act. Conservatives remained hopeful of moderate accessions, as the exact intentions of Palmerston and of radicals such as Bright and Roebuck, including their attitude to Russell, remained unclear. As always, local issues dominated the hustings. Even so, reform remained more a concern than Italy, despite Russell taking up the lofty cry of Italian liberty. By May Russell's worsening plight brought the engaging subplot of Palmerston's intentions back into centre stage. It was clear that the longer Russell's difficulties persisted the better Palmerston's prospects became.

Those, like Graham, favouring Russell's cause, urged an immediate move against the government once the new parliament met. Russell himself compared the opposition to 'the Irishman's blanket; if you want to strengthen the top you must cut off the bottom; if the bottom, you must cut off the top'.[37] Throughout May, Whigs, Peelites, Liberals, and radicals closeted themselves, negotiators scurrying between Pembroke Lodge and Cambridge House, Russell and Palmerston's London residences. Russell entered negotiation with two bargaining points. First, that any new government must contain Peelites and radicals, as well as Whigs and Liberals. Secondly, that any new reform bill must be a substantial measure. These conditions he saw as the safeguards of his position. Palmerston, meanwhile, blocked any opposition motion carrying a specific commitment to the immediate introduction of a reform bill, or passing judgement on Conservative foreign policy. A general motion declaring want of confidence in the government was agreed. But Bright remained silent and aloof, while Gladstone's intentions were shrouded in mystery. This further weakened Russell's position.

Finally, at a momentous meeting at Willis's Rooms on 6 June 1859, attended by about 280 Whig, Liberal, Peelite, and radical MPs, both Russell and Palmerston called for support of a general opposition motion. Each agreed to serve under the other depending upon whom the Queen sent for; each competing with the other in expressing disinterestedness and readiness to cooperate. At the beginning of the proceedings Palmerston helped Russell, because of his short stature, up onto the platform, to the accompaniment of much laughter – a moment of poignant symbolism. A discrete and moderate, if noncommittal, Bright advocated union, but his fellow radical Roebuck threw a shell into the proceedings by expressing disbelief in the cordial union of the various sections of the Liberal party, doubting that Palmerston and Russell could long cooperate in the same cabinet, and decrying factious opposition attacks on the government. Most, though not all, of the speakers that followed, however, urged support for Russell and Palmerston's general motion of want of confidence in the government. This was proposed in the Commons by the young Lord Hartington (heir to the Duke of Devonshire) upon parliament assembling on 7 June. The opposition motion produced three nights of fervent debate. The diarist Greville saw Palmerston's contribution, pro-French and anti-Austrian, as 'the last act of his political life'.[38] Disraeli was brief, fluent, and epigrammatic. In the fullest House for years, on 10 June, the opposition want of confidence motion passed by 323 to 310 votes; a narrow opposition majority of 13. The following day Derby resigned.

In the first instance the Queen charged Lord Granville with the formation of a government. She disliked Russell and feared Palmerston would inflame feelings in Europe. In exasperation at royal interference in foreign policy Palmerston had once told Prince Albert 'that he was a German, and did not understand British interests'.[39] But the Queen's attempt at compromise failed. Russell refused to accept Palmerston as leader of the

Commons under Granville's premiership in the Lords; an unacceptable relegation. On 12 June Palmerston agreed to form a government, with or without Russell. It only remained for Russell to insist on the Foreign Office – the cause of liberal Italian nationalism being one issue on which Peelites, Liberals, and radicals might unite. Granville accepted the Presidency of the Council. Cornewall Lewis took the Home Office. While Gladstone, finally surrendering his hopes of Conservative reunion, insisted on becoming Chancellor of the Exchequer as the condition of his joining the cabinet. Though voting for Derby's ministry in the crucial division on 10 June, Gladstone privately confessed that he did not wish to be 'the one remaining Ishmael of the House of Commons'.[40] The Italian question he presented as his justification for joining Palmerston's ministry. Fellow Peelite Sidney Herbert, having helped organise the Willis's Rooms meeting, entered Palmerston's cabinet as Secretary for War. The Duke of Newcastle, while chairing a Commission examining schooling for the children of the labouring classes, became Colonial Secretary. The radical Cobden was offered office, but declined. Upon Russell's insistence the radical Milner Gibson was given the Board of Trade and Clarendon's radical brother, Charles Villiers, the Poor Law Board. Bright, to his chagrin, was offered nothing. Impotent, Bright continued to rail against the lofty pretensions of the ruling class. In private conversation Bright talked of being duped; claiming that he alone, of all prominent Liberals, was excluded from office.

In retrospect, the momentous Willis's Rooms meeting and Palmerston's subsequent second ministry can be seen as the formal foundation of the parliamentary Liberal party. In Palmerston's cabinet of 1859 those vital ingredients of Victorian Liberalism, Peelite morality and administrative expertise, Whig traditions of disinterested governance and legislative reform, notions of moral, economic and efficient government, and radical enthusiasms, came together. This was a heady and potent blend. It was an amalgam that was to provide a political focus for nearly all the dynamic forces of change in Victorian Britain, giving expression to an extraordinary range of progressive aspirations. It was the particular arrangement of non-

Conservative opinion produced by the climactic events of 1859; a parliamentary alignment of Liberal opinion, moreover, under Palmerstonian rather than Russellite leadership. Palmerston's success forcefully demonstrated his formidable resources as a domestic politician. The recovery of his position during the early months of 1859 was a triumph of patience and astute judgement. Conversely, Russell's failure should not be allowed to conceal his near success. The patronising references to 'little Johnny' employed by his detractors ignored those genuinely liberal impulses, as well as keen ambition, that drove him. But it was to the victor, Palmerston, that went the profitable spoils of Liberal leadership, as 1859 shaped the pattern of parliamentary politics for the next twenty-six years. The great Liberal party of the Victorian age came into being under Palmerston's command.

3

PALMERSTON AND LIBERALISM, 1859–65

In 1859 Palmerston faced a formidable parliamentary challenge. He had to hold together a progressive alliance made up of Peelites, Whigs, Liberals, and radicals, constituting the newly-minted Liberal party – what Clarendon described as 'a great bundle of sticks'.[1] Parties are held together as much by shared attitudes to opponents as by common principles. Dislike and aversion cement allegiances as firmly as ideals, with shared hatreds often the basis of political friendships. Prior to 1859, Whigs and Liberals had shared an easy contempt for Conservatives and a hostile disparagement of radicalism. Radicals, meanwhile, had found common purpose in decrying the oligarchic assumptions of Whiggism. Peelites had assumed a self-adulatory sense of superiority, enshrined in the pious cult of a dead leader. After 1859 none of these attitudes survived as a ready means of defining a common Liberal purpose.

'It became necessary in 1859', Palmerston later informed the former Whip Lord Ernest Bruce, 'to reconstruct the government upon a different principle and . . . out of a larger range of political parties.'[2] It was the supreme achievement of Palmerston's last years to blend the rich mix of ingredients comprising the broader Liberal party after 1859 in a way which affirmed it as the natural party of government. Belief in responsible aristocratic leadership, administrative efficiency, free trade, national prestige abroad, and civil and religious liberty at home, was the core of Liberal executive credibility. Palmerston's standing as a genial and prudent pair of safe hands proved the indispensable presence binding the Liberal bundle of sticks together. Palmerston offered well-ordered social, material, and moral progress as the antidote to social conflict and political tensions. His geniality symbolised a society at ease with itself. Thus he came both to define and to personify the robust self-confidence, material prosperity, and liberal inclinations of the mid-Victorian age.

Palmerston's Liberal Leadership

In fusing the parliamentary elements of Liberalism together Palmerston enjoyed two great advantages. First, he was not a Whig. Second, he was old. As an Irish peer and a member of Tory governments prior to 1828, Palmerston had embraced Canningite policies. By 1829 he was attacking the illiberality of the Duke of Wellington's foreign policy. Alongside Lord Melbourne, he led the Cannningites into Grey's reform ministry of 1830, taking the Foreign Secretaryship. Championing a robust liberal foreign policy during the 1830s and 1840s, he carried Canning's foreign policy forward with a distinctive and resilient jauntiness. After 1850 he proved himself a resourceful domestic politician, claiming, to the surprise of his rivals, the premiership in 1855. In 1859 he outflanked Russell to head a government for the second time. Yet Palmerston was not by background or temperament a Whig. His sense of political possibilities was not, like that of Russell and Derby, constrained by Whig sensibilities to the half-closed world of Westminster and St James's. He saw public opinion outside parliament as the true foundation of political power. 'The strength of the government', Palmerston reminded his whip Henry Brand in 1863, 'consists not simply in the balance of votes . . . in the Commons, but mainly in favourable public opinion.'[3] In his *Times* obituary of 1865 Palmerston was praised for acknowledging the power of public opinion: 'Lord Palmerston bowed to this deity, recognised its power, and used it as he could.'[4]

During the 1850s Palmerston's successful courtship of public opinion took two main forms. First, he skilfully used the expanding cheap daily press to influence popular opinion. He ensured that his views were floated in editorials or basked in the glow of press tributes. Repeal of the advertisement duty in 1853, the stamp duty in 1855, and paper duties in 1861, encouraged the establishment of new newspapers, particularly in Lancashire and Yorkshire. Development of the railways, telegraph, and more efficient printing presses facilitated the process. Palmerston's speeches were extensively quoted in these papers. At the same time, longer-established Liberal papers such as the *Leeds Mercury* under the proprietorship of Edward Baines, enjoying a wide provincial circulation, also reported Palmerston's speeches. Palmerston described members of the press in 1860 as the 'favourites and ornaments of the social circles into which they enter'.[5] At Lady Palmerston's parties it was noticed that John Delane, editor of *The Times*, and Palmerston often made themselves conspicuous by standing aside in deep conversation: 'a little affectation, which both enjoy: it tells the world of their close alliance'.[6] By the 1850s the term 'the fourth estate' to describe the press had entered common usage.

Secondly, Palmerston embraced extra-parliamentary speaking, directly addressing eager popular audiences in the provinces. During 1856 he spoke to large enthusiastic crowds in Manchester, Salford, Liverpool, and Glasgow. He drew his listeners into a vision of national economic and moral improvement; social stability and prosperity standing on the forthright defence of British interests abroad. This defined a domestic community of shared interests, subsuming offensive class hostilities and divisive social grievances. As he told an audience at Chester in May 1865, the Liberal party was that body committed to the removal of conflict between the classes. At the same time, the triumphal air attending Palmerston's provincial speeches, celebrated with Union Jacks and bunting, was always accompanied by careful flattery of local civic pride. The energy and industry of the men of Manchester, Liverpool, or Glasgow being complimented for ensuring the material and moral progress of the nation. Palmerston's characteristic insouciance and easy manner reinforced the message of social amelioration. He presented himself as the embodiment of national pluck, the British mastiff personifying the nation's influence in the world. In 1863 Palmerston toured the Clyde eliciting enthusiastic popular responses; he also returned again to Lancashire and Yorkshire. Following a narrow Commons victory over the Danish question in 1864, Palmerston undertook another speaking tour, managing public opinion in the country. It was noticed how Borthwick, editor of the *Morning Post*, was 'closeted nearly every day with Lord Pam'. Frustrated radicals such as Bright and Cobden could only despair at the snobbish 'flunkeyism' of the provinces.[7]

Palmerston's advanced age also served him well. As a young man he often fell short of expectation. In old age he constantly surpassed it. Russell suggested that Palmerston, aged seventy-one in 1855, only reached maturity after his Biblical span of three score years and ten. 'Had he died at seventy he would have left a second class reputation. It was his great peculiar fortune to live to right himself.'[8] A disarming *présence d'esprit*, good-natured suavity and an enviable vigour enhanced Palmerston's administrative talent. When examining Foreign Office papers in 1852 Lord Stanley found 'Palmerston's activity and restlessness are extraordinary: there is no subject, however dry or trivial, on which long minutes in his handwriting may not be found. This is the more remarkable, because he has always borne, and rather carefully assumed, the manner of an idler.'[9] And for all his statements that power lay with public opinion, Palmerston devoted himself with extraordinary conscientiousness to managing the Commons. Eschewing pleasure he stuck to the Commons, 'as a diligent tradesman sticks to his shop', tirelessly observing and measuring the fluctuating bearings of parties and sectional associations. During debate in June 1860, after being at Ascot all day, 'Palmerston outdid himself in gay and sparkling fancy and skilful banter. He was radiant. In an enormous House, after one o'clock [in the morning], his stentorian voice rang through the anterooms where many a far younger man was stretched at length and sound asleep. Cheers and laughter followed almost every sentence.'[10] In a similar demonstration the following session, Palmerston gave a number of successful speeches in the Commons, after having ridden to Harrow to lay a foundation stone and deliver an address, riding back through heavy rain. This triumph of social manner and stamina was admirably complemented by Lady Palmerston's parties at Cambridge House; Lady Palmerston being an accomplished political *grande dame* with the 'remains of great beauty'.

Yet Palmerston's advanced age enabled others to accept arrangements from him on the assumption they would be short-lived. Between 1855 and 1865 Palmerston's health was a constant preoccupation. His age entered as an element in all calculation. Palmerston was tolerated, the historian Lord Acton observed in 1862, 'because he is cheerful and wounds no pride, and because he is old and excites no envy'. In June 1859 the elderly Whig Lord Broughton noted the 'general impression that [Palmerston's] government will not last – not a year many say. Indeed, Palmerston's age forbids a long term of office for him.'[11] Palmerston's achievement was to live for far longer than expected. That expectation, meanwhile, helped him hold together Liberal opinion in Westminster.

Palmerston's final decade was a triumph of diligence, style, longevity and luck. That accomplishment melded together those varied parliamentary elements that came together at Willis's Rooms; forging a progressive alliance which survived Palmerston's eventual death in October 1865. Within that alliance was contained Peelite administrative expertise, self-confidence, and hard-headed efficiency, as represented by Gladstone, Herbert, and Cardwell. Patrician Whiggery, the tradition of progressive reform legislation overseen by an enlightened aristocracy, the rule of law protecting property and prosperity, was represented by Russell, Granville, Charles Wood, and Cornewall Lewis. Whiggery embodied a broad, undogmatic Anglican tolerance and the commitment to economic and responsible government. In addition, after 1859, radicalism no longer led to that political wilderness to which Cobden and Bright were condemned during the 1850s. After 1859, radicalism became a means to office as well as an emotive cause. The radicals Thomas Milner Gibson, Charles Villiers, T. E. Headlam, Charles Gilpin and Henry

Layard all held posts under Palmerston. On accepting office in Palmerston's ministry in 1863 the radical MP for Halifax, James Stansfeld, declared that to refuse to share in the management of affairs was an act of 'moral cowardice', not an assertion of independence.[12] Radicalism became respectable. It lost its urban coarseness and acquired a sleeker gloss as personified by clever ambitious young men such as Charles Dilke and G. O. Trevelyan. Thus radical populism and links with militant Nonconformity became further ingredients in the rich parliamentary mix that made up the Liberal party in Westminster.

In May 1860 Gladstone referred to 'our strangely constructed cabinet'.[13] Palmerston's supreme achievement was to blend these elements into a lasting political compound. The achievement was evident, at one level, in the fact that after 1859 non-Conservative MPs increasingly used the term Liberal to describe their party affiliation. Approximately 30% of non-Conservative MPs in the parliament of 1852–7 used terms other than Liberal to describe themselves. In the parliament of 1859–65 barely 7% of non-Conservative MPs used any term other than Liberal to describe their political affiliation. Only 9 MPs called themselves Whigs, none Repealers, and 22 MPs declared themselves to be Reformers or Radical Reformers.[14] Despite embracing a spectrum of views, the term Liberal became, after 1859, the accepted party designation under which non-Conservative MPs acted together.

The shaping of a common Liberal purpose prior to 1865 was to some extent deferred by Palmerston's longevity. Old Pam's popularity and his centrist inclinations did not prompt a dramatic change in the Liberal Party at the parliamentary level. In social composition the Commons Liberal party remained throughout the 1860s largely landowning and patrician in character. Just over 50% of Liberal backbenchers were landowners, approximately 30% of Liberal MPs having direct family connections with the aristocracy. A mere 16% of Liberal MPs were from business backgrounds (the majority of radical leanings), and roughly 12% were lawyers by profession.[15] It was also the case that 11 of the 15 ministers Palmerston appointed to his cabinet in 1859 were territorial magnates.

Yet, of far greater importance was that this parliamentary party gradually became, during the 1860s, the focus of the aspirations of an astonishing range of increasingly powerful groups and interests outside Westminster. Whig landowners established profitable relations with groups socially wholly unlike themselves, while perpetuating conflict with those socially most like them – the general body of landowners comprising the Conservative back benches. As Trollope described it in his 1869 political novel *Phineas Finn*, 'as gallant a phalanx of Whig peers as ever were got together to fight against the instincts of their own order in compliance with the instincts of those below them'. The Liberal party appealed to progressive aristocrats, ambitious industrialists, artisans seeking the vote and labour activists, as well as Anglican high churchmen and Nonconformists. It came to speak to those in the provinces and industrial towns.

The burgeoning cheaper daily press of the 1860s proved overwhelmingly Liberal in its politics. National daily newspapers such as the *Daily Chronicle* and the *Daily News*, London evening papers such as the *Star* and the *Sun*, and provincial newspapers such as the *Birmingham Daily Post*, *Western Daily Press*, *Halifax Courier*, *Leeds Mercury*, *Liverpool Mercury*, *Manchester Guardian*, and *Dundee Weekly News* swelled the ranks of Liberal journalism. Militant Nonconformity, the Liberation Society, calling for Anglican disestablishment, and the United Kingdom Alliance, campaigning for temperance, harnessed their energies to the Liberal Party. In 1851, 40 per cent of churchgoers in England and 75 per cent in Wales attended Nonconformist chapels. Organised labour and trade unions looked to Liberals in parliament as their champions at Westminster.

A small, youthful Liberal intelligentsia, inspired by John Stuart Mill and Matthew Arnold, gave a cutting edge to arguments for Liberal reform. University men such as James Bryce, Leslie Stephen, Goldwin Smith, Henry Sidgwick, Henry Fawcett, and Albert Dicey gave flair and incisive intelligence to Liberal debate. Young cosmopolitan intellectuals, sensitive to the obligations of privilege, learnt from John Stuart Mill that it was the duty of the educated, rather than the propertied, to govern. Thus Liberalism embraced the spectrum of progressive opinion; a continuation of the Whig ideal of brokering the advance of differing dynamic social and economic interests. Palmerston's contribution to this process was to accustom Liberal MPs of all persuasions increasingly to act together in parliament.

Gladstone: the 'People's Chancellor'

Heightened moral vision was not part of Palmerston's detached worldly response to practical affairs. It was another non-Whig, Gladstone, who most successfully came to inject intense moral zeal into Liberal purposes. This marked Gladstone's transformation after 1859, as Chancellor of the Exchequer, from an executive Peelite politician into a charismatic tribune. His budgets of 1860 and 1861, pushed through in the face of cabinet reluctance and Lords opposition, reduced indirect taxation and purged the fiscal system of protectionism. Free trade was proclaimed as the basis for future social harmony, economic prosperity, and popular political maturity. As *The Times* declared in 1859, free trade, like parliamentary representation and ministerial responsibility, was now an article of national faith. Gladstone saw his fiscal policy as the 'social contract' of the mid-Victorian state. This was complemented by the repeal of the paper duties in 1861. The Anglo-French Commercial Treaty of 1860, whose political symbolism was as important as its free trade economic consequences, also buttressed Gladstone's vision. Free trade and minimal indirect taxation liberated the people economically, encouraged their diligence and self-reliance, raised civic maturity, and stimulated political responsibility.

The enthusiasm of working men for economic liberalism sprang less from doctrinal devotion to the theories of political economists, than from a deep-seated antipathy to elitist control and dislike of the morally degrading tendencies of paternalism. The commitment to *laissez faire* and distaste for state regulation among working men stood upon moral as much as economic foundations.[16] In 1862 Gladstone was triumphantly received by huge crowds in Newcastle, the banks of the Tyne lined with people for twenty miles cheering him as he sailed by. He was idolised as the 'People's Chancellor'. Like Peel, Gladstone looked to a public opinion outside Westminster as the true embodiment of the nation's legitimate aspirations. In his Tamworth Manifesto of 1834 Peel had described authentic public opinion as enshrined in those moderate, intelligent, and responsible voters less interested in the partisan postures of party than in the nation's true interests. After 1859, Gladstone saw authentic public opinion embodied in the aspirations of the virtuous and industrious middle classes and working men. Striking the keynote in a London speech of October 1859, Gladstone declared that the mass of people desired thrift and economy in government, which required him to lift the fiscal burden on the artisans and peasantry of England. At Manchester in 1864 Gladstone told his audience that public opinion was the best restraint on extravagant government. Peel in the 1840s had contented himself with expressing similar thoughts in Westminster. Gladstone, during the 1860s, discovered the exhilarating power of directly addressing such sentiments to popular audiences. He praised the industry of the working man who, through his skill and discipline, secured his own comfort and respectability.

The Christian terms in which Gladstone expressed his admiration for the humility and simplicity of working men, complementing the obligations of aristocracy, struck powerful chords of popular appeal suggesting strong ties of moral affinity. Gladstone's speeches conveyed a powerful sense of consecration; a compliment to which popular audiences responded with adulation. The growing force of evangelical Nonconformity in the 1860s found in Gladstone, as well as Bright, an eloquent voice acknowledging a higher Providential authority overarching man's earthly affairs. Like Palmerston, Gladstone's links with the press, particularly the liberal *Daily Telegraph*, also greatly assisted his popularity. By his journalistic advocates Gladstone was portrayed as a manly and straightforward politician, above intrigue and chicanery, who combined financial acumen with religious principle and honour.

Palmerston's longevity and skill, alongside Gladstone's popular transformation, left Lord John Russell as an increasingly marginal and spent force. Russell's reform bill of 1860 was received in parliament with apathy. In July 1861, he went up to the Lords as Earl Russell. His Under-Secretary at the Foreign Office, the young Lord Kimberley, saw Russell's elevation as the *coup de grace* to Lord John's career: 'his position in the country is nothing apart from the House of Commons'.[17] At the same time, death savagely thinned the ranks of the experienced and talented. A succession of obituaries reinforced the sense of the passing of an age. The elder Peelites in both Houses were struck down. In 1860 Lord Aberdeen died, followed a year later by Sir James Graham. The former Chartist and MP for Finsbury Thomas Duncombe died in 1861, as did the Peelite Secretary for War Sidney Herbert, aged a mere 51. Prior to his death Herbert was Lord Granville's preferred successor to Palmerston as Liberal leader in the Commons. Late in 1861 Prince Albert passed away, aged 42, leaving a distraught Queen in self-imposed seclusion. His death, Disraeli remarked, destroyed 'that long-meditated plan of re-establishing Court influence on the ruins of political party'.[18] The Peelite first Viceroy of India, Lord Canning, died in 1862. The elderly Whig patriarch Lord Lansdowne died in 1863. The same year George Cornewall Lewis, Gladstone's rival for the Exchequer, died aged 57. Cornewall Lewis was mourned by *The Times* as the most learned Englishman of his generation. Prior to 1863 Cornewall Lewis had held the strongest claim to the post-Palmerston Commons Liberal leadership; though Trelawny, from the radical benches, saw Cornewall Lewis as 'a gauche doctrinaire', full of knowledge, but unable to steer clear of damaging words and topics.[19] Another Whig grandee, Palmerston's Lord Lieutenant of Ireland, the Earl of Carlisle, died in 1864. The Duke of Newcastle, a Peelite and Colonial Secretary after 1859, died in 1864 aged 53. Between 1861 and 1864 Gladstone's path to prominence was cleared. In May 1865, bereavement brought a moment of poignant symbolism as the former Peelite Gladstone walked beside the Manchester radical John Bright leading the cortège at Richard Cobden's funeral.

Liberal Government: Finance, Reform, Religion and Foreign Policy

In 1860 Gladstone described the Liberal cabinet as a kaleidoscope: 'as the instrument turns the separate pieces adjust themselves and all come out in perfectly novel combinations'.[20] Across a whole range of public questions ministers found themselves in differing alignments. Over Italy Palmerston, Russell, Gladstone, Milner Gibson, and Argyll were pro-Italian, favouring an active policy assisting liberal nationalism in the region. Their colleagues strongly urged strict non-intervention. In foreign policy, more broadly, Palmerston, Russell, and Newcastle were generally combative, while the rest of the cabinet, particularly Gladstone and Milner Gibson, favoured more pacific policies. Likewise Palmerston, Russell, and Newcastle wished for greater defence expenditure, against the preferences of their colleagues for economy. Over finance, Russell, Newcastle, Granville, and Argyll broadly supported Gladstone's plans for extensive free trade reforms, though only Russell and Milner Gibson supported the Chancellor's desire to repeal the paper duties. On parliamentary reform Russell, Milner Gibson, Newcastle, Argyll, and Gladstone favoured extending the franchise. Palmerston, Herbert, and Villiers, however, were reticent about expanding the electorate. Only Newcastle and Villiers favoured extensive redistribution. While on Church matters Gladstone, Herbert, and Newcastle's conservatism contrasted with the greater flexibility of the rest of the cabinet.

Certainly Derby, from the opposition benches in the Lords, retained a conviction that a broad non-Conservative alliance in the Commons was by its nature inherently impermanent. Bouts of illness confirmed Derby's commitment to killing the Palmerstonian alliance with kindness. Frequent Conservative assaults on the government would, he believed, only bind the various elements of the Liberal party more closely together. Support given to the Whigs and moderate Liberals, on the other hand, would severely test their sense of a common purpose with extreme Liberals and radicals. In the parliament of 1859–65 Derby enjoyed the support of just under 47 per cent of MPs.

Splits in the Palmerstonian alliance and adhesion of support to the Conservatives did not need involve large numbers of MPs for Derby to acquire a Commons majority.

Two threats existed to this strategy. First, Palmerston himself was an attraction for discontented Conservatives; those frustrated by inactivity or contemptuous of Disraeli's leadership. A small group of Conservatives led by G. W. Bentinck, MP for West Norfolk, and including the Ultra Tory Charles Newdegate, MP for Warwickshire, openly loathed 'the Jew'. Their Anglican fervency, hatred of Catholicism and suspicion of Disraeli rendered them, Derby noted, 'loose fish'.[21] Secondly, the absence of frequent pitched battles itself tested the Conservatives' own sense of common purpose. Holding the party together, without exciting partisan emotions, while quietly awaiting fractures in Palmerstonian support, made heavy demands on Conservative loyalty to Derby. What strengthened Derby's hand after 1859 was the record of the 1858–9 Conservative ministry, which dispelled the easy characterisation of the Conservatives as reactionary bigots and substantiated their claim to policies of safe, responsible and progressive moderation.

During late 1859 and 1860 the majority of the cabinet won the case for abstaining from involvement in the Italian question, despite Palmerston, Russell and Gladstone's wishes. The signing of the Treaty of Villafranca in July 1859 brought fighting between French, Piedmontese, and Austrian forces to an end. Austria retained Venetia, while Lombardy was ceded to France for transfer to Piedmont. Both Russell and Palmerston seized the opportunity to speak in parliament in a high liberal tone of Italian freedoms. Gladstone, however, alarmed many in the Commons with impassioned statements that seemed to overstep the bounds of discretion. In January 1860, though personally prepared to enter an alliance with France to drive Austria out of the peninsula, Palmerston and Russell, under the weight of cabinet pressure, agreed to the more limited course of asking both France and Austria not to interfere in the region. But the announcement in March 1860 of the French annexation of Nice and Savoy, while Piedmont annexed central Italy, produced an outburst of Francophobia. Palmerston found himself forced to condemn French expansionism, and 100,000 British civilians, fearing a French invasion, armed themselves in what was called the Volunteer Movement. Then attention dramatically shifted to the south of the peninsula as Garibaldi's guerrillas marched through the Kingdom of the Two Sicilies. The Bourbon dynasty in Naples collapsed and Papal sovereignty in Umbria and the Marches was overthrown.

British policy followed breathlessly behind the astonishingly rapid course of events. In recognition of Garibaldi's *fait accompli*, in October 1860, Russell congratulated the Italians on throwing off their oppressors. Liberal nationalism seemed to have triumphed and British hopes for the overthrow of a corrupt Neapolitan regime and the curtailment of Papal temporal power, albeit at the cost of French expansion and Austrian humiliation, appeared realised. All that was left to Russell and Palmerston was to claim the importance of their moral support in the success of Italian unification. The majority of Palmerston's ministry had not wished to intervene. In practical terms the ministry, without large military resources, could not do much. None the less, the success of Piedmont and Garibaldi, a popular hero to many British liberals and radicals, enabled Liberals to declare the effectiveness of the government's moral influence abroad. This fortuitous outcome enabled Liberals to take up Italian unification as a badge of honour. In particular, it brought Palmerston and Russell shoulder to shoulder in a common cause. By early 1861 lofty liberal speeches on Italian affairs were the chief mainstay of the government. Italy did much more for Liberal unity than the Liberals did for Italian unification.[22]

Finance and expenditure, meanwhile, proved more dangerous to the unity of the Palmerstonian alliance. Early in 1860 Gladstone, supported by the radicals in the cabinet, confronted Palmerston and others on the need for retrenchment, repeal of the paper duties, and the reduction of indirect taxation. In 1853 Palmerston had opposed Gladstone's budget. In 1860 financial differences looked dangerously like the split in ministerial ranks predicted by Derby. Cobden, having declined a place in Palmerston's cabinet, acted as the British negotiator at Paris in a free trade Anglo-French Commercial Treaty agreed in early

1860. Both Gladstone and Cobden saw the treaty as a great boon to the commercial classes in Britain: Cobden becoming the subject of celebrations of 'bourgeois triumphalism' upon his return. Gladstone also saw the Treaty as an important buttress to his broader fiscal policy. Income tax was increased to cover reductions in import duties. Palmerston, however, refused to countenance Gladstone's proposal to reduce defence expenditure; fears of hostilities with France were still running high. Gladstone threatened to resign. Cobden feared the crisis would destroy the newly-minted Liberal party.[23] But Palmerston stood his ground. Gladstone, with his memories fresh of political isolation, backed down. The repeal of the paper duties, another integral part of Gladstone's financial package, meanwhile barely passed the Commons by a slim majority of nine votes. Much of the speaking against repeal betrayed personal dislike of Gladstone. Disraeli accused the Chancellor of rashness, inconsistency, and intolerance. While listening to Disraeli's accusations Gladstone leaned on the ministerial front bench white with rage. Repeal of the paper duties was subsequently thrown out by the Lords. Palmerston avoided a clash between the two Houses by referring the procedural question, of whether the Lords could reject a finance bill approved by the Commons, to a Committee of Privileges. The report of the Committee, that the Lords did have such power, was presented by Palmerston to the Commons in July 1860. He allowed himself in his speech to imply some hesitation about the merits of Gladstone's budget.

The Conservatives sought subtly to exploit these fissures in ministerial ranks. Using Lord Malmesbury as an intermediary, Derby communicated to Palmerston his willingness to support the premier over finance, as long as the government brought in a moderate, rather than extensive, parliamentary reform bill. The pledge to legislate on reform during the 1860 session, despite Palmerston's own apprehensions, was part of the understanding between the government and radical MPs. In May 1860 Malmesbury also ascertained that Palmerston would welcome Conservative support in defeating Gladstone's repeal of the paper duty. Malmesbury's *sub rosa* negotiations were intended by Derby to exacerbate Palmerston's differences with Gladstone and cabinet radicals, while also forcing a cabinet split over reform. A limited reform bill, Derby anticipated, would alienate both Russell's and Palmerston's radical support in the Commons. Derby intended to demonstrate to Palmerston that his real friends sat opposite, not alongside him, in parliament. Every obstructive motion, Derby privately declared in May 1860, must come from the Liberal side of the House.[24]

In the event, the reform bill introduced by Russell to the Commons in March 1860, a simplified version of his 1854 plan, was stillborn. Disraeli and the Conservatives remained largely silent, leaving it to Liberals and radicals to find fault with the bill. Received with profound indifference in the country, yet honouring the pledge to introduce a measure, Russell's reform bill was withdrawn in June. Listening to Russell smothering his offspring, Palmerston looked nervous, Wood and Cornewall Lewis exchanged chuckles of evident delight, while Gladstone busied himself with papers. Yet the blow to Russell from the failure of his reform bill was less than Derby had anticipated. Foreign affairs now occupied Russell's attention more. No mention of reform was made in the Queen's Speech for the 1861 session, it being moderate and conservative in tone. Palmerston replied to Locke King's motion for extension of the county suffrage in February 1861 with an opposition speech from the Treasury bench. Russell responded to another similar radical motion with ironic banter, some pleasantry, and caustic humour. The radical champions of private reform motions, Locke King, Berkeley, and Baines, remained largely quiet during 1862 and 1863. When Berkeley did bring forward a ballot motion in May 1862 it was not taken seriously. A despondent Bright came to believe that nothing could be done on reform while Palmerston lived. Symptomatic of the mood was the election of the Whig Lord Hartington unopposed for North Lancashire, with a moderate and on the whole conservative hustings speech, in March 1863. Indeed, in a mimicry of the Palmerstonian style, Hartington, with a heavy appearance and a drawling slowness of utterance which resembled affectation, seemed the embodiment of insouciant moderate good sense. From domestic reform, radical attention shifted to liberal movements abroad in Poland,

Hungary, Greece, and the North American States. Quiescence on domestic reform eased Palmerston's immediate difficulties. But both Derby and Disraeli retained a firm belief that the reform issue, if revived, must create incurable splits in the Liberal party.

In January 1861 Derby planned to continue his 'patience policy'; a strategy Malmesbury described as keeping the 'cripples on their legs'.[25] Derby anticipated that doing nothing, but quietly supporting Palmerston, would prise the premier away from Gladstone, if not Russell. Disraeli believed Palmerston's death or retirement could not now be long delayed; an event that would bring general disruption to Liberal ranks. The tensions between Whigs and radicals, he maintained, were irreconcilable. In mid-February the government Whip Brand had conversations with Lord Stanley and talked of the agreement between Whigs and moderate Conservatives, regretted that divisions between them gave power to the radicals, and spoke of fusion.[26] Yet the 1861 session also saw the easing of the government's difficulties over finance, with Gladstone emerging the victor. Gladstone again brought forward an ambitious plan of fiscal reform, including repeal of the paper duties. Palmerston's continuing reluctance to repeal the paper duties was overborne in cabinet by other ministers.

Then in May, believing the government to be on the verge of disintegration, the Conservatives decided to deal what they confidently hoped would be the deathblow to the Palmerstonian alliance. Abandoning passivity they launched a Commons assault on the budget. They were encouraged by the vehemence of the Whig Sir John Ramsden, a member of Palmerston's first ministry, in denouncing Gladstone's plans. But on 30 May the government succeeded in gaining a majority of 15 votes on the critical paper duties clause. To Disraeli's intense anger, a number of Conservatives absented themselves from the vote in protest against his leadership. The ministry did not split. The Conservative Commons Whip Colonel Taylor talked of treachery. Derby was also much angered by the failure to defeat the government, speaking with particular irritation of Gladstone. Their bolt shot, the Conservatives fell back demoralised. Rumours subsequently circulated in the Commons of Disraeli's impending resignation as opposition leader.

The crucial paper-duties vote in May 1861 proved a watershed in the unity of the Palmerstonian alliance Ministerial divisions dissipated. Gladstone went on to face down Lords opposition, securing the passage of his fiscal reforms. Protective duties on raw produce, food and manufactured goods were removed. This restored Gladstone's position in Westminster and extended his popularity in the country. By 1861 Gladstone confessed his puzzlement that he seemed to be at both the conservative and radical ends of the cabinet. The motion of the radical James Stansfeld, MP for Halifax, in June 1862, calling for a reduction in defence expenditure, failed, despite being supported by 65 advanced Liberal and radical MPs. None the less, this further strengthened Gladstone's hand in forcing Palmerston to accept retrenchment. To do otherwise, Brand warned the premier, would create a dangerous alliance between radicals, Gladstone and the Conservatives. Gladstone's association with radicals such as Milner Gibson and Stansfeld in pursuing fiscal reform further enhanced his reputation among provincial Liberals.

Religious issues were skilfully played by Palmerston. His continuing to favour evangelicals and moderate broad-church-men in his Anglican appointments, acting on the advice of his son-in-law Lord Shaftesbury, gained Palmerston general support from evangelicals and other groups such as Wesleyan Methodists. The earlier appointments of Tait and Bickersteth to the sees of London and Ripon were followed by Charles Baring's being made Bishop of Durham in 1861. Palmerston's hostility to Catholicism, particularly the Pope's temporal power in Italy, on the other hand, enabled him to endorse liberal movements abroad while being seen as the champion of Protestantism at home. Palmerston was less responsive to Irish Catholic claims than Derby's 1858-9 government had been, which had benefited by gaining Irish seats. Anti-Catholicism remained an important ingredient in British national identity and was a patriotic card Palmerston was happy to play. Since the sixteenth century, and on through the eighteenth century during successive wars with

France, Protestantism was central to British national identity: a conviction that manifested itself in both radical and Tory traditions. Protestant images of the Pope as the Anti-Christ or the Beast of Revelation were given new force in the early ninteenth century by the colourful and apocalyptic language of evangelicalism. In the 1860s, Palmerston saw Irish Roman Catholics as the natural enemies of his Liberal government.

At the same time, Palmerston sought to defuse militant Dissent, whose ultimate aim, he recognised, was the disestablishment of the Church of England. Through parish church rates Nonconformists, as well as Anglicans, were required to pay for the upkeep of the Established Church. After 1859 Palmerston made the issue of church rates, the abolition of which was being demanded by the Liberation Society and championed by Sir John Trelawny in the Commons, an open question for the government. This was consistent with his wish to avoid making religious questions the basis of party differences. It was also part of the understanding Palmerston had established with the Conservative opposition. As much as a reflection of Palmerston's own pragmatic views on religion, this was a shrewd response to the passions which religious issues excited. Nonconformity was showing itself to be a powerful political force in the constituencies, while the development of liberal theology spurred on wide-ranging discussion of doctrinal matters. The rise of ultramontane power in Rome, as Pope Pius IX promulgated his Syllabus of Errors in 1864, intensified Catholic and anti-Catholic feelings. In an age of religious revival religion was too important, Palmerston sensed, to be too prominent in defining party differences. Geniality and good fellowship were usually notably absent from religious debate.

Derby shared Palmerston's preference for not exciting religious feeling. Derby carefully refrained from marshalling the Conservative party as the ardent champion of Anglicanism. Excessive Protestant zeal was a double-edged sword able to inflict injury on both opponent and advocate – as Russell discovered after penning the Durham Letter during the Papal Aggression crisis of 1850. In his letter to the Bishop of Durham in November 1850, Russell had denounced the Pope's plan to re-establish a Catholic hierarchy in England. But Russell's defence of Protestant national interests had only brought upon him barbed allegations of religious intolerance. Derby declared the Pope's pronouncement insolent, but not insidious. Both Palmerston and Derby remembered how, during the 1820s and 1830s, it had been religious issues that had split moderate opinion. Centrist coalescence between Whigs and liberal Tories, based upon common social and economic views, had been denied by the force of religious controversies. In February 1855 Derby, unlike Wellington in similar circumstances in 1834, had not used Protestantism to rally his party: 'It appears to me that the present moment would be singularly inopportune for the agitation of any question connected with such a subject'.[27] The accord of moderate men, Palmerston and Derby believed, required reticence and caution on religious questions. The religion of all sensible men, as Disraeli phrased it, was the same. But what comprised that religion sensible men did not say.

The practical effect of Palmerston and Derby's reserve on religious issues was to highlight the moral intensity which Gladstone brought to political questions. To many whose religious belief was the driving force of their political conviction, the moral intensity and Christian context which Gladstone brought to matters prosaic in other hands struck a deep resonance. At the same time, during the 1860s, Gladstone stepped back from direct partisan involvement in public sectarian conflict. In 1857, his vociferous opposition to the Divorce bill had only emphasised his political isolation. After 1859, his growing personal contact with Nonconformist ministers helped to broaden the denominational range of his political appeal. In 1864 Gladstone began holding private meetings with leading Nonconformists establishing areas of mutual understanding. While maintaining his own personal religious beliefs, Gladstone found the moral basis of his policies, his private piety and evident devotion, established broad points of sympathy. Palmerston was patently a man of the world. Gladstone was, equally clearly, a man of God. Should Gladstone succeed Palmerston as Liberal leader it was to be anticipated that religious issues would come to the forefront of political debate.

The pattern of strong rhetoric and inaction which characterised the response of Palmerston's government to Italian
unification carried over into subsequent foreign crises after
1860, such as the American Civil War and the Schleswig-
Holstein affair in 1864. The discrepancy between words and
deeds grew. Palmerston left the Poles to their fate in 1863 after
they revolted against Russian rule, having given indirect encouragement to their national aspirations. Palmerston refused to
join France in condemning Russo-Prussian mutual aid in suppressing the revolt; a policy that Derby denounced as 'meddle
and muddle'. As Palmerston's former Under-Secretary at the
Foreign Office, Lord Wodehouse privately recorded: 'The whole
affair has I fear been mismanaged, Lord P. and Lord R[ussell]
have been overborne by their pacific colleagues backed by the
mischievous influences of the Court; the result has been a
miserable vacillating undignified policy – we have either done
too much or too little'.[28]

A strong wish to avoid entanglement underlay Palmerston's
reaction to the American Civil War. But declarations of neutrality were put under pressure by Bright's powerful denunciations of the moral iniquity of slavery; diplomatic embarrassments
created at the arrest by the North of two Southern envoys on the
British ship *Trent* in 1861; and by the government's failure to
detain the *Alabama*, a ship built in Liverpool for the Confederate
navy, in 1862. Bright saw the Union's fight as not only against
slavery, but also for labour and democracy. Certainly, after
President Lincoln's Emancipation Proclamation in 1863,
Bright's call to free working men to support the Union united
old radicals and young labour activists, although in the upper
levels of society sympathy for the Confederacy, as a beleaguered
property-owning society, also existed.

Some country gentlemen simply wished the American Civil
War to be prolonged so that both sides might be humbled.
Wodehouse noted in August 1862: 'My sympathies are with
neither party, but I wish for the break up of the Union. If the
Union had lasted, the insolence and aggressive temper of the
Americans would have led to war with England before long.
Two or more independent States in N. America will balance

each other and give Europe less trouble.' For others, sympathy for the Confederacy was prompted by a degree of class jealousy, the popular egalitarianism of the Unionist cause being seen as corrosive of aristocracy, monarchy, and church establishments. Notoriously, during a speech at Newcastle in October 1862, Gladstone praised Jefferson Davis for creating a nation out of the Confederacy. In dinner table conversation Gladstone expressed astonishment at 'the eagerness of the "negrophilists" as he called them, their readiness to sacrifice three white lives in order to set free one black man, even after it was shown that there was no disposition among the negroes to rise in their own defence'. The 'fanaticism' of English sympathisers he found hard to understand.[29]

Cobden indulged Bright's ardour for the Unionist cause, while deploring the waste of blood and money brought on by the war, and preferring a joint European mediation of the conflict. The thoughtful Conservative Lord Stanley found Bright's vehemence 'hardly compatible with sanity: peace, economy, human life, free trade, personal liberty, all are as nothing compared with the one paramount idea of bringing the great popular republic out of the struggle triumphant'.[30] Economic distress, meanwhile, tested popular commitment to the moral arguments of Bright and others. The Civil War brought widespread suffering to Lancashire, as the cotton industry collapsed during 1863–4. While the workhouses filled and cotton prices rose, however, there were over fifty demonstrations by working men during 1863 in London, Lancashire and Yorkshire, in support of the North. In the face of all these contrary pressures Palmerston sought to preserve a policy of neutrality.

Popular radicalism was given further momentum by Garibaldi's brief visit to Britain in April 1864. Support for Garibaldi had been evident when he visited Newcastle in 1854. In 1860 a volunteer British Legion joined his army in southern Italy. In 1862 a meeting of his supporters ended in riots in Hyde Park. The man who overthrew tyranny and Popery was lionised in 1864 by the London trades unions, as huge crowds turned out to cheer him. Such was the density of the London crowd that it took Garibaldi's coach five hours, to the accompaniment of bands and processions, to travel three miles; though Lord Stanley thought the crowd 'mostly of the poorer sort, dirty and many of them drunk'.[31] Nervous of democratic incitement, Palmerston called upon Gladstone to keep Garibaldi under control. Garibaldi became a guest of the Duke of Sutherland at Stafford House and Gladstone persuaded him to give up a provincial tour. Despite his disagreeable habits of spitting and smoking indoors, Garibaldi was feted by London society, who received him with much curiosity. While the chaperoning of the Duke of Sutherland kept the revolutionary leader away from 'bad company', in particular the trades unions, Garibaldi did manage to meet Mazzini during his stay. The General's original national itinerary of four to six weeks, however, was curtailed to a stay of under two weeks in London, and, with reasons of health given as the official explanation, Garibaldi returned to Italy before the end of the month. There remained, however, the radical celebration of Garibaldi as a simple sublime man of the people fighting for democratic freedoms, overthrowing privilege, and destroying tyranny. The breaking up of pro-Garibaldi working men's meetings by police in the following months led to the formation in March 1865 of the National Reform League under the leadership of the barrister Edmond Beales and former Chartist George Howell.

The Schleswig-Holstein crisis during the summer of 1864 again showed the limits to translating the government's rhetoric into effective action. Following Prussia's attack on Denmark, statements were made implying support for Danish sovereignty. But Palmerston and Russell found themselves diplomatically isolated in Europe. Nor did the cabinet, with the exception of Palmerston and Russell, see just cause for a military entanglement. This diplomatic humiliation prompted the Conservatives, in July 1864, to move a Commons motion of censure condemning the government for it's inept handling of the affair. Since the beginning of the year Derby had been drawing up possible cabinet appointments, anticipating a government defeat during the 1864 session. To the laughter of the House, in July Cobden tellingly described Palmerston as doing Tory work better than Derby, with the Conservatives after Palmerston's death becoming his residuary legatees. In the event, Palmerston narrowly escaped defeat by 313 to 295 votes. Amid the deafening cheering and waving of hats which accompanied the announcement of the vote, Palmerston appeared in an ecstasy of delight. Palmerston was, ironically, only saved by praise from radicals supporting him for keeping Britain out of war. There seemed little party unity on either side of the House. In the Lords, the style and policy of Russell's despatches were openly attacked by Lord Grey; a split in Whig ranks seen to have ominous implications. Russell's reputation was seriously damaged.

At a European level the Italian Risorgimento, the Polish revolt of 1863, and the Schleswig-Holstein crisis demonstrated the absolute collapse of the European settlement of 1815. The map of Europe was redrawn. Garibaldi and Bismarck represented the harsh new realities of European power politics. Britain's international role in this new diplomatic setting was unclear. What was apparent was that Britain was becoming increasingly powerless on the continent. Palmerston and Russell were repeatedly left impotent and isolated, their humiliation masked by a liberal rhetoric that often belatedly endorsed, though rarely influenced, events. All too often Palmerston blustered while Russell lectured. Yet domestically the success of the government in the Danish vote of July 1864 strengthened their position in public esteem. It countered the impression that Palmerston only held office on the sufferance of the Conservatives. The likelihood of a dissolution, to the relief of many MPs, became more remote.

Bright Resurgent and Gladstone 'Unmuzzled', 1863–5

The Italian Risorgimento, the American Civil War and final Union victory in 1865, provided inspiration and heroes for radical activists, who found their audiences relatively indifferent to domestic reform. Lincoln, Mazzini and Garibaldi joined the pantheon of popular icons in the struggle for freedom and democratic liberty. 'John Brown' became a common rallying song at popular meetings. The immediate beneficiary of this mobilisation of radical energies was John Bright. During the mid-1850s Bright's futile denunciations of the Crimean War were followed by a nervous breakdown that left him a crippled and lonely figure. During 1858–9 he stepped forward, a man recovered, championing the radical demand for parliamentary reform; despite the misgivings of colleagues like Cobden who, from rustic seclusion in Sussex, believed Bright to be pushing the wrong issue at the wrong time. During 1859 Milner Gibson became Cobden's voice in Westminster, representing radical interests in Palmerston's second cabinet. In private Bright caustically described Milner Gibson as having become a Whig.

During 1860–1 the flame of reform flickered and died. But after 1863 the torch was relit as Bright arose a giant refreshed. His thinking on reform had undergone change. No longer was redistribution the primary condition for real reform. It was better, he decided, to defer redistribution and deal with it on the basis of a wider suffrage. The ballot was less important and the separation of franchise reform from redistribution accepta-ble. After 1863 suffrage reform became Bright's touchstone. His celebration of the Union's cause, as an inspiration to popular struggles for freedom in all countries, complemented an un-flinching commitment to enfranchisement for the British work-ing man. In 1864 Bright helped to form the Manchester-based National Reform Union, whose mainly middle-class member-ship, campaigning for household suffrage, initially worked along-side the artisan National Reform League. In January 1865 Bright gave a forceful speech at Birmingham calling for reform. In March 1865 he delivered powerful Commons speeches exalt-ing Abraham Lincoln and the Union, giving a vivid sense to fellow radicals of his own power and indomitable courage.

Bright's grand theme during 1863–5 was the importance of the people as the source of true political morality. It was the people who must overthrow corrupt privilege and the smothering condescension of oligarchy. As the 1860s progressed, Bright's language came to resonate, in a profoundly important way, with Gladstone's celebration of the virtuous integrity of the industri-ous working man. During his fight for retrenchment and moral integrity in financial policy after 1860, Gladstone found solace and support, compensating for frustrations with ministerial and parliamentary colleagues, in those popular audiences who idolised him as the 'People's Chancellor'. The flattery was exhilarating and mutual. By addressing them directly Gladstone gave his audiences a potent sense of their own worth. His statements etched themselves on the popular mind. As Gladstone gave them self-respect so his audiences delivered to him their aspirations and loyalty. He portrayed them as the responsible constraint on government extravagance. Between 1861 and 1866, despite inflation, Gladstone reduced public expenditure by approximately 10 per cent.

The Biblical overtones of Gladstone's language re-inforced, among Nonconformists and others, the sense that he spoke for them. Such popular acclamation compensated for the widespread suspicion with which Gladstone was viewed within Westminster. His crushing power and command of words, sometimes more evident than his command of his temper, seemed to carry him on in a torrent of declamation. Gladstone's prolix style struck listeners within the House as wordy, diffuse and unclear. Often he seemed caught in a maze of his own verbiage. His restlessness and overbearing dogmatism stood on the bedrock of his religious faith in apparent defiance of more pragmatic concerns; whereas outside Westminster, it was less the substance than the occasion and manner of Gladstone's extra-parliamentary speeches that suggested exciting new alignments of political support. This was less to do with policy than with public expectation. Nevertheless, it suggested the outline of a Liberal purpose mobilising new constituencies of feeling. By 1864 Gladstone favoured enfranchising those new constituencies. He had been impressed by the trades union and artisan deputations he received as Chancellor. The stoicism of the Lancashire operatives during the cotton famine and their unwavering support for the North in the American Civil War also moved him. He believed extending the suffrage would strengthen the call for retrenchment in the Commons. It would bring into alignment the electorate and payers of income tax. Fiscal liability and political respectability would be merged.

In May 1864 Gladstone famously declared in the Commons that 'every man who is not presumably incapacitated by some consideration of personal unfitness or of political danger is morally entitled to come within the pale of the Constitution'.[32] The qualifications to this statement Gladstone held in his own mind and the vague terms in which the principle was expressed were less immediately striking than the radical populist sympathies it suggested. The subtle discrepancies between Gladstone's meaning and the impact of the words he used were drowned out by prolonged cheering from the radical benches. At one level the statement was consistent with the development of Gladstone's thinking since 1860. But Trelawny noted the curious hiatus on the Treasury bench while Gladstone made his 'Chartist speech'.[33] Gladstone declared himself puzzled by the parliamentary sensation his declaration created. Ineffectively, he belatedly tried to make explicit the qualifications he entertained to his general conviction. He had stated that his principle of fitness for the franchise would bring only a select portion of the working class within the pale of the constitution.

In the Clubs, however, the speech was seen as Gladstone's break with the old Whigs and his placing of himself 'at the head of the movement party'.[34] It was noted that, among parliamentarians, Gladstone was respected and admired, but because of his arrogance, want of tact, and his pedantic stiffness in adhering to his own opinions, except among Bright and other radicals he was disliked. The excessive irritability of his attacks on Cornewall Lewis in 1857 were recalled. A rattled and gout-ridden Palmerston, despite Gladstone denying his views were extreme, accused him of laying down the doctrine of universal suffrage. Rather than a privilege to be earned, Gladstone had suggested that the vote was a right to be claimed. Gladstone's genuine puzzlement was a measure of the distance his own subtle and complex reasoning created between him and his colleagues, who placed a simpler more literal interpretation on his words. The impact in parliament and in the country was also a measure of the gap Gladstone's popularity placed between him and Whigs and moderate Liberals. Clarendon dismissed Gladstone's statement as one of the Chancellor's odd inexplicable freaks. The old high and dry Whigs were supposed to be frantic: some, in order to retain office, willing to eat Gladstone's distasteful offering, others looking to join the Conservatives. Lord Stanley observed that the speech showed that, once Palmerston was gone, Gladstone's succession as Liberal leader in the Commons was both inevitable and dangerous.[35]

The general election of July 1865 returned a Palmerstonian parliament; there being no particular question which dominated the hustings. Liberals won the majority of seats not just in Scotland and Wales, but in England as well. Liberal candidates were particularly successful in the large English boroughs, with over 2,000 electors, winning 49 out of a total of 59 seats. The Conservatives lost 15 seats, including some of the Irish gains of 1859. Approximately 290 Conservative MPs (44% of the Commons) faced a Liberal majority of about 360 MPs (56% of the Commons).[36] Typically of mid-Victorian elections 303 Commons seats (47%) were uncontested. The 1865 election was quiet, even by mid-Victorian standards. A total of 922 candidates stood for election, 30 less than had stood in 1852, though the level of split voting among the electorate fell to 8.5%, as compared to 19% in 1857.[37] At the same time, 150 MPs were elected to the Commons for the first time; a large number of new faces replacing those who had chosen to retire.

This reinforced the sense, as Palmerston approached his 81st birthday, of a generational shift. A number of Liberal MPs declared a general support for a measure of reform. But Palmerston told Brand 'it is not for us to begin an agitation on a subject on which there are many different opinions, even among men who on other subjects act cordially together'.[38] He privately hoped reform might remain a dead letter. What made Palmerston's course the more difficult was the number of radical intellectuals elected to parliament for the first time; John Stuart Mill most notably, but also Henry Fawcett, G. O. Trevelyan, Thomas Hughes, and Duncan McLaren. Bright thought this development 'remarkable considering the state of our electoral system and the treachery of the Whigs'.[39]

The 1865 election also brought a separation between Gladstone and his old constituency of Oxford University, which he had represented since 1847. As early as 1853 his re-election was contested; a clear indication of serious tension in the constituency. In 1860 Gladstone considered not standing for his old University. The subsequent development of his views, particularly his 'pale of the Constitution' statement of May 1864 and a Commons statement in March 1865 countenancing disestablishment of the Church of Ireland, created intolerable strains. In July 1865, rejected by Oxford, he was returned for the large populous constituency of South Lancashire. Out of a total constituency electorate of just over 22,000, exactly 8,788 voters returned Gladstone as the third member for South Lancashire; the other two successful candidates both being Conservatives. Palmerston had described Gladstone as a 'dangerous man': 'keep him at Oxford and he is partially muzzled; but send him elsewhere and he will run wild'. In similar vein, in 1860, Clarendon had predicted that Gladstone's 'insatiable desire for popularity' and 'fervent imagination' would drive him to 'subvert the institutions and the classes that stand in the way of his ambition'.[40] In July 1865 Gladstone was unmuzzled.

Palmerston's Departure

On 18 October 1865, just two days short of his 81st birthday and in harness to the end, Palmerston died. His last audible words related to the acknowledgement of Belgian independence by France. In Gladstone's phrase, the tallest antlers in the forest had now fallen.[41] An era seemed to have passed. Palmerston entered the Commons in 1807. For the 30 years prior to his death he served as MP for Tiverton. As Foreign Secretary in every Whig government after 1830 until 1851, he came to personify a vigorous liberal British policy abroad; his name becoming synonymous overseas with British pluck. Yet it was after 1855 that Palmerston blossomed into a domestic politician of genuine weight and stature. His diligence within Westminster and his popularity in the country held together during his final years those varied dynamic forces comprising provincial and parliamentary Liberalism. This was to be his supreme achievement. An unlikely triumph for one who, as a Regency buck, had been better known for his romantic escapades and social élan. After 1855, dressed in his buttoned-up coat, dark trousers and black necktie, Palmerston combined extraordinary stamina with a tough presence and engaging joviality to command the Commons with an authority that dominated his contemporaries. Looking like 'a retired old *croupier* from Baden', Palmerston had a 'racy, buoyant and facetious' manner that charmed popular audiences.[42] For journalists, such as Bagehot, he seemed to embody the pragmatic and undoctrinaire moderation of the national character. To many he was a shrewd and safe pair of hands. To his popular audiences in Salford, Manchester and Glasgow he merged British pride with domestic prosperity and social ease.

Palmerston's passing opened up the Pandora's box of Liberal aspirations. Following Palmerston's death the Queen immediately agreed that Russell should succeed as premier. As widely predicted Gladstone became Liberal leader in the Commons; an event Palmerston had warned would lead to 'strange doings'. Clarendon replaced Russell as Foreign Secretary. Gladstone and Russell began preparing a reform bill for the 1866 session. With Palmerston gone, both felt strongly that Liberal government could not simply be a comfortable continuation of that which had gone immediately before. 1866 should mark a new beginning. Palmerston's death, Bright remarked, signalled the break with the old generation. But, while for Russell reform was about safely extending the suffrage, for Gladstone reform was essentially about strengthening the call for economic government.

In August 1865 a disconsolate Derby had feared Palmerston's longevity would hold off indefinitely Gladstone's Liberal leadership. This would defer what Derby anticipated would be radical government, middle-class alarm, and an inevitable Conservative reaction, bringing his party back into power. 'Our game', he told Disraeli, 'must be purely defensive' – support being offered to the moderates in the cabinet, while watching for opportunities to widen the breach between them and the radicals. Derby believed he would not hold office again. A despondent Disraeli declared that 'the leadership of hopeless opposition is a gloomy affair'.[43] Two months later political circumstances were transformed. Disraeli immediately recognised that 'the truce of parties' was over: 'I foresee tempestuous times, and great vicissitudes in public life'.[44] The Liberal MP Robert Lowe feared that Palmerston had 'left his party without tradition, chart or compass, to drift on a stormy sea on which their only landmark was his personal popularity'.[45] Coming away from Palmerston's funeral Sir Charles Wood was similarly apprehensive: 'Our quiet days are over; no more peace for us.'[46]

4

'A LEAP IN THE DARK', 1866–8

The turbulent events of 1866 brought to a head those party tensions deferred, since 1859, by Palmerston's longevity. The dramatic outline of what occurred reveals the powerful undercurrents that surged just below the calm surface of Palmerston's genial dominance. In March 1866 Russell and Gladstone introduced a modest reform bill. They proposed a £7 borough franchise qualification and a £14 household county franchise. Subsequently they proposed that 49 seats be taken from small boroughs for redistribution. Yet, despite its cautious character, the bill prompted vigorous opposition from a group of dissident Liberals, labelled by Bright the 'Adullamite Cave', which included Robert Lowe, Edward Horsman, Lord Elcho and Lord Grosvenor. Bright's jibe was a Biblical reference to the Book of Samuel and the cave in which David sought refuge from Saul. In June 1866 the Liberal reform bill was brought down by a hostile amendment moved by the Adullamite Lord Dunkellin. Some 48 Liberals voted with the Conservatives. Russell resigned and Derby formed his third ministry. Gladstone had pushed for a dissolution, the election to be held on the reform issue; but Brand warned that this would be a fatal mistake, putting the Conservatives in power for years. As it was, while handed the poisoned chalice of reform, Derby's government was in a Commons minority.

At the end of June 1866 riots broke out during a reform meeting of 20,000 people in Hyde Park, organised by the

National Reform League under Beales and Howell. One police-
man was killed and over 100 people were seriously injured. The
Conservative Home Secretary, Spencer Walpole, banned subsequent meetings. In late August an estimated 150,000 people
attended a reform meeting in Birmingham at which Bright
spoke, jointly organised by the National Reform Union and
National Reform League. Similar meetings occurred in other
cities around the country, including those organised by the
London Working Mens' Association and the London Trades
Council. Through September to December 1866 Bright undertook an extensive speaking campaign, addressing large crowds in
Manchester, Leeds, Glasgow, Dublin, and London. Yet what
degree of enfranchisement Bright favoured was unclear. While
the Reform Union hoped for household suffrage and the Reform
League seemed to want manhood suffrage (paupers, criminals,
and the insane being excluded from the vote), Bright talked of
'the people' being given power and independence from an
aristocratic class. He was opposed to universal manhood suffrage. Household suffrage stood as 'the ancient franchise of the
country'; though, in private, Bright talked of a £5 rating
franchise in the boroughs as being acceptable.

Despite Disraeli's initial indifference to the question, Derby
insisted, in October 1866, that the government must deal with
the reform issue, preferring to proceed with general resolutions
rather than a specific bill. A Royal Commission was also
considered as a delaying tactic. In December 1866 Derby
proposed the principle, subsequently introduced to the Commons, of a household borough suffrage, hedged around with
restrictions and safeguarded by plural votes for various propertied and professional categories of the electorate. In February
1867 Disraeli committed the government in the Commons to
moving ahead with a reform bill, the cabinet's resolutions being
abandoned. On 2 March, three cabinet ministers, Lord Cranborne (formerly Lord Robert Cecil), Lord Carnarvon, and
General Peel, resigned in protest at an urban household suffrage
forming the basis of a Conservative reform bill.

During subsequent rapidly-moving Commons debate, Disraeli
abandoned many of the restrictions that hedged this central

clause. Plural voting was dropped, the two-year residential qualification was reduced to one year, and a £10 lodger franchise in the boroughs was accepted. The most startling concession, however, was the acceptance of the advanced Liberal Grosvenor Hodgkinson's amendment on 17 May 1867, which, by abolishing the compounding of rates, removed the largest single obstacle to small urban tenants receiving the vote. This one amendment, it was estimated, added a further 500,000 voters to the electorate. The county suffrage was also extended from a £15 to a £12 annual rental qualification, while those owning land worth £5 or more a year were given the vote. At the same time, on 8 April 1867 the 'tea room revolt' and a backbench rebellion of 52 Liberal and radical MPs on 12 April prevented Gladstone offering a consolidated opposition to the Conservative measure. This ensured the success of the Conservative bill – transformed as restrictions to household suffrage were stripped away.

When the much-altered measure passed through parliament in August 1867 it effectively almost doubled the electorate, enfranchising about a third of the adult male population in England and Wales. During debate in the Lords, using a phrase coined by the Conservative election manager Philip Rose in a letter to him of 1860, Derby famously described the reform act as 'a leap in the dark'. A modest redistribution of 45 seats gave an additional 25 members to county constituencies. Reform Acts for Scotland, also based on an urban household suffrage doubling the electorate, and Ireland, less extensive in nature, followed in 1868. A measure dealing with electoral corruption was also passed in 1868, introducing heavier penalties for bribery and transferring jurisdiction over disputed elections from Commons committees to the High Court.

At the end of 1867 Russell resigned the Liberal leadership, to be succeeded by Gladstone. In February 1868, for reasons of ill health, Derby also retired, handing over the premiership to Disraeli. During April 1868 Gladstone carried against the Conservative ministry resolutions proposing the disestablishment of the Church of Ireland. Irish disestablishment fractured the Conservative cabinet more bitterly than parliamentary reform.

High churchmen like Gathorne Hardy vehemently opposed it; moderates such as Stanley and Pakington argued for accepting its inevitability with good grace; while low churchmen such as Cairns were hostile to disestablishment and any compromise reform that provided an endowment for the Catholic Church in Ireland. Upon the success of Gladstone's first resolution Disraeli denied the moral competence of the Commons to settle an issue which had not been part of any hustings speeches at the previous election. Despite Gladstone objecting to a 'penal dissolution', Disraeli declared a general election necessary so that the country could express an opinion on this important question. Disraeli thereby granted the new electorate created in 1867 the power to determine government policy. Unifying the Liberal party around Irish disestablishment, Gladstone subsequently led the Liberals to a resounding victory in the general election of November 1868. Facing a crushing Commons majority of 110 Liberal MPs, Disraeli chose to resign the premiership before meeting the new parliament. Both this decision and Disraeli's declaration of a dissolution were significant departures from the conventions of parliamentary government. According to Erskine May this was 'the first open acknowledgement of the truth that a ministry in reality derives its commission from the electorate'.[1] In December 1868 Gladstone became prime minister at the head of his first Liberal administration.

The Myths of 1867

The extraordinary and dramatic events of 1866–68 were given by politicians, in retrospect, differing interpretative glosses. Either a measure of democracy was delivered in 1867 by popular agitation (the radical myth), effective opposition (the Liberal myth), or by generous design (the Conservative myth). In the radical version of events the reform agitation of 1866, echoing the popular protests of 1831–2, forced a reluctant government to deliver an extensive and far-reaching measure. The powerful voice of artisans and respectable working men seeking the vote, articulated through organisations like the London Working Men's Association and London Trades Council, saw Conservative reticence overcome by populist enthusiasm. The story, possibly apocryphal, of a browbeaten Spencer Walpole breaking into tears when confronted by a deputation of Reform League leaders during the Hyde Park riots, symbolised the collapse of Conservative nerve. From August to December 1866 Bright spoke to huge reform meetings in Birmingham, Manchester, Leeds, Glasgow, and London. Bringing both the Reform Union and Reform League behind him, in a well-organised and powerful movement for radical reform, middle-class and respectable working-class opinion came together. The Conservative government was awed into submission. On 6 May 1867, as the Conservative measure went into committee in the Commons, a large Reform League demonstration in Hyde Park, reasserting its right to assemble, drove home the necessity for a far-reaching reform of the suffrage. Thus 1867 marked the domestic culmination of those popular struggles for liberty witnessed in Italy, Hungary, Poland, Greece, and America during the early 1860s. By delivering urban household suffrage the Reform Act restored the ancient franchise of 'the people', long lost to oligarchy and aristocratic Whig privilege.

In the Liberal version of events, 1867 marked the cynical and hypocritical appropriation of Liberal policy by the Conservative leadership. In an act of reckless irresponsibility Disraeli, after helping to kill the moderate Liberal measure of 1866, caved in to radical demands during 1867 in order to stay in power. As a result, the Conservatives found themselves compelled to give effect to advanced Liberal principles. Retribution awaited in November 1868. Disestablishment of the Church of Ireland proved a transcendent issue galvanising Liberal opinion in the country. The powerful Liberal majority that brought Gladstone to office demonstrated that Liberal policy, even in the hands of usurpers, could only benefit its legitimate advocates. The landmark reforming Liberal ministry of 1868–74, therefore, was the true legacy of Conservative opportunism. This, in turn, revealed the moral shallowness of Conservative thought; prejudice and self-interest posing as principle.

The Conservative version of events became a cornerstone of Disraeli's legacy to the party; the Beaconsfield tradition later extolled by Tory apologists such as the journalist T. E. Kebbel. The 1867 Reform Act stood as a dazzling act of faith in the inherent conservatism of the British working man. Beneath the Liberal and radical inclinations of middle-class and artisan opinion, Disraeli discerned in the mass of the population a body of innate conservative sentiment, tapped by the urban household suffrage. Thus Disraeli perceived the electoral basis of what Conservatives of a later generation called 'Tory Democracy'. Lord Malmesbury prior to 1867, it was noted, had advised Derby of his belief that labourers, once they had the vote, would be very likely to vote Conservative. Derby himself startled some of his followers by using, during the 1867 debates, the phrase 'Conservative democracy'. Vindication for 1867 came with the Conservative electoral success of 1874, producing the first Conservative Commons majority since 1841. Between 1885 and 1918 the Conservatives never had less than 48 per cent of the popular vote, holding office (with the exception of 1892–5) continuously from 1885 to 1905. For over 77 years of the 110-year period from 1886 to the present the Conservative party, either alone or in coalition, has held power. Thus the consequence of Disraeli's short-term tactics in 1867 was to produce long-term electoral dominance. In the process, the Conservative party was transformed from being the narrow representative of a class to being a truly national party; 1867 had provided, Disraeli recalled, 'the happy opportunity' to 'enlarge the privileges of the people of England'.[2] During the 1870s he went on to define the national appeal of Conservatism in terms of social reform, Empire, and preservation of the constitution.

All these versions of the events of 1866–8 contain some partial truths. But all were primarily shaped by the political needs of later generations, lending false retrospective coherence to complex events. None stands as a single authoritative explanation of what occurred. A more satisfying historical explanation lies in posing those questions raised by the events of 1859, but deferred by Palmerston's genial longevity. Upon what common basis could the Willis's Rooms alliance be preserved and the Liberal party act together? If Liberal unity was not possible, what configuration of parties might follow? To what extent was radicalism tamed or frustrated by Palmerstonian constraint? What response could or should Conservatives adopt to Liberalism? Finally, how were extra-parliamentary forces, such as the press, Nonconformity, and labour, to align themselves with the party dynamics of Westminster?

Liberal Dissension, 1866

In the first instance, the events of 1866 seemed to confirm Derby's long-standing belief that a broad party alliance of non-Conservatives was an inherently unstable alignment. As soon as Palmerston died, the word 'reconstruction' sprang to Conservative lips. Derby anticipated the Liberals proposing disestablishment of the Irish Church and prepared for its defence. Certainly Russell's discussions in November 1865 about the membership of his cabinet showed him anxious to appease all sections of the Liberal party. Known sceptics of further reform, like Robert Lowe and Edward Horsman, were considered as cabinet additions. Lord Stanley, the rising hope of progressive Conservatives, was invited to join the government, but upon Disraeli's advice declined. In conversation with Clarendon on reform Russell spoke moderately, only anxious at the idea of losing credibility if he did nothing. Meanwhile, middle-class radicals such as G. J. Goschen, W. E. Forster, and James Stansfeld were brought into the ministry.

Russell rejected Gladstone's suggestion of bringing Bright into the government. Yet the importance of radical support committed Russell to an immediate measure of reform. From outside the government Bright primed ministerial radicals, as well as Gladstone, with the requirements of a genuine reform measure. Whig preferences for a delay, while a Commission gathered information, were pushed aside. By December 1865 Russell was clear about some of the main features of his bill. But in January 1866 cabinet Whigs, Lord Clarendon, Sir George Grey, the

Duke of Somerset and Lord Stanley of Alderley, renewed their efforts to stave off reform. Russell persevered; his difficulties in keeping the cabinet together resulting in some details of the bill still being undecided days before its introduction to the Commons. At the same time Russell and Delane quarrelled, *The Times* now no longer enjoying privileged information. Russell's liking for seclusion further compounded his difficulties.

Liberal lack of unanimity on reform was magnified after Gladstone presented the government's bill to parliament on 12 March 1866. While extending the vote to £14 county householders and £7 borough householders, a lodger franchise in boroughs of £10 was also proposed, as well as enfranchising those with deposits of at least £50 in savings banks. It was calculated such franchises would add approximately 400,000 to the electorate. Under subsequent redistribution clauses 49 small boroughs were to be disfranchised, and 26 county seats, 22 borough seats, and 1 MP for London University were to be created. No immediate support was forthcoming from moderate Liberals, while radicals (dismissing it as too limited) and Conservatives (depicting the prejudices of working men) spoke out against the measure. Believing the basis of the government's bill to be 'a fraud of the worst character', Bright noticed how he was being portrayed as 'the great "terror" of the squires', who seemed 'seized with a sort of bucolic mania in dealing with me'.[3]

Many Liberals, meanwhile, became resentful of Gladstone's bullying and overbearing manner. During acrimonious reform debate in March Gladstone, for the first time since assuming the leadership, lost his temper, his angry utterances cited as proof of his lack of self-control. Rather than lead the Commons Gladstone seemed determined to drive it. Gladstone's effectiveness as Commons leader was further hampered by a series of economic crises which, as he was Chancellor of the Exchequer, diverted his attention. A cattle plague, a bad harvest, and the collapse of the Overend and Gurney Bank all claimed his time during 1866. By June some anticipated Gladstone himself collapsing under the strain, such was his extraordinary state of mental excitement.

This cleared the way for Robert Lowe's strident and powerful

116

denunciations of the case for reform. Far from being a reactionary, Lowe had a firm, almost doctrinaire, belief in rational administrative efficiency, disliked amateurish aristocratic mores in public life, but also believed expertise and intelligence could too easily be swamped by ignorant prejudice and popular superstition. In what became classic statements of the argument against democracy, Lowe defended the existing balance of classes within the representative system. This delicate balance, he argued, would be thrown into disequilibrium by a preponderance of working-class votes. Government, Lowe continued, was a practical matter, not susceptible to sentimental, metaphysical, or abstract theories. What worked was, in turn, safeguarded by the ability of the educated and wealthy, enjoying intellectual and material freedom, to recognise what was in the true interest of society as a whole. Dependency and impractical doctrine only delivered power to demagogues. Extending the franchise would give way to ignorance, drunkenness, intimidation, violence, and venality. It would violate a sacred trust. The weaknesses of democracy in America, with selective arguments taken from Alexis de Tocqueville's classic study, warned of diffuse authority, inefficient bureaucracy, and the debasement of political debate. In devastating fashion, drawing further examples from mob politics in Australia, Lowe abrasively demonstrated the crippling absence of a progressive consensus among Liberals on the question of reform. Moreover, the terms of the mid-Victorian debate on parliamentary reform were now clear. In 1831–2 discussion of the franchise had focused, in distinctly Whiggish terms, on the alignment of political intelligence with property. During 1866–7 consideration of enfranchisement centred on the respectability and moral character of potential new voters.

Around Lowe's job of demolition, during May and June 1866 the Adullamite Cave gathered themselves. The former Peelite, Scottish landowner and MP for Haddingtonshire, Elcho provided the organisational impetus to the group's activities. Elcho drew in Lord Grosvenor to provide respectability, used Clanricarde's Irish connections, and ensured Lowe's devastating oratory was backed with votes. Disraeli, meanwhile, enlisted Lord Carnarvon's help in marshalling opposition to the bill among

Whig magnates. Clarendon, Lord Grey, the Dukes of Cleveland, Somerset, and Sutherland, and Lords Lansdowne and Spencer entertained deep anxieties about the measure. Strong distrust of Gladstone and the government's intention to introduce an Irish land bill aggravated their concerns. Elcho, with Lowe's help and Conservative assistance, persuaded the young Whig Lord Grosvenor, as heir to the vast Westminster estates, to move a hostile amendment forcing the ministry to merge franchise reform and redistribution. It was seconded by Lord Stanley who, along with Carnarvon, maintained Conservative communication with the Adullamites. Despite the government making concessions, they barely survived Grosvenor's amendment with a dangerously slim majority of 5 votes. The Adullamites, with Lowe flushed with triumph, shared in the delirium of the opposition benches. Palmerston's Commons majority evaporated; 36 Liberal MPs, most of them close relatives or protégés of Whig magnates, voted against the ministry, a further 6 abstained from the vote. A badly shaken cabinet considered resignation. They were urged by Sir George Grey to withdraw their legislation, while at the same time being advised by Milner Gibson, on Bright's encouragement, to call an election.

This prepared the way for Dunkellin (Clanricarde's son) to move in the Commons the hostile amendment in June 1866 which finally killed the bill. Drafted at a meeting between the Conservative leadership and Whig dissidents, held at Lansdowne's house, the amendment proposed that the borough franchise qualification be based on payment of rates rather than on rental value. This would markedly reduce the degree of enfranchisement contained in the bill and provided a rallying point for all sections of opposition. The ministry were defeated by a majority of 11 votes, 315 to 304, the Liberal rebels of Grosvenor's motion being joined by a further 15 Liberal MPs. Following the vote, celebration broke out on the Conservative benches, while Gladstone sat looking both perplexed and disconcerted. Brand's desperate subsequent attempts to repair party unity failed. Many Whigs did not conceal their satisfaction at Gladstone's defeat. A divided and bitter cabinet resigned on 26 June 1866 amid much recrimination.

Conservative Reform, 1866–7

Derby and Disraeli's long-held conviction that the Palmerston alliance must founder on reform was vindicated. The impassioned and pungent arguments of Lowe on the one hand, and advanced Liberals like Bright on the other, revealed the irreconcilable differences embraced by Liberal opinion. From April to June 1866, in contrast to Russell and Gladstone's aloofness from their own backbenchers, Disraeli energetically devoted himself to organising the opposition; flattering and coaxing Conservatives, while befriending Liberal malcontents. Russell, by contrast, always seemed secluded at Pembroke Lodge, while Gladstone appeared to many to be lacking in tact, temper, or common sense. The opportunity existed, Disraeli believed, to form 'an anti- revolutionary party on a broad basis'. In keeping supporters up to the mark Disraeli declared that, if the Liberal measure passed, 'the aristocratic settlement of this country will receive a fatal blow'.[4] In private he admitted his fear that the success of the bill would seat the Whigs in power for a lifetime.

During the spring of 1866 both Derby and Lady Derby were seriously ill; at one moment of crisis the bedridden Conservative leader sending a message of farewell to his wife who appeared to be dying in a neighbouring room. None the less, by letter during March, Derby urged Disraeli to resist the government bill to the utmost; even if, in anticipation of Liberal disintegration, this meant being still and silent. Derby remained doubtful, however, whether the Adullamites would support a Conservative government once the Liberal measure was thrown out. Conceivably, Russell might call a vote of no confidence and win an extension of power. By June 1866 the deep divisions in Liberal ranks were patently obvious; though by following Brand's advice and not calling an election, nor bringing forward a vote of confidence, but by resigning and putting a minority Conservative ministry in office, Russell firmly put the Conservatives on call. Arguably, a dissolution or a vote of confidence might have better suited the Conservatives' medium-term interests. Derby privately indicated his reluctance to become again, as in 1852 and 1858, premier on sufferance.[5] Meanwhile, as always, Disraeli was eager to take

119

office. Russell's decision to resign, Liberal differences having been demonstrated, brought to the forefront the question of how the Conservatives should respond to the fragmentation of their opponents.

Derby's doubts about the willingness of the Adullamites to join a Conservative government were well-founded. The Adullamites themselves hoped for a centrist ministry headed by Clarendon and led by Stanley in the Commons. Elcho saw them as a patriotic band rising above party and holding the balance between Whigs, radicals, and Tories. Through Malmesbury they let Derby know that they would even be willing to support Stanley as premier, if his father agreed to make way for him.[6] Delane joined the campaign for a Stanley government. As it was, Clarendon refused to be Derby's Foreign Secretary, and Derby was adamant he would not surrender the party leadership. Despite Derby's second son being married to Clarendon's daughter, and though no significant differences of policy existed between them, the old Whig heartily disliked the Conservative leader. Clarendon may have been playing a deep game, anticipating becoming prime minister himself should Derby fail. Derby courted Lansdowne, Grosvenor, Clanricarde, the Duke of Somerset, and other Adullamites without success. It soon became clear that the Liberal dissidents, playing for high stakes, would only consider a coalition with the Conservatives if Derby and Disraeli stood down. Disraeli was, as always, vulnerable. Yet neither man, particularly Derby, was willing to entertain such a relegation. Neither regarded himself as dispensable. Nor was Derby prepared to pursue a centrist coalition without some prominent Whig names as elements of the fusion. An offer of the Duchy of Lancaster to Lord Shaftesbury was also unsuccessful. Thus a centrist coalition, widely anticipated from March to June, failed to materialise in July 1866.

The failure to bring non-Conservatives into the ministry disappointed, though it did not surprise, Derby and Disraeli in their wish to establish a broad basis for support. Piqued by Whig and Adullamite aloofness and strongly urged on by Disraeli, Derby decided, none the less, to form a ministry as best he could. Familiar faces from 1858–9 filled up cabinet posts with Disraeli returning to the Exchequer, Stanley taking the Foreign Office, Malmesbury accepting the Privy Seal, Carnarvon the Colonial Office, Pakington the Admiralty, Peel the War Office, and Lord John Manners the Commission of Works. One new young doctrinaire Conservative presence was the intellectual and vehemently anti-Disraeli Lord Cranborne at the India Office.

Restricted to Conservative resources and lacking a Commons majority, the policy of the new ministry remained unclear. Cattle plague, a banking crisis, and the implications of Bismarck's crushing of the Austrians at the Battle of Sadowa in July preoccupied many minds. In the immediately following months, however, two things did become apparent. First, no deeply-held vision of Tory Democracy was driving ministers forward. What did exist, as in 1858–9, was the intention to prove Conservative government responsive, enlightened, and capable of reform. Secondly, the Hyde Park riot of the late summer did not propel the cabinet onward with an urgent sense of necessary action. Rather than panic, the incident induced in Conservative ministers regret at Spencer Walpole's lachrymose ineptitude. Stanley's response was characteristic. In June 1866 he did not believe that the political excitement among the upper classes over reform was shared to any considerable extent by the people – a view he still held six months later. Witnessing the large reform meetings of July 1866 he thought the crowds drawn by curiosity as much as reforming fervour, while the Hyde Park disturbance displayed more mischief than malice, and more of mere larking than either. Stanley found Walpole's reaction, on the other hand, ludicrous.[7] Popular clamour merely stimulated Conservative instincts for order.

What more forcefully influenced Conservative official thinking was the disturbing fact that the 1865 election had left Conservatives in a minority throughout the country. The English and Welsh counties survived as Conservative strongholds, though the Liberal dominance of the boroughs meant England and Wales generally returned 266 Liberal MPs as against 236 Conservatives MPs. In Scotland, Liberal domination was overwhelming, 41 Liberal MPs representing a total of 53 Scottish county and borough seats, as against 12 Conservative MPs; while in Ireland the Conservative majority of 1859 had given way to Liberal control in the majority of both counties and boroughs, 55 Liberal MPs representing Irish seats as opposed to 50 Conservative MPs.[8] Both in parliament and in the country Derby faced minority support and power on sufferance. In blunt tactical terms, remedying this situation meant having 'to destroy the present agitation and extinguish Gladstone and Co'.[9]

If in opposition Derby favoured a passive policy encouraging non-Conservatives to argue among themselves, in office in 1852 and 1858 he consistently sought to establish the Conservatives as a credible and moderate party of government. In 1866 precisely the same intention shaped Derby's response to the serious difficulties which he faced. Having taken the premiership he meant to keep it. As he declared to Pakington: 'If one wished to commit political suicide, it is not difficult to do so and, as far as I am personally concerned, I have no particular objection; but politically I have a very strong objection. I accepted office very unwillingly, but having accepted it, I mean to keep it as long as I can.'[10] Derby well understood that reform was an issue on which his government must act. During September and October 1866 Derby overruled Disraeli's reluctance to take up the question. He insisted Disraeli give the matter serious consideration and committed the cabinet to discussion of reform in November. As he stated in the Lords in July 1867:

> I did not intend for a third time to be made a mere stop gap until it would suit the convenience of the Liberal party to forget their dissensions and bring forward a measure which would oust us from office and replace them there: and I determined that I would take such a course as would convert, if possible, an existing minority into a practical majority.[11]

Derby was the engine propelling Conservative reform. Not that he anticipated the necessity for a radical bill. Indeed, he welcomed the alarm excited by Bright's violent language as enabling the genuine demand for reform to be met with a more moderate measure. What was needed was some intelligible principle upon which a new settlement might be based. In the event of defeat and a dissolution, such a principle would provide a definite issue on which to go to the country. By December 1866 Derby had hit upon such a principle in the form of urban household suffrage, safeguarded by plural voting. The support of the Queen, her cooperation being necessary if a dissolution were to be called, buoyed up Derby's hopes.

During the 1866 recess Gladstone departed for Italy, leaving the divided Liberal party 'to the healing powers of nature'.[12] The holiday provided Gladstone with much-needed rest and an excuse to put distance between himself and Bright. Many moderate Liberals, while admiring Gladstone's eloquence, energy and intelligence, felt him to be unreliable and feared he had been captured by Bright. In such circumstances, a moderate reform bill from Derby might be preferable to choking on an extreme reform measure from the radicals. Bright and leaders of the Reform League such as Beales and Howell, meanwhile, organised mass reform meetings around the country. Their primary theme was the respectability of the working man; an impassioned refutation of Lowe's calumnies against the drunkenness and depravity of the lower social orders. Bright accused Lowe of having a Botany Bay (the Australian penal colony) view of the great bulk of his fellow countrymen. If the intelligent Whig nobility were severed from the popular party, he warned, then the nobles would go down. The discipline and decorum of the great majority of reform meetings was cited as concrete proof of mature political responsibility deserving enfranchisement. The vindication of the moral character of 'the people' was usually more prominent than claims for specific franchise arrangements. This suited Bright, enabling him to appeal to both middle-class audiences, seeking household suffrage, and Reform League gatherings espousing a wider manhood suffrage. The ambiguity of Bright's views on democracy were cloaked by a high moral assertion of the rights of 'the nation' to power; the selfish immoral interests of one class denying the ancient and God-given rights of the people to raise an Eden amid waste wilderness. If reform was not enacted, Bright repeatedly warned, violence and social conflict would inevitably follow. The apocalyptic intensity of such language drew inspiration, while helpfully blurring radical differences. Meanwhile, Whigs and less advanced Liberals stepped back from such oratory. Gladstone feared the reform agitation was complicating the issue, exciting unreasonable demands for extensive reform. Elcho saw Bright's game as squeezing the Whigs and moderate Liberals between the Conservatives and radicals, a new franchise smashing the Conservatives and leaving Bright triumphant. Brand politely refused invitations to attend Reform Union meetings.

But while it heightened the expectation of reform, Bright's campaign left the Conservative government relative freedom of action. Derby's adoption of rated urban household suffrage, safeguarded by plural voting, provided recognition of the moral respectability of 'the people'. At the same time, it was a principle which could face both ways. Accompanied by suitable safe-guards, it could reassure Conservatives and Adullamites that a clear defence against manhood suffrage had been constructed; while to Liberals and radicals, it embodied principles espoused by the Reform Union and other earnest advocates of reform. Having decided the main principle of Conservative reform, Derby's procedural preference was to propose a series of general resolutions to parliament. In early February 1867 the cabinet agreed on resolutions, number 5 reading: 'That the principle of plurality of votes, if adopted by parliament, would facilitate the settlement of the borough franchise on an extensive basis.'[13] That an urban household suffrage was not specifically mentioned appeased Peel, whose eyes, Disraeli observed, lit up with insanity at mention of the phrase.

The resolutions presented by Disraeli to the Commons on 11 February 1867 remained substantially the same as those drafted by Derby the previous November. Though containing some striking passages Disraeli's speech was uneven, Gladstone's lukewarm reply deliberately equivocal. The option of appointing a Royal Commission to gather information was still open. But under immediate opposition attack Disraeli, without consultation, promised to bring forward an outline of a reform bill, rather than proceed with resolutions. This *volte face* forced the cabinet to quickly draft an outline reform measure for presentation to the Commons on 25 February. Derby and Disraeli had hoped that discussion of general resolutions would exacerbate

Liberal divisions. It was reported that Russell, increasingly ill and unpopular, favoured turning out the government immediately, while Gladstone, now anxious to appear moderate, wished for a delay. It became clear, however, that in fact Liberals were uniting in criticising this procedure and ignoring the substance of the resolutions. Seeing this, Disraeli immediately decided to adopt a less contentious procedure; thereby redirecting debate to the content of the government's recommendations.

This sudden change in procedural strategy highlighted a significant shift in cabinet control, once Commons debate on reform commenced. During the recess Derby, as in 1859, had skilfully controlled ministerial discussion. It is striking how successfully in February 1867 Derby brought the cabinet behind resolutions he had penned four months earlier. After February, however, the initiative quickly passed to Disraeli. Derby, both ill and distanced in the Lords, was unable to influence directly the rapid course of events in the Lower House. The hasty drafting of a bill necessitated by Disraeli's declaration, moreover, threw cabinet discussion into confusion. Lord Cranborne (formerly Lord Robert Cecil and later Lord Salisbury), Lord Carnarvon, and General Peel (brother of the premier of 1841–6) indicated their wish to resign. Abandoning household suffrage, Derby desperately sought alternative schemes which might preserve cabinet unity. The compromise so-called 'Ten Minutes Bill' suggested by Stanley, proposing a £6 borough franchise and a £20 county franchise, was drawn up. But it immediately became clear that such a measure would be vehemently opposed by both Liberals and many Conservatives. At a meeting at the Carlton Club on 28 February a large number of Conservative backbenchers indicated their readiness to accept rated residential household suffrage in the boroughs, as a clear principle of reform short of, so a defence against, manhood suffrage and democracy. On 2 March, the cabinet decided to revert to urban household suffrage and take the consequences. The bold line, which would undercut Gladstone's position, now seemed the safest course to adopt. Cranborne, Carnarvon, and Peel promptly resigned.

Control now slipped from Derby's increasingly frail hands. The Dukes of Richmond and Marlborough and Henry Corry were taken into the cabinet. At a party meeting on 15 March 1867, where Derby explained the bill to be introduced to the Commons, a general support for the measure was expressed. He also indicated that the plural-voting proposal could be dropped if strong objections were raised in debate. Privately Derby was clearly 'bent on remaining in power at whatever cost, and ready to make the largest concessions with that object'.[14] But after 18 March, when Disraeli presented the bill to the House, initiative was, of necessity, handed to Disraeli. A strong Commons speech by Disraeli on 26 March gave the Conservatives the upper hand. Disraeli attacked Gladstone for now denouncing reform proposals which the cabinet, of which he had been a member, in 1854 had approved. As Liberal opposition unravelled during April, Disraeli seized the opportunity for tactical dexterity. An Adullamite rump (less Lowe and Horsman), led by Lord Grosvenor, diligently assisted Disraeli and sought to cripple Gladstone. The wish to settle the reform question, fear of a dissolution, and a deep dislike of Gladstone now tore apart Liberal ranks. They became paralysed by dissension. A combination of Grosvenor's followers and advanced Liberals defeated Gladstone's attempt on 12 April to substitute a £5 rating borough franchise for the Conservative proposal.

This failure, Gladstone felt, was 'a smash perhaps without example'.[15] He temporarily surrendered the Liberal leadership in the Commons, talking of retirement to the back benches. The increasingly ill-tempered Gladstone then took to speaking in the Commons early in the evening during subsequent reform debates, indicating he did not wish to assume the prerogative of a leader in closing the debate on his side. Opposition demoralization cleared the way for Disraeli's audacity to play on the confused state of party feeling. Carnarvon declared his wish not to make mischief by fomenting Conservative divisions, while most backbenchers seemed prepared to settle the reform issue conclusively with a comprehensive measure. Stanley thought it 'wonderful how the [Conservative] party has held together under all its difficulties'.[16] By May 1867 Disraeli had clearly become the directing mind of the ministry. With surgical precision he dissected the Liberal opposition.

During May 1867 Disraeli responded to and incorporated far-reaching amendments to the government's bill. Bright, watching Disraeli's tactical dexterity in the Commons, grudgingly observed that Disraeli was such a good juggler that the Liberals did not know a real thing from a trick. Disraeli's 'subtle wickedness' even snared conscientious radicals such as John Smith (MP for Stockport and first chairman of the Anti-Corn Law League) and Duncan McLaren, pitting them against other Liberals. Quite simply Disraeli was seeking to shatter party discipline by stepping in advance of the Liberals.[17] The safeguards placed around urban household suffrage were removed. Plural voting was dropped, the residential qualification was reduced from two years to one (moved by the radical A. S. Ayrton), a £10 lodger franchise in the boroughs was accepted (moved by the advanced Liberal William Torrens), and Hodgkinson's amendment, abolishing the distinction between personal payment and compounding the payment of rates, added at least 500,000 householders to the electorate. Disraeli declared the personal payment of rates as the real test of a man's fitness to have the vote. This was the Conservative view, carried further and at a local level, of Gladstone's argument that financial probity and political responsibility be merged. Having swallowed the broad principle of household suffrage, Conservative backbenchers tamely accepted amendments transforming the government bill; the radical Locke King's amendment to reduce the county franchise from a £15 to a £12 annual rental qualification also being incorporated into the bill.

Cranborne's fulminations against Disraeli's treachery found little support as prolonged debate became increasingly wearying and intricate. Cranborne expressed his astonishment at the Conservatives adopting the ethics of a political adventurer. But the bulk of MPs now simply wished to see the question settled for the foreseeable future. The Reform League demonstration in Hyde Park on 6 May, as six months earlier, failed to produce alarm among Conservative ministers. Stanley thought the meeting 'went off quietly, without excitement, the numbers at no time great', the speeches 'not much listened to'. Once again, for Stanley, it only highlighted Walpole's weak character in the face of mischief rather than malice.[18] The great majority of MPs were now prepared to enfranchise sober and responsible artisans as long as it did not mean the vulgarisation of politics. The only Commons amendment of note which Disraeli did reject was John Stuart Mill's call for women's suffrage. By July the Commons had agreed to a bill far more extensive than Gladstone believed prudent and going beyond what Bright had demanded. Indeed, Bright feared that a 'residuum' of unregenerate poor, unfit for the vote, would benefit from the measure. But the Commons third reading passed without a division.

On 19 July 1867 Derby addressed a meeting of Conservative peers, calling for party unity in support of the bill. It was his object, he declared, 'to act so as to place the Tory party permanently in power and not to place them in a position to be beaten as soon as they had served the purpose of the opposition'.[19] Lord Grey moved a Lords amendment against the bill. Carnarvon, Cranborne, and Lowe, with the support of *The Times*, encouraged Grey. A weary and nervous Derby rallied himself to repulse the attack, calling the bill a large, extensive, and Conservative measure, likely to put the matter of reform to rest for many years. Unable to secure Russell's support, Grey's assault on the bill failed. Lord Cairns, Derby's Solicitor General in 1858 and appointed Lord Justice of Appeal in October 1866, did carry a motion safeguarding minority representation in large cities by giving each elector only two votes in three-member constituencies. Then, once again raising himself from his sick bed, on 6 August, Derby marked the passage of the measure through the Lords by declaring his confidence in the sound sense of his fellow countrymen. The extended franchise was, he stated, the means of establishing the institutions of the country on a firmer basis, while increasing the loyalty and contentment of a great portion of Her Majesty's subjects.

The complex history of the 1867 Reform Act reveals a number of truths. As Derby had predicted, reform exposed those deep fissures within the Liberal party that Palmerston had papered over. During 1867 Gladstone's opposition leadership collapsed amid the ruins of Liberal unity. Yet, even in these circumstances, intense personal distrust of Disraeli and dislike of Derby blocked the ready adhesion of Liberal dissidents to the Conservative party. The refusal of Clarendon, Grosvenor, Lansdowne, Elcho, and Lowe to join Derby's ministry condemned the Conservatives, once again, to the travails of minority government. Once in power, Derby and Disraeli were adamant that Liberals should no longer be allowed to be the monopolists of all plans for social amelioration. Both wished firmly to smash Gladstone. As premier for a third time, Derby was resolved to prove the Conservatives capable of introducing progressive reforms meeting the changing demands of society.

Disraeli was to claim that in 1867 he 'educated' the Conservative party. In truth, this was Derby's achievement. It was Derby who transformed the protectionist rump of the 1840s into a moderate party, prepared to support far-reaching reform as a lasting settlement. In 1866, as in 1858, it was Derby who forced Conservative attention on parliamentary reform. This was not propelled by a vision of 'Tory Democracy', beyond anecdotal accounts of conservative sensibilities among the lower social orders; nor was it a panic response by unnerved ministers to popular demonstrations and radical invective. Derby believed there existed a genuine demand for reform, but it was not voiced by the Reform League. If the destructive slide to manhood suffrage and radical fomenting of extreme aspirations was to be prevented, a clear defensible line demarcating a responsible electorate had to be drawn. By December 1866 Derby believed that, in the case of the urban electorate, household suffrage provided such a principle. Disraeli's conversion followed.

Derby demonstrated his skill and unobtrusive mastery of Conservative discussion during the recess of 1866–7. But by March 1867 age, illness, and his peerage wrested control of events from him. If, in origin, 1867 was Derby's bill, after March it became Disraeli's measure. Disraeli's triumph in the reform debates of 1867 safeguarded, despite the insecurity of his position, his succession to Derby as Conservative party leader the following February. The bill in its final form launched parties into a new world, where familiar features of the political landscape were much altered. Disraeli and most other Conservatives hoped that the newly-enfranchised would honour their benefactors; though Tory sceptics like Cranborne, fired with disgust for Disraeli, only saw a disgraceful opportunistic surrender of Conservative principle. In his determination not to become a stopgap, Cranborne pronounced, Derby had merely become a weather-cock blown hither and thither by gusts of political pressure; delivering everything and believing in nothing.[20] In this scheme of things Disraeli stood as the arch-villain. But the vast bulk of Conservative backbenchers lacked Cranborne's acerbic intellectual edge. Though unable to trust Disraeli completely, they were prepared to celebrate the Reform Act as a great measure because delivered by their own hands.

Predictably, Liberals were scathing in their judgements of the 1867 reform measure. Clarendon feared Disraeli had destroyed the constitution. 'Where we lifted the sluices of democracy an inch,' Lord Dalhousie declared, '[Derby] and Dizzy have raised them a foot. My only hope is that they will be the first to be washed away in the flood.'[21] Lowe believed the Conservative leader had, for the most sordid motives, deceived everyone. Cultivated Englishmen, Lowe declared, who were not slaves to the trammels of party, could only feel shame, rage, scorn, indignation, and despair. But it was not true that the Conservatives had simply stolen Liberal policy for their own purposes. That the 1867 Reform Act went further than either Gladstone or Bright had wished showed Derby and Disraeli striking out on a line of their own. Though bemused by the manner in which urban household suffrage had been achieved, Bright saw no need for further agitation on the franchise question. Future activities, he believed, should now concentrate on the ballot. The radical Reform League leaders were generally enthusiastic about the final form of the bill; particularly once Hodgkinson's amendment had been incorporated. Resident householders had regained their long lost rights, League literature claimed, though manhood suffrage was yet to be achieved. None the less, a people's parliament was coming to life, as a popular franchise, contended for amid obloquy and proscription, was obtained. Radical attention shifted from extension of the franchise to the secret ballot, redistribution, and the right to public assembly. But it was Lowe, toward the end of the reform debates, who identified the critical import of the 1867 Act. A new era in English politics, he declared, had been inaugurated. Numbers had won over wealth and intellect. Previously there had existed a party of attack and a party of resistance. Following 1867, 'we have instead two parties of competition who, like Cleon and the Sausage-seller of Aristophanes, are both bidding for the support of Demos'.[22]

Securing a Reform Act for England and Wales in August 1867, Reform Acts for Scotland and Ireland, and a Boundary Act (extending the boundaries of 70 English and Welsh boroughs) in 1868, did not bring the Conservatives immediate benefit. After March 1868 Gladstone united the scattered Liberal party around the cry for disestablishment of the Church of Ireland. In November 1868 the Liberals won a resounding victory in the first general election to be held under the new enfranchisement. After the election, 384 Liberal MPs faced a reduced Conservative party of 274 MPs; 80 per cent of the seats the Conservatives held were in England; the vast majority of their victories in county seats. On 3 December 1868 Gladstone became prime minister for the first time.

The Impact of Reform

What then was the effect of the 1867 Reform Act? In 1867 no politician had a precise idea of what would follow. In Carlyle's famous phrase, they were 'shooting Niagara'. The Liberal Chief Whip George Glyn warned Gladstone that 'all is new and changed and large and I must say in some respects *dark*'.[23] The borough electorate in England was increased by 134 per cent, the county electorate increased by 46 per cent. Whereas it was estimated that on average 1 in 5 adult males in England and Wales possessed the vote prior to 1867, after the Reform Act an average of 1 in 3 adult males were enfranchised. In Birmingham an electorate of 15,000 in 1866 was increased in 1868 to 43,000. Similarly, Manchester's electorate of 22,000 in 1866 was expanded to 48,000 in 1868. The distribution of seats and redrawing of constituency boundaries completed by June 1868 comforted Conservatives as Disraeli intended. Of the 52 seats taken from corrupt boroughs or those with fewer than 10,000 inhabitants, 25 extra seats were given to counties; 20 seats went to new borough constituencies; London University obtained an MP (all graduates receiving the vote); Merthyr Tydfil and Salford (major industrial centres) acquired a second member each; while Leeds, Birmingham, Liverpool, and Manchester became three-member constituencies.[24] Cairns's amendment protecting minority representation, Conservatives hoped, by giving electors only two votes in such constituencies, would enable Conservatives to return at least one member.

Through a Commission redrawing constituency boundaries, packed with Conservatives, Disraeli also managed to reduce urban intrusion into the counties. This segregation of urban and rural voters, it was anticipated, would protect Conservative domination of the increased county representation. In this respect election results in 1868 and 1874 were encouraging. In 1868 Conservatives won 127 English county seats, as compared with 99 seats in 1865. In 1874 the number of English county seats won by Conservatives was 145. During the same period Liberal representation in the English counties dropped from 48 seats in 1865 to 45 seats in 1868, and then 27 seats in 1874.

The disparity between borough and county constituencies was also evident in the impact of enfranchisement. While a household suffrage, subject to a one-year residency qualification, operated in the boroughs, the county franchise operated on the occupation of land worth £12 a year, or a property franchise for those with lands worth £5 a year. In England, at the 1868 elections, 1 in 8 of the total borough population had the vote; in the counties the ratio was 1 to 15. A similar picture existed in Scotland where the borough ratio, in 1868, of voters to non-voters was 1 to 9, the county ratio 1 to 27. None the less, in Scotland after 1867 the total proportional increase in voters was even greater than in England and Wales. Again, however, redistribution limited the impact of the enlarged electorate. Of the 7 new seats given to Scotland, 3 went to counties, 2 shared seats went to the Universities of Edinburgh, St Andrews, Glasgow, and Aberdeen, with just the remaining 2 seats going to the large urban constituencies of Glasgow and Dundee.

As important as the legal right to the vote, moreover, was the recognition of that right by the compilers of the electoral register. It is easy to assume that legislative intent was precisely translated into well-defined electorates. But in fact the mechanical complexity of the registration system injected an arbitrary element into the identification of voters. Unreliable returns by landlords, shifting urban populations, and simple apathy could produce significant variation in the constituencies. Subsequent legislation, such as Goschen's 1869 Act enabling some indirect ratepayers to be classified as householders and Dilke's 1878 Act entitling many previously considered lodgers to claim the household franchise, further complicated the process. And as the complexity of the registration system increased so the margin for random and unforeseen variation was extended. After 1868 both parties intensified their activities to ensure that their supporters entitled to vote were registered. At the same time party activists sought the removal from the register of their opponents' supporters. This battle for the electoral register often had a crucial effect on election results. In many cases it was necessary for lodgers to have party backing to help them complete the annual process of registration. For many, the time and effort involved was a strong deterrent. Applications had to be made in person to the revising barrister during office hours, usually leading to loss of wages for time away from work, among other disruptions. One authority estimates that in the London boroughs in 1868 between two and three hundred thousand lodgers were entitled to vote, but the names of only about fourteen thousand appeared on the register. Local disparities in the efficiency and commitment of register compilers exacerbated difficulties.

At the constituency level this system was clearly a strong inducement to increasingly professional local party organisation. It gave impetus to the appointment of professional party agents (rather than solicitors acting in an amateur, part-time capacity), and the establishment of party-sponsored clubs and formal party associations. As the size of the electorate expanded so party bureaucracy grew. None the less, the 1867 Reform Act did increase significantly the number of artisan and respectable working-class voters. This was particularly the case in new industrialized urban boroughs such as Oldham, South Shields, Bolton, Halifax, Leeds and Birmingham. In established constituencies in Liverpool and the London boroughs the increase was less striking.

The 1868 election offers an opportunity to analyse voting behaviour before the ballot drew a veil over electors' choices; public votes being recorded in many constituencies in poll books. Though poll books cannot record the motivation for any individual vote, some general conclusions can be drawn; particularly where voting is recorded alongside occupations. Doctrine, deference, fear of recrimination, bribery, and business interests could affect an individual's choice. Though it is usually difficult to say positively *why* a vote was cast, it is often possible to show what was *not* happening. For example, poll studies show voting patterns did not follow strict class lines. Nor are occupational categories a sure guide, though certain groups such as publicans tended to vote Conservative. Butchers also generally proved Conservative supporters, and grocers, for some reason, Liberal in their politics. Similarly, flax spinners and engineers tended to vote Liberal. More strikingly, religion continued to play an important part in voting behaviour. Nonconformists, for example, tended to support advanced Liberal candidates: though the increase of non-church or non-chapel-going voters in the boroughs was slowly eroding denominational loyalties. In the industrial towns of Lancashire and Yorkshire a form of industrial deference existed, where the political affiliation of factory owners influenced employees' voting. In Preston and Blackburn, for example, in 1868 the influence of Tory mill owners secured the election of Conservative MPs; though increasing sections of the electorate, even in these communities, were employed outside the factories. What the poll books reveal most strikingly is the complexity of voting behaviour.

Again and again the efficiency of local party organisation appears increasingly crucial. In 1860 Palmerston had encouraged the formation of the Liberal Registration Association. His intention was to disarm dangerous popular influences in the constituencies. During the 1857 election Palmerston had been angered and alarmed by the radical tendencies of many local Liberal groups, who were generally supportive of Russell's leadership. By 1868 the Palmerstonian Registration Association was being remodelled into a more broadly-based Liberal Association. What is striking is how effectively the established parties drew new electors into their orbit. The fate of the Reform League after 1867 is typical of a wider pattern. During 1866–7 the League enjoyed a membership of 65,000 in 600 branches around the country. Conceivably, it might have aspired to become the independent mouthpiece of working-class activism, seeking redress of the specific class grievances of its supporters. But, in fact, it was absorbed by the Liberal party and any class-based programme it might have formulated was mitigated. Financially, the League was always dependent on more moderate middle-class sponsors such as the textile manufacturer Samuel Morley, often members of the Reform Union. After 1868 Liberal party managers found George Howell and other League leaders compliant partners in constituency affairs. In return for a secret subsidy from the Liberal Whip Glyn the Reform League helped Liberal organisation. In 1868 and 1874 Howell stood as a radical Liberal candidate for Aylesbury.

The broad community of moral sentiment which formed popular Liberalism, well before formal organisation defined its parameters, accommodated bodies like the Reform League within its embrace. Similarly, emergent trades unions generally harnessed their aspirations to the Liberal party. In 1874 the first working-class MPs entered the Commons. Thomas Burt, MP for Morpeth, and Alexander MacDonald, MP for Stafford, were miners whose candidature had been supported by the Labour Representation League formed in 1869. Both men were from trades union backgrounds. Both proved loyal Gladstonian Liberals.

While the Liberal party domesticated the institutions of organised labour, the Conservatives after 1867 expanded their constituency organisation through local Conservative Clubs. John Gorst's success in extending the network of the National

Union of Conservative and Constitutional Associations offered party affiliation to Conservative working men. As with the Liberals, Conservatives found many working men keen to associate with the established parties, with minimal concessions demanded of them in terms of policy. Local party clubs and associations offered not only participation in the political life of the community, but also sporting facilities, newspaper rooms, libraries, concerts, and lectures, supplying the full cultural and intellectual needs of citizenship.

Rather than the parties having to debase themselves in pursuit of working men's votes, as many anti-democrats such as Lowe had feared, working men showed themselves pleased to join the established parties if a door was opened to them. This meant that the enlarged electorate changed the parties less in terms of policy and parliamentary personnel than in terms of rhetoric and organisation. For many politicians reared in the world of mid-Victorian parliamentary government the prospect of organised popular party support censoring those in Westminster was new and unpalatable. During the election of 1868 the young Whig Lord Hartington found canvassing extremely distasteful; 'almost all the gentlemen being on the other side, the society is not agreeable'.[25] But the activities of those such as John Gorst for the Conservatives showed the electoral dividend to be readily available to party managers willing to extend a hand to the newly enfranchised. Frederich Engels, running the family business in Manchester, could only lament in 1868 that 'everywhere the proletariat is the rag, tag and bobtail of the official parties'.[26]

Yet those who lamented attacks on parliamentary government recognised the single most important effect of the 1867 Reform Act. The constitutional structure that had framed party politics since 1832 was significantly modified by the extension of the suffrage – 1867 did not immediately dismantle the edifice of parliamentary government, but it did mark a significant step in the loosening of that constitutional fabric. Drawing the newly-enfranchised into the established parties and getting supporters on the electoral register gave firm impetus to the growth of professional constituency organisations. The formalisation of constituency politics also reduced the opportunities for the unenfranchised to participate in the rituals of electoral contests. Meetings attended by ticketed audiences began to replace open-air hustings carnivals. Print began to replace older oral and visual symbols of political partisanship. The move to render constituency politics more sober and respectable, while not eradicating beer and brawling, did begin to constrain the boisterous participation of the unenfranchised. Thus, while formal male political participation was extended, informal involvement was reduced. At the same time, the necessary integration of local organisation into a national structure created centralised party bureaucracies.

At another level, during the 1870s, the emergence of 'caucus' politics in large urban constituencies, such as Birmingham under the sway of the screw manufacturer Joseph Chamberlain, further demonstrated the growing importance of organisation. Originally a derogatory term associated with American democracy, the phrase 'caucus' politics described the tight control of local constituency parties by a committee – a system of wire-pulling, critics maintained, which led to the manufacture of popular agitation and the undermining of legitimate electoral influence. But the benefits of the 'caucus system' were shown when, despite Cairns's minority clause applicable to three-member constituencies, in 1868, 1874, and 1880 all three Liberal candidates were returned for Birmingham; Liberal votes being carefully distributed so as to keep out Conservative challengers. Here were the beginnings of the modern party machine. The Liberal government's 1869 Municipal Franchise Act, moreover, strengthened the local base of popular politics, encouraged further municipal party organisation, and provided a civic model for demands for greater national democracy by enfranchising all compound ratepayers after one year's residency, unmarried women on the same terms as men.

Similarly, bodies such as the Liberation Society and United Kingdom Alliance, drawing on the organised conviction of Nonconformists, and in the 1870s, the National Education League and National Liberal Federation, exercised increasing influence. 'Sectionalism' became a fear of many parliamentarians; pressure groups committed to single issues, 'faddists' in the vocabulary of the day, threatening to unbalance broad party objects. The Liberal party after 1867, to the alarm of many Whigs, proved itself especially prey to the divergent particular aims of sectional support. The autonomous sovereignty of Westminster was slowly broken down.

Gradually, but perceptibly, after 1867 sovereignty began to shift from parliament to the electorate. Or, to be more precise, power shifted to the national party organisations through which the opinion of the electorate was conveyed. Sovereignty passed from parliament to the platform. Politicians were 'standing on the threshold of a new career', Bright told an Edinburgh audience in 1868. 'We need no longer have recourse to the arguments which we have often heard from platforms in times past. . . . We now have to appeal to you.'[27] While Bright perhaps over-dramatised the case, the pitch of his observation was true. Whereas before 1867 governments were generally brought down by Commons defeats, in 1868, 1874, and 1880 cabinets, defeated at the polls, resigned before meeting parliament. Dismissing ministries increasingly became a matter of electoral mandate, rather than party dynamics within Westminster. In Lowe's words, MPs were no longer advocates of principle, but supplicants for popular favour. After 1867 the number of uncontested constituencies fell significantly. In 1865, 195 constituencies were uncontested. In 1868 that number fell to 140, in 1874 it dropped further to 118, and in 1880 only 67 constituencies were uncontested. In 1865, 46 per cent of MPs faced no contest. In 1880 only just over 16 per cent of MPs were so fortunate.

Party contests in each constituency became the norm as electoral judgement came to determine the identity of the government. The increasing number of candidates standing for seats at general elections confirmed the trend. In 1868, for the first time since 1832, more than 1,000 candidates stood for election. At no time after 1868 did less than a 1,000 candidates put themselves forward at a general election. MPs found themselves required more and more frequently to address their constituents. Individual election manifestos became formulated around the pressing national questions of the day. In November 1868 Gladstone appealed to the nation on the question of disestablishment of the Irish Church. He succeeded, with Disraeli's compliance, in imposing this issue on the hustings platforms and placards of constituencies throughout the country. Increasingly, thereafter, local contests were fought around a national agenda, though the Liberal and former Peelite Duke of Argyll, in 1873, believed the 'policy of looking out for a 'cry' before a dissolution . . . odious if not immoral'.[28] The beginnings of the mass merchandising of party leaders reinforced this development as effigies of Gladstone and Disraeli appeared on plates, toby jugs, and teaspoons. Party leaders became popular icons; while Conservative partisans delighted in placing Gladstone's portrait on the inside of chamber pots.

When Whigs deplored the Conservatives' destruction of the constitution in 1867 it was the demise of parliamentary government they mourned. No longer were constituency contests and parliamentary politics distinct levels of political activity. They were to be gradually merged. Politicians were to be increasingly drawn out from their parliamentary seclusion. The encroachment of party organisation, the restricted scope for statesmanlike independence, and the requirement for popular flattery rendered politics, for those such as Clarendon, less appealing and gentlemanly. Even the recently retired radical MP, A. H. Layard, disappointed in his ambitions, in 1873 bemoaned politicians being trammelled by constituents and colleagues.[29] After 1867 the power of the electorate progressively usurped parliament's sovereignty and MPs found themselves having increasingly to act as delegates. In the decades after 1867 national parties, enjoying mass membership and the resources of central bureaucratic organisation, gradually assumed the power to make and unmake governments, define the national agenda, and direct parliamentary debate. As Cranborne discerned in October 1867: in passing the Reform Act ministers renounced all pretension to independence. Rather than govern, ministers now had to lead. Yet they were leaders 'in no other sense but that in which the first horse in a team is called a leader: he is the first to be driven'. National parties increasingly came to wield the constitutional whip hand. Cranborne's verdict was characteristically terse. 'If the practice that has been recently pursued shall be sustained, it is difficult to believe that our system of parliamentary government can long survive.'[30]

5

GLADSTONE AND LIBERALISM, 1868–74

The exuberant energy of the 1868–74 ministry marked the heady flush of Gladstonian Liberalism in power. The extensive legislative achievement of this government indicated the broad sweep of opinion and powerful reforming impetus embraced within the progressive movement of Liberal belief. The Church of Ireland was disestablished, an Irish Land Act passed, elementary education reformed, competitive examinations for entrance to most areas of the civil service introduced, the purchase of military commissions abolished, the judicial system overhauled, religious tests for Oxford and Cambridge Universities abolished, local government reformed, and the secret ballot introduced for parliamentary elections. Between 1869 and 1873 major areas of British society were overhauled. The ties between the state and the Established Church were loosened, the patronage system was reformed, and greater efficiency and professionalism were sought within the framework of economic government. By 1873 the Liberal party was tearing itself apart as Gladstone's leadership faltered. But for the first three years of its existence Gladstone's government proved itself, arguably, the greatest reforming ministry of the century.

Gladstone's Liberal Leadership

Gladstone did not see the achievements of his first government as the initial instalment of further far-reaching Liberal reforms.

141

Rather, he believed his appointment as premier in 1868, aged 59, marked the climax of his career. Retirement and the private pleasures of scholarship were to follow. A sense of closure became an increasingly common theme in the self-reflection of his journal. Inevitably, Gladstone was unaware of the drama that the next twenty-five years of his public life would bring. Instead, he saw the reforms of 1868–74 as the culmination of his policies so far. For example, his financial reforms of the 1850s and 1860s had established the Chancellorship of the Exchequer as a pre-eminent executive office, second only to the premiership. Public expenditure and inter-departmental relations were framed by rules drawn up by the Treasury and enforced by the Public Accounts Committee of the Commons. Thus were established the fiscal foundations of the mid-Victorian state. The financial measures of Gladstone's first government were the completion of this financial structure. That, between 1868 and 1874, the nation's *per capita* net income rose, supported this perspective. Buttressing the central tenets of economic government and retrenchment, accompanied by increasing national prosperity, were those measures bringing greater efficiency and administrative professionalism to government; institutional reform recognising the morality of merit, removing barriers of Anglican exclusivity, and encouraging a civic and moral individuality. In broad principle Liberals could easily subscribe to such ideals. But translating these broad ideals into the detail of legislation embroiled them in complex and intricate difficulties.

In 1868 Gladstone aligned his charismatic leadership with the transcendent cry of Irish Church disestablishment. This united the powerful forces of popular Liberalism behind a parliamentary party, articulating the aspirations of most of the dynamic forces transforming mid-Victorian society. During the 1860s a broad community of moral sentiment, yet to be defined through formal organisation, had coalesced around such Liberal cries as 'religious and civil liberty', 'peace, retrenchment and reform', free trade, economy, improvement and progress. In part, this was because Liberalism struck an historic resonance, emotional as much as intellectual, with some of the deepest concerns of mid-Victorian moral culture. In his *Chapter of Autobiography*

Gladstone declared that 'the action of man in the state is moral, as truly as it is in the individual sphere'.[1] Liberalism upheld that the means to a worthy life was through individual character surmounting hardship, deprivation, and adversity. The strong and righteous exhibited self-reliance, forethought, and the deliberate exercise of free choice. Weakness of will and the deterioration of individual moral fibre was that to be feared. Self-discipline, dedication, patience, strength of purpose and the free exercise of rational choice were that to which to aspire.

Such ideals were often encapsulated in the ethos of 'manliness'. Liberalism offered a vision of a meritocratic society of self-reliant and responsible male citizens who, through enlightened and free cooperation, could secure not just social and material progress, but also collective moral regeneration. This required extending civil liberties to all religious denominations and slackening the ties between the Anglican Church and the State. At its most emotionally direct, therefore, Liberalism offered each voter a public affirmation of his individual self-worth. Paternalism corrupted both patron and recipient, fostering a debilitating dependence. As much as an end in itself liberty was an essential means to moral self-reliance and the triumph of character over adversity. As a doctrine of 'manliness', with its watchword of civil and religious liberty, retrenchment, and reform, Liberalism offered powerful emotional identification to a wide range of aspiring sections. It was not concerned with class or the narrow material interests of particular social groups. Rather, it evoked a broad moral vision, deliberately embracing all classes and denominations, through which popular Liberalism might discover an uplifting common purpose with its parliamentary representatives. Palmerston and Derby had avoided basing party alignment on sectarian differences. Gladstone's succession to the Liberal leadership promptly brought moral and religious issues to the forefront of debate.

Gladstone's taking up of Irish disestablishment in 1868 perfectly matched Liberal sensibilities. It provided an uplifting common purpose. Indeed, it appeared the one issue able to restore Liberal unity. That Liberal electoral support was largely based in Scotland, Wales, and Ireland reinforced the point. It also characterised Gladstone's leadership in aligning the twin poles of progressive opinion within the traditional ruling class with the 'virtuous passion' of popular feeling around a single morally charged issue. Momentarily resting on his axe while felling a tree on the Hawarden estate, Gladstone declared with deep earnestness, on being invited to form a government in December 1868, that it was his mission to pacify Ireland. He felt an intense and appropriate personal sense of incandescence: 'the Almighty seems to sustain me for some purpose of his own, deeply unworthy as I know myself to be. Glory be to His name'.[2]

Irish disestablishment chimed in with the Whig and Liberal wish to separate the state from Anglican exclusivity. It followed in the tradition of Catholic Emancipation, repeal of the Test and Corporation Acts, Irish educational reform in 1831 and the Irish Church Temporalities Act of 1833. Irish disestablishment complemented the anti-clerical stance of Liberal foreign policy and distaste for the growth of ritualism in the Church of England during the 1860s. Moreover, Ireland blatantly breached the principle of an Established Church nourishing the spiritual needs of the majority of its population. In 1861, 12 per cent of the Irish population were members of the Church of Ireland. An overwhelming 78 per cent of the Irish population were Catholics, the remaining 10 per cent being Ulster Presbyterians. An Established Church, Whigs and Liberals believed, should be a national church. For many Nonconformists the issue also touched on their wish for disestablishment throughout the United Kingdom: Ireland providing a precedent for further disengagement of Church and State. By 1870 the term the 'Nonconformist conscience' was entering political parlance. The 1868 election doubled the number of Nonconformist MPs in the Commons. Approximately 62 Liberal backbench MPs were Nonconformists, drawn largely from the older sects (Unitarians, Baptists, and Congregationalists) and generally radical in their opinions. And while divided on other issues, all were agreed on Anglican disestablishment as a common goal.

The Liberation Society enthusiastically threw its sizeable propaganda resources into the Irish disestablishment campaign. From the mid-1860s Catholic-Irish MPs, via the National

Association campaigning for Irish disestablishment as well as Irish land reform and endowments for Catholic education, established an alliance with the Liberation Society. Similarly, radicals who were not Nonconformists supported disestablishment as part of a broader attack on vested interests, privilege, and religious exclusivity as obstacles to meritocratic reward and moral regeneration. Around Irish disestablishment, after March 1868, Gladstone effectively reassembled the scattered fragments of the Liberal party in the call for an instalment of real justice for Ireland. From being thoroughly disorganised, the Liberal party was transformed by the commanding force of the Irish Church question.[3]

The unanimity of Liberal opinion on Irish disestablishment in 1868, however, was not evident on other issues. Agreement did not even exist on the general principle of disestablishment beyond Ireland. While prepared to disestablish the Irish Church, Whigs and Liberals generally opposed disestablishing the Church of England itself. Further parliamentary reform, in the form of the ballot, advocated by radicals, alarmed Whigs and moderate Liberals, including Gladstone himself. The religious aspect of elementary education reform rendered that issue contentious. The vexed and long-standing question of church rates reform, non-Anglicans also being required to make payment to support the parish vestry, occupied much radical and Nonconformist energy. Motions for reform of church rates from Clay and Trelawny during the 1860s were supported by Russell. Palmerston also voted for these motions, confident that Conservative opposition would defeat them. But this Liberal rallying cry was resolved during the 1868 session, at Gladstone's initiative and with Conservative compliance. The issue of Irish disestablishment remained, possessing the merit of unifying Liberals as well as potentially pacifying Ireland.

Derby's retirement in February 1868, meanwhile, enhanced the strategic benefits to Gladstone of an Irish initiative. Derby, having served as Lord Grey's resolute Irish Chief Secretary from 1830 to 1833, had long experience and authority on Irish matters: Disraeli had none. Moreover, since the 1860s Disraeli had been building a reputation as a stalwart champion of the established Anglican Church. In speeches to his constituents in Buckinghamshire he called for the defence of the Church's legal rights against Nonconformist agitation. The Anglican Church he portrayed as a 'majestic corporation' endowed with 'the sanctity of a long tradition'.[4] Church establishment stood as part of the historic fabric of English life. In his 1865 election address Disraeli made defence of the Church his foremost concern. In 1868 Disraeli, strongly supported by cabinet colleagues such as Gathorne Hardy, turned the Conservative government's face against any reform of the Irish Church. This was despite the fierce distaste of some other colleagues, such as Stanley, for the zealous intransigence of the Tory high church party. In tactical terms, therefore, justice for Ireland offered Gladstone firm ground on which to distance himself from Disraeli; parliamentary reform having blurred party distinctions.

Gladstone's concern for Ireland was first awakened in the 1840s. In 1845 he described Ireland as 'that cloud in the West, that coming storm, the minister of God's retribution upon cruel and inveterate and but half-atoned injustice'.[5] During 1865, Gladstone somewhat ambiguously declared he could no longer defend the establishment of the Church of Ireland; his stating what he could not do leaving to veiled inference what he might be prepared to do. Privately Gladstone described Irish establishment as a 'hideous blot'.[6] Outbreaks of Fenian violence in 1867 pressed Ireland to the forefront of concern. Attempted Fenian uprisings in southern Ireland in March 1867 were followed by two attacks in England, at Manchester and Clerkenwell, which killed 13 people. Public opinion was outraged. The 'cloud in the West' darkened menacingly. By early 1868 Gladstone believed Ireland's problems required disestablishment of the Irish Church, revision of the land laws, and reform of Irish university education. But only disestablishment offered the immediate prospect of unified Liberal action. Displaying his tactical acumen in March 1868 Gladstone proposed from the opposition benches Commons resolutions calling for Irish disestablishment. Deep rifts in the Conservative cabinet were immediately created. The strong church party in the cabinet, headed by Gathorne Hardy, clashed with those ministers seeing the necessity and justice of reform, such as Stanley. Disraeli favoured a strong Protestant line, which some of his colleagues sought to temper. These religious divisions proved more debilitating to Conservatives than any traumas over parliamentary reform.

In old age Gladstone reflected that there had been four critical junctures in his career when he had experienced real political insight. Not, he was anxious to explain, simply an intuiting of public opinion. Rather, 'an insight into the facets of particular eras, and their relations one to another, which generates in the mind a conviction that the materials exist for forming public opinion, and for directing it to a particular end'.[7] The first occasion when he saw in an historical moment the materials to form public opinion toward a particular end came in 1853, when he presented his landmark budget. The second critical juncture came in 1868 with Irish disestablishment. The other two occasions, both failures, were Irish Home Rule in 1886 and reform of the House of Lords in 1894. But in 1868 it was Irish disestablishment which Gladstone sensed as a luminous transcendent issue, born of the historical moment and a Providential will. Gladstone's ability to communicate, through his oratory, the passionate intensity of his conviction of the historical and divine justice of his cause, raised Liberal unity afresh from the chaotic ruins of 1867. Anxious not to be seen as too pro-Catholic, Gladstone declared himself an 'ardent Protestant' who wished to remove public financial support from all denominations in Ireland.[8] Thus religious freedom, divine justice and economic government were all served.

The single-issue moral crusade, binding together the differing strands of Liberal opinion, became characteristic of Gladstone's leadership. From May to October 1868 Irish disestablishment monopolised Liberal energies and disrupted Conservatives. It dominated the hustings in November, forcing a national agenda on local platforms to an extent previously unknown in mid-Victorian elections. It produced an overwhelming Liberal victory. Whig distaste for electioneering was more than compensated for by the overpowering enthusiasm for the campaign amongst British Nonconformists and Irish Catholics. In November 1868 Liberals increased their hold on those borough constituencies enlarged by redistribution, the Welsh, Scottish, and Irish constituencies, and those large English urban constituencies with electorates of over 2000. In Scotland Liberals won 52 out of a total of 60 seats, while in Wales, reflecting the growing militancy of Nonconformity, Liberals won 22 out of a total of 30 seats. A crushing Commons majority of 110 Liberal MPs forced the Conservatives back into their electoral heartland of the English counties. Of a total of 274 Conservative MPs, 217 sat for English constituencies.

The sole crumb of comfort for the Conservatives was the anti-Catholic aspect of the election in Lancashire, where Protestantism provided some Conservative gains. In Lancashire the Conservatives returned 21 MPs against 13 Liberal MPs; Conservatives taking Salford, Bolton, Preston and Blackburn. Bright's impassioned reform speeches during the 1860s also contributed to the growth of Conservative opinion in Lancashire. Stanley noted that 'Bright is more feared by the leading mill owners than by the aristocracy – the trades unions have caused the change.'[9] Gladstone himself was defeated in the newly-created constituency of South West Lancashire, his surprise at his defeat bringing on a public burst of ill temper on the hustings platform. But he was immediately elected for the London borough of Greenwich.

Despite the Queen's fear that Gladstone was inflaming old sectarian feuds, which complemented Clarendon's private doubts as to whether the Liberal leader was quite sane enough for the premiership, Gladstone took office in 1868 with the largest Commons majority of any Victorian prime minister to date. This powerful Liberal majority was firmly united on Irish disestablishment. In late November Gladstone published his *Chapter of Autobiography* explaining his changing views on Church/State relations. He placed his opinions in the context of the political and theological debates of the 1840s, the Maynooth grant, and the Oxford Movement. Despite giving little consideration to the religious issues of the 1860s, the pamphlet laid out Gladstone's personal logic on Irish disestablishment, underlining the imperative need for the Liberal commitment to religious equality in Ireland. The views of this Liberal majority on other issues, however, were far less clear. By 1872 some Liberals were regretting the narrow focus of the 1868 campaign.

Liberal Reform, 1868–73

Gladstone's 1868 cabinet, in spite of a preponderance of aristocratic members, reflected the broad nature of Liberal support in the country. Nearly half the Liberal front bench had not served in cabinet before. At the same time, in comparison with Gladstone's later cabinets, there was a strong sense of collegiality. No single minister saw himself as a strong rival to Gladstone. Clarendon as Foreign Secretary, Granville at the Colonial Office, and Hartington as Postmaster General provided a continuing Whig presence in the government. Hartington, heir to a Dukedom, was already establishing himself as the rising natural leader of the Whigs. Granville, in particular, proved an emollient partner in cabinet counsel, enhancing a harmonious sense of cooperation. As government leader in the Lords Granville spoke in an easy and conversational style, never rising to great eloquence, but always sensible and clear. The loquacious Earl of Kimberley (formerly Lord Wodehouse), became Privy Seal. Russell, Lord Halifax (formerly Sir Charles Wood), and Sir George Grey declined invitations to join the government. The former Peelites Argyll and Cardwell took the India Office and War Office respectively. Bright's appointment to the Board of Trade, despite illness, signified the importance of radical support. Bright became the first Nonconformist to be a cabinet member, after a two-hour discussion with the new premier. Gladstone took care to flatter him, though Bright retained a fear of becoming a prisoner, rather than an ally, in the Whig camp. The radical MP Trelawny commented in his diary: 'Samson has lost his hair.'[10] The young and capable banker George Goschen, a radical middle-class critic of aristocratic patronage and inefficiency, took over the Poor Law Board. His manner in the Commons was quiet, practical and well-informed. Outside the cabinet, W. E. Forster, MP for Bradford, Matthew Arnold's brother-in-law and a fellow spirit to Goschen, was given Education. The Adullamite Lowe, who shared Goschen and Forster's wish to purge the state of aristocratic inefficiency and establish administrative expertise and rational government, became Chancellor of the Exchequer. The Palmerstonian Liberal, former Peelite, and South Wales industrial landowner H. A. Bruce was appointed Home Secretary.

The presence of the Quaker John Bright and Forster, a Quaker by upbringing, on the front bench ensured ties with popular Nonconformity. In 1871 the Unitarian James Stansfeld, friend and admirer of Mazzini, joined the cabinet in charge of local government. The presence of Goschen, Forster, Bruce, and Bright also linked the ministry with those Liberal MPs who had commercial backgrounds and interests. In 1868 the proportion of Liberal MPs with careers in manufacturing, trade or banking rose to over 24 per cent. The number of Liberal MPs who were lawyers also rose slightly to 13 per cent. The vast bulk of Liberal MPs remained from landed backgrounds, either aristocratic or gentry, comprising nearly 45 per cent of the Commons party.[11] But the Liberal electoral base in England gave strength to the growing number of Liberal MPs associated with business. These were men such as Samuel Morley, wealthy Nottingham hosiery manufacturer and MP for Bristol; William Rathbone, Unitarian Liverpool merchant and MP for the city; Anthony Mundella, Nottingham manufacturer and MP for Sheffield; and Jacob Bright, younger brother of John, chairman of the family cotton firm in Rochdale and MP for Manchester. Whig grandees like Granville had industrial interests on their land which bridged country-house Whiggery with growing commercial interests. Moreover, as much as their middle-class origins, it was their belief in rational efficiency in government that lent a keen reforming edge to Goschen, Lowe and Forster's views. That Gladstone put the Poor Law Board, the Exchequer, Education and the Home Office into the hands of such men indicated the clear reforming impetus of his administration.

As noted above, in December 1868 it was Irish disestablishment that dominated the government's agenda. Irish legislation was to continue to engross the prime minister's energies throughout 1869 and early 1870. Gladstone appointed the compliant

Chichester Fortescue as Irish Chief Secretary to be his partner in Irish policy. During the New Year in seclusion at Hawarden, Gladstone prepared an extensive and complex Irish Church bill, discussed in cabinet during February and presented to the Commons on 1 March 1869. To Liberal backbenchers Gladstone's speech was a 'marvellous exposition', though, as always, his intellect seemed to revel in fine distinctions. It was a measure designed to enlist support from British Nonconformists and Irish Catholics. Even so, immediate controversy attended the issue of the amount of endowment to be left to the disestablished Church of Ireland. Both Whigs and the Queen supported the Church retaining all post-Reformation endowments. Bright and the Liberation Society, on the other hand, criticised this as too generous. Intense Commons debates during April were closely monitored by a nervous and fidgety Gladstone whose pallid features betrayed his passionate concern and anxiety. From the front bench a caustic and impassioned Bright denounced the tyranny of priests. A compromise settlement allowed the Church continued possession of donations made after 1660. Not wishing to be forced into an anti-Catholic corner, Disraeli acquiesced in the principle of disestablishment. The Liberal evangelical Archbishop of Canterbury, A. C. Tait, anxious to cooperate with Nonconformists and remove vestiges of Anglican exclusivity, assisted in private negotiations.

While these events secured the Irish Church bill's passage in the Commons, Derby and Cairns moved a rejection of the measure in the Lords. From the beginning Gladstone had anticipated that the Lords would be the stumbling block to Irish disestablishment. A split in Conservative ranks, led by Carnarvon, Bath, and Devon, however, combined with the solid support of Whig peers, carried the measure through its second reading in the Upper House. The ranks of Whig peers did split, none the less, in committee stage, as Cairns proposed amending the preamble of the measure to include concurrent endowment: the distribution of the assets of the Anglican Church in Ireland between the Anglican, Catholic, and Presbyterian Churches; alternative state subsidies for the latter churches, through the Maynooth grant and the Regium Donum, being ended. Cairns's success prompted Gladstone to threaten abandonment of the bill, Cairns's proposal being a 'great, moral and political evil'.[12] This, the prime minister anticipated, would leave the Lords to their fate as the target of popular vilification. The calmer heads of Granville, Halifax, and Grey, however, persuaded the prime minister to accept a compromise which, none the less, avoided concurrent endowment. Disraeli also put pressure on Cairns to allow the issue to be settled; disestablishment being, as Disraeli saw it, the sole cement of the Liberal majority. The Irish Church bill received the royal assent on 26 July 1869. The Liberal press welcomed it as a great triumph. The strain upon Gladstone had been immense. At times during the session he appeared close to nervous collapse. The victory over Irish disestablishment was his; but the question became, whither Liberal reform now?

Initial Nonconformist and Irish Catholic elation at the securing of Irish disestablishment was to give way in subsequent months to increasing Liberal discord. Disraeli believed the Irish land question was the chief difficulty facing the cabinet; an issue over which the radicals would give Gladstone a good deal of trouble. Cabinet members such as Clarendon, Argyll, and Lowe were, by 1869, beginning to express concern over Gladstone's Irish policy. The nature of a proposed Irish Land bill, the proposed release of Fenian prisoners, and alarm at the political activities of the Catholic hierarchy, were causing them serious disquiet. Fortescue, Clarendon, Argyll, Spencer, and Hartington argued the need for some coercive Irish legislation to maintain order; the demand for the release of imprisoned Fenians prompting mass rallies throughout south and west Ireland. But Gladstone, under what Kimberley thought a 'happy delusion', insisted land reform would kill Fenianism.[13] None the less, following rural outrages and murders during January and February 1870, and facing mounting Whig pressure within the cabinet, Gladstone acceded to a Peace Preservation bill. The premier stopped short, however, of suspending Habeas Corpus.

The Vatican's pronouncement of Papal infallibility in 1870 also exposed dangerous divisions within the cabinet. The announcement dashed Gladstone's ecumenical hopes of an eventual union of the church catholic and brought into question the civic loyalty of Catholic populations. Indeed, ultramontane pronouncements from Rome struck at the heart of the Liberal vision of civic individuality. Gladstone wished to register a strong protest in Rome, hoping to save the Catholic Church from itself and forestall an anti-Catholic backlash in Britain. Such a domestic reaction could only further complicate the passage of Irish land reform. Granville, Clarendon, Argyll, and Lowe as well as Bright, however, persuaded Gladstone against such a course. The Pope's goodwill, Clarendon observed, would be important in discouraging disorder in Ireland.

As it was, the Government's Irish Land bill was, though complex, far from being a radical measure. Certainly it stopped short of the 'Three Fs' (fixity of tenure, freedom of sale, and fair rent) being demanded by the Irish Tenant League and Catholic bishops. The bill also showed that Liberals were able to act more easily on questions of institutional reform, such as disestablishment, than on social or economic issues touching on property. No less than eight ministers, at Gladstone's invitation, submitted schemes for Irish land reform to the cabinet. Bright's suggestion that public money be devoted to help buy out landlords was dismissed by Granville as a great land-jobbing speculation.[14] Prolonged collective discussion milked Gladstone's own proposals of their bite. In February 1870 the premier introduced to the Commons a bill which avoided giving universal protection to tenant rights, but gave tenants property in any improvements they carried out, compensation for disturbance while rent was paid, and the possibility of purchasing the land with state aid, if 20 per cent of the purchase price was laid down by the tenant. The latter clause was what survived of Bright's more far-reaching proposal. The moderation of the measure secured its passage through the Commons. As Trelawny observed: 'both sides feel that a measure of some sort is indispensable, yet the vastness of the difficulty represses hasty conviction; still more, enthusiasm'.[15] Amendments to safeguard landlords against tenants abusing the powers given to them by the bill were inserted by the Lords. Again, Gladstone fulminated against the Lords' cramming amendments down the throat of the Commons. But by August 1870 the amended Irish Land bill was passed.

Institutional reform remained much safer ground on which Liberals could act together in response to the call for meritocratic efficiency. The Order in Council of 1870, requiring entry by examination for junior posts in the civil service, fulfilled the recommendations of the Northcote–Trevelyan Report of 1853. With the exception of the diplomatic service, open competitive examination replaced nomination as the normal means of entry. This reform owed much to Lowe's advocacy. Gladstone was confident, however, that the recognition of merit would only serve to strengthen the claims of the aristocratic classes to superior gifts of administrative ability; polished by education at Oxford or Cambridge. Similarly, the abolition of religious tests for fellowships at Oxford or Cambridge passed in 1871 espoused the morality of merit. But while Gladstone was sensitive to the accusation of secularism and had initially hoped that a compromise would preserve some of the Anglican character of the two ancient universities, he also believed reform would consolidate the claim of the upper classes to the responsible exercise of public duty. Men like Benjamin Jowett at Balliol might thus all the more effectively prepare an intelligent ruling class for the duties of government. Intellectual meritocracy was decidedly not synonymous with social egalitarianism. Rather, in Gladstone's mind, meritocracy was a fair and efficient means of legitimising the natural hierarchy of society.

The legislative successes of individual ministers supplemented the accomplishments of the government. During 1870 Forster, a well-known proponent of popular education, passed an Education Act which was very much his own achievement. Demand to allow local authorities to use ratepayers' money to establish new elementary schools had been growing, but the religious curriculum to be used in such schools dogged the issue. Liberal convictions enforced the need, particularly as the electorate broadened, for an educated public able to act in an economic, political, and morally responsible manner. Dependency and prejudice flourished on ignorance and posed the real threats to merit and efficiency. The establishment of the National Education League in 1869, at the instigation of the Unitarian mayor of Birmingham, Joseph Chamberlain, led the call for free, compulsory and secular elementary education. Churchmen within the Liberal party feared the rise of secular amorality in such 'Godless' schools. Gladstone himself favoured giving extra money to existing 'voluntary agencies', mainly the Church of England, to expand educational provision. Forster's measure initially proceeded on this basis. Introducing his bill on 17 February 1870, Forster guided his measure through parliament, alongside heated discussion of the Irish Land bill, demonstrating considerable stamina in seeing his scheme through.

Thoughtful Conservatives such as Derby (formerly Lord Stanley) welcomed Forster's scheme as moderate and probably as fair a solution of the question as could be found.[16] But the demands of those Liberals supporting the National Education League's call that Anglican domination of state elementary education be surrendered, prompted impassioned debate. Nonconformists, fearing Anglicanism more than secularism, joined the attack on 'voluntary agencies'. As some of the government's supporters feared, the bill was 'rudely handled'. Indeed, Trelawny noted that 'the Conservatives seem to be more favourable to the ministerial plan than the radicals'.[17] The resulting compromise increased central funding of voluntary schools, while allowing, where provision remained inadequate, for the establishment of non-voluntary schools supported by a local rate to be administered through popularly elected School Boards. The Cowper–Temple amendment, agreed to by the cabinet in June, prohibited the teaching of particular formularies or catechisms in the religious curriculum of Board Schools.

Thus the 1870 session was brought to a close with two major legislative reforms, Irish land and elementary education, secured; though the National Education League's disappointment at Forster's Education Act had seriously undermined his standing as leader of radical opinion. Forster's evident diligence and honesty were offset by his vanity and lack of tact. Similarly, the Education debates of 1870 exposed ominous divisions within the Liberal parliamentary party. Moreover, the divisive vehemence of the education debates among parliamentary Liberals was no less damaging to Liberals in the country. Both within Westminster and in the constituencies deep divisions over educational reform during 1870 caused the impetus of Liberal reform to falter.

In 1871 Edward Cardwell carried through army reforms abolishing the purchase of commissions and reorganising the military reserve; the same policy of merit and efficiency that underlay civil service and university reform.[18] The Austro-Prussian War of 1866, particularly the massive battle at Sadowa involving half a million troops, and the Franco-Prussian war of 1870, demonstrated the need for a professional and well-trained officer corps. Memories of costly débâcles in the Crimea haunted the minds of military reformers. Economy and morality also argued for a reduction in the size of the military, improving conditions of service, and emphasising the role of the reserve. The possibilities for engaging in large-scale military adventures overseas, it was anticipated, would thereby be reduced. This implied a less aggressive foreign policy, the avoidance of military intervention abroad, and a pacific moral diplomacy based upon Britain's economic interests in an international community of free trade. Between 1868 and 1873 Gladstone and Lowe reduced defence expenditure by £4 million; the lowest level of spending on defence since before the Crimean War. Although the army reform measure was very much Cardwell's own, Gladstone lent these military reforms his powerful oratorical support in the Commons. They were, he pronounced, part of the reform of the morality of a 'vast and leisured class'.[18] When, in July 1871, the Lords seemed intent on rejecting the measure, Gladstone negotiated with the Commander-in-Chief and the Queen to proceed with the abolition of the purchase of commissions by way of a Royal Warrant. This forced the Lords, including Russell and Grey who had supported Conservative opposition, to capitulate and the Army Regulation bill was passed.

Yet Gladstone's wish for less military intervention abroad could not prevent a campaign in Canada in 1870, the Looshai expedition of 1871–2, and the onset of the Ashanti war in 1873. Kimberley thought Gladstone found foreign affairs 'uncongenial'.[19] Cabinet colleagues feared that, following Clarendon's death in June 1870, only Granville, on the front bench, really understood foreign affairs, and that Gladstone really believed in

Cobden's theory that men were growing too civilised for war. Hence the cabinet found themselves surprised and perplexed by the outbreak of hostilities between France and Prussia in 1870.[20] None the less, Britain immediately declared its neutrality upon the outbreak of the Franco-Prussian War in July 1870, and negotiated a treaty at the Conference of London in March 1871 resolving disputes over navigation of the Black Sea, which had flared up between Russia and the other parties to the 1856 Treaty of Paris.

The Liberal government's reform of the judicial system, though discussed in 1869, waited until the Judicature Act of 1873 and Selborne's succession to Hatherley as Lord Chancellor. The Judicature Act bore the marks of Selborne's considerable skills in drafting legislation. It brought a strong dose of efficient rationalisation to the variety of existing law courts, enforcing the premise that justice delayed was justice denied. The Courts of Common Law, Chancery, Admiralty, Probate, and Divorce were merged into one Supreme Court of Judicature, divided into the High Court of Justice and the Court of Appeal. The appellate jurisdiction of the House of Lords was also abolished, only to be restored by Disraeli's Conservative government in 1876. Nevertheless, Selborne's judicial reforms were an impressive and long-standing achievement, complementing the policy of rational efficiency evident in changes to the civil service and the military.

During 1871 and 1872 Goschen oversaw the reforms embodied in Local Government and Public Health Acts. These created a Local Government Board, rationalising the administration of the Poor Law, public health and other local government matters. Local sanitary authorities were established devolving the administration of public health to local professional bodies. These reforms allowed local authorities increasing financial discretion and encouraged the expansion of municipal powers in rapidly growing urban areas. Increasingly, most notably under Joseph Chamberlain's mayoralty in Birmingham, but also in Manchester, Bradford, Rochdale and Liverpool, municipal authorities oversaw the provision of gas and water supplies, sanitation, hospitals and public libraries, among other local services. As the conditions of urban life were improved by this municipal activism, so growing civic confidence was expressed through the large and impressive municipal buildings, town halls, and magistrate's courts, constructed in the cities of the Midlands and the North. Men of business and commerce undertaking the improvement of social conditions and moral welfare within their own communities, reliant on neither the finance nor the authority of central government, fulfilled an important part of the Liberal vision of a self-sufficient and self-disciplined citizenry.

The efforts of H. A. Bruce to reform trade union legislation in 1871 and the licensing law in 1872 were far less successful. In 1869 the radicals Thomas Hughes, author of *Tom Brown's Schooldays*, a Christian Socialist and MP for Frome, and Anthony Mundella, MP for Sheffield, attempted unsuccessfully to pass private members' legislation giving trade unions security for their funds. Gladstone promised them government action and in 1871 Bruce saw through a measure granting trade unions full protection for their funds. But, while this affirmed the legal status of the trade unions, Bruce's attempts to legalise peaceful picketing, through the Criminal Law Amendment Act, was promptly overthrown in the courts. Thus, while acquiring legal recognition, trade unions were denied the right to any practical demonstration of their grievances. George Howell, as secretary of the Parliamentary Committee of the Trades Union Congress (established in 1868), complained of Liberal indifference and warned of artisans turning to the Conservatives for political support. Strikes demanding higher wages or shorter hours followed. In 1874, the Labour Representation League, founded in 1869, put forward 16 of its own candidates at the general election. Bruce's licensing legislation in 1872, meanwhile, offended one section of society, the publicans and brewing interest, without securing the support of the temperance movement. Regulations were applied to the granting of new licences while the opening hours of public houses were restricted. A bungled attempt to legislate on the issue in 1871 had only inflamed the feelings of interested groups, the hostility of the drink interest being blamed for Liberal by-election losses in East Surrey, Yorkshire, and Plymouth. Bruce's 1872 Act disappointed the

United Kingdom Alliance, which criticised it for being too mild. During 1873 the Alliance also put up candidates against official Liberal nominees in a number of by-elections.

Robert Lowe also proved a serious disappointment at the Exchequer. He managed to introduce a cautious budget in 1869, Gladstone sending him a list of proposals. *The Times* praised the budget for substituting a simple and comprehensible tariff of duties for a labyrinth of imposts. But in 1871, becoming increasingly unpopular in the House, the fussy Lowe suffered the humiliation of having his budget revised by the Commons. His proposed tax on matches prompted protest demonstrations on behalf of the match girls, orchestrated by the firm of Bryant and May and supported by radical MPs. At the same time, Lowe's proposed increase in succession duties angered landed Liberal MPs.[21] Forced to drop his tax increases, Lowe resorted to raising income tax by twopence. Lowe's ineffectiveness was all the more damaging because after 1871, as Liberal disagreements on other issues multiplied, Gladstone hoped that sound finance might be the key to the government's survival. In dinner-table conversation Granville recalled that Palmerston had always refused to see any talent or power in Lowe.[22] Under Gladstone's Chancellorship during the 1860s the Liberals had been seen as the party of responsible and economic government. After 1871 Gladstone was hoping to play this strong card once again. But subsequent outcries alleging incompetent supervision of the Treasury, involving the use of Post Office Savings Bank money, and irregularities in the Zanzibar telegraph contract, finally compelled Gladstone to move the inept Lowe to the Home Office in 1873. The prime minister described the petulant and maladroit Lowe as 'wretchedly deficient'.[23] The discredited Bruce, removed from the Home Office, was elevated to the Upper House as Lord Aberdare and given the sop of the Lord Presidency of the Council.

Liberal Discord, 1872–4

The ineptitude of ministers such as Bruce and Lowe highlighted growing discontent within the Liberal parliamentary party. As early as May 1871 George Glyn, Brand's successor as Liberal Whip, was warning Gladstone of 'the apathy and political discontent' within Liberal ranks.[24] At one level this reflected the unpopularity of ministers such as Lowe and Bruce in the Commons. The First Commissioner of Works, the radical A. S. Ayrton, MP for Tower Hamlets, also offended backbench support by an acerbic manner as displeasing as Lowe's pungent sarcasm. Yet it was also true that by 1871 the sheer volume of legislative reform undertaken by the Liberal government was taking a heavy toll on ministers and MPs. Increasingly the pleasant but rather ineffectual Glyn began to complain about the difficulty of getting ministers to attend debates. In 1871 the evangelical Liberal Hugh Childers resigned the Admiralty, owing to political strain aggravated by family bereavement. After taking up the Duchy of Lancaster in 1872, Childers resigned again in 1873. In 1870 Bright had already resigned the Board of Trade, pleading ill health. Three years later he agreed to the less onerous appointment of the Duchy of Lancaster in succession to Childers. Cardwell also began to show early signs of his subsequent mental collapse.

After 1873 Gladstone took over the Exchequer himself, adding considerably to his own executive labours. Derby noted that 'with all [Gladstone's] splendid talent, and his great position, few men suffer more from the constitutional infirmity of an irritable nature: and this is a disease which hard mental work, anxiety, and the exercise of power, all tend to exacerbate'.[25] In February 1871, for example, during Commons debate on the Black Sea conference, Gladstone exploded in a damaging display of bad temper. Trelawny found Gladstone to be wanting in temper, discretion and straightforwardness.[26] Yet, on the other hand, there was no replacement for Gladstone within the cabinet. Lowe was inept and unpopular, Bright disabled, Cardwell not highly regarded, Clarendon was dead, Granville too easy-going, and Childers appeared a spent force. Gladstone, meanwhile, 'would give himself no rest, leave nothing to any subordinate or even colleague but do all in person: the result being that he is overworked, and the rest not being employed, get into the habit of leaving everything to him'.[27] The radical

MP Trelawny recorded the mood in his diary in February 1872: 'Gladstone's government is on the wane. He wants judgement and moderation – in short, ballast. As to his subordinates, they are with few exceptions not first rate men'.[28] Ignoring accusations of reckless cuts in defence spending, the premier during 1873 doggedly persisted in a policy of strict economy and retrenchment in government expenditure. Complaints about niggardly cheese-paring increased.

The government's reforming zeal brought on legislative congestion in parliament. The time allocated to government bills became clogged. Yet the very wide number of issues on which different sections of the Liberal party expected government action demanded legislative initiative. To put forward too little legislation would have been seen as ineffective. Yet to attempt too much, with consequent failure, was to be seen to be inefficient. As a result, MPs found themselves sitting through longer late night sessions and voting in increasingly frequent divisions. The Conservatives began prolonging debate or putting forward adjournment motions, as on the army regulation or ballot bills, deliberately wearing down Liberal stamina. Liberal by-election losses put further pressure on government supporters. In August 1871 the Conservatives regained, for the first time since 1841, the constituency of East Surrey. Their victory was ascribed variously to the victuallers' dislike of Bruce's licensing bill, the landowners' dislike of Goschen's rating bill, and the alarm created by Gladstone's apparent radical tendencies. By 1872 the ministry's Commons majority was effectively reduced to some 50 votes. Government measures fell into arrears under the pressure of business. As early as June 1869 the item 'Bills Abandoned' began to appear on the agenda of cabinet meetings. Some relief in the legislative log jam was provided by the ministry first introducing measures to the Lords. But by 1873 MPs were vocal in their complaints at being forced to consider major legislation under intense pressure of time.

The temper of parliament began to fray – a mood not helped by Gladstone's driving rather than leading the Commons with threats of prolonging the session. Cooperation had given way to ill-tempered coercion. Even more importantly, the very success of the government in addressing a number of issues removed much of the ground upon which Liberal unity had stood. Disestablishment of the Irish Church provided the transcendent cry which had galvanised Liberals in 1868. Although even here tensions existed between those Whigs and moderate Liberals who saw the measure as a conclusive settlement of Irish grievances, and radicals and Nonconformists who saw it as a first step, either towards further Irish reforms or towards Anglican disestablishment in other parts of the United Kingdom. Gladstone had not come into office with an agreed programme of reforms beyond Irish disestablishment. Measures on Irish land reform, elementary education, trade unions, and licensing laws, had inflamed Liberal dissensions. While battling the obstinacy of the Lords, Gladstone's ministry had, most noticeably, lost the loyalty of much radical and Nonconformist opinion. In particular, the debates on elementary education and licensing laws had fomented Nonconformist dissatisfaction. In April 1871 Lord Derby listed a long catalogue of the resentments accumulated by Liberal reform.

> The state of the House [of Commons] is indescribable: ministers have managed to offend nearly every important interest in the country by some one of their measures, and collectively the opposition they have provoked is too strong for them. The army dislikes abolition of purchase: the publicans are furious at Bruce's bill: the country gentlemen think Goschen's new plans of rating revolutionary: the middle class dread an increased pressure of income tax: the farmers have been warned by Lowe that he will tax their houses and carts if he could: the East End is disgusted by the (now abandoned) match tax: the Dissenters have not recovered their good humour at last year's education bill; the clergy oppose the removal of university tests: and all the property-holding classes are uneasy at the proposed doubling of succession duty'.[29]

Derby's final verdict was that there was 'no one of their proposed reforms that might not have been carried singly: but no government can fight the whole community at once'.

By 1872 the Ballot Act was the price Gladstone had reluctantly to pay for Bright's continued support. During Commons debates Disraeli made much play on Gladstone's change of opinion on this issue. A Ballot bill had been thrown out by the Lords in 1871. Once again, in 1872, the Ballot measure was opposed by the Lords; in part because the Upper House was forced to discuss it as the end of the session pressed upon them. Former Palmerstonian ministers such as the Duke of Somerset and Lord Lyveden (Vernon-Smith of the Board of Control, 1855–8) argued it was the responsibility of the Commons to educate public opinion, not simply to cave in to radical demands. In private Lord Grey condemned the government for chasing the 'fleeting public opinion of the hour'. Whig alarm increased when, in a speech in Whitby, Gladstone proclaimed the ballot to be 'the people's bill', the Lords being wise to yield to the legitimate aspirations of 'the people'.[30] Such democratic language led George Grey to fear that unless Gladstone took a 'firm stand against the extreme views now openly professed by many members below the gangway', then 'some of our institutions will be in great danger'.[31] Gladstone's increasing use of ultra-democratic language was noted on all sides, while a few speculated on his going mad before the next general election. In private by February 1872 an embittered and alienated Lowe was declaring 'Gladstone is mad, but he is cleverer in his madness than almost any other man in his sane mind.'[32] The final passage of the Ballot Act of 1872 reinforced growing distrust of Gladstone in his reliance on his extreme supporters. Such disquiet echoed Chichester Fortescue's conviction that 'the constitutional Whigs are not going to be dragged into the abyss of wild democracy merely to keep out the Tories'.[33] Their comfort was a belief that even many radicals did not trust Gladstone entirely and followed his lead unwillingly.

Gladstone's apparent submissiveness to the United States in resolving the *Alabama* question in 1872 further aggravated Liberal discontent. The North having won the Civil War, the United States after 1865 pressed for compensation from the British government for supplying the warship *Alabama* to the Confederacy. Gladstone's Newcastle declaration in 1862, praising Jefferson Davis for forging a nation out of a confederacy, haunted diplomatic discussions. Following Clarendon's death in July 1870 Granville succeeded to the Foreign Office. Granville's skill and restraint secured the agreement of all parties to the Washington Treaty of May 1871, outlining the conditions upon which the arbitration of disputes between Britain and the United States could be undertaken. In the preamble to the Washington Treaty Gladstone agreed to insert a near-apology for the *Alabama* affair; though the United States still argued for further 'indirect claims' of compensation, beyond direct compensation for the *Alabama* incident, on the basis that Britain's actions had prolonged the war and caused unnecessary destruction and loss of life. In March 1872 Trelawny saw this question as 'the great rock' in the path of the government, over which they might well fall victim to a vote of censure.[34] In August 1872 arbitration at Geneva concluded that Britain should pay the United States a large indemnity of £3,750,000. Anglo-American relations were repaired; but the domestic political cost was high. Delane described the American claims as 'monstrous', accusations circulating of the arbitrators being bribed.[35] Within the cabinet, Lowe, Cardwell, Goschen, Halifax, and Kimberley sharply criticised Gladstone and Granville's handling of the whole affair. In the Lords, Russell, Grey, and Somerset attacked government policy. Gladstone's putative weakness in dealing with the *Alabama* affair was seen as confirmation of his alleged shortcomings in handling foreign affairs. A shaken premier acknowledged his gratitude, during the *Alabama* debates, to the Conservatives for their forbearance. But this did not prevent Disraeli subsequently attacking the government for their alleged weakness in negotiations. The government survived the 1872 session having barely escaped defeat rather than achieving much success.

By 1873 radicals and Nonconformists were becoming dangerously alienated by the limits to Gladstone's reforming zeal. At the same time, Whigs and moderate Liberals were increasingly unsettled by the premier's apparent willingness to incite popular fervour. Kimberley noted in March 1873 that 'our old programme is completely exhausted: and Gladstone is not the man to govern without "measures", nor is he at all suited to lead a party in difficulties. He must have a strong current of opinion in his favour.'[36] As Liberal opinion became more weary and combustible, Gladstone saw an Irish University bill, discussed in cabinet since 1869, as essential. 'No bill, no government', he told Hartington in January 1873. Colleagues such as Argyll saw the Irish University issue as likely to bring the government down. It was significant that Granville, fatigued by over four exhausting years in office, almost welcomed such a prospect; the question affording 'an admirable opportunity for honourable defeat'.[37] The Queen's Speech, opening the 1873 session, was tame.

Gladstone had particular views on Irish University reform. He envisaged a number of Colleges in Ireland, to include Trinity College, Dublin, the Queen's Colleges, and Catholic and Presbyterian denominational Colleges, coming together under the 'neutral' authority of a federal University. Funding for the University would come from Trinity's existing endowments, from surplus left after the disestablishment of the Irish Church, and from the government. As with the Irish disestablishment bill, Gladstone withdrew to the seclusion of Harwarden to draw up an Irish University bill, calling on the advice of a few individuals on particular points. Following cabinet discussion in November 1872, Hartington, as Chief Secretary for Ireland in succession to Chichester Fortescue, denounced the plan. Feeling it would estrange Trinity, while giving priests too much influence over Catholic education, Hartington threatened to resign. Argyll and Kimberley also expressed disillusionment with the plan. None the less, a weary cabinet agreed to a measure altered only in detail, which was introduced to parliament on 13 February 1873.

Gladstone presented the measure to the Commons in a speech, even by his own voluble standards, of prodigious length. To avoid contention no professorships in modern history, theology, or philosophy were to be established within the University, made up of the constituent Colleges of Trinity, the Queen's Colleges of Belfast, Cork and Galway, and such 'voluntary' colleges, Newman's Catholic College in Dublin and the Presbyterian Magee

College, as wished to join. Faculty, moreover, could be reprimanded for offending the conscientious scruples of those they were teaching. Nonconformists cautiously welcomed the outline of the bill. Protestant opinion in Ireland divided over the merits of the measure, while Irish Catholic leaders quickly expressed opposition to the plan, primarily because it made no direct provision for the endowment of a Catholic college. Secular radicals such as Henry Fawcett, MP for Brighton and a disciple of John Stuart Mill, blasted the bill for not abolishing religious tests or establishing religiously mixed institutions.[38] Gladstone declared the bill to be a matter of confidence in the government; a move Disraeli thought unwise.

As criticism of the bill hardened during February 1873 the Conservatives sensed an opportunity to humiliate the government. Privately Disraeli dismissed the Irish University bill as 'humbug'. The Conservative Gathorne Hardy could 'never remember so growing an opposition from all quarters'. By early March Gladstone reported 'much coldness' on the Liberal benches and found Glyn to be 'downcast'.[39] In an attempt to rescue the situation Cardwell, on behalf of the government on 10 March, declared their willingness to accept amendments to the bill. But Disraeli drew together the measure's opponents by attacking Gladstone for not proposing a system of concurrent endowment. The government were defeated on the second reading by 287 to 284 votes; 38 Irish Liberals, radicals such as Fawcett, and a number of Whig–Liberals (objecting to the reduction of Trinity College's endowment) opposing the bill; 22 Irish Liberal MPs abstained from the vote. There was 'now no *cause*' or 'great public object', Gladstone observed, 'on which the Liberal party are agreed and combined'.[40] From the Liberal back benches Trelawny attributed the government defeat mainly to bad judgement and mismanagement. 'The measure was not one on which the existence of a government ought to turn. Gladstone ought to have been more sure of his ground before committing his party so far.'[41]

Seeing no cry on which an election might be fought and won, rather than dissolve parliament, Gladstone, suffering ill health, chose to resign. The topic of retirement had become an increasingly common theme in the private reflections of his journal. In late 1871 Gladstone was lamenting the unceasing pressures of public affairs. These demanded all the moral force of his soul, leaving nothing for his own spiritual sustenance. As a result, he felt he was living only half a life. During 1872 a haunting sense of spiritual barrenness, and the need to tend to his own inner life away from public office, permeated his thoughts. On the last day of 1872 he noted that an 'anxious and eventful year' had come to an end: 'probably the last of the present cares, and coming near the last of all'.[42] Disraeli, however, refused to release the Liberals or Gladstone from their predicament in March 1873. Upon Gladstone's insistence the Queen invited Disraeli to form a government three times, the Conservative leader declining on each occasion. Disraeli's thinking was simple and sound. To come into office, once again in a minority, would provide exactly the circumstances for Liberals to reunite; a short-lived Conservative tenure of power on sufferance promptly giving way to prolonged opposition. Sir Stafford Northcote, Disraeli's lieutenant and Gladstone's former private secretary, was convinced that the Liberal party was rapidly disintegrating and only precipitancy on their part would prevent it. Moreover, taking office before a dissolution was, Disraeli commented, 'a delusion and a snare'. Northcote confirmed Disraeli's strategic analysis.[43]

[Gladstone] has expended the impetuous force which brought him into office, and is now brought face to face with new, or rather old, difficulties which he can hardly surmount without alienating one or other wing of his party. If he goes with the Extreme section, a large body of his moderate supporters will rank themselves with the Conservatives: if he quarrels with the Extreme section, they will become the opposition, while the conduct of affairs will fall to the acknowledged Conservatives, who obtain the support of the moderate Liberals. But if we appeal to the country before the breach in the Liberal ranks is fully made, and before the policy of the Extreme men is fully developed, we shall consolidate them; the Extreme men will hold back a little, the moderates advance a little, and there will be more confusion and confiscation.[43]

Some Whigs, fearful of Gladstone and distrusting Disraeli, sought out moderate Conservatives exploring the possibility of a centrist ministry under Derby, as Lord Stanley had become upon the death of his father the former premier in 1869. As in 1866, however, Derby refused to be drawn.[44]

While Disraeli held his nerve, to the general approval of his supporters, an angry Gladstone struggled, denied the comfort of opposition. In explaining to the Commons his reasons for declining office, Disraeli outlined a Conservative manifesto. The period when fiscal issues had dominated politics was coming to an end, he declared, the great questions of trade, taxation, and political economy now being settled. But new issues, 'not less important, and of deeper and higher reach and range', were now 'burning' questions.[45] The future of the constitutional monarchy, the aristocratic principle of the constitution, and the maintenance of a national church were now pressing issues. Moreover, the principle of property, upon which the country had secured its free and famous union of order with liberty, was now being impugned. The sacredness of endowments and the tenure of landed property needed defending. A 'great constitutional party, distinguished for its intelligence as well as for its organisation', was now coming forward to safeguard these fundamental principles. But the premature formation of a minority Conservative ministry would have betrayed this destiny. In the near future, Disraeli predicted, a powerful Conservative party, supported by a majority of the Commons, would in time acquire power in triumph.

Gladstone limped back into office. Kimberley noted in his journal: 'we can hardly hope to escape discredit, and our faces, no wonder, looked very gloomy when we found ourselves again in a cabinet'. The relief of some Liberals at having narrowly escaped a Disraeli government helped. The dangers of courting Irish Catholic opinion, by proposing denominational education, had been clearly demonstrated. Irish Liberal support for the government was now lost. Nonconformist MPs, however, had largely remained loyal to Gladstone during the crisis. These considerations provided some comfort; though the groundswell of popular enthusiasm among provincial Liberals for further disestablishment and radical educational reform, as well as the rattled nerves of moderate Liberals, anxious at a frenetic Gladstone being held hostage by the radicals, on the other hand, defined the premier's immediate difficulties. Kimberley noted that 'Gladstone seems utterly weary of office and few of us I think will be sorry for rest.'[46] The remainder of the 1873 session proved largely barren.

A bill introduced by Henry Fawcett abolishing religious tests for Trinity College was supported by the government and passed in the face of protest from some Irish MPs. The O'Keeffe case, however, revived Liberal divisions on Irish policy, exacerbated by an increasing fear of growing ultramontane forces within the Catholic Church. A Catholic priest in Callan, Ireland, O'Keeffe was also manager of the Callan National Schools. For disobeying two Papal Bulls O'Keeffe was suspended by the Catholic hierarchy and in April 1872 the Commissioners of National Education agreed he should be replaced as manager of the schools by his successor. This was portrayed by some, including Whigs and moderate Liberals, as an intolerable intrusion into temporal affairs by the agents of a foreign ecclesiastical power; ultramontane forces within the Catholic Church challenging the state's authority. Many Nonconformists, on the other hand, believed a church had a right to require obedience from its members without interference from the state. In mid-May 1873 E. P. Bouverie, son of Lord Radnor and Liberal MP for Kilmarnock, proposed a censure motion on the commissioners. Hartington, as Irish Chief Secretary, forestalled a crisis by appointing a select committee to investigate the matter. Bouverie withdrew his censure motion; though 'Hartington seemed justly indignant when Bouverie compared the course taken as analogous to "roping", a process resorted to on the Turf. The process is to press a horse towards the ropes.'[47] Even so, in the Lords Russell decried the threat of ultramontane interference and the pandering to Catholic leaders evident in the Irish administration.

Disagreements within the cabinet about the release of further Fenian prisoners, anxiety about the rise of ritualism in the Church of England, modifications made to the system of elementary education set up by Forster's Act of 1870, and dislike of certain of Gladstone's high church ecclesiastical appointments, maintained ferment within Liberal ranks. At a cabinet meeting in June 1873 an exhausted Gladstone 'spoke of the present position of the government in the House as "deplorable". Constant difficulty and danger – opposition active to damage – enemies on our own side – or members thinking only of their electioneering interests – (how unlike '69 and '70!)'.[48] The government staggered on to the end of the session; a combination of languor and indiscipline debilitating the ministerial front bench. To his diary Gladstone confessed that all seemed 'constant tumult'.[49]

Between May 1873 and January 1874 ten Liberal seats were lost at by-elections. One of these losses occurred in Gladstone's own constituency of Greenwich in August 1873; the other sitting Liberal member for Greenwich, Sir David Salomons, having died. This haemorrhaging of electoral support drained the life-blood of the ministry. Fear of Liberal extremism seemed the main cause of by-election losses. The Conservative V. F. Stanford ended long-standing Liberal representation in Shaftesbury in August 1873, with the support of the dowager Marchioness of Westminster, who, in the name of Whig principles, wished to protect religion and the monarch. An increasingly confident Disraeli, picking up on his Commons statement of the previous March, made a speech in Glasgow in November 1873 denouncing the Liberal urge for perpetual change and the harassment of historic interests. The country yearned, he declared, for tranquillity. Gladstone's career of 'plundering and blundering', Disraeli privately commented, was coming to a close.[50]

Disraeli's Glasgow speech, intended to whip up party zeal, also picked up on themes drawn from his famous Crystal Palace address of June 1872 to the National Union of Conservative and Constitutional Associations. Since 1832, he stated, the Liberals had imposed alien cosmopolitan ideas upon national institutions. As the guardian of those national principles, upon which the greatness and glory of the country stood, the Conservative party, he expounded in 1872, had seen its inheritance appropriated by Palmerston. But now Conservatives were ready as a powerful national party to retrieve their inheritance.[51] The party looked to 'three great objects': to maintain the institutions of the country, to uphold the Empire, and to elevate the condition of the people. While Liberals might disparage the last objective as 'the policy of sewage', the merging of the national theme with the imperial theme, the closing of fiscal debate as now settled, and the vague promise of general improvement for 'the people', forged a strong base for Conservative electoral appeal. Though some progressive Conservatives feared that by making their manifesto too reactionary Disraeli would deter the support of moderate Liberals frightened by Gladstone and the radicals.

Gladstone's response to reviving Conservative fortunes during 1873 was ineffective. A reshuffling of ministerial appointments brought familiar tired faces into new positions. A Commons declaration in favour of county franchise reform in July 1873 and proposed further fiscal reforms failed either to unite or to reinvigorate Liberals, though 'the radicals seemed to chuckle amazingly and to joyfully accept the taunt that the [county franchise] measure is to be a new Liberal "platform" (as the term is) for the next election'.[52] On 24 January 1874, to the surprise of the party and most cabinet colleagues, Gladstone announced the immediate dissolution of parliament. His subsequent electoral address made clear his wish to lay aside divisive religious and educational issues, concentrating on finance, the possible repeal of income tax and a reduction in the rates. As he had earlier confessed to Bright, if Liberals were implacably divided on things to be done, then fiscal reform 'may end us in a way at least not dishonourable'.[53] In 1869, religion had strained Liberal party connection; in 1870, Irish land reform and elementary education; in 1871, Lowe's finance; in 1872, the *Alabama* question, local taxation, and the ballot; and again religion in 1873. By 1874 financial orthodoxy, the Peelite trump of the 1860s, was the only card Gladstone had left to play. Abolition of income tax, moreover, would remove the possibility of an electorate, roused by radicals, using the tax as a mechanism for stripping the rich of their wealth and destroying the mid-Victorian minimalist state. Gladstone's sudden decision to dissolve, however, highlighted the fact that Liberal organisation in the country was far less advanced than the Conservative structure overseen by Gorst. In 1868 Liberals had won an over-whelming victory based upon the 'virtuous passion' excited by a single moral issue. In 1874 there was no single transcendent cry and no party organisation to fall back upon. Popular Liberal support collapsed.

The general election of February 1874 smashed the Liberal hegemony that had characterised electoral politics since 1847. A gain of 82 seats, affirming the trend of recent by-election results, gave the Conservatives a Commons majority of 50 votes over Liberals and Irish Home Rulers combined. The Home Counties in south-east England became almost exclusively Conservative territory. This confirmed Disraeli's capture of Palmerstonian opinion, as held by the expanding suburban middle classes. In the English counties generally Conservatives won all but 27 of a total of 170 seats. In London Conservatives increased their representation from 3 to 10 seats, out of a total of 22 seats, making significant inroads into traditionally Liberal constituen-cies. Protestant opinion in Lancashire, where anti-Catholicism was an important factor, again indicated strong Conservative rather than Liberal preferences, as in 1868. Conservative gains were made in Manchester, Oldham, Stalybridge, Warrington, and Wigan. Markham Spofforth, the Conservative party's prin-cipal electoral agent, relayed to Disraeli on 8 February 1874 the belief of Sir Algernon Borthwick, owner and editor of the *Morning Post*, that if Disraeli were to 'adopt a Palmerstonian policy you will be prime minister for life – and that seems to be the general impression'.[54]

The election in 1874 pushed Liberal electoral support back into Northern England, Scotland, and Wales. Ireland was lost by the Liberals in devastating fashion. As early as April 1870 Disraeli and Derby had predicted that the Fenians would cause the Liberals far more trouble as constitutional repealers than when preaching armed insurrection. In November 1873 the Home Rule League was formed in Dublin dedicated to the winning of self-government for Ireland. In February 1874 Home Rulers, under the leadership of Isaac Butt, won 60 seats, though only two of them were in Ulster. Home Rule victories came in Catholic areas, while Protestant constituencies became the base

for anti-Home Rule sentiment. In 1868 Liberals had won 65
Irish seats. In 1874 they won only 17. After March 1873 Irish
Liberal MPs had abandoned the government. The immediate
effect of the influx of a large Home Rule contingent in February
1874 was, however, unclear. Butt himself had entered parliament as a Derbyite in 1852, did not enjoy a high reputation,
though possessing a talent for a rather florid style of oratory,
suffered from financial difficulties, and was a Protestant. What
was clear was that Liberalism in Ireland was devastated as a
political force. While Conservative support in Ireland became
consolidated in Ulster, Home Rule ended the electoral significance of Liberal Unionism in the rest of the island.

Gladstone's defeat in 1874 was, however, principally the result
of the defection of moderate support. This was evident, at one
level, in the increasing presence of businessmen on the Liberal
back benches after 1874. For the first time, less than half of the
Liberals elected in 1874 had aristocratic or landed backgrounds;
though they remained the single largest social group, accounting
for 46 per cent of Liberal MPs.[55] Nonconformism and radicalism
remained largely loyal to Gladstone during the election,
although some losses were due to pressure-group radicals. Nonconformist disillusionment with Forster's Education Act and
Bruce's Licensing Act, the alienation of the temperance movement, and the desire for further disestablishment prompted the
putting up of candidates who split the Liberal vote. Most
disastrously, at Leeds a radical candidate advocating Irish
Home Rule divided the Liberal vote and two Conservatives
were returned. Liberal post-mortems into the election often
emphasised the disastrous effect of 'faddists', 'crotchet mongers',
and organisations such as the NEL, on the results.

But it was Whig and moderate Liberal anxieties which were
played upon by Conservative rhetoric. Concern intensified that
Gladstone's financial reforms might lead to further attacks on
property. Gladstone's indication that he would like to reform
local government encouraged misgivings that in Ireland such a
policy would be a sop to Home Rulers and stimulate nationalist
sentiment. Gladstone's refusal to condemn Home Rule during
the campaign strengthened Whig and moderate Liberal fears

that he might sanction nationalist aspirations. Even more importantly, dread of disestablishment and radical educational reform unsettled moderate Liberal opinion. In a well orchestrated campaign Conservatives exploited moderate Liberal foreboding. Gladstone's administration was portrayed as restless, unpredictable, and prey to popular agitation. The constant ferment of great questions and 'sensational' politics had exhausted the country, which now desired calm and steady government. In contrast to Liberals' imputed lack of firmness, Conservatives declared a steadfast commitment to defence of the established church and the monarchy. Liberal candidates were put on the defensive. They generally avoided commitments with regard to future policy, reciting the legislative achievement of the Gladstone ministry and Gladstone's proven mastery of financial affairs, while declaring an unspecified dedication to 'Liberal principles'. Yet little flesh, in terms of either policy or legislation, was put on the bones of Liberal principle. Unlike 1868, Liberals in 1874 had no irresistible sense of mission driving them on.

As the extent of Liberal defeat became apparent Cardwell, Argyll, and Halifax blamed growing fear of radicalism for the party's failure. 'Faddists' and 'crotchet mongers' became the targets of Liberal anger and frustration. Whigs cited the widespread impression that Gladstone would 'accept any measure that extreme Liberals would require as the price of their support'.[56] *The Times* gave equivocal support to the Liberals, less from enthusiasm for Liberal government than because of distrust of Disraeli. Argyll, Kimberley, and Spencer even welcomed the extent of the Conservative victory as preventing the balance of power being held by Home Rulers. In the Whig house journal, the *Edinburgh Review*, the editor Henry Reeve denounced Gladstone's parsimony at the Treasury, his weakness in a foreign policy that ran counter to the policies of Palmerston, Russell, and Clarendon, and the premier's feeble administration of Ireland. Reeve called for the revival of historic Whig principles, which had been debased by Gladstone into surrender to the avowed enemies of the Church of England, ultramontane priests, and Home Rulers. In his own constituency of Greenwich

Gladstone came second in the poll to the Conservative distiller T. W. Boord. On 17 February 1874 Gladstone resigned as prime minister, following Disraeli's example in 1868 and surrendering the seals of office before meeting parliament. The constitutional inference was clear; it was the electoral verdict, not the vote of the Commons, that decided the identity of the government.

Disaffected Whig and moderate Liberal opinion in 1874 had a natural leader in Lord Hartington, heir to the Duke of Devonshire. Aged 41, Hartington had impeccable social credentials, an easy parliamentary manner, and a firmly Palmerstonian sense of policy. Committed to maintaining the Whig aristocracy as the natural leadership of the Liberal party, Hartington emanated sound sense and good judgement. On one hand, he possessed an aristocratic pedigree that reassured those who thought Gladstone 'neither honest, moderate or gentleman enough . . . to be the Whig minister'.[57] On the other hand, Hartington's blunt manner, evident sense of duty, and dependability enabled him to inspire loyalty, not to mention snobbish gratification, in middle-class Nonconformist MPs. Like Palmerston and Derby, Hartington concealed commitment behind a pose of aristocratic languor. When, as a young MP, he yawned mid-way through his maiden speech, Disraeli predicted he would do great things. Duty was to be borne without obvious effort. Yet nonchalance was not be confused with dilettantism. A pose of indolence and a passion for shooting and horse racing were not to be understood as lack of commitment; while an impressively impartial rudeness, whatever the station of the person he was talking to, rested on the secure self-regard of being the heir to a Dukedom. Only those seen to pose a radical threat to property and the rule of law were beyond the pale of Hartington's Whiggish sensibilities.

Gladstone saw Reeve's attack in the *Edinburgh Review* as an attempt to incite a leadership coup on behalf of Hartington. In March 1874, an embittered Gladstone announced he would take no part in parliamentary affairs during the coming session. He also reserved, until a later date, his position regarding the leadership of the Liberal party.[58] Gladstone's growing sense of isolation was then intensified during July 1874 by general Liberal support for Archbishop Tait's Public Worship Regulation bill, meant to suppress ritualism within the Church of England. Voices from within the party, such as Forster, Goschen, Harcourt, and Samuel Morley, as well as *The Times*, argued for the measure, which Gladstone strongly opposed. The bitterest debate of the session occurred between Gladstone and Harcourt on the Liberal benches over the merits of Tait's bill. Gladstone opposed the bill for leading almost certainly, he believed, to disestablishment of the church itself. Disraeli's attack on ritualism as 'the Mass in masquerade' played to the staunchly Protestant mood of the Commons. Harcourt praised Disraeli's 'dignified decency' and 'talents'. A Conservative measure abolishing patronage in the Church of Scotland also bitterly divided Liberals. 'What on earth [Gladstone] means on church matters', Halifax commented in August 1874, 'puzzles us all.'[59]

Gladstone immersed himself in theological scholarship and pamphlet writing, addressing the issues raised by the Vatican Decrees of 1870. Visitors to Harwarden in November 1874 found Gladstone unable to talk or think of anything but ecclesiastical questions. That month he published his impassioned anti-Papal pamphlet *The Vatican Decrees*, in which his own sense of betrayal found ecclesiastical vent in denunciations of the Papacy, Irish Catholic bishops, and English Catholic leaders such as Manning and Newman. Gladstone objected to a civil authority imposing religious conformity, either in its Catholic form of ultramontanism or in its Protestant form in the Public Worship bill. He believed an ultramontane conspiracy existed to re-establish the Pope's temporal power; anti-Romanism offered him a bridge to Dissent. He was also anxious to refute allegations of his own sympathy for Anglo-Catholicism.

In January 1875 Gladstone publicly informed Granville that he was resigning the leadership of the Liberal party. He later commented that he felt 'out of touch with some of the tendencies of the Liberal party, especially in religious matters. I thought they leant to the dethronement of the private conscience and to a generalised religion'. Gladstone spoke of handing over 'his trust' to Granville. Liberals understood this act as a retirement from active politics. Gladstone declared the Liberal party would benefit from a period of review before appointing his successor; it had 'peccant humours to purge and bad habits to get rid of'.[60]

Within three weeks a meeting of Liberal MPs at the Reform Club, chaired by Bright, unanimously endorsed Hartington as the new party leader in the Commons. Forster's name had also been canvassed, but the MP for Bradford withdrew his candidature. Forster's natural support within the party, the radicals, were divided against him following his Education Act. Hartington's merit, on the other hand, was that he divided Liberals least. The Liberal Whip W. P. Adam worked hard to avoid a public expression of Liberal differences in a contested election for the party leadership. The notion of MPs openly electing a leader was innovatory and threatening. That only one candidate, Hartington, eventually stood for endorsement at the Reform Club meeting was the gratifying result of Adam privately persuading Forster to withdraw his hopeless candidature. Harcourt welcomed Hartington as 'the best constitutional sovereign in the party after the fall of [Gladstonian] despotism'.[61] Gladstone himself advised his successor to avoid division and scandal, while providing 'light and negative, rather than positive', leadership. Hartington was to share the Liberal leadership with his cousin, Granville, in the Lords. Aristocratic Whiggery, amenable and ameliorating, reasserted itself as the natural leadership of the Liberal party. The axioms of parliamentary government enjoyed a new potency. As Reeve was to declare in the *Edinburgh Review* in 1880: 'the first and plainest of Whig principles is to maintain the authority of parliament'.[62]

6

DISRAELI AND CONSERVATISM, 1874–80

1874 brought Conservatives into the sun-lit uplands of real parliamentary power. For the first time since 1841 they took office with a Commons majority: 350 Conservatives looked across the chamber at 242 Liberals and 60 Home Rule MPs sitting on the opposition benches. Their triumph was, in part, a result of the collapse of Liberal unity after 1870. The desertion of moderate Liberal support, in particular, had exposed widening fissures in progressive opinion. The transformation of Irish Liberal MPs into Home Rulers created further opposition disarray. Disraeli's avoidance of haste, in not seizing office in 1873, had accelerated the process of Liberal disintegration. But Conservative victory was also a measure of the effectiveness of the rhetoric with which Disraeli clothed the Conservative party after 1872. He donned Palmerston's mantle and captured new constituencies of electoral support.

Disraeli's Conservative Leadership

Approaching seventy years of age and suffering from gout, bronchitis, and asthma, in February 1874 Disraeli at last achieved supreme office with power. The struggle had been prolonged and exhausting; a powerful Byronic impulse driving him on. His grip on the Conservative party leadership had never been secure. From dandy poseur, via Young England romantic, in 1846 Disraeli had, with devastating sarcasm, made Peel look ludicrous. Disraeli's audacity, a gift for self-dramatisation, and oratorical talent pitched into the strong head-winds of prejudice, contempt, and suspicion. Though his parvenu manner and exotic past offended them, his talent for razor-edged ridicule gratified the Protectionists' desperate desire to hit back at their apostate leader. Thereafter, the urgent Conservative need for oratorical talent finally obliged Derby, by 1850, to recognise Disraeli as Conservative leader in the Commons.

The arrangement suited Derby well. Disraeli devoted himself to the thankless task of maintaining an opposition without exciting a cry upon which their opponents might unite; marshalling men to do nothing. Moreover, he led the Commons without posing the slightest possible threat to Derby's own position. The backbench frustrations and resentments created by Derby's passive opposition strategy found in Disraeli a natural and diverting target. In opposition from 1859 to 1866, Ultra Tories, such as George Bentinck (MP for West Norfolk), Sir Rainald Knightley (MP for South Northamptonshire), and Charles Newdegate (MP for North Warwickshire), constantly plotted Disraeli's overthrow. Henley and Walpole often gave them encouragement, while Lord Robert Cecil happily flirted with the malcontents. Throughout the 1850s and 1860s Disraeli's position remained wholly dependent on the grace of Derby's endorsement. Between 1863 and 1865 despondency rendered Disraeli an apathetic and fading political presence. It is interesting to note that during the 1863 session Disraeli only voted in 8 out of a total of 188 Commons divisions. In 1864 he voted in 17 of a total of 156 Commons divisions during the session. In early 1864 Disraeli seemed to be growing old and in weak health, losing his former vivacity and given to sleeping in his seat. Subordination and inactivity was a hollow role for an ambitious man, who in 1865 turned 61 years of age.

Only Disraeli's reform triumph in 1867 ensured his succession to the premiership upon Derby's retirement the following year. Yet even that success confirmed for many Disraeli's lack of principle. Cynical opportunism, a willingness to act with anyone to achieve power, seemed all too apparent. A confidant of Disraeli noted that one of his peculiarities was to view a temporary success as an end in itself. He 'either does not care, or thinks it useless to struggle, for distant results: and, indeed will sacrifice these for the advantage of the moment.'[1] This harked back to Disraeli's tactical promiscuity of the 1850s. At different times, he had advocated alliances with Manchester radicals, discontented Whigs, and the Irish Brigade; proposals Derby quashed. Anti-semitic prejudice amplified distrust. Derby's death in October 1869 finally removed the protective cloak of Disraeli's patron and made his position the more vulnerable.

The electoral defeat of November 1868 led on to a period of apathetic opposition leadership during 1870 and 1871. Lord Salisbury, as Cranborne became in 1868, continued to fire savage journalistic salvoes into Disraeli's sagging leadership, decrying the treachery of 1867. Disraeli's own intermittent performances in the Commons during 1869 and 1870, though occasionally still displaying sparkle and brilliance, nevertheless seemed to lack firm conviction or earnestness. Disraeli privately admitted to a diminished interest in politics. Having achieved his ambition of becoming premier, he felt that if he never held office again he should not feel his life had been a failure. During 1870 rumours were rife within Conservative circles as to Disraeli's imminent retirement. Not until the end of the 1872 session did any real vehemence return to his parliamentary speeches. Only slowly did he seem again eager, animated, and in good health.

The publication of Disraeli's novel *Lothair* in 1870, despite its popularity among the general public, did nothing to repair his reputation as a serious politician within his own party. The novel's aristocratic hero Lothair represents the traditional social harmony embodied in the natural hierarchy of landed estates. Lothair is contrasted with the restless spirit of middle-class modernity, which subverts mutual affection and trust in the name of rootless abstractions and selfish merit. The wiles and cunning of Catholicism are shown undermining the legitimate social, as well as religious, authority of Anglicanism. The simple dignity of repose struggles with the impatient modern desire to be constantly doing. The novel entertained, but was easily dismissed as vulgar and superficial. Though seen as original, ingenious, and striking in places, it displayed, critics claimed, a certain tawdriness and a childish love of the gorgeous. 'The same oriental turn of mind', Derby imparted to his journal, 'that induces my friend like most of his race, to take pleasure in striking exhibitions of colour.'[2]

In January 1872 a small private meeting of prominent Conservatives at Burghley House discussed who should replace Disraeli as party leader. Some members of the last Conservative cabinet were joined by a few representative backbenchers and Gerard Noel the Chief Whip. Lord Cairns immediately floated the name of the new Earl of Derby, as Lord Stanley had become in 1869, to replace Disraeli. Noel believed Derby's leadership would gain the Conservatives 40 or 50 seats. Only Lord John Manners and Sir Stafford Northcote defended Disraeli.[3] This Burghley House meeting marked the nadir of Disraeli's standing as party leader. It appeared he could not win elections, inspire confidence, or effectively challenge Gladstone. Yet sufficient doubts existed about Derby's own thinking to ensure that nothing was done. In November 1869 the newly-elevated Derby had declined to succeed his father as Patron of the National Union of Conservative Associations. When speaking to Carnarvon of the Conservative party he declared that 'I shall certainly not tie myself to that dog's tail.'[4] To his journal Derby confided his wish to maintain some independence from his party as a moderate man of aristocratic sympathies who detested religious enthusiasts and political extremists.[5] Moreover, Disraeli's most likely successor as Commons leader, should Derby become head of the party, was Gathorne Hardy; a man whose eloquence and energy Derby admired, but whose strong Anglican partisanship he deeply disliked.

Disraeli's two great speeches of 1872, at Manchester in April and Crystal Palace in June, signalled the recovery of both his personal reputation and Conservative party fortunes. Again, as in 1846, it was Disraeli's talent with words that propelled him forward; although his oratory always remained better suited to the tastes of the Commons than to popular audiences. At Manchester, in the oppressive heat of a packed Free Trade Hall, he memorably described the debilitated Liberal government, now the 'unnatural stimulus was subsiding' and their 'paroxysms ended in prostration', as sunk in melancholy, with Gladstone alternating between 'a menace and a sigh'.

> As I sat opposite the Treasury bench the ministers reminded me of one of those marine landscapes not very unusual on the coasts of South America. You behold a range of exhausted volcanoes. Not a flame flickers on a single pallid crest. But the situation is still dangerous. There are occasional earthquakes and ever and anon the dark rumbling of the seas.[6]

Brilliant mockery led on to his portrayal of Liberal policy as 'plunder and blunder'. He declared the Conservatives, by contrast, to be a united national party committed to the defence of the Established Church, preservation of the constitution, pride in Empire, and the improvement of the social condition of the people. An immense crowd of 6,000 within the Hall listened to a speech that lasted 3 hours and 20 minutes. On his way to the Hall the horses were taken off Disraeli's carriage, the crowd drawing the carriage along, after he found himself mobbed on arrival at the station. Such popular enthusiasm surprised many Conservatives as well as Liberals.

Disraeli's message in 1872 was not a new departure in his thinking. Rather it represented a reworking of established themes. Since 1860 he had been putting forward his claim as a champion of the Established Church. As a political rallying-cry defence of the Anglican Church had failed in 1868. But in 1872 the 'Church in danger' was a call to action given new potency by Gladstonian reform. By October 1873 Disraeli was much preoccupied with the danger and unpopularity of the Catholic movement abroad and the Ritualist movement at home. He anticipated an imminent test of strength and was clearly prepared to confront the advocates of ritualism within the Anglican Church. Similarly, Disraeli's call for defence of the monarchy reflected a warming of relations between the Conservative leader and the Queen evident from the early 1860s. In January 1861 Disraeli and his wife received their first invitation to stay at

Windsor Castle. In April 1863, after an invitation to attend the marriage of the Prince of Wales, Disraeli was honoured with a personal audience with the Queen. The stiffness of Gladstone's relations with the monarch left the Queen the more susceptible to the flattery and charm Disraeli so effectively employed.

By 1872 a personal rapport with the Queen infused Disraeli's call for the maintenance of the monarchy and the constitution. Also, his celebration of Empire in 1872 was not, as often represented, the proclamation of a new era of aggressive Imperialism. Again, it was rather the reworking of an element in Disraeli's thinking traceable back to his 'Runnymede' letters published in *The Times* in 1836. It was only in the early 1850s, when challenging Gladstone as the guardian of fiscal probity, that he had made anti-colonial statements. In 1862 Disraeli had forcefully denounced the Liberals for a hasty colonial policy of self-government which was weakening the ties between Britain and her colonies. Relations should be strengthened, he maintained, between Canada, Australia, New Zealand, South Africa, and India. A strong Empire, founded on sound principles of freedom and equality, enforced the power, prestige, and spirit of the national community. In 1872 Disraeli declared that the Liberals were working to bring about the disintegration of the British Empire. Before 1865, such themes were a weak weapon against Palmerston. By 1872 they provided a powerful antidote to Gladstonian Liberalism.

Stability, repose, and national celebration, Disraeli declared, were to replace restless exertion, constant flux, and miserly penny-pinching. Promises of social reform, though vague apart from the desirability of sanitary legislation (pure air, pure water, unadulterated food, and healthy habitations), offered an escape from divisive and contentious political issues. The term 'social reform' remained an awkward innovation during the 1870s. While some talked of measures of social amelioration or social improvement, others simply referred to miscellaneous, as opposed to political, legislation. Social questions, it was implied, should be considered apart from party feeling. Again, it should be noted that the argument for measures of social improvement was not a new element in Disraeli's thinking. In December 1864 he declared the health of the nation to be crucial to the greatness, liberty, and wealth of the country. None the less, the call for such reforms substantiated the Conservative claim to be a truly national party; energy being devoted to the provision of useful legislation building consensus, rather than divisive political issues. At Edinburgh in October 1867, Disraeli proclaimed the Conservatives to be a party formed of all classes, from the highest to the most homely, upholding the nation's institutions, security, and rights.[7] In 1872 he appealed to the pride of the working classes in belonging to a great imperial nation: a pride denoting Conservatism in its highest and loftiest sense. The nation's greatness stood upon Britain's ancient institutions. The 'cosmopolitan' ideals of Liberalism, on the other hand, produced humiliation in foreign affairs, disintegration within the Empire, and division and fractiousness within the nation itself. His Reform Act of 1867, Disraeli claimed, merely restored the electoral privileges enjoyed by working men before 1832 through the old scot-and-lot borough franchises. In 1832 the Whigs had swept away these ancient rights, the loss of which caused, he asserted, the Chartist movement.

After 1872 Disraeli captured Palmerstonian opinion as the current of middle-class and suburban feeling began flowing strongly towards the Conservatives. Liberal by-election defeats confirmed the trend. The general election of February 1874 delivered the suburban vote *en masse*; London and the Home Counties becoming solid Conservative territory. Radicals denounced the complacent Conservative propensities of those living in 'smug villas', making up the rapidly growing suburbs of London, Manchester, and Liverpool. Yet it was this achievement which transformed Disraeli from a dispensable liability into an inspiring leader. Even Salisbury, by 1873, was no longer publicly pillorying him. The death of Disraeli's wife in December 1872 of cancer, left the Conservative leader with the sole preoccupation and comfort of renewed political exertion.

The growth of Conservative constituency organisation after 1868 facilitated the party revival. In 1874 approximately 60 per cent of all English and Welsh constituencies had some kind of active Conservative Association operating within them. While, most importantly, monitoring the electoral register, such Associations also distributed pamphlets, held meetings and provided a social and cultural centre for party supporters. In April 1870 the barrister and former MP for Cambridge, John Gorst, succeeded Markham Spofforth as principal Conservative party agent.

The cantankerous Gorst energetically built upon the work of his predecessors. He made it clear that his first priority, given firm Conservative support in the counties, was to organise the Conservatives in the larger boroughs.[8] Immediately he established the Conservative Central Office in Parliament Street, Westminster, to oversee the National Union of Conservative and Constitutional Associations inaugurated in 1867. Created under the watchful eye of Lord Abergavenny, to whose powerful patrician sway and intense partisan feeling fell primary responsibility for fund-raising, the National Union trod carefully. It assisted local organisations when requested, while avoiding exciting local suspicion of central control. Gorst encouraged Associations to draw up lists of possible Conservative candidates well before elections (which began to break the inhibiting local influence of electioneering solicitors) and sought to control campaigning expenditure. In 1874 these efforts were repaid by Conservative gains in the populous boroughs of Marylebone, Chelsea, Greenwich, Southwark and Tower Hamlets, as well as in the taking of three of the four seats for the City of London.

Undoubtedly Gorst saw his activities as the basis for a genuinely popular Conservatism. But he could do no more than assist in a movement of opinion already under way. Gorst believed that the ballot had neither harmed nor helped the Conservative vote, nearly all voters being prepared to say beforehand which candidate they would support.[9] But the growth of Conservative Associations should not be seen as a more democratic development than it was. The control of local Associations usually remained in the hands of a small number of middle-class businessmen. Moreover, as noted above, organisational efforts were concentrated in urban borough constituencies. Conservative county strongholds largely remained under the traditional dominance of local landowners.

The victory of 1874 was to establish Gorst's high reputation in the traditions of the party. Gorst himself later sought to propagate the myth that he had single-handedly won the victory of 1874. This was unfair on Gorst's predecessors. The important work of Spofforth and Jolliffe was thereby overshadowed. Equally, it overestimated the impact of organisation in moulding, as opposed to merely channelling, opinion. Yet it was also true that while, during the early 1870s, popular Liberalism operated through militant interest groups, such as the Liberation Society or National Education League, it was the Conservatives under Gorst at Central Office who first moved towards a centralised party bureaucracy harnessing the popular enthusiasm of the constituencies.

Conservative Reform

Disraeli's 1874 cabinet was composed so as to heal Conservative party wounds. The scale of his electoral victory helped the new prime minister to disarm his opponents within the party. The moderate Derby, a hesitant Salisbury, and wary Carnarvon were all given office. In 1870 Salisbury and Carnarvon, after pleas from the Duke of Richmond, had agreed to rejoin the Conservative front bench in the Lords, though Salisbury continued to insist he was not a follower of Disraeli. In 1874 one rival, Derby, at the Foreign Office, and Disraeli's two foremost Conservative critics, Salisbury at the India Office and Carnarvon at the Colonial Office, were drawn into the cabinet. Northcote, able and industrious, though a heavy speaker, accepted the Chancellorship of the Exchequer. Loyalty was rewarded when Lord John Manners became Postmaster General and Gathorne Hardy took the War Office. The party stalwarts Lord Cairns and the Duke of Richmond took the Lord Chancellorship and Privy Seal respectively. Cairns's low church opinions, if not his intellectual arrogance, were the cabinet counterweight to the strong high churchmanship of Salisbury. Thus, despite middle-class electoral support, the cabinet remained overwhelmingly aristocratic and landed in character. This reflected Disraeli's own social views. *Lothair*, after all, had been a celebration of birth and property. Disraeli 'neither understands nor likes the middle class'.[10]

Under pressure from Derby the premier did, however, make one middle-class cabinet appointment. The Lancashire solicitor and businessman Richard Assheton Cross, despite his not having any previous ministerial experience, was placed at the Home Office. Cross had been a near-contemporary of Derby at both Rugby and Trinity, Cambridge. Outside the cabinet W. H. Smith, heir to the family newsagency business, was made Financial Secretary to the Treasury. Lord Sandon, the eldest son of the Earl of Harrowby, was appointed Vice President of the Council, and as MP for Liverpool, was seen as another connection with middle-class opinion. Clearly Disraeli would have preferred a simple re-instatement of his 1868 cabinet. But it was pressure from Derby that secured Cross and Smith places in the government, and ensured the demotion of the amiable but ineffective Lord John Manners. Posts given to men such as Cross and Smith, moreover, were a cheap enough price to pay to enlist bourgeois compliance in maintaining the aristocratic settlement of the country. Blatant partisan use of government patronage, civil service and ecclesiastical appointments, as well as the dispensing of honours such as Lord Lieutenancies of counties, further consolidated Conservative support.

If middle-class allegiance was acquired easily in terms of ministerial appointments, so too had broad rhetoric secured electoral votes without any difficult commitment to specific measures. In Disraeli's mind no fixed legislative programme accompanied his rousing Palmerstonian call. The return to normality, after a disruptive period of Gladstonian frenzy, indeed, did not seem to require an extensive package of legislative proposals. A rather naive Cross was dismayed at their first cabinet meeting. He had expected Disraeli to be full of legislative schemes. Instead, the prime minister looked to his colleagues for suggestions and they had difficulty in framing the Queen's Speech. The one firm decision taken was not to mention the issue of Irish Home Rule. With the exception of foreign policy this set the pattern for the rest of the ministry. While Disraeli provided the rhetorical tone, he looked to department heads to supply the legislative substance of domestic policy. The prime minister was bored by details. He did not initiate proposals. Throughout his premiership Disraeli's grip on his cabinet was loose, legislative timetables becoming easily delayed, and ministerial discussion often bogged down in details or irrelevancies.

As a result, during the 1874 session, the actions of others caused ecclesiastical difficulties to temporarily unsettle the government. Archbishop Tait brought forward a private measure to suppress growing ritualism within the Church of England. The anti-ritualism of the Public Worship Regulation Bill inflamed the high-church sensibilities of Salisbury and Carnarvon. When agreeing to serve under Disraeli, Salisbury had expressed his earnest hope that no attacks on Anglican ritualism would be undertaken by the government. Salisbury admitted that the folly of the ritualist party had done damage to the Church, but could not countenance any threats to the Church's authority. Despite the apparent popularity of Tait's measure, initially Disraeli attempted to keep the government neutral. Then on 15 July he played the popular Protestant card, speaking out against the 'Mass in masquerade'.[11] The previous October, before taking office, Disraeli had anticipated just such a confrontation. Cross pressed upon the prime minister the widespread support for the measure in Lancashire, Derby urged Disraeli to put himself at the head of the movement, and the Queen bombarded the premier with requests for assertions of Protestantism from the government.

Gladstone, coming out of semi-retirement to oppose the bill, gave further prompting to Disraeli to champion the measure. This secured the bill's triumphant passage through the Commons and Gladstone's isolation. It also, however, brought on a crisis with Salisbury. With no apparent trace of irony, Disraeli, despite his own reputation, described Salisbury as 'a great master of gibes and flouts and jeers'.[12] Carnarvon took to the country, dismissing Disraeli's statements as offensive. An open rupture was barely averted. Yet relations were restored, Disraeli's reputation for skill in handling the Commons was enhanced, and the government's popularity in the country strengthened.

With cabinet harmony regained by late 1874, the ministry's stock was even higher at the end of the session than six months earlier. Subsequent cabinet meetings were mainly good-tempered, with ministers anxious to avoid ill-humour and the creation of ministerial factions, though submerged resentments did linger. Gorst shrewdly observed the parallel to the Liberals' relationship with Nonconformity:

> The High Church party has always seemed to me to occupy on our side a position somewhat analogous to the ultra-dissenters on the other: it has an electoral importance beyond what is due to its mere numbers, and holds opinions and principles to which party interests are subordinated.[13]

As the old Lord Derby, as party leader, had maintained 20 years earlier, the Protestant cry was always a seemingly attractive one for the Conservatives. It was, however, a cry that could disrupt as much as consolidate party ranks.

It was Cross at the Home Office who improvised during 1874 a series of initiatives giving concrete form to Disraeli's heightened social rhetoric. And where the initiative was seized substantial political rewards were reaped. Electoral debts were also repaid. Cross established a Royal Commission to review trades union legislation. He passed a Factory Act giving a statutory reduction in the hours worked by women and children to no more than 56½ hours a week. Particularly in Lancashire, Conservative borough candidates during the election had pledged themselves to the nine-hour cry. Finally, just as he attended to Bruce's ineffectual trades union legislation, so Cross also revised the Liberals' unpopular Licensing Act. In cabinet Salisbury had strongly supported Cross's Licensing bill for religious reasons, it was supposed, as the teetotal party were for the most part Dissenters or free thinkers. Brewers and publicans had voted solidly Conservative in the 1874 election and Cross responded to their interests. The Home Secretary's subsequent popularity was attested to by a contemporary jingle:[14]

189

For he's a jolly good fellow,
Whatever the fools may think;
For he has shortened the hours of work
And lengthened the hours of drink.

That Northcote's budget reduced the income tax, while not adopting Gladstone's panacea of total abolition, and offered remissions on brewers' licences, sugar, horses, railways, police subsidy, and relief for lower incomes, further bolstered Conservative popularity.

In 1875 Cross built on his initial social reform measures with more considered legislation. Most important was his Employers and Workmen Act, which Disraeli believed would 'gain and retain for the Tories the lasting affection of the working classes'.[15] This was despite the prime minister spending part of the cabinet discussion of Cross's legislation in May 1875 fast asleep. Trade union leaders such as George Howell found Cross not only conciliatory, but also sympathetic. Cross's measure freed striking workers from liability to criminal prosecution for breach of contract. At the same time, the Home Secretary's Conspiracy and Protection of Property Act legalised peaceful picketing. This was precisely what Liberal legislation had failed to do. Cross's success, Howell celebrated, was 'a political *coup* which astounded the trade union world'.[16] An Artisan's Dwellings Act encouraged, to a modest degree, local authorities to improve working-class housing. This was seen as a capstone to preceding mid-Victorian public health reforms. In cabinet Cross, drawing on examples in Edinburgh and Glasgow, had persuaded colleagues that model housing saved space and lodged more residents without overcrowding. The back slums in London provided some of the worst examples of atrocious and unhealthy living conditions. A Friendly Societies Act, prepared jointly by Cross and Northcote, sought to safeguard funds: not by regulating the Societies' funds directly, but by encouraging them to make more information available to potential subscribers.

Howell's overall verdict on the Home Secretary's activities was striking: 'Mr Cross has dished the Whigs once again.'[17] The

Trades Union Congress held at Glasgow in October 1875 moved, amid loud applause, a vote of thanks to Cross; his legislation being hailed as 'a great boon to the industrial classes'. Cross's success allowed ministers to preen themselves. In a Mansion House speech in August 1875 Disraeli provided a broad rhetorical gloss to Cross's legislation. The government had acted on their 'sincere convictions that the time had arrived when political change was no longer the problem to solve in this country, but that its intelligence and energy should be directed to the improvement and elevation of the condition of the people'. Thus was increased 'the great total of national happiness'.[18]

Other legislation during 1875 and 1876 filled out the government's achievement. A Public Health Act consolidating in one measure earlier statutes, and a Sale of Food and Drugs Act, intended to prevent adulteration, were passed by George Sclater-Booth, President of the Local Government Board. Yet, as with Cross's Artisans' Dwellings Act, under Sclater-Booth's legislation local authorities were enabled, but not compelled, to carry out reform. Sclater-Booth also oversaw the River Pollution Act intended to clear up Britain's waterways. Lord Sandon passed an Education Act in 1876 giving effect to his conviction that elementary education should be to some degree compulsory and that in small county communities the expansion of Board Schools, as opposed to voluntary Anglican schools, should be held in check. Board Schools, he feared, were simply a platform for Nonconformist ministers. In cabinet he spoke with a kind of pious horror of the growth of School Boards in country areas. One cabinet colleague regretted that Sandon, despite his diligence, acted under such parsonic influences as rendered him unfit for most government offices.[19] None the less, as a result of Sandon's legislation, after 1876 children between the ages of ten and fourteen could not be employed without a certificate either of school attendance or of academic attainment.

Difficulties over education, however, echoed increasing complications in the ministry's other legislation. The ease with which Cross realised his own initiatives began to dissipate. Disraeli's rapidly deteriorating health during 1875 weakened the premier's control of the Commons. At times he seemed half asleep and only speaking with great effort. The charming but inept Sir C. B. Adderley, at the Board of Trade, mishandled the call of the advanced radical Samuel Plimsoll, MP for Derby, for greater safety regulations for merchant shipping. Despite the anger of shipowners, Adderley found himself obliged in July 1875 to adopt a version of Plimsoll's proposed legislation. Even so, Adderley stopped short of compulsory regulation, insisting that legislation should only create the conditions for responsible men to manage their own affairs. Adderley, Derby concluded, had bungled the issue. As a result colleagues began to push for Adderley's replacement. At the close of the session, in August 1875, Hartington delivered a carefully prepared and skilful criticism of the government's blunders, justifying his claim to the Liberal leadership.[20]

Similarly, the government's Agricultural Holdings Act, touching on tenant rights, inflamed the anger of Conservative landowners. Disraeli's contribution to debate was a notable failure, his performance betraying his feeble physical condition. Ministers, meanwhile, feared mounting agitation among tenant farmers. Some Whigs sought to stir the farmers against their landlords, which the cabinet worried would break up Conservative strength in the counties. Stopping short of compulsion, and preserving landlords' freedom of contract and rights, the Act established a voluntary framework for resolving disputes between landlords and tenants.

The Conservative legislation of 1874–6 appears the single greatest package of social reforms passed by any nineteenth-century government. At one level this was an impressive substantiation of Disraeli's Crystal Palace rhetoric. In retrospect, for later generations of Conservatives, these measures assumed a warm inspirational glow. For some they became a mature expression of Disraeli's early philosophy as laid out in his 1845 novel *Sybil*, which had decried the splitting of the country into the 'two nations' of rich and poor. 'One Nation' Toryism was born. For other Conservatives, particularly Lord Randolph Churchill in the 1880s, Disraeli's social reforms were an expression of that elusive entity 'Tory Democracy'. None of these retrospective readings of the Conservative legislation of the

1870s are convincing, however. With the help of hindsight it was easy to give a false coherence and doctrinal impetus to these social reforms. Disraeli's interest in their details had been slight. No strong collectivist commitment saw him requiring a broad package of social reforms from ministers. By November 1875 he was wearily hinting at excessive ministerial exertions. In cabinet he declared himself anxious not to have a large programme for the forthcoming session. Nor were these Conservative measures radically different from those a Liberal government might conceivably have introduced. Later suggestions that they marked a dramatic new departure are misleading.

Though impressive in sum, the measures passed during 1875–6 arose more from pragmatic responses to particular problems rather than issuing forth from underlying doctrine. Conservatives did pronounce that property had its responsibilities as well as rights. While disliking increased public expenditure, they sought social and political stability; unanswered legitimate grievances only providing ammunition for agitators. Elements of social responsibility, humanity, and the desire to preserve the social hierarchy based upon a consensus of feeling, all coalesced in Conservative minds around the reforms of 1875–6 – just as the same elements came together in many Liberal minds. Rather than striking off in a new political direction, these social reforms were seen as executive common sense in a period of political repose. Significantly, Derby thought the social legislation of 1875 useful, though dull. Certainly sections of the press and the public, looking for excitement, considered the 1875 session a barren one. 'What they look to', Derby noted, 'is not the importance of the law when passed, so much as the noise made in passing it.'[21] Social legislation was seen as unostentatious and sober business attending to matters of practical utility.[22]

Nor did this legislation mark a collectivist departure from the principles of political economy. State intervention and regulation were not enthusiastically embraced. The reforms were designed to enable voluntary improvement, not compel compliance. The Factory Act did not violate the market principles governing employment because it merely gave legislative protection to those who were not, in any case, free agents, namely women and children. The Artisans' Dwellings Act was permissive legislation empowering, not compelling, local authorities to clear slums. Moreover, new housing was to be built by private enterprise. The Agricultural Holdings Act set up an entirely voluntary legal framework, while Cross maintained that his Conspiracy and Protection of Property Act did not breach the principles of political economy, but simply placed employers and employees on an equal legal footing. If Disraeli was particularly sensitive to the electoral benefits of such legislation, other Conservatives shared in a wish simply to strengthen a sense of social consensus. After addressing a meeting of 2,000 working men in Edinburgh in December 1875, Derby believed there was no reason why working men should not be Conservative in their politics 'since they have . . . nothing more to get or expect from agitation'.[23] Labour, Disraeli had written in his 1844 novel *Coningsby*, was the twin brother of property.

The 1870s legislation was *not* a new departure or a dramatic revitalisation of Tory paternalism; though it did offer the opportunity for drawing flattering contrasts with the divisive and overbearing restlessness of Gladstonian Liberalism. If some regarded the 1875 session as dull, it was also worth noting that Liberal unity remained very fragile. As a stopgap Hartington had done better than expected, but his backbenchers were not in the mood for vociferous opposition. Like Goschen and Thomas Hughes on the Liberal benches and his fellow Conservative the young Derby, Cross had been schooled at Rugby in the rigours of practical efficiency. It was in this bipartisan spirit that much of the detail of the social legislation of 1875–6 was framed.

Disraeli's great achievement was to provide a rhetorical context for the Acts of 1875–6. Disraeli's genius lay in the use of words. His speeches of 1872–3 established the Conservatives as a national party with a positive anti-Liberal message. He raised them above the narrow advocacy of sectional interest. He successfully placed the social condition of the people near the top of the political agenda. The period of controversy over fiscal issues, he declared, was over. Gladstone's executive forte was marginalised. Unity and calm were themes that emphasised the broad consensus upon which social reform might be quietly pursued. It was his public statements, his skill with words, that constituted Disraeli's real legacy to the Conservative party. His language gave wider meaning to the substantive detail of the legislation of others. The alchemy of Disraeli's rhetoric transformed the base metal of conventional social legislation into the gold of party triumph.

Yet, by 1876, Disraeli's failing health rendered him a pale shadow of his former parliamentary self. In late 1874 he was suffering from a disagreeable combination of gout and bronchitis. In June 1875 cabinet colleagues found the premier 'wearied and out of spirits'. By November 1875 he was 'visibly an old man'. Derby noted of cabinet discussion in late January 1876 that Disraeli 'often appears asleep, takes no part, and much time is wasted in loose talk'.[24] As the session proceeded, cabinet meetings became increasingly less business-like. Disraeli's audacity and ease of manner gave way to weariness and an ill-tempered rudeness. In June Disraeli told the Queen he could no longer continue in the Commons. At the end of the 1876 session Disraeli entered the Upper House as the Earl of Beaconsfield. Subsequently asked how it felt to be in the Lords Disraeli declared: 'I feel I am dead, but in Elysium.'

Empire and Foreign Policy

The trump Disraeli played in his rhetorical hand after 1874 was the patriotic card. Disraeli presented himself as the custodian of Palmerston's legacy; although that legacy was shorn of Palmerston's talk of liberty and support for liberal nationalism in Europe. Disraeli's speeches of 1872–3 established the Conservative party as the champion of patriotic honour.[25] Palmerstonian esteem was injected with imperial ardour. This reflected Disraeli's personal interests. The grand stage of foreign policy, as opposed to the intricacies of domestic affairs, fully engaged the sweep of Disraeli's romantic imagination. The premier 'dislikes details, detests the class of business he calls parochial, and takes peculiar pleasure in turning over and discussing all sorts of foreign questions, on which action is not necessary and often not possible'.[26] His intellectual interests and cultural influences were broadly European. His father's literary salon had exposed him, as a young man, to cosmopolitan tastes beyond the narrower horizons of English culture. In foreign affairs the mature Disraeli came to see a heroic role for himself that embraced those wider interests. It provided him with a theatre for action. At the height of the Bulgarian crisis, in October 1876, Derby observed that for 'the premier the main thing is to please and surprise the public by bold strokes and unexpected moves: he would rather run serious national risks than hear his policy called feeble or commonplace'.[27] Disraeli did not sleep in cabinet during the discussion of foreign affairs. As Foreign Secretary Derby preferred to restrain imperialist ardour, keep Britain free of continental entanglements, and dampen down Carnarvon's excitability as Colonial Secretary. As a result Disraeli much preferred to have foreign policy discussed outside of the cabinet, so that it remained a sphere of policy largely directed by himself and those ministers directly concerned. This, Derby noted, was one of Disraeli's 'peculiarities'.

The Asiatic empire held a special place in Disraeli's romantic sensibilities. As a young man he had undertaken a grand tour of the Near East. This was a formative experience whose exotic and vivid sensations had excited his romantic imagination and shaped his views on race, religion, and civilisation: the 'great Asian mystery' as he called it. The world's great religions and civilisations had all emerged, he believed, from the Near East through the Semitic race, both Jewish and Arab. 'God has never spoken to a European', the hero of his 1847 novel *Tancred* learns. Race contained the genius of history.[28] Nationalism, particularly in its radical form, and the cool legal niceties of the nation state were far less important to Disraeli than the dynamic cultural impetus of vital human communities. For him institutions held little fascination. A regard for the Turkish Empire, under whose rule he claimed Jewish merchants were treated generously, and an affection for Turkish culture remained with Disraeli for all his life. This was despite the fact that subject peoples under Ottoman rule in the Balkans in reality more often experienced cruelty tempered only by incompetence. Turkish tastes, he confessed in

1830, suited his own natural indolence and melancholy. He even considered volunteering for the Turkish army to help suppress the Albanian revolt of 1830. Such predilections continued to shape Disraeli's responses to foreign, in particular Asian, affairs.

In 1875 Disraeli secured, via a loan from the Rothschilds, the government's purchase of 44 per cent of the shares in the Suez Canal. This protected access to India and secured Britain's position in the Eastern Mediterranean. Doubts about the constitutionality of the decision were pushed aside. Intense cabinet discussion during November 1875 ensured firm government unanimity on the matter. Ministers were all agreed they could not allow nearly half the Canal shares to pass to a French company; the purchase was seen as an act of self-defence. Derby was gratified when, following the announcement of the purchase, public enthusiasm far exceeded what he judged to be the real importance of the transaction. In 1876 Disraeli also persuaded parliament to grant the Queen her long-existing wish for the title of Empress of India. A Royal whim was indulged, Conservative support for the monarchy demonstrated, and Imperial commitment given a symbolic boost. Again, Derby judged that 'never was more fuss made about a matter so utterly unimportant'.[29]

But such actions were relatively easy political successes. Despite traditional Whigs having a final fling, from their historic distrust of prerogative power, in opposing the Royal Titles bill. The government's successes played to elements of the public mind eager for British successes abroad; 'a strength of feeling', Derby observed nervously, 'which might under certain circumstances take the form of a cry for war'.[30] In 1875 a much more complex and dangerous crisis threatened, which eventually did whip up a popular cry for war. It also roused the sleeping giant of Gladstone to virulent opposition. Already, in May 1875, Gladstone had spoken with unusual vehemence against Northcote's budget. The Chancellor was widely regarded as having come off best in these clashes, while a few suspected Gladstone of wishing quietly to resume his old post as leader.

Disraeli happily inherited the Crimean policy of Palmerston, which recommended Britain support the Turkish Ottoman

Empire against Russian expansionism. This defined British interests, as laid out in the Treaty of Paris of 1856, as the guarantee of the independence and integrity of the Ottoman Empire. This policy matched Disraeli's own sensibilities. He also saw, as did most Conservatives, continued Turkish control of Constantinople as 'the key to India'. Russian usurpation would open the way for Russia to push further south, severing British links with the Asian subcontinent. British interests remained, he firmly believed, best served by shoring up Ottoman sovereignty. When, during 1875, revolts against Turkish rule broke out in Bosnia and Herzegovina, predictably Disraeli was unsympathetic to what he dismissed as dangerously destabilising nationalist ferment.[31] As Foreign Secretary Derby, during August, was coolly deprecating the tendency of the press to represent the crisis as much more serious than it had yet become. 'Insurrections are always apt to look bigger at a distance than they really are.'[32] By November 1875 Disraeli was seeing the question as primarily an opportunity, while maintaining traditional British policy, to put his name in the annals of history as the statesman who settled the vexed Eastern Question. Like his fictional character Sidonia, a Judaic Byron, Disraeli hoped to solve 'with a phrase some deep problems that men muse over for years'.[33] Diplomatic initiatives to defuse the situation, led by Germany, Austria–Hungary, and Russia, pursued mediation. But wishing to steer an independent British line and 'dreaming of Palmerstonian glories', Disraeli refrained in May 1876 from endorsing the Berlin Memorandum calling for the Turks to concede. British public response to this sequence of events, and the attempt to resolve the crisis peacefully, remained restrained.

Then, during 1876, the crisis rapidly escalated. Accompanying confusion in Constantinople, as a coup espousing reform placed the young and feeble-minded Murad V at the head of the Ottoman Empire, revolt in Bulgaria was brutally suppressed by the Turks. Between 12,000 and 15,000 Christian men, women and children were massacred; mainly at the hands of irregular Muslim Turkish bands, the notorious *bashi bazouks*. By June 1876 vivid press reports were appearing in Britain describing the full horror of the torture, rape, and other atrocities that had occurred. Again, Disraeli's response was predictably cool. It was also to prove inept. The despatches of the British ambassador in Constantinople, Sir Henry Elliot, who was in ill health, affirmed the premier's instinctive response to the crisis. Elliot pointed out that violence and cruelty were endemic to Ottoman misrule and that the Bulgarian horrors, though horrific, were not unusual. Disraeli chose to express publicly his scepticism regarding reports of violent massacre. Two unfortunate statements made in the Commons during July came to haunt him. Tales of atrocity he dismissed as 'coffee-house babble'. And he made the observation that Oriental people, rather than resort to torture, 'generally terminate their connection with culprits in an expeditious manner'.[34] The callous indifference to the tragic fate of fellow Christians, which seemed evident in these statements, prompted disbelief followed by outcry. Derby regretted Disraeli's habit of being 'too anxious to excite interest, to astonish or puzzle his audience by an air of mystery'.[35] In turn Disraeli wrote sharply to Derby accusing the Foreign Office and Elliot of misleading him over the massacres. On 9 August the cabinet decided to send a consular agent into Bulgaria.

In the final debate of the 1876 session, on 11 August, a wearied Disraeli tried, with the tact and skill he could muster, to repair the situation. He declared the government ready to bring Turkey to task once the facts of any atrocities had been firmly established; while the paramount concern of the ministry remained firmly to maintain the interests of the British Empire. The following day it was announced that Disraeli was to be elevated to the Upper House as Lord Beaconsfield. Carnarvon described the premier's decision as 'political suicide'.[36] The conciliatory Northcote was named Disraeli's successor as Conservative leader in the Commons. A disappointed Gathorne Hardy acquiesced, his high-church and clerical interests rendering him an unsuitable candidate. None the less, severe political damage from the Bulgarian question had already been done.

As during the Indian Mutiny in 1857, lurid reports in the press of the horrors inflicted on the Bulgarians whipped up popular outrage. Nature mirrored the warmth of public feeling as extreme heat and a long drought baked the country during the summer of 1876. The popular moral outcry touched on two potent aspects of the Victorian sensibility. First, the firm belief that Britain stood at the vanguard of progress enabled the Turks to be portrayed as infidel fiends whose cruel immorality violated the standards of civilised peoples. Secondly, sexual sensibilities and belief in the sanctity of women were outraged by the stories of Christian women being dishonoured; details of rape on a vast scale confirming that the Turks lay far beyond the pale of civilisation. A high-minded alliance of churchmen, Nonconformists, university dons, and journalists voiced their disgust. The pro-Liberal *Daily News*, owned by Samuel Morley, printed graphic reports of what had occurred, fuelling popular excitement.

The outbreak of intense moral outrage that marked the Bulgarian agitation threatened Disraeli's hope of pursuing a national Palmerstonian policy based upon domestic consensus. Indeed, the popular outcry did permanent damage to the credibility of the Conservative ministry. By late August Derby, as Foreign Secretary, was warning Elliot of the universal feeling of indignation created by reports of the Bulgarian atrocities. Such reports made Derby feel uncomfortable, there being too little substantiated information available. A huge public agitation involving hundreds of meetings around the country denounced Turkish barbarity and Disraeli's pro-Ottoman policy. Lord Shaftsbury, in early September, recorded with gratification the 'universal fever at blood-heat' driving popular anger against the Turks.[38] Conservatives stood by the government. The Foreign Secretary comforted himself with the thought that the agitation occupied so much public attention partly because there was nothing else for the press to write about. Moreover, 'at this time of year [it] can do little harm'.[39] Most Whigs supported a traditional Palmerstonian policy as best serving British interests. But those primarily Nonconformist popular forces, which had galvanised Gladstone's politics of conscience in the provinces in the late 1860s, began again to give voice, during July and August, to a powerful sense of moral outrage.

Only belatedly did Gladstone recognise the full force of what was occurring. As a member of Aberdeen's coalition he had supported the Crimean policy of the 1850s. He retained a belief that Ottoman territorial integrity should be protected against the rise of an independent Slav state. Moreover, during the summer of 1876 he was more concerned with the theological issue of Future Retribution than with the Eastern Question. Leaders of the popular agitation expressed intense frustration at Gladstone's apparent aloofness from events. Unlike 1868, Gladstone in 1876 was not shaping public opinion. He believed the politics of conscience had been smothered by the Tory reaction of 1874; moral politics anaesthetised by Palmerstonian platitudes. Only after the Bulgarian agitation was under way, as an outcry in full spate, did Gladstone recognise the opportunity presenting itself. 'There is now', he told Granville, for 'the first time for many years, a virtuous passion'.[40] In the course of three days a bed-ridden Gladstone wrote and then published in early September, a pamphlet called *The Bulgarian Horrors and the Question of the East*; 200,000 copies of this virulent attack on Ottoman savagery and Disraeli's foreign policy were sold by the end of the month. Characteristically, Gladstone's language often suggested more than he meant. When he wrote that the Turks should be ejected 'bag and baggage' from the Balkans he was calling for administrative reform not, as some understood, the forced repatriation of recently arrived Turkish communities. None the less, with this one public act Gladstone immediately placed himself at the head of those claiming to represent the reawakened conscience of the nation. He effectively hijacked the Bulgarian agitation.

Though weak from gout, Disraeli forcefully responded to Gladstone's attack in a speech, on 20 September 1876, questioning Gladstone's patriotism and denouncing Slav secret societies. Privately Disraeli declared that all that was not faction in Gladstone's essay was froth. Derby judged Gladstone's pamphlet to be religious zeal appearing under the guise of sympathy for oppressed races. Gladstone's conclusions seemed to fall short of the vehemence of his premises. The official leaders of the Liberal party, Hartington and Granville, meanwhile, declined to follow Gladstone's sudden leap to the forefront of the agitation. Signs of dissension among the Liberal leadership began to emerge:

Gladstone and Lowe rival each other in the vehemence of their abuse of everything Turkish: but one proposes to place Turkey under a sort of joint control of all the Powers, the other to leave it to be absorbed by Russia. There can hardly be a more fundamental difference of policy.[41]

Within the cabinet Salisbury, Carnarvon, and Northcote began to pressure the premier to modify his position, while Derby stood staunchly by Disraeli. The Foreign Secretary was convinced a strong reaction to the agitation would soon set in. The ministry had 'nothing to unsay or undo'. Indeed, in the following months traditional domestic anti-Russian feeling did emerge. The momentum of the Bulgarian agitation faltered and Conservative nerves were steeled. At the opening of the new parliamentary session in February 1877 Whigs, including Hartington and Granville, declined to endorse the 'virtuous passion' headed by Gladstone.

While the government majority held firm the opposition failed to find any plan of common action. The Queen gave the lead to London society by denouncing Gladstone's activities as shameful and mischievous. It was supposed that, should Gladstone return to office, he would form a purely radical government. Delane attributed the violence of Gladstone's language to his admiration for the Greek Orthodox Church. Gladstone, in response, praised the virtuous outrage of 'the people', whose integrity spoke out, despite the moral limpness of the upper classes. His attempt to move five strongly-worded anti-government resolutions in the Commons in early May 1877 failed. Whigs and moderate Liberals continued to be unnerved by the popular moral zeal and religious fervour the Bulgarian agitation brought to bear on foreign policy. They were disgusted by Gladstone's insistence upon moving his resolutions, while the radicals seemed doubly satisfied. Gladstone's resolutions both condemned moderate Whig policy and seemed to mark Gladstone out as the radicals' future leader. Yet a Liberal defeat in the Salford by-election, despite the confident expectation of victory, suggested Gladstone's agitation was failing in provincial towns as well as London. Gladstone's decisive Commons defeat in May 1877 openly advertised deep Liberal divisions.

Disraeli, meanwhile, tried to square the diplomatic circle of not breaking completely with a concerted European resolution of the question, while also not closing off the possibility of becoming the architect of an independent British settlement. He began talking in a swaggering vein of the great weight of English opinion upon foreign powers. In January 1877 the six-power Conference of Constantinople sought and failed to impose reforms on the Turks. Salisbury was despatched as a plenipotentiary to Constantinople, though his earnest attempts to force reforms on Turkey, over the head of Elliot, were hampered from London by Disraeli and Derby. Then in April 1877 Russia declared war on Turkey. During the following months a pale and enfeebled Disraeli became more bellicose. In June he told the cabinet that 'the upper classes and the working classes were united against Russia. The middle classes would always be against war: but fortunately the middle classes did not now govern.'[42] By July the war fever was taking increasing hold on the cabinet. Disraeli now pushed forward British prestige as the one thing most needful in foreign policy. As the bitter conflict escalated and the Russians advanced on the Turkish capital, in January 1878 the cabinet despatched a British fleet to Constantinople, only to recall it the following day. 'Twitters' Carnarvon, the most strongly Turcophobe member of the cabinet, resigned in protest. A replay of the Crimean War, Carnarvon declared, would be 'insane'; his high church beliefs encouraged him to see a Russian war on Turkey as a crusade.[43]

Meanwhile passions in the country intensified as war hysteria mounted. Despite signs of economic distress, domestic issues seemed unnoticed. The word 'jingo' came into the English language to express the bellicose nationalism that swept domestic opinion. Blatant anti-Russian prejudices were now resurgent. On 24 February a 'jingoistic' mob gathered outside Gladstone's London residence in Harley Street breaking windows and jeering. The strength of anti-Russian feeling also prised Derby away from Disraeli; the Foreign Secretary holding frequent private meetings with Count Schuvalov, the Russian ambassador, in the hopes of securing peace. Derby feared jingoistic passions pitching Europe into war before diplomacy was given time to work. Since the beginning of 1877 Derby had been increasingly unsettled by Disraeli's careless talk of war. By early January 1878 Derby was close to a nervous breakdown, suffering from ill health and drinking heavily. The Queen, meanwhile, was putting intense pressure on the premier to declare war against Russia and stop the Russian advance towards Constantinople. In February a British fleet was finally stationed at Constantinople.

Derby found himself profoundly disgusted by Disraeli's swaggering talk and his 'evident enjoyment of an exciting episode of history, with which his name was to be joined'.[44] But by March the Russians were attempting to impose a punitive peace on the prostrated Turks, which proposed the creation of a large, independent pan-Slav Bulgarian state. In late March the cabinet discussed the seizure of Cyprus as a military base from which to exert British control in Asia Minor. As Disraeli secured cabinet agreement to the transfer of British troops from India to the Mediterranean and the calling up of reserves in England, Derby resigned.

Derby's resignation on 27 March 1878 ended a political friendship with Disraeli that had lasted thirty years. In 1882 Derby was to enter a Liberal cabinet. More importantly, Derby's departure marked a gradual, though significant, shift in the higher levels of the Conservative party. Salisbury, who succeeded Derby as Foreign Secretary, was prepared to work with Disraeli despite his differences with the premier. With the threat becoming very real of Russian troops marching into Constantinople, Salisbury was prepared to adopt a more bellicose Disraelian policy. In March Salisbury emerged as the most ardent cabinet supporter for the proposal to occupy Cyprus by force. It is possible he acted knowing that this was a policy guaranteed to eject Derby from the cabinet. Thereafter, it was hardliners such as Salisbury and Lord Cranbrook who stood closest to an old and ill Disraeli marooned in the Lords. Moderate centrists, like Derby who left the party, or Northcote experiencing increasing isolation, lost influence. Salisbury subsequently characterised Derby's policy as one of weakness and indecision. The appointment of the Duke of Northumberland to the Privy Seal in February 1878 had already added a strong supporter of Salisbury to the cabinet. From 1878 the Conservative leadership became noticeably more reactionary and more belligerently anti-Liberal. Responsible centrism was replaced as the keynote of Conservative policy by a harder-headed Toryism. Doctrinal sclerosis in Disraeli's old age was to help in Gladstone's subsequent revitalisation of the Liberal politics of conscience.

The Russians' punitive Treaty of San Stefano, unacceptable to the other European powers, was in June 1878 submitted to the Congress of Berlin for modification. Under that shrewd master of European *Realpolitik* Count Bismarck, the Congress dismembered the proposed extended Bulgarian state eagerly sought by Russia. Yet the Berlin Congress also finally provided Disraeli, accompanied by Salisbury, with an historic diplomatic stage upon which to play his long-cherished role as an international statesman. He became the 'Lion of the Congress', earning the admiration of Bismarck and fighting against his own exhaustion and ill health to ensure his presence was a prominent one. With Salisbury he brought back from Berlin in mid-July, he declared, 'peace with honour'. This meant not just the curtailment of pan-Slav ambitions, but also the formal transfer from Turkey to Britain of the island of Cyprus.

This moment marked the high point of Disraeli's political career. Atop 'the greasy pole' he basked in his triumph as an elder European statesman. A grateful Queen gave him the Order of the Garter, the offer of a Dukedom being declined. In *Coningsby* Disraeli wrote that 'a great man is one who affects the mind of his generation'. Disraeli's performance at Berlin in 1878 imprinted on the minds of successive generations the image of the Conservative party as the champion of patriotic honour; led by a man whose shrewd judgement and astute negotiating skill had secured both British interests and lasting European peace. Since youth the Byronic desire to be a hero in the world, the spur of an indefatigable ambition, had driven Disraeli on. In July 1878 Disraeli glimpsed the fulfilment of that Byronic dream. As he boasted to Lady Bradford: 'The party is what is called on its legs again, and jingoism triumphant!'[45]

But the harsh realities of 1878, both diplomatic and domestic, belied the glory in which Disraeli momentarily basked. The Congress of Berlin marked the conclusive demise of that European system upheld by Palmerston and enshrined in the Congress of Vienna of 1815. The European events of 1859–71, in Italy, Austria, Russia and France, had already dismantled much of the 'concert' system. By 1878 Palmerstonianism was diplomatically bankrupt. Disraeli's triumph at Berlin was more a matter of public relations than of hard diplomacy. At home, the events of 1876–8 also demonstrated the serious obstacles to securing domestic consensus in support of a nationalist foreign policy. The 'virtuous passion' of the Bulgarian agitation forcefully revealed those sections of the public mind hostile to a purely pragmatic foreign policy seemingly indifferent to morality. At the same time, the agitation had restored Gladstone's belief in the popular appetite for the politics of conscience. While the agitation itself faded during 1877, the intensity of the outcry left an indelible mark on the political landscape.

The personal antipathy between Gladstone and Disraeli was brought to a new level of intensity. Their mutual hatred affected the emotions of their followers. It helped Disraeli during 1877 that Gladstone's moral crusade had also split Liberal opinion. Moreover, the development of the Eastern crisis during 1877–8 prompted a shift, signalled by Derby's resignation, in the Conservative leadership. The hardening of Tory sensibilities after 1878 suggested a polarisation of party sentiment. Partisan passions intensified. For individuals like Derby on one side, and Whigs like Hartington and Granville on the other, a retreat from centrism promised only increasing discomfort. For a rapidly fading Disraeli, resting on his laurels, it marked a collapse back into the ease of inactivity.

Conservatism Becalmed, 1878–80

During 1878–80 the Conservative ministry seemed to drift rudderless, subject to the current of unpredictable events. The onset of an economic depression in 1879 affected agriculture, manufacturing, and trade. Harvest failures and falling prices unsettled farmers and gentry, while also embittering relations between landlords and tenants. The prolonged torrential rains that devastated the 1879 harvest reflected the gloom descending on the government. Evictions in Ireland brought on by arrears of rent prompted violent agitation, inspired by the powerful oratory of the former Fenian Michael Davitt. Popular Irish anger at the escalating number of evictions was vented in agrarian outrages, bringing increasing levels of violence to the Irish countryside. In England, Conservative support in the larger boroughs waned as commercial depression produced falling profits and growing unemployment. The incidence of bankruptcies sharply increased. Northcote's credibility as Chancellor came under increasing pressure as he found himself forced to raise income tax.

Increased military expenditure placed further demands on Northcote's financial management. Wars in Afghanistan and South Africa involved expensive military expeditions. In both cases the Conservative government found itself drawn into imperial adventures by local impetuosity; neither campaign being the direct result of a commitment to imperial expansion in London. In India the headstrong Lord Lytton, as Viceroy, oversaw two military invasions of Afghanistan during 1878–9 intended to establish British influence in the region. During the course of hostilities the British mission in Kabul was massacred. Similarly, in South Africa, Sir Bartle Frere provoked a war with the Zulus, leading to the annihilation of a British force at Islandhluwana in January 1879. Finally, in July 1879, the Zulus were defeated at Ulindi. Yet the elimination of the Zulu threat still left the Dutch Boer settlers in a high state of resentment at British annexation of the Transvaal. The Afghan and Zulu wars did more than strain Northcote's Exchequer. They also provided Liberal critics of Disraeli's allegedly reckless imperialism, primarily Gladstone, with ample material with which to decry imperialist oppression. Charges of immorality and financial extravagance, in a potent Gladstonian blend, came together. If such accusations somewhat unfairly placed full responsibility for events on ministers in London, the damaging impact of such criticism was no less effective for that. Waste and incompetence, as well as military humiliation in the early stages of both conflicts, seemed all too evident.

The obstructive tactics of Irish Home Rule MPs in Westminster also clogged parliamentary proceedings. Isaac Butt's low-key leadership was challenged by those Home Rule MPs desiring more forthright action. Under Joseph Biggar and Charles Stewart Parnell, Irish members began disrupting business by interminably prolonging debates. This strategy reached its climax during the 1877 session when the Commons was kept sitting in Committee for 26 hours; a disruption of business which brought the Speaker close to actually suspending seven Irish MPs from the chamber. In 1877 Charles Parnell, a charismatic young Protestant landowner, became President of the Home Rule Confederation of Great Britain. At the same time, after 1878, the Irish land war, with which Parnell maintained an ambiguous connection, promised to give Home Rulers the momentum of a mass movement, broadening their appeal within Ireland. In alliance with Davitt's rural campaign, Parnell's displacement of Butt (who died in 1879) as leader of the Home Rule MPs brought organisation, propaganda and inspirational leadership together. A strong power base was forged which gave a keen political edge to Irish grievances. Parnell emerged as Ireland's new Daniel O'Connell, fusing mass agitation with astute parliamentary tactics. In October 1879 the Irish National Land League was founded with Parnell elected as President.

Conservative difficulties prepared the ground for the extraordinary phenomenon of Gladstone's Midlothian campaigns. This was the Bulgarian agitation writ large. Gladstone sought to ignite the 'virtuous passion' of the people against the moral vacuity of Disraeli's policies, what Gladstone termed 'Beaconsfieldism'. Taking advantage of improvements in railway travel and telegraph communication Gladstone undertook during November and December 1879 a series of impassioned outdoor speeches denying the whole system of government policy. Imperial adventures, both financially extravagant and politically unnecessary, had brought about the brutal suppression of noble Zulus and led to the protracted deaths of Afghan women and children. This was consistent with that callousness which had characterised Disraeli's response to the Bulgarian atrocities. Such moral culpability was contrasted by Gladstone with the 'right principles' that should underpin British policy. Foreign policy, Gladstone asserted, should be inspired by 'the love of freedom', needless and entangling engagements being avoided, the equal rights of all nations being acknowledged, and peace preserved. Wherever possible cooperation between the Great Powers of Europe should be maintained, thereby Britain's moral standing internationally being restored.

Conservative credibility, weighed down by the worsening economic situation, began to collapse under Gladstone's onslaught. The prime minister, however, exhibited a dangerously slack grasp on events. Disraeli did not dissolve parliament in the summer of 1879, as he might have done; though deferring the dissolution until 1880 merely gave Gladstone further opportunity for denunciations of 'Beaconsfieldism'. Conservative party managers remained optimistic about an impending election. Disraeli spiritedly dismissed Gladstone's indictments as 'a waste of powder and shot'. But failure to take the first Midlothian campaign seriously, and misplaced complacency about Conservative electoral prospects, proved significant errors. Like Gladstone in 1874, Disraeli looked to a popular budget as the government's most promising vote-winner. But by January 1880 the cabinet was laid low by illness: Disraeli, Salisbury, and Northcote forced to their beds, Lord John Manners injured in a hunting accident, and Lord Cairns fleeing the London fog on account of his asthma. Government vigour was now drained to dangerously low levels. Unexpected Conservative by-election victories in Southwark and Liverpool in February 1880 sparked the cabinet into life. Ministers promptly took the disastrous decision on 6 March to announce an immediate dissolution. Six years of office, weariness, age, bad advice, and incapacity had distanced them from reality.

The April 1880 election, preceded by a second Midlothian campaign from Gladstone, ruthlessly slashed Conservative representation in the Commons. Disraeli's election manifesto dwelt mainly on the danger of Irish separatism. But the sudden alighting on the imminent threat of Home Rule ignited no

Unionist fervour; the Liberal party being officially as committed to the Union as the Conservatives. Disraeli anticipated 16 to 18 Conservative losses in the election. In fact, Conservative numbers fell from 352 to 238 MPs, a devastating loss of 114 seats. The Liberals won 353 seats, with Home Rule candidates gaining 61 Irish seats. The deterioration of Conservative party organisation, the economic slump, the passion excited by Gladstone's Midlothian campaigns, greater Whig commitment to the Liberal campaign, and improved Liberal party organisation were all cited as factors in the crushing Conservative defeat. The election result hit the Conservatives like 'thunder . . . from a clear blue sky'.[46] Unable to campaign because of his peerage, Disraeli maintained a public face of dignified imperturbability. In private, however, he described his position as 'discomfited, defeated, and, if not disgraced, prostrate by a singular anomaly and irony of fate'. Salisbury called the result 'a perfect catastrophe'.[47] The Conservative gains of 1874 were eradicated. Only the Tory strongholds in London and the Home Counties remained intact. The Liberals made inroads into traditional Conservative counties outside the south-east, as well as strengthening their domination in Scotland and Wales. Both Gladstone and Hartington themselves won county constituencies.

On April 15 1880 the cabinet decided to resign, rather than meet the new parliament. The novel precedents of 1868 and 1874 were followed. The formal communication of this decision to the Queen on 21 April forced on her the distasteful possibility of inviting Gladstone to form a government. Both Granville and Hartington, despite comprising the official Liberal party leadership, recognised the impossibility of Gladstone taking a subordinate office under them. A distraught Queen found she could not avoid appointing Gladstone premier; a man she privately despised as a 'half mad firebrand who would soon ruin everything and be a Dictator'.[48]

Disraeli's Legacy

Just over a year after resigning the premiership Disraeli was dead. His last novel, *Endymion*, some of which was written while prime minister, was published in November 1880. It was set in the political world of Disraeli's youth, 'describing the art of creating a career'. This was an ambition to be realised through fashionable society as much as in parliament. At the end of March 1881 an attack of bronchitis forced him to his bed. Four weeks later he died. Thus ended the exotic career of that most unlikely of Victoria's premiers.

In the aftermath of electoral disaster in 1880 Disraeli observed that the Tories 'have existed for more than a century and a half as an organised political connection and having survived the loss of American colonies, the first Napoleon and Lord Grey's Reform Act, they must not be snuffed out'.[49] In August 1882 his arch-enemy, Gladstone, privately recorded the Conservatives' continuing sources of strength. The Conservative party possessed great wealth available for the expenses of elections. In comparison with the Liberals, Conservatives had far less 'explosive matter' within their party. The powerful professional classes, such as the Army, the Law, and the Clergy, were generally Conservative in disposition; while the powerful influence of the landed classes, the difficulty of keeping the public mind intent upon great national issues, and the association of higher social influences with Toryism, provided the Conservative party with its resilience.[50] What was Disraeli's own contribution to his party's survival?

In part this depends on one's view of Disraeli's personality. What were the springs of action that drove him tirelessly on? For the historian of Peel, Norman Gash, Disraeli was the most cynical and unscrupulous of all Conservative leaders. For Robert Blake, in his magisterial biography, Disraeli was essentially a politician seeking power. 'Politics was the breath of Disraeli's life.' Politics was the essence of his being; the arena of public affairs the all-consuming object of his ambitions and aspirations. In 1851 a confidant observed that, 'whether in town or country, politics constitute [Disraeli's] chief, almost his sole, pleasure'.[51] Calculating opportunism, more than commitment to particular ideas, served those aspirations and most commonly characterised his actions. In 1854 *The Times* attacked Disraeli 'as the impersonation of an intellect alone, without feeling or sense of right: one to whom politics are a game of skill only'.[52] A pose of cynical worldly detachment, Blake argued, cloaked a purely pragmatic response to political affairs. In 1835 Disraeli had declared it a fallacy to think that theory produced circumstances, it was circumstances that produced theory. Neither Disraeli's Jewish heritage nor his early Romanticism figured largely in Blake's portrait.

More recently Peter Ghosh has argued that while the 'opportunist' view of Disraeli is clearly evident at moments of crisis, such as in 1867, at other periods consistent views did influence his actions. This was particularly true in terms of financial policy during the 1850s and 1860s, when Disraeli was Chancellor of the Exchequer three times. Disraeli's fiscal views were consistent, but not distinctive. In other words, he subscribed to the mid-Victorian consensus of peace, retrenchment, and reform.[53] Disraeli saw the opportunity to achieve what Gladstone in fact delivered. But brief periods of minority government were insufficient to displace his rival's masterful dominance of financial affairs. Paul Smith has helpfully emphasised Disraeli's Jewishness as an integral part of those ideas which underpinned his policies; while John Vincent, in a stimulating short study, has linked these elements with Disraeli's literary output and the refutation of later attempts, primarily after 1945, to find in Disraeli an inspiration for Conservative flirtations with collectivism.[54]

But it is also important to recognise the extent to which Disraeli remained, as in his *risqué* youth, a Byronic Romantic. It was the heady cultural ferment of Romanticism during the 1820s that shaped Disraeli's imagination and moral sensibilities. During his Grand Tour of 1826 he befriended Byron's boatman, re-enacting a scene from Byron's life on Lake Geneva. He later arranged for Byron's manservant, in whose arms the great poet had died, to be brought to England to live at his father's house. Throughout his life, in conversation Disraeli referred to Byron as the great genius who had died before realising his full gift. The whole spectrum of Romantic enthusiasms for adventure and mystery enthralled Disraeli. His reading of Goethe, Wieland, and Heine in translation introduced him to the ironic tones of German Romanticism and the turbulent realisation of both self and artistic truth in life. Institutions, constitutional systems, and the prosaic detail of domestic legislation bored him. 'England should think more of the community and less of the government', he wrote in his novel *Coningsby*. It was the vivid manifestations of vital human communities that fired his imagination; the definition of his own genius through individual struggle that gave impetus to his sense of destiny. His was a career pursued as art.

Disraeli remained throughout his life a Romantic looking to be a hero in the world. He entertained, as he wrote in his 1832 novel *Contarini Fleming*, 'a deep conviction that life must be intolerable unless I were the greatest of men'. He sought, like his fictional hero Alroy, 'a mind to whose supreme volition the fortunes of the world would bow like fate'. The inspiration and creativity of language was his medium and the source of his genius. His novels, with their elements of mystical fantasy, were not literary diversions; the psychological equivalent of Gladstone's passion for cutting down trees. They were an integral part of his sense of himself as an heroic individual valiantly overcoming the prejudices and obstacles of a turbulent hostile world. With typical precocity he declared in 1833 that his life was a struggle 'with moments of rapture – a storm with dashes of moonlight'. In 1851 the young Stanley marvelled at Disraeli's 'singleness of purpose; contempt of obloquy; energy which no labour can exhaust; indifference to the ordinary pleasures and pursuits of men, which he neglects in search of power and fame'. Thus was the Romantic hero to fulfil his destiny. To a lady admirer in 1862 he declared it the grossest error to see themselves as living in a utilitarian age. Rather, they lived in a period of great drama and infinite romance.[55]

Traditional Tories were right to sense in Disraeli something exotic and alien. This was despite his assuming gravitas after 1846, shedding the trappings of dandyism, and becoming to all appearances a typical country gentleman ensconced in the Hughenden estate that friends bought for him. His ironical distance from such appearances was evident in his comment that 'the British People being subject to fogs and possessing a powerful Middle Class require grave statesmen'. Disraeli privately sneered at the country squires on his own back benches.

'They had good natural ability, he said, taking them as a body: but wanted culture: they never read: their leisure was passed in field sports: the wretched school and university system was at fault: they learnt nothing useful and did not understand the ideas of their own time.'[56]

Deference to authority was antithetical to much in Disraeli's temperament. His early novels, he hoped, would corrupt public taste. With the Queen, in the 1870s, his conscious laying on of flattery with a trowel enforced his own sense of being master of the situation. In private he described the Queen as troublesome, wilful, and whimsical, like a spoilt child. It was he who manipulated the reclusive and lonely Queen's feelings. Disraeli possessed to a remarkable degree the art of listening, or seeming to listen, and sending visitors away well pleased with themselves. But it was rebellion that had made him. Prominence was achieved through his overthrow of Peel. Thereafter, it was his oratory which sustained his often precarious position. 'We govern men with words', he wrote. Language was the pliable medium of his art; his own career his most compelling creation.

Disraeli's legacy to the Conservative party, therefore, was not primarily a matter of substantive policies – though some Conservatives later built the elusive notion of Tory Democracy around his legislative achievements. The main responsibility for the 1867 Reform Act lay with Derby. It was Derby, rather than Disraeli as later Tory apologists such as T. E. Kebbel claimed, who 'educated' the Conservative party during the 1850s and 1860s. The survival of the Conservative party during those long bleak years of opposition was Derby's achievement. Rather, Disraeli's legacy to the party was to provide it, after 1872, with a potent language about itself that defined a Conservative – or anti-Liberal – identity to be carried forward by succeeding generations. The wisdom of ancient manners was portrayed in combat with modern legislation. In seizing upon the collapse of Gladstonian Liberalism in 1872–4, Disraeli brought the Conservatives forward as a national party. They became Englishmen at large, not merely landed proprietors. They were committed to Empire, a robust foreign policy conducted in the light of British interests, associated with support for the monarchy, the defence of property, and protection of the Established Church. As already noted, these were consistent strands in Disraeli's thinking. They provided links between his subversive youth and his role as the pragmatic elder statesman. From the beginning of his career to his death Disraeli was also consistently anti-Whig. He would not condescend, he declared, to be a Whig. The Whigs embraced alien and cosmopolitan ideas. Since 1688 they had burdened England with Venetian politics (an exclusive oligarchy), Dutch finance (a national debt), and French wars. He sought, in contrast, an authentically national party rooted in the ancient institutions of the country. Love of these institutions, Disraeli proclaimed, embraced all classes of society. Self-interested Whigs, he argued, merely sought the preservation of an oligarchy. Through the Conservative claim to be a national party, rather than merely the representation of the landed interest, lay a commitment to the improvement of the social condition of the people. From his youthful radicalism to his mature Toryism Disraeli consistently praised the good sense of the great mass of the English people. It was the national community, as an organic whole, that was to be brought behind Britain as a great imperial world power; her historic institutions integrating social cohesion with national identity. British civilisation was the 'ornament and honour of the world'.

The potency of Disraeli's words inspired timeless abstractions, such as 'One Nation Conservatism'. In part this was because of the ambiguity of his words, in part because his phrases gave powerful expression to sufficiently generalised thoughts. His literary imagination defined Conservatism during the 1870s in a way that served well the purposes of successive Conservative leaders. His death in 1881, moreover, provided the party faithful with a venerated image upon which to call for legitimacy. Other candidates for canonisation were, for various reasons, unsuitable. Peel was an apostate, Derby too dull. The recurring call upon the posthumous endorsement of his resonate language ensured Disraeli's enduring place in posterity. The Primrose League, named after what was supposed to be his favourite flower, was founded in 1883. Dedicated to Disraeli's memory, the Primrose

League enshrined a popular cult, providing the opportunity for ordinary Conservative supporters, both men and women, to promote Tory principles. By 1891 it enjoyed over a million members, including many from the working class. Disraeli's greatest artistic success, his own political career, and the words through which he created it, emblazoned a venerated image on successive Conservative minds: an image made up of differing proportions of romance and nostalgia.

Disraeli's solid achievements as Conservative leader were relatively few, although he certainly regarded almost all issues from an exclusively parliamentary or party point of view. Lord Randolph Churchill was to summarise Disraeli's career as 'failure, failure, failure, partial success, renewed failure, ultimate and complete victory'. The only election Disraeli won for his party was in 1874. On only two occasions, in 1867 and 1877, did he convincingly achieve his political aim of breaking the Liberal party down into its constituent parts. The countless alliances and tactical manoeuvrings his fertile mind envisaged largely failed to materialise. But he did provide Conservatives with a potent language about themselves that enabled them to be a national anti-Liberal party. The diverse and disruptive expectations excited by Liberal fervour, he asserted, were best calmed by reverence for ancient institutions, pride in Empire and a quiet faith in the good sense of the English people. Disraeli thereby rescued the Conservatives from both narrow sectionalism and atavistic bigotry. His rhetoric gave the Conservative party a future. And if governing men was a matter of words, such a legacy was the most valuable gift of all.

7

THE CRISIS OF LIBERALISM, 1880–6

Crisis was not a word that immediately leapt to the minds of Liberal commentators in April 1880. The 1880 election returned the Liberal party to power with their largest nominal Commons majority since the 1832 Reform Act. Gladstone's powerful denunciations of 'Beaconsfieldism' appeared to reignite popular passions, the Liberal politics of conscience reinvigorated with a transcendent moral cry. Crisis seemed more prevalent in Conservative circles as painful post-mortems inevitably followed electoral disaster. Disraeli's death in 1881 compounded Conservative difficulties. Yet, within six years, the Liberal party was split asunder. The Home Rule crisis of 1886 stands alongside 1846 as a dramatic moment of fundamental party realignment. Party connections were redrawn as Liberal Unionists, including Hartington and Chamberlain, split away from Gladstonian Home Rulers. The crisis recast party sentiment for decades to follow.

What was the nature of this crisis and what did it reveal about the inherent tensions within the Liberal party? Understanding this issue requires prior discussion of the nature of the Liberal victory in 1880 and Gladstone's subsequent leadership. Recent important work, particularly by T. A. Jenkins, has emphasised the danger of reading the events of 1879–80 backwards.[1] It can too easily seem that an inevitable chain of events followed Gladstone's assault on Disraeli's foreign policy in 1876; the Bulgarian agitation leading ineluctably to the passions of the Midlothian campaigns, an overwhelming Liberal electoral victory, and Gladstone's irresistible return to power. This facile reading contains a number of inferences. First, that the joint Whig leadership of Hartington and Granville after 1875 was hesitant and ineffective. Thus a vacuum at the head of the party irresistibly drew Gladstone back into the centre of affairs. Secondly, that Gladstone's ability to arouse the moral passion of popular Liberalism demonstrated his unique status as the true embodiment of Liberal belief. It was Gladstone's historic role to hold together the Whig and radical sections of the party, despite their mutual antipathy. Thirdly, that the victory of 1880 restored the natural Liberal hegemony that, with the exception of 1874, had characterised electoral politics since 1846. Each of these inferences requires revision.

Liberal Opposition and the Midlothian Campaigns, 1875–80

The leadership of the Whig duumvirate of Hartington and Granville was not as feeble as later Gladstonian myth suggests. In 1875, as the Liberal Chief Whip observed, it was sensible for the Liberals to bide their time. Despite the relative quiet of the opposition during 1875 and 1876 the Speaker noted Hartington's 'good temper, firmness [and] moderation'.[2] Liberal backbenchers remarked on Hartington's straightforwardness and avoidance of subterfuge. The contrast with Gladstone in such comment was implicit. Hartington's more solid qualities being emphasised by his lack of humour and his mediocre oratory. The fact that Gladstone continued to intervene in Commons debates, on occasions of his own choosing, did not make Hartington's position easier.

Gladstone's dramatic hijacking of the Bulgarian agitation in late August 1876 highlighted the ambiguities of his relationship with the official party leadership. Gladstone refused to admit that his actions threatened the position of either Hartington or Granville. As he explained to Granville, he was 'an outside workman, engaged in the preparation of materials, which you and the party will probably have to manipulate and then build into a structure'.[3] Yet the subsequent reluctance of Hartington and Granville to take up those materials, and so abandon a Palmerstonian policy, incited Gladstone to rail against the moral limpness of the political elite and the metropolitan press. Distaste for the agitation was confined, Gladstone declared, to 'the clubs and Upper Circle'; the spirit of 'Fitzwilliamism' being at odds with 'the people's' unchanging sentiments which lay at 'the heart of the Liberal party'.[4] For Gladstone the agitation became a matter of 'the masses' against 'the classes'. As the crisis developed Whigs and moderate Liberals found themselves trapped with no firm distinctive ground on which to stand. Hartington limited his criticism of the ministry to their failure to endorse the Berlin memorandum. By December 1876 Hartington feared that Gladstone was precipitating a break-up of the party.

The failure of Gladstone's five Commons resolutions in May 1877 helped Hartington reassert his authority over Liberal backbenchers. Gladstone noted in his diary that his resolutions did not have 'a single approver in the *Upper* official circle'.[5] The strong Commons support for the Berlin Treaty, which Disraeli and Salisbury brought back from the Congress in July 1878, confirmed Hartington's conviction that 'the magnanimous and patriotic line will be the best'. The *Leeds Mercury* praised Hartington and others because, 'in deciding upon their duty as Liberals, they have not forgotten that they were Englishmen'.[6] Again, the critical comment on Gladstone was implicit. In December 1878 Hartington won plaudits from the left of the party for his strong criticism of government policy in Afghanistan.

The following year Hartington proposed a range of domestic reforms on land law, the county franchise and county government. A leading radical, Joseph Chamberlain, elected MP for Birmingham in 1876, was keen to encourage Hartington's reform plans as a basis for Whig–radical cooperation. Chamberlain regarded Gladstone, by 1878, as an erratic and unreliable old man. Another rising young radical and Chamberlain's close ally, Sir Charles Dilke, was similarly happy during 1879 to foster Whig–radical relations. In November 1879 Chamberlain assured Harcourt that while 'differences do and always will exist' between Whigs and radicals, 'they won't prevent cordial union for common objects'.[7] Hartington's moderate proposals for domestic reform appeared a practicable basis for cordial union. The more so as, by 1879, the Conservative government's interest in domestic legislation had evaporated.

In October 1879 Hartington appeared on a platform alongside Bright in Manchester. The *Manchester Guardian* commented that the noble marquis had, by his good temper, good judgement, and honesty of purpose, attracted to himself the ungrudging support of every section of the party. What was *not* apparent by late 1879 was a vicious Liberal schism between Whig and radical factions, demanding the presence of Gladstone to restore party unity. The 'virtuous passion' of Midlothian was not an obvious necessity to repair a shattered Liberal solidarity of purpose.

Nor was a Gladstonian moral crusade, by the late 1870s, the only means of mobilising popular Liberal support. Chamberlain's rise to national politics, from his local power base in Birmingham, stood on the emergence of 'caucus' politics. In 1877, under Chamberlain's auspices, the defunct National Education League transformed itself into the National Liberal Federation (NLF). This offered for popular Liberal activism an alternative model to the Gladstonian pattern of broad moral alliances. Organisation and programme politics might replace the kinship of conscience. The NLF offered popular membership to Liberal activists through local Liberal Associations. Each local organisation democratically elected representatives to attend the annual assembly. The authority and force of the NLF annual assembly arose from its claim to embody, in a direct democratic fashion, the views of Liberal activists in the country.[8] Ninety-five Liberal Associations sent representatives to the inauguration of the NLF in 1877.

But it is easy to overstate both the democratic and the national character of the NLF. Local Associations were usually controlled by a small number of middle-class activists with the time and money for politics. Moreover, Liberal Associations in Scotland, Wales, the Home Counties, London and Manchester resented the dominance of Birmingham. Despite its claims, the NLF remained, in many ways, the vehicle of a sectional group within the Liberal party. For Chamberlain the NLF was a means of bringing about the radicalisation of the Liberal party. Yet Chamberlain's dominance of the NLF and jealousy at its Birmingham orientation, particularly in Manchester, created serious tensions. The suspicious radical Sheffield MP Mundella believed that 'Birmingham is to pull the strings of the Liberal boroughs, and the puppets are to dance in response to the wires', the NLF acting 'as Birmingham deems desirable, and Chamberlain moves Birmingham'.[9]

The launching of the NLF at the height of the Bulgarian agitation prompted Gladstone to address its first annual assembly. Thereafter, he recognised the NLF as a radical power base whose objects and methods were hostile to his own. The best cure for 'Beaconsfieldism', he maintained, was a prescription of 'virtuous passion', offered in the form of the Midlothian campaigns. Whigs and moderate Liberals shared Gladstone's suspicion of the NLF. It was feared it would force specific pledges on parliamentary candidates, dominate constituency organisation, and actually impose an agenda on the party leadership. Such dangers were all the greater if an uncontrollable impetus was given to a popular demand for county franchise reform, and public opinion on foreign affairs became more volatile.[10]

Such fears, however, were not realised. The radical cure was not worse than the disease. After 1877 the NLF's programme proved predictable radical fare. Internal tensions sapped its potential power. Hartington shared initial Whig concern at a body outside the control of the official party leadership. But by 1879 he was sufficiently confident to extend an olive branch to Chamberlain. In a speech at Liverpool, in February 1879, he declared that 'I can conceive nothing more unjust than the abuse which is being lavished upon [the caucus system] on the ground of tyranny and dictation.' In large urban constituencies such as Birmingham, Manchester, and Liverpool, where the NLF enjoyed broad support, Hartington believed 'nothing can be more conducive to the interests of the Liberal party'.[11] As Gladstone's anxieties about the NLF increased, Hartington's disquiet eased. Similarly Granville, in January 1880, was confident that the radical leaders were very aware that they needed moderate support.

The 1880 election was not, except in Gladstone's mind, a replay of 1868. In 1868 Gladstone's moral crusade on the issue of Irish disestablishment had galvanised the scattered fragments of the Liberal party. But in 1879 Hartington secured broad support for his leadership. A vicious schism between radicals and Whigs was not evident. Hartington himself fought a successful campaign during 1879–80 with a message similar, though more sober in tone, to Gladstone's Midlothian addresses. Disraeli's foreign policy, Hartington declared, was not Palmerstonian, but 'the bastard imperialism of the Second Empire'.[12] The extravagance and incompetence of the Conservatives' financial and foreign policies, he repeatedly argued, violated the traditional principles of Liberal government. A return to those principles would secure the moral and material improvement of the people. Moreover, the rise of the NLF, although contentious, showed organisation and programmes of reform to be a viable alternative means of tapping popular activism, in contrast to the Gladstonian politics of conscience. Gladstone's position in 1879 was much more ambiguous than in 1868. The more so as he stood outside the official leadership of the party. One thing, however, was clear. After Gladstone boarded the train for Midlothian on 24 November 1879 his subsequent speeches not only brought a moral indictment against 'Beaconsfieldism'; they also subverted Hartington's authority as party leader and reasserted the politics of conscience as the authentic expression of popular Liberal sentiment. In 1868 Gladstone had rescued the Liberal party. As he rushed forward again in 1879, it was far from clear that the Liberal party needed rescuing.

Gladstone himself saw the Midlothian campaign as the most important and formidable political challenge to which God had yet called him. It was 'a crisis of an extraordinary character'. The 'battle to be fought was a battle of justice humanity freedom law, all in their first elements from the very root, and all on a gigantic scale', he recorded in his journal in December 1879.[13] It was an assault on the 'strongholds of Anti-Christ' and 'the obscene empires of Mammon and Belial'. A campaign 'on grounds, not of political party, not even of mere English nationality, not of Christian faith, but on the largest and broadest ground of all – the ground of our common humanity'.[14] And certainly, on 24 November, Gladstone felt he had 'never gone through a more extraordinary day'. On the way to Edinburgh he stopped off to speak at Carlisle, Harwick and Galashiels, the journey being 'more like a triumphal procession'.[15] Meeting Lord Rosebery on arrival at Edinburgh he was received by a huge crowd with fireworks and torches. Over the next two weeks he made thirty speeches to a total, he estimated, of nearly 87,000 people. One listener observed how 'Gladstone simply maddened his audiences. He welded them into a unity, wild with passion, ready to follow him even to the death.'[16] In his diary Gladstone noted: 'Fervid crowds at every station. The torchlight procession at Glasgow was a subject for Turner.' Even on his return journey to Harwarden the popular, spontaneous, yet orderly excitement continued. 'At Chester we were met by a torchlight procession of working men, some thousands, with bands: probably 20,000 men in the streets. No police visible.'[17]

This was a new kind of politics. Gladstone was not joining a public agitation already under way. He was shaping, with a sense of historic purpose, a militant popular mood moulded by the charismatic force of his impassioned oratory. The Midlothian campaigns were a direct challenge to the sufficiency of parliament. In appealing directly to the virtuous instincts of the people, Gladstone made the suspect moral sensibilities of the 'upper ten thousand' and the metropolitan press irrelevant. By decrying the loss of moral equilibrium inherent in 'Beaconsfieldism', whose 'strange excesses, and profligacy' set up 'false phantoms of glory', the narrow specific claims of radical reform were transcended. The immediate audience for Gladstone's oratory, moreover, was secondary to the national readership he spoke to through the press. Midlothian provided him with a platform from which to speak to the nation, with a Holy wrath as a tribune of the people.

At the beginning of December 1879 Hartington threatened to resign the Liberal leadership because of the humiliating and unconstitutional position in which he had been placed by Gladstone. The Chief Whip, however, persuaded Hartington to stay in place. Gladstone's succession would, he feared, split the party. The Liberal Catholic convert Lord Ripon believed it was in 'the true interest of the party to keep Hartington as leader' and 'let the Scotch excitement calm down'. Granville feared that Gladstone's Scottish campaign would alienate moderate Liberal voters in the event of a general election. The *Edinburgh Review* declared that 'the most important and influential portion of English political society' esteemed 'sobriety of language, dignity of demeanour, and steadfastness of action', disliking 'exuberant powers of eloquence and mysterious artifices of policy'.[18]

The Liberal leadership anticipated some Conservative losses and Liberal gains at the forthcoming election. What they most feared, however, was the return of a weak Conservative government with the balance of power in the Commons held by Irish Home Rulers. Since February 1879 Chamberlain and Dilke had been holding secret meetings with Parnell. On the basis of a modified form of Home Rule, giving the Irish control of local business, Chamberlain and Parnell saw the possibility of radical–Home Rule cooperation. An inconclusive election result would give both Parnell and Chamberlain a strong hand. In January 1880, Hartington indicated his readiness to support further Irish land law reform. What very few in the opposition anticipated was a spectacular Liberal electoral victory. This underestimation of Liberal feeling in the country naturally led, after the election, to the attribution of overwhelming victory to the personal contribution of Gladstone and his two Midlothian campaigns.

The triumph of April 1880 forced the leadership issue. Significantly, it was still not settled who would lead a Liberal government. Much speculation focused on a Granville ministry with Gladstone in an honorary advisory position within the cabinet. Chamberlain, Dilke, and John Morley rejected suggestions made by followers that a separate radical party might be formed, indicating their willingness to join a Whig-led administration. The fact that, during the election, Gladstone stated his disinclination to push Granville and Hartington aside unless extraordinary circumstances demanded it, fuelled speculation. But on 12 April Gladstone conveyed to Hartington and Granville, via Lord Wolverton, his now firm conviction that the extraordinary reception accorded him during his second Midlothian campaign, as fervid and impassioned as that the previous November, required him to lead the government. This left Hartington and Granville no choice. Once assured that the Queen would accept Gladstone as premier, both men immediately made way for the Grand Old Man's return.

Later Gladstonian myth laid a gloss of certainty over the events of 1879–80. It became one of those historic moments when Gladstone sensed the 'ripeness' of an issue, his personal conviction imparting an incandescence to his actions as the instrument of a Providential will. In truth, the events of 1879–80 were far more complex. Rather than simply restoring Liberal unity Gladstone had overlaid Hartington, Granville, Dilke, and Chamberlain's negotiations with a barn-storming campaign that focused popular support on himself. Gladstone's pre-eminence had not been a necessary condition for Liberal unity. These ambiguities permeated the tensions within Gladstone's second cabinet. They were tensions, moreover, that did not always follow a simple Whig–radical divide.

Two further considerations haunted Liberals after 1880. First, Gladstone's leadership in 1880 was understood to be temporary. Once the special circumstances that had compelled him to come forward had passed, and British policy was purged of 'Beaconsfieldism', it was anticipated he would once again retire. The general expectation in 1880 was that this would probably occur in about two years time. What form would a post-Gladstonian leadership take? Secondly, at some unknown time, the death of his elderly father would promptly elevate Hartington to the Lords as the new Duke of Devonshire. The official arrangements of 1880 were, from the beginning, provisional.

Liberal Government: Ireland, Egypt, Bradlaugh, and Reform, 1880–5

In April 1880 Gladstone resumed both the premiership and the Chancellorship of the Exchequer. Hartington and Granville were placed at the India Office and Foreign Office respectively. Argyll became Privy Seal and Harcourt took the Home Office. Kimberley returned to the Colonial Office. The Whig presence in cabinet was strong. Six frontbench peers sat alongside four commoners with strong aristocratic or landed connections. Only three cabinet ministers – Forster, Chamberlain, and Bright – might claim middle-class radical credentials. Forster became Chief Secretary for Ireland, while Chamberlain was brought into the cabinet as President of the Board of Trade. The radical elder statesman John Bright resumed the Duchy of Lancaster. Outside the cabinet Dilke became Under-Secretary at the Foreign Office and A. J. Mundella took charge of Education. But Gladstone's second cabinet never enjoyed the camaraderie of his first administration. In 1868 no individual minister was in a position to challenge Gladstone's leadership. In 1880 too many anticipated promotion, once Gladstone was gone, for equanimity to prevail.

Despite surrendering the leadership to Gladstone Hartington headed a strong Whig presence in the Commons. A significant part of the Liberal electoral victory, particularly in the counties, was due to the renewed commitment of Whig landowners to the campaign. This was Hartington's achievement. After the election, of the total of 346 Liberal MPs, 41 were heirs, sons or brothers of peers, with a further 28 being baronets and 11 MPs being sons of baronets. Adding to these the 71 MPs who were great landowners or members of the gentry, a total 151 Liberal MPs belonged to the aristocratic or gentry landowning section of the party – just over 43 per cent of all Liberal MPs. This was a slight *increase* on the proportion of such MPs returned for the Liberal party in 1874. The number of industrial or business Liberals, 114 MPs in all, actually fell to just under 33 per cent of the Commons party.[19] The bulk of Liberal MPs in 1880 had no wish to see Gladstone abducted by the radicals. They looked to

226

Hartington to ensure Gladstone's safety. Hartington, meanwhile, faced the demands of two, often conflicting, roles. As heir
apparent to Gladstone he sought to maintain contact with all
sections of the party, a quiet continuation of his policies during
1878–9. At the same time, he had to act as leader of the Whigs,
making sure that Gladstone and the radicals did not take the
Liberal party off in dangerous directions. Reconciling these two
roles was Hartington's political dilemma after 1880.

The apparently confident, but inwardly insecure, Chamberlain had not assumed he would be given a cabinet post prior to
April 1880. Indeed, Dilke seemed to have better prospects.
Privately Chamberlain stated that if Hartington had headed
the ministry both he and Dilke would have been in the cabinet.
As it was, by giving Dilke a junior post and Chamberlain one of
the more humble cabinet appointments, both men were at once
muzzled by office yet denied pre-eminence. Gladstone had no
wish to appear in servitude to radicalism. Yet the organisational
resources of the NLF had undoubtedly made a contribution to
electoral success in 1880 and a position in cabinet gave encouragement to Chamberlain's well-proven ambition. He remained
aware of the resources provided by the NLF upon which he
might call. In cabinet discussion he subtly reminded ministerial
colleagues of the leverage this gave him. Most cabinet members
saw themselves acting as part of an executive body at some
distance from the party support which had placed them in
power. Derby noticed, however, Chamberlain's 'odd, peculiar
manner, of referring everything to the judgement of friends
outside, rather than giving an opinion of his own: as though
he considered himself in cabinet less as an adviser, than as the
representative of a party or section: which indeed is the case'.
This served to impress on colleagues his self-created role as
spokesman for Liberal activists in the country. Although at least
one former Liberal whip remembered that the 'structural defect
in the NLF' was that 'the Executive was at too great a distance
from its base'. But such a 'design . . . suited Mr. Chamberlain's
purposes'.[20]

Cabinet radicalism did not speak with one voice. It was not,
despite Chamberlain's claims, a united movement. Indeed,

radicals often directed their most intense animus against fellow radicals. Bright represented the moral free-trade traditions of the Manchester School. Forster's bid for the Commons leadership in 1874–5 had been scuttled by lingering resentments over Education and the hostility of Chamberlain's National Education League. Ireland, after 1880, was to strip Forster of all his credentials as a radical statesman. Meanwhile, in early 1880, Chamberlain was directing insinuations against Joseph Cowen, the independent-minded MP for Newcastle and critic of the Birmingham 'caucus' system. Similarly, another radical given a junior appointment by Gladstone, Mundella, had strained relations with Chamberlain and Dilke. The latter privately dismissed both Mundella and Fawcett as 'windbags'.[21]

Upon meeting parliament on 20 May 1880 Gladstone noted in his journal: 'It almost overpowered me as I thought by what deep and hidden agencies I have been brought back into the midst of the vortex of political action and contention.'[22] Ireland proved an immediate difficulty. But this was a topic to which Gladstone had given little attention during his Midlothian campaigns. As in previous Liberal governments, ministerial differences arose over the balance between coercive and conciliatory legislation. The traditional Whig view was that concessions were only safe if the rule of law and civil order prevailed. Property rights remained sacrosanct. Otherwise reforms merely encouraged lawlessness, mob politics and violence, while suggesting executive weakness. Hartington's willingness to see further land reform in Ireland was set in this context. Advanced Liberals, on the other hand, pushed for immediate conciliation to meet the mounting grievances of Irish nationalists. The violent tactics of Davitt's Land League and Parnell's deliberately ambiguous relations with the League, struck at the root of ministerial differences.

In the first instance Forster, as Irish Chief Secretary, proposed a hastily drawn up Compensation for Disturbances bill. This aimed to put a brake on evictions by penalising landlords for ejecting their tenants, even for non-payment of rent. Whig ministers objected strongly to the measure. Passed by the Commons, despite 20 Liberal MPs voting against the bill and a further 50 abstaining, it was forcefully rejected by the Lords; the majority of Liberal peers present opposing the measure and imposing a crushing defeat of 282 to 51 votes against the bill. Then, as the situation in Ireland rapidly worsened during 1880, the call for coercive legislation strengthened. Whereas in 1877 there were recorded 273 rural outrages, ranging from cattle maiming to murder, by 1880 there were 2,590 such incidents. Coercion was strongly opposed by Bright and Chamberlain, who enjoyed Gladstone's support. A fracture of the ministry threatened as Hartington's language hardened. The time was approaching, he warned, when further concession would be impossible; objections to the use of force by the authorities being sentimental and illogical.

During 1881 government policy uneasily combined coercion with concession. The Land League appeared to control large areas of the Irish countryside. Rural outrages continued to escalate. An Arms bill attempted to prevent the further distribution of weapons. Habeas Corpus was quickly suspended. The 1881 Coercion Act gave the Irish authorities powers to detain those suspected of treasonable practices without trial. Only a handful of radicals supported the resistance of Nationalist MPs to the measure. In October Parnell himself was arrested, along with two other Irish MPs, for breaches of the coercion legislation, and imprisoned in Kilmainham Gaol. Conciliation, meanwhile, was offered through the 1881 Land Act, which sought, through land courts, to implement fair rents. 'Fixity of tenure' for tenants was secured for fifteen years and the 'free sale' of an outgoing tenant's 'interest' in his holding protected. Forster successfully overcame Whig opposition to the measure during the committee stage, though a flood of litigation immediately clogged the workings of the Act. The Land League, meanwhile, campaigned against the delays and inefficiencies in implementing the measure.

Gladstone was profoundly troubled by his government's policy. The suspension of Habeas Corpus and suppression of freedom of the press offended his Liberal sensibilities. Parnell's imprisonment, moreover, he found an embarrassment. In early 1882 Gladstone encouraged Chamberlain, via the Irish MP

Capt. W. H. O'Shea, to enter into secret negotiation with Parnell. Initially Parnell had welcomed imprisonment. It made him a martyr in Nationalist eyes, while also conveniently distancing him from continuing Nationalist outrages. But by April 1882, for both personal and political reasons, Parnell wished to be released. His mistress, Kitty O'Shea, Capt. O'Shea's wife, was in the last stages of pregnancy with his child. He also feared his control of the Nationalist movement was being undermined by more extreme elements. In the so-called 'Kilmainham Treaty' Gladstone agreed to release Parnell from prison in return for the Irish leader undertaking to promote peace in Ireland. Parnell agreed to facilitate the workings of the Land Act and hinted at future support for the government, while the premier introduced an Arrears bill. This provided public money to pay off rent arrears, enabling tenants to make use of the land courts created by the 1881 Land Act. But the prospect of conciliation was swiftly and tragically dashed. Parnell's release on 2 May 1882 caused Forster to resign. On 6 May Lord Frederick Cavendish, the newly appointed Irish Chief Secretary, and T. H. Burke, the permanent Under-Secretary, were savagely attacked while walking across Phoenix Park in Dublin. Both men were slashed with surgical knives and their throats cut. As well as being Hartingon's younger brother, Cavendish had been Gladstone's private secretary and was married to Mrs Gladstone's niece. Private grief and public anger demanded further rigorous coercion. The passing of the subsequent Prevention of Crimes (Ireland) Act repaired Gladstone's relations with cabinet Whigs. Goschen rejoiced that a possible 'Gladstone–Parnell alliance' had been 'shattered'.[23] While for Gladstone himself Cavendish's murder was a personal blow from which he never fully recovered.

Ireland revealed one dimension to the tensions within Gladstone's cabinet. Colonial affairs and foreign policy produced another pattern of ministerial differences. During the Midlothian campaign Gladstone had forcefully denounced the moral evil of Disraeli's imperialism; but once in office he was constrained to work within formal agreements such as the Treaty of Berlin and the Cyprus Convention. Some modification to policy was possible by attending to the unfulfilled clauses of the Berlin Treaty. Goschen was sent on a special mission to Turkey to secure full implementation of the Treaty, which required Montenegro being given access to the sea, and the extension of Greece northwards. In contrast to Disraeli, Gladstone worked hard to act in concert with the other European powers and agreement was obtained to the remaining clauses of the Treaty. Goschen also pressed the Turks to reform the government of their Asiatic provinces. Equally importantly, however, Gladstone did not withdraw from British occupation of Cyprus, which he had strongly condemned in opposition. In the autumn of 1880 he did secure Britain's military withdrawal from Afghanistan. But events in South Africa brought on serious cabinet conflict. In February 1881 the Boers of the Transvaal inflicted a defeat on British troops at Majuba Hill. Hartington called for a military suppression of the Boer revolt. With considerable skill Gladstone succeeded in pursuing a more conciliatory policy, embodied in the Convention of Pretoria of August 1881. This granted the Transvaal independence under a general claim of British suzerainty.

No sooner was the South African crisis resolved than an emergency in Egypt brought Hartington and Chamberlain together in condemnation of Gladstone's instinct for non-intervention. A nationalist revolt led by Arabi Pasha prompted Hartington, Kimberley, and Northbrook (at the Admiralty) to call for military action to protect British commercial and strategic interests. Chamberlain supported intervention. From outside the cabinet Dilke also called for a robust response. A reluctant Gladstone was forced to acquiesce. On 14 July the Commons voted money to undertake the military occupation of Egypt and the protection of the Suez Canal. Alexandria was bombarded. Bright, remaining true to his Manchester School principles, resigned in protest. The split between Radical Imperialists such as Chamberlain and Dilke, on the one hand, and radical 'Little England' MPs such as Bright, John Morley, Henry Labouchere, and Sir Wilfrid Lawson, on the other, revealed deep divisions within radical ranks. These differences became more bitter as military operations in the Sudan against the Madhi ensued. The Egyptian crisis brought Hartington and Chamberlain together in opposition to Gladstone. While Irish issues aligned ministers in one pattern, Egypt produced an alternative orientation of frontbench opinion. The fervour of Midlothian quickly ran into the Egyptian sand.

Gladstone's vigour weakened under the heavy demands of being both prime minister and Chancellor of the Exchequer. His health broke down in 1880. Serious illness compounded the damage done by Gladstone's habitual reclusiveness from his parliamentary supporters during debate of the Irish Land bill. The backbench Whig William Cartwright, MP for Oxfordshire, complained in his journal:

> Unfortunately Gladstone holds no general intercourse with men in the House. He comes in from behind the Speaker's chair – sits on the Treasury bench – conferring with Bright or Forster – never going amongst the members generally – and what is still more deplorable, consulting at home with his own familiars. He acts on the impulse of his own consciousness and with intensified impulsiveness.[24]

In December 1881 Gladstone confessed he was 'quite unable to recover and extricate my mind from the cares of government and the state of Ireland in particular'. The personal tragedy of Lord Frederick Cavendish's murder five months later brought him close to collapse. From July to September 1882, showing signs of nervous exhaustion, the prime minister seemed a shadow of his former forceful self. During October and November Gladstone wrote repeatedly to Granville of his 'inability, inability of brain, to face the legislative work that must come on'.[25] On medical advice in January 1883 he went to Cannes, where he stayed until the beginning of March. Granville presided over the cabinet in the premier's absence. Cabinet reshuffles exacerbated a sense of instability. Argyll resigned from the front bench in May 1881 in protest at the Irish Land Act. Forster resigned in May 1882, while Bright followed suit in July. In December 1882 Gladstone passed the Exchequer over to Childers. Hartington replaced Childers at the War Office. Lord Derby was brought into the

Liberal cabinet to head the Colonial Office. Having abandoned Conservatism Derby appeared to new Liberal colleagues to have become a dutiful schoolboy to Gladstone's headmaster. Meanwhile Dilke, despite the Queen's objection to his republicanism, entered the cabinet as President of the Local Government Board. This new ministerial alignment discussed business, in the prime minister's absence during early 1883, in expectation of Gladstone's imminent retirement. This encouraged the ambitious, such as Chamberlain, to strike distinctive postures of their own.

Within parliament a deep sense of uncertainty prevailed. Ireland, mercifully, grew quieter as the Land Act and the Arrears Act soothed rural grievances. But no legislative centrepiece was brought forward by the cabinet around which to arrange government business in the 1883 session. Before leaving for France Gladstone had commented on the necessity for local government reform in Ireland. In subsequent correspondence with Granville he proposed a broad reform of local government in Britain and a parliamentary reform bill as major measures for the coming session. He added that, if either were announced in the Queen's Speech, the way would be clear for him to retire at Easter. In the event, the government proposed the reform of local government in London, while Hartington quashed any possibility of similar reforms in Ireland.

Once the 1883 session was under way much time was then taken up resolving the problem of Charles Bradlaugh. Repeatedly elected MP for Northampton, Bradlaugh, a republican and openly-declared atheist, refused to take the Commons oath containing the words 'so help me God'. In the face of staunch resistance from the opposition, the government attempted to amend the parliamentary oath. Between March and May the Commons timetable became hopelessly bogged down.

Meanwhile Gladstone, returning from France in March, did not retire, but entered into a dispute with Harcourt as the minister responsible for London local government reform. Harcourt refused to accept Gladstone's proposal that control of the police in the metropolis should be passed from the Home Secretary to the Municipality. As a result Harcourt, at the end of May, abandoned his bill; there being insufficient time to pass it that session.[26] The general impression grew that increasing parliamentary energy was being expended to diminishing legislative effect. The passage of the Corrupt and Illegal Practices Act did provide an effective measure against electoral corruption. Election expenditure was limited and the penalties for corrupt practices increased. The abolition of the old system of paid canvassers encouraged the organisation of volunteer support. None the less, Liberal backbench unease and a desire for firm leadership intensified.

Parliamentary malaise promoted ministerial rows. After June 1883 a new cabinet dispute broke out over parliamentary reform. In a speech at Birmingham on 13 June, Chamberlain called for a further extension of the franchise and other parliamentary reforms. Since January 1883 Francis Schnadhorst, secretary of the National Liberal Federation, had been advising Chamberlain to drop Irish local government and to go for parliamentary reform. In October Chamberlain drove the message home at the Leeds conference of the National Liberal Federation. In November this led to a clash between Chamberlain and Hartington, the former insisting the Irish must be included in a broader suffrage, the latter equally insistent on their exclusion. While Hartington stood as the heir apparent to Gladstone, equally Chamberlain saw the need and opportunity to assert radical policy. The uncertainties created by Gladstone's anticipated imminent retirement only encouraged such ministerial division.

Yet the very tensions created by the expectation of Gladstone's departure enabled the Grand Old Man to argue that he must reluctantly continue as leader in order to preserve Liberal unity. In 1880 Gladstone declared that the need to purge government of Beaconsfieldism was a special circumstance requiring his interim leadership. By late 1883 the need to see through a Liberal measure of parliamentary reform supported by both Whigs and radicals was cited as requiring the unforeseen continuation of his leadership. Gladstone's continuing claim on the Liberal leadership by 1883 depended on a persistent sense of emergency. Yet it was precisely the temporary nature of Gladstone's leadership that did much to foment divisions. Thus, while stating that he was mentally unequal to preparing any large and complex measure, Gladstone found ready justification for not stepping down. Reform, unlike Egypt, brought Hartington and Chamberlain to loggerheads and suggested a fundamental schism between Whigs and radicals within the Liberal party; a rupture only to be healed by Gladstone's unique authority. Liberal government was becoming an exercise in crisis management. The cabinet did not meet during most of August 1883 and during September Gladstone left, in the company of Tennyson, for a cruise in Scotland and Norway.

Then in cabinet, on 22 November 1883, a refreshed Gladstone provided firm direction on the reform issue, presented as the pressing question of the day. The franchise was to be equalised in counties and boroughs, in Ireland as well as the rest of the United Kingdom, while redistribution was to be deferred for attention later. While assimilating Chamberlain's desires, Gladstone reassured Whigs with the thought that a household county suffrage would not swell the ranks of borough radicalism, but rather create a rural counterpoise to dangerous urban forces. Carlingford, Selborne, and Northbrook were comforted. Hartington, however, remained unhappy. Some suspected the disruptive influence of Hartington's mistress, the Duchess of Manchester. In cabinet Hartington's observations were 'frequent, but generally more growls of dissent. He does not like his position, and makes the fact evident.'[27] The solace that Irish franchise reform would split Parnellite ranks failed to soothe Hartington. He threatened resignation. Reform was inappropriate to what Hartington pressed as the most urgent questions; the restoration of efficiency in the Commons and order in Ireland. Reform of the franchise was 'a rather lazy electioneering trick'.[28] Hartington saw it as an artificial creation got up by Gladstone and Chamberlain. Other moderate Liberals responded with the subversive thought that, without accompanying redistribution, the Lords might be relied upon to reject a franchise bill.

Gladstone's reform proposals of 22 November 1883, as intended, tamed Chamberlain and isolated Hartington. Despite continued protestations of his physical frailty, Gladstone forcefully reasserted his authority. Indeed, Gladstone's energy responded to the stimulation of crisis, his doctor concluding 'that excitement is indispensable to an old man's health'. Ministers submissively fell into line. Hartington did not resign. He behaved, Gladstone noted, 'extremely well'.[29] By the New Year Hartington had acquired from Gladstone an undertaking that the premier would indicate his preferences regarding redistribution when introducing the franchise bill to parliament. Hartington also came to fear that resigning would simply concede ground to Chamberlain. If a split was to occur, better that Chamberlain be prised away from Gladstone than Hartington abandon Gladstone to the radicals. Others meekly acquiesced in the firm Gladstonian course of franchise first and alone. Granville's natural geniality was reinforced by his advancing age and fatigue. Derby was anxious to demonstrate his new Liberal loyalties, while Carlingford and Selborne, conscious of their own modest talent, recognised their reliance on Gladstone's favour. At the Bristol conference of the National Liberal Federation on 26 November 1883 Chamberlain pronounced Gladstone's proposal as radical policy; suffrage reform without redistribution and including Ireland.

Gladstone pressed forward hard on the franchise question during the 1884 session. Possible rival claims to parliamentary attention, increasing difficulties in Egypt and Irish disorder, were played down. The government survived a Commons censure motion on its Egyptian policy on 19 February 1884 by 311 to 262 votes. The franchise measure was introduced by Gladstone on 29 February. Just as cabinet fractures had been carefully avoided during the preceding recess, so Commons opposition was assiduously minimised. The inclusion of Ireland helped neutralise the Parnellites, though Irish Nationalists were ambivalent about the prominence given to suffrage reform. While prepared to welcome it as an instalment towards self-government, Parnellites feared a wider franchise would increase anti-Irish sentiment in some English and Scottish constituencies, while increasing the cost and labour of electioneering in Ireland itself. A minority of moderate Liberals, flirting with the ingenious attractions of proportional representation, were appeased by hints of subsequent redistribution. From the back benches

Goschen, opposed to extending the county suffrage, pursued an independent line drawing the discredited Forster into his orbit. But franchise reform now seemed inevitable. At the same time, the enduring difficulties of the Conservative party leadership following Disraeli's death continued to inhibit the opposition. On 7 April the franchise bill passed its second Commons reading by 340 to 210 votes. By 20 June, as the measure approached its third Commons reading, Gladstone commended the Liberal rank and file for having shown 'great firmness of purpose'. Evil predictions had been falsified, no caves formed, crotchets had vanished, and small or critical divisions had been avoided.[30]

But on 8 July 1884 the Lords rejected the franchise bill; Lord Cairns's wrecking amendment securing 205 to 146 votes. Franchise reform, it was asserted, must be accompanied by a measure of redistribution. After parliament was prorogued on 14 August predictable positions were taken by each party, suggesting a clear polarisation of political sentiment. Liberals denounced the obstacle to the national will represented by the Upper House, while Conservatives decried Gladstone's impetuosity and recklessness. In tactical terms this undercut well-meaning or ambitious centrists such as Goschen, Lord Randolph Churchill, or Lord Wemyss. It also prepared the way for a 'very queer solution' of the crisis, once parliament reassembled in October 1884.[31] It was a solution which affirmed Gladstone's and Salisbury's ascendancy within their respective parties. In return for allowing the franchise bill – reintroduced in November – passage through the Lords, Salisbury met in private session with Gladstone and Dilke to draft a mutually acceptable redistribution measure. Though Hartington, Northcote, and Granville attended early meetings they were effectively side-lined. Thus, behind closed doors in Downing Street during November, Gladstone, Dilke, and Salisbury constructed a reform settlement. It was a solution that confirmed their own respective standing and compensated Conservatives for a wider suffrage with favourable adjustments to constituency boundaries. Parliamentary compliance swiftly followed.

Gladstone's franchise bill was given the royal assent on 6 December 1884 and a redistribution bill was granted the royal assent on 25 June 1885. Household suffrage became the uniform basis of the vote throughout the United Kingdom in both counties and boroughs, though some older county franchises survived. A sweeping redistribution of seats reshaped the old county divisions into single-member constituencies, Lancashire received 15 additional MPs, the West Riding 13 more MPs, Liverpool was divided into 9 single-member constituencies, and the representation of London constituencies increased from 22 to 62 MPs. The principle of relating parliamentary representation to population was acknowledged and two-thirds of adult males in England and Wales were given the vote. In Scotland approximately three-fifths and in Ireland one half of adult males enjoyed the vote after 1886. A total of over two million voters was added to the electorate, but 1884 did not deliver democracy. That had to wait until 1918 when all adult males and women over the age of 30 were enfranchised. But it was a significant step towards popular sovereignty.

The reform crises of 1832 and 1867 were largely played out in Westminster. In 1884 the settlement was largely decided in Downing Street. At one level this confirmed the increasing authority of the party leadership as the sovereignty of parliament gave way to an expanding party system. It affirmed the growing power of the executive, resting upon party support, and the diminishing role of ordinary MPs. In 1867 the character of reform emerged from the mêlée of Commons debate. In 1884 it was decided in conclave by Gladstone, Dilke, and Salisbury; their backbenchers reduced to a supporting cast dutifully endorsing the agreements of leading men. The resolution of the reform question in 1884 affirmed Gladstone and Salisbury's authority. Chamberlain was excluded from critical meetings in Downing Street during November 1884. Not only was he surprised by the agreements that emerged, he feared the electoral implications of single-member constituencies for the future. This, in turn, exacerbated his disagreements with other radicals. Hartington, similarly, played a peripheral part in crucial discussions during the autumn. On the Conservative side, Salisbury's authoritative role in Downing Street deliberations revealed Northcote, as Conservative leader in the Commons, to be a broken reed, and the audacious impetuosity of Lord Randolph Churchill to be an entertaining side-show. In 1884 it was the intentions of Gladstone and Salisbury that truly mattered.

The new electoral regime created by the legislation of 1884–5 suggested to many that they stood on the threshold of 'a new world'. As Derby anticipated, 'an unknown world, possibly a world which some of us will not care to explore'.[32] Gladstone and Salisbury between them may have largely decided the structure of that new electorate. But the strange and unfamiliar nature of what might lie ahead gave many pause for thought. Proven patterns of behaviour provided reassurance. In the first instance, during 1885, some politicians responded to the unknown by resorting to the familiar. In January 1885, having safely delivered franchise reform, Gladstone relapsed into talk of failing health and imminent retirement. As always, such statements stirred others, particularly Chamberlain, to action. It was assumed Granville, Derby, and Selborne would retire with Gladstone. Hartington remained Gladstone's obvious successor. This left the crucial question of future arrangements between Hartington, Chamberlain, and Dilke. All three believed a mutually acceptable arrangement possible. Harcourt and Dilke busied themselves as intermediaries negotiating the composition of a Hartington ministry.

Yet difficulties mounted in the following months. Conservative inaction emphasised ministerial differences. Childers warned of a £2 million deficit. Most dramatically, news was received in early February 1885 of General Gordon's death at Khartoum. An outburst of intense public anger was directed against Gladstone for supposedly abandoning Gordon to the Madhi; Wolseley's relief-force having arrived within days of the General's death. Once again Gladstone's physical resources rallied in the face of attack. In cabinet on 28 February Gladstone overrode the wishes of Granville, Hartington, Derby, Selborne, Spencer, Northbrook, Dilke, and initially, Chamberlain that the government resign. But the decay of the ministry continued to gain momentum.

Characteristically the impulsive Chamberlain responded to the uncertainties of early 1885 with a dramatic programmatic initiative. This reflected his conviction that, following 1884, the 'centre of power has been shifted, and the old order is giving place to the new'.[33] As early as May 1883 Chamberlain had discussed with John Morley their need for a broad radical programme. Between August 1883 and July 1885 a series of articles in the *Fortnightly Review*, overseen though not written by Chamberlain, laid out the basis of a 'new departure'. This Radical Programme combined traditional aims with some new elements in radical thinking. Church disestablishment remained essential, the disendowment of the Anglican Church releasing money for the provision of free education. New proposals included the introduction of graduated taxation on incomes, the more equal distribution of wealth being a benefit to the whole community. In a speech at Birmingham in January 1885 Chamberlain made it clear that such tax reform was directed primarily against the inequities of landownership. In provocative terms he described landownership as a form of robbery, denying the natural rights of men to the land of their birth. Such inflammatory language, though later tempered and promptly incurring a reprimand from Gladstone, signalled Chamberlain's strong sense of entering a brave new world. 'What ransom', he declared 'will property pay for the security it enjoys?'[34] Landed ministers such as Derby and Selborne were outraged.

This was Chamberlain's attempt to define debate in a new political landscape on issues of his own choosing. Chamberlain sought to dictate the terms of future party conflict; an election under the new dispensation of 1884–5 being a certainty in the near future. Through the *Fortnightly Review* Jesse Collings argued for the compulsory purchase of land to provide smallholdings for labourers. The slogan 'three acres and a cow' encapsulated a vision of independent yeomen reinforcing the assault on landlordism. In the cities this required additional powers for elective local authorities to clear slums and to fine landlords for misuse of property. Also implicit in Chamberlain's 'new departure' was a criticism of other radicals who more narrowly sought to identify advanced Liberalism with some hobby of their own. Radicalism, Chamberlain's collaborator T. H. S. Escott had written in the *Fortnightly Review*, was 'not so much represented as it is burlesqued' by radicals such as Sir Wilfrid Lawson, Joseph Cowen, Samuel Storey, or Henry Labouchere.[35]

Chamberlain hoped the Radical Programme he spearheaded in January 1885 would subsume narrow 'fads' within a broad radical assault on property and landlordism. He also hoped it might assimilate and thereby neutralise emergent socialist opinion. In 1881 H. M. Hyndman, Frederich Engels' friend and disciple, founded the Democratic Federation. In 1884 the Fabian Society was formed. As trade and industry descended into recession during 1885 the conditions for the spread of militant socialism among working men seemed favourable. 'Parasitic' landlords became the target of urban discontent. Chamberlain's attack offered an alternative to crude class revolution; although Chamberlain placed more emphasis on rural inequalities: a logical response to the extension of the household suffrage to the counties. Chamberlain's initiative generated much discussion in the press; but it failed to have any impact at cabinet level. The Sudan crisis in February 1885 and Russia in March and April occupied ministerial attentions.

Ireland, meanwhile, returned in April 1885 to dog the ailing Gladstone ministry. The question of whether to renew the Crimes Act sharply divided the cabinet. Gladstone stood aloof. Hartington felt strongly that Chamberlain and Dilke must agree to some form of renewal. Then, while momentarily laying his Radical Programme aside, Chamberlain brought forward a scheme of Irish devolution giving elective county boards greater local responsibilities, and a national council, a Central Board, responsibilities currently carried by the Dublin administration. This Central Board scheme split the cabinet. Chamberlain refused to support a renewal of the Crimes Act without it. It was, Chamberlain maintained, the only way of avoiding Home Rule. Gladstone initially supported the Central Board scheme as the 'only hope for Ireland', but undercut his advocacy by expressing his growing determination to retire. The premier's eyesight, voice, and hearing were failing. Spencer, as Lord Lieutenant of Ireland, forcefully opposed the plan. Hartington and a majority of the cabinet also rejected Chamberlain's scheme. By mid-May Chamberlain was expressing his eagerness to quit office. A majority of the cabinet, including Hartington and Dilke (who both offered to resign on 20 May), Harcourt, and Childers, came to share the wish to leave office. Hartington's gloom included weary talk of impending revolution – though by this he meant not socialist insurrection, but the capture of the Liberal party by Chamberlain and Dilke.

On 8 June 1885 the opposition moved a Commons amendment on the budget, condemning the proposed increase in duties on beer and spirits, which was carried by 264 to 252 votes; 62 Liberals were absent from the division, of whom only 14 were paired. In cabinet the following day the decision was quickly taken to resign. The budget defeat was both unexpected and, for most members of the government, timely. Only Gladstone of those around the cabinet table, it was noted, looked other than thankful. Release from office allowed Chamberlain, for one, to take up the opportunity of meeting the new electorate campaigning on a purely radical platform. The Conservative MP W. H. Smith observed that the out-going ministers 'all appear to be in roaring spirits at their escape from the intolerable position in which they found themselves'.[36]

'Elijah's Mantle'

Since April 1881 Conservatives had been grappling with the question of who should succeed Disraeli. Upon whose shoulders should 'Elijah's Mantle' fall? The 'Dual Control' of Northcote in the Commons and Salisbury in the Lords proved unsatisfactory, in large part because the arrangement emphasised Northcote's weaknesses. In 1876 Northcote had beaten Cranbrook to become Conservative leader in the Commons; but he seemed temperamentally incapable of forceful attack. As a young man in the 1840s Northcote had been Gladstone's private secretary. This, it was believed, inhibited his criticism of the Grand Old Man. Caution and an instinctive preference for conciliation gave the debilitating impression of timidity. As Derby observed in 1876: 'Northcote is safe, moderate, makes no enemies, and never discusses any subject of which he is not master'.[37] It was North-cote's achievement to give competence a bad name.

Northcote's flaws were ruthlessly exposed by the Conservative *enfant terrible* Lord Randolph Churchill. Between 1881 and 1885 Churchill, despite illness, achieved a dazzling rise to prominence characterised by audacious irreverence. Northcote was labelled 'the Goat', Gladstone 'the Moloch of Midlothian', and Chamberlain a 'Pinchbeck Robespierre'. Around him Churchill gathered a small group of fellow spirits. This so-called 'Fourth Party' included the elegant and cool A. J. Balfour, Salisbury's nephew, the disappointed and sour Sir John Gorst, Disraeli's party manager of the early 1870s; and the experienced, suave, and well-connected former diplomat, Sir Henry Drummond Wolff. They first came together over the Bradlaugh case in 1880, deriding Northcote's ambivalence and exacerbating Gladstone's predicament. Thereafter this subversive group lost no opportunity to portray Northcote as inept. With patrician disdain Churchill dismissed the middle class Conservative stalwarts R. A. Cross and W. H. Smith as 'Marshall and Snelgrove'. From 1880 to 1882 Churchill and his colleagues attacked the 'Old Gang's flaccidity', fit only for 'mere clogged opposition'; derision aimed at 'old men crooning over the fire at the Carlton Club'. The 'Old Gang' were a 'superannuated oligarchy'.[38] Churchill's youthful arrogance played arch insubordination as high art.

After a prolonged and serious illness from March to October 1882, Churchill returned to the parliamentary fray in 1883 with renewed impatience and urgency. As the mischievous schoolboy of Conservative politics, after October 1882 Churchill began a concerted broad assault on the party leadership, despite the death of his father in July 1883 temporarily forcing him back to Blenheim Palace. Relations with the press were carefully cultivated, particularly with Algernon Borthwick of the *Morning Post*, Thomas Chenery of *The Times*, and Thomas Gibson Bowles of *Vanity Fair*. In 1880 Churchill had mounted a speaking tour courting provincial audiences. In 1882 he returned with new vigour to the task of establishing a power base outside parliament. He talked of organising large popular meetings over the Egyptian issue: Gladstonian means to attack the Grand Old

Man's policies. The power base Churchill sought he found in disgruntled sections of the National Union of Conservative Associations. Aided by the aggrieved Gorst, Churchill began espousing the cause of 'Tory Democracy'. Always a nebulous concept, 'Tory Democracy' was presented by Churchill as the true legacy of Disraeli's flair, vision, and persistence. Pious invocations were blended with ridicule of Northcote's apathy. Maintenance of the constitution and anti-radicalism were combined with appeals to democracy. Imperial rule and social reform were the policies Conservatives must embrace. At the Birmingham conference of the National Union of Conservative and Constitutional Associations (NUCCA), in October 1883, the mercurial Churchill urged the party to regain the confidence of the working classes.

The year 1884 saw the climax of Churchill's campaign to wrest control away from the Conservative Central Committee and pass it to the National Union. Courting the voters of Birmingham he declared his intention to represent the intelligent, independent, and instructed mass of electors. Then in July 1884 Salisbury forcefully brought Churchill to heel. Salisbury agreed to abolish the Central Committee, in return for Sir Michael Hicks Beach, Disraeli's last Colonial Secretary and a thorough politician, being appointed chairman of the National Union Council, and official recognition being given to the rapidly growing Primrose League. Having established himself at the forefront of national politics Churchill's cry of 'Tory Democracy' had served its purpose. After July 1884, as Churchill again concentrated his attentions on party realignment at Westminster, provincial Conservatives fell away from his gaze. Some, having enthusiastically responded to his blandishments, nurtured a shoddy sense of having been used.

After 1880 Salisbury allowed Churchill to destroy Northcote's credibility. The 'Fourth Party' generally praised Salisbury, while disparaging 'the Goat'. As a result Salisbury, with his gloomy cynicism and fatalistic grandeur, found his ascendancy within the party affirmed. The reform episode of 1884, with Northcote marginalised and Churchill partially tamed, strengthened Salisbury's authority. By the beginning of 1885 Salisbury stood at the head of the party, recognising Churchill's erratic talents, yet deeply distrustful of his demagogic proclivities. Salisbury himself found public speaking an aggravation; although the daunting power of his intellect shone through such public statements as he made. By 1885 the Conservative succession struggle had been conclusively won by Salisbury. Salisbury and Churchill's success during 1884 highlighted the incapacity of their colleagues; incompetence being underlined or disguised by old age and illness. Cranbrook and Cairns were dying. Cross was sliding into decrepitude, while Manners and Richmond were looking towards quiet retirement. In December 1884 Churchill left for India, not to return to Westminster until April 1885. In his absence the disarray within Conservative ranks in the Commons increased. In February 1885 the rank and file, following a meeting at the Carlton Club, condemned Northcote's weak lead during the Khartoum debate. By March Northcote was unable to maintain control of Conservative votes on the Redistribution bill. Beach assumed Churchill's lead of backbench malcontents, 47 Conservative MPs defying Northcote's arrangements with Dilke. Another Carlton Club meeting on 16 March effectively ended Northcote's leadership of the Commons party. The following month Churchill returned to England. In the aftermath of Northcote's demise Churchill was clearly looking to play a creative part in the reformulation of Conservative policy.

All parties now prepared for the unknown electoral consequences of the 1884–5 legislation. Upon the Liberals' awkward resignation from office in early June 1885 Salisbury rather reluctantly formed a caretaker Conservative government. Like many Liberals, the Conservative 'Old Guard' preferred facing imminent electoral uncertainties unhampered by office. Salisbury himself became premier and Foreign Secretary. The enfeebled Northcote, elevated to the Lords as Earl of Iddesleigh, became First Lord of the Treasury. Churchill entered the cabinet heading the India Office, though Salisbury was careful not to give Churchill any say in the allocation of offices. Indeed, Salisbury hoped the India Office would isolate the bumptious Churchill and prevent him causing wider mischief. The middle-class party stalwarts Cross and W.H. Smith took the Home Office and War Office respectively. Hicks Beach, seen as Northcote's natural successor, became Chancellor of the Exchequer and Carnarvon Lord Lieutenant of Ireland.

Carnarvon was eager to restore good feeling in Ireland. By September he was describing militant Ulster Unionists, the Orangemen, as 'demented'.[39] Yet beyond reconciling the Catholic hierarchy to his education policy, Carnarvon had no specific programme. Sir William Hart Dyke, as Chief Secretary for Ireland, but not a member of the cabinet, was seen as a compliant and reliable partner for Carnarvon. From June 1885 to the end of the year Salisbury's government avoided commitment, seeking to keep options open in the face of an unknown future. In August 1885 Parnell came away from a private conversation with Carnarvon with the impression that a Conservative Home Rule bill was not out of the question. In return for Irish Commons support the Conservative cabinet agreed not to renew the Crimes Act. But in cabinet meetings on 14 and 15 December Salisbury's government decided to do nothing and say nothing further about Irish policy. Gladstone's sounding out of Balfour as to a bipartisan settlement of Irish grievances was resoundingly snubbed by Salisbury. Churchill played his usual game of brinkmanship with skill, holding both the Orange Unionist and Green Nationalist cards in his hand. In late 1885 an extraordinary fluidity prevailed over the political scene.

The Home Rule Crisis, 1886

What was clear during 1885 was that Irish Home Rule MPs held a pivotal position in parliamentary politics. Salisbury's caretaker government was in a minority in the Commons. Parnell's 60 Home Rule MPs, helped by Liberal divisions, held the balance of power. Yet the ambiguities that surrounded Parnell's leadership of Irish nationalist opinion remained. When Parnell called for Home Rule what precisely did it mean? What was the relationship between popular insurrection and the constitutional struggle? Throughout his career Parnell stood astride these ambiguities, shifting his weight and exploiting vagueness to extract maximum political advantage. Gladstone's principal private secretary, while noting Gladstone's continuing faith in Parnell, believed the Irish leader to be 'as slippery as an eel and cunning as a serpent'.[40] In October 1882 the Irish National League was formed, replacing the Land League, providing Parnell with a powerful well-organised popular base linking rural agitation with the disciplined Parnellite parliamentary party. The 1884 Reform Act increased the Irish electorate from 4.5 per cent to 16 per cent of the total population. Redistribution reduced Irish borough representation. By 1885 Parnell was convinced that a broader, more rural Irish electorate was moving decidedly behind Home Rule.

The uncertainties of late 1885 encouraged some English politicians to be imaginative. Already, in May, Chamberlain had floated his Central Board scheme; a proposal which O'Shea encouraged him to believe Parnellites would accept and which Gladstone had privately endorsed. After June 1885 Carnarvon produced a Land Purchase measure, the so-called Ashbourne Act, and an Intermediate Education Act. This showed that Conservatives too could be conciliatory, particularly such Conservatives as the irrepressible Churchill who knew Ireland well. In the autumn of 1885 Churchill recognised in the question of Ireland the opportunity to reconfigure British party alignment. Private conversations between Parnellites and others, as well as fevered rumours of various *sub rosa* negotiations, flourished. Some Liberal MPs claimed to have witnessed Parnell and the Conservative Chief Whip, Rowland Winn, deep in conversation in June. Likewise Churchill was glimpsed privately engaging in intense discussion with Parnellite MPs. It is impossible for historians now to recover the extent, significance, or nature of many of these secretive conversations. What is important is that they emphasised the fluidity of the political situation. Awareness of the dramatic course events actually took in 1886 should not obscure the wide range of creative opportunities that, prior to commitment, presented themselves.

Gladstone's thinking, like others', was shaped by the firm expectation that the next election would increase Parnellite strength in the Commons. In November 1885 parliament was dissolved and a general election called under the terms of the 1884–5 Franchise and Redistribution Acts. Polling occurred between 24 November and 9 December 1885. It returned a new Commons of 335 Liberal, 249 Conservative, and 86 Home Rule MPs. The parliamentary arithmetic was close and crucial. The numerous Parnellites held the critical balance of power. The number of Liberal Commons votes was exactly matched by Conservatives and Irish Nationalists combined. This opened up new strategic possibilities as much as closing off options; particularly as during the election the Irish National League, on 21 November, and Parnell in subsequent speeches, had called on Irish electors to vote against the Liberal party. This forcefully established Parnellite independence of both the Liberals and Conservatives.

Chamberlain's attempt, moreover, to impose a radical agenda on the Liberal party during the election failed woefully. In September 1885 Chamberlain launched what critics dubbed his 'Unauthorised Programme', three issues being selected from his Radical Programme of earlier in the year: free education, graduated taxation, and compulsory powers for local authorities to purchase land to provide allotments and smallholdings. Whigs and moderate Liberals swiftly moved behind Gladstone to oppose such radical reforms. Many radicals also proved either indifferent or hostile to Chamberlain's programme. They saw 'socialistic' tendencies in Chamberlain's wish to extend state regulation, while many Nonconformists feared that Chamberlain's plans for free education, without the accompaniment of disestablishment, would actually strengthen the position of the Church of England. The election revealed Chamberlain's isolation. Tensions between Liberals were taken by Gladstone as conclusive proof of the indispensability of his leadership.

Liberal attentions focused on Ireland. By early August 1885 Gladstone was persuaded that Chamberlain's Central Board scheme was an inadequate response to Irish nationalist grievances. Indirect communication with Parnell, through Kitty

O'Shea, confirmed that the Central Board proposal was no longer acceptable to Home Rulers. During August, seriously ill with a throat infection, Gladstone convalesced on a cruise to the Norwegian fjords; taking advantage of the withdrawal from London to ponder more fundamental responses to Irish grievances. By September, having returned to England, Gladstone was coming to believe that Pitt's Act of Union had been 'a gigantic though excusable mistake'.[41] In mid-November he received from Parnell, via Kitty O'Shea, a 'Proposed Constitution' outlining a form of Irish self-government. Gladstone immediately drafted a secret memorandum sketching out his own Home Rule scheme. It proposed a separate Dublin parliament to deal with all Irish, as opposed to Imperial, affairs. Irish representation in both Houses at Westminster was to remain for Imperial subjects only. There were to be unspecified provisions to secure minority views in the Irish parliament through nominations and proportionate representation. Officers of state and civil functionaries in Ireland were to cease to be under British authority. Yet Gladstone's public election pamphlet made no mention of Home Rule, raising only those issues upon which it was known Liberals were agreed. Then, on 17 December 1885, in the so-called 'Harwarden Kite', Gladstone's youngest son Herbert leaked to the press notice of his father's intention to endorse Home Rule. This dramatic announcement immediately overshadowed Chamberlain's 'Unauthorised programme'. It also drew the Parnellites back towards the Liberals, although Gladstone continued to avoid any official pronouncement.

The recovery of a possible Liberal–Parnellite alliance was reinforced by Conservative backbench calls for coercive legislation to restore law and order in Ireland. In his own election address Churchill had avoided any mention of Ireland at all. Instead, he concentrated his invective on Hartington, as the embodiment of moderate opinion, denouncing his 'disreputable evasion, stammerings and stutterings, and haltings and hesitations'.[42] While taunting the Whigs, Churchill portrayed the Chamberlainite radicals as straightforward and honest men. On 26 January 1886, following defeat on an amendment to the Address moved by Jesse Collings, Salisbury's government resigned. The Queen was distraught at the thought of recalling Gladstone, whom she called 'a half-mad and really in many ways a ridiculous old man'.[43] Some anticipated a Hartington ministry. Nevertheless, on 1 February 1886 Gladstone formed his third administration, committed, he declared, to examination of the union with Ireland. There was still, at this stage, no official public declaration of commitment to Home Rule.

Thereafter the 76-year-old Gladstone's handling of Home Rule formed the central axis of the 1886 session, around which other Liberals, radicals, and Conservatives manoeuvred. In the process the Liberal party suffered a cataclysmic and irreparable split. Alarmed by the 'Harwarden Kite' Hartington refused to join Gladstone's third cabinet, although, during January 1886, he played with the idea of making Ireland 'a subject province'. While not conceding Home Rule this proposal had the advantage of removing troublesome Irish Nationalist MPs from Westminster. Other leading Liberals, mostly Whigs, followed Hartington's lead. Lords Selborne, Carlingford and Northbrook associated themselves with Hartington, while Derby and Goschen also declined office. Similarly Lord Richard Grosvenor made his Unionist feelings apparent. Likewise Bright rejected Gladstone's move towards Home Rule as an immoral surrender to violence.

Chamberlain did accept cabinet office, as President of the Local Government Board, but only after being assured that an enquiry into Irish affairs would precede any ministerial commitment to Home Rule. In fact no subsequent enquiry took place. Should Gladstone commit himself to Home Rule, Chamberlain anticipated that a majority of Liberals would desert the premier. At the same time Chamberlain was talking of Churchill as a man he could work with. As a cabinet minister Chamberlain continued to confide in Churchill, their intimacy becoming the subject of journalistic comment. Gladstone, for his part, found Chamberlain wanting in straightforwardness and not to be trusted. Chamberlain's radical colleague John Morley, who was open to Home Rule legislation, became Chief Secretary for Ireland. Morley's inexperience, it was supposed, would render him a compliant partner in Irish policy, which would remain very much in Gladstone's hands. The radical G. O. Trevelyan took the Scottish Office. But involvement in the scandal breaking over the Crawford divorce case made it impossible for Chamberlain's colleague, Dilke, to be appointed to the cabinet.

The loyal Gladstonians Granville, Spencer (a staunch Home Ruler), Childers, Rosebery, and Kimberley provided weight to the Liberal front bench, as did Lord Ripon, the first and only Catholic to sit in a Liberal cabinet. Harcourt took the Chancellorship of the Exchequer where he became an apostle of economy. Henry Campbell Bannerman became War Secretary and A. J. Mundella took the Board of Trade. But the 'Harwarden Kite' ensured that Gladstone's third cabinet was very different from that which had resigned just seven months before. Hartington, Dilke, and Goschen were serious losses to the Liberal front bench, Granville was now old, haggard, and widely regarded as past serious exertion, while Gladstone had considerable difficulty in filling the Royal Household appointments.

During March 1886 Gladstone pushed forward in cabinet on two Irish reforms – the 'Siamese twinship' as he called it.[44] The first was a plan to modify the land purchase scheme established by Carnarvon, the second, a proposal creating a separate Irish legislature in Dublin. Gladstone hoped that land purchase reform would secure the continued support of important ministerial Whigs, such as Spencer, while the precise form of Home Rule to be adopted by the government was to be left unspecified, for the moment. But in cabinet, on 13 March, Chamberlain forced a confrontation with the prime minister which led Gladstone to declare his clear intention to legislate for a separate Irish parliament. At this both Chamberlain and Trevelyan resigned from the government. The premier did not try to persuade Chamberlain to remain. When Gladstone introduced his Home Rule bill into the Commons on 8 April both Hartington and Chamberlain joined the Conservatives in attacking the scheme. The Commons atmosphere was electric as Gladstone spoke for three and a half hours in a *tour de force* which was loudly cheered by his own backbenchers. The Conservative benches pointedly cheered Hartington and Goschen.

The fracture of the Liberal party was now inevitable. The bill contained no provision for the Protestant Unionists in Ulster. Irish MPs were no longer to sit at Westminster: a clause mainly brought about by pressure from John Morley. The bill, therefore, differed in important ways from Gladstone's private Home Rule sketch of November 1885. Additional earlier safeguards removed from the 1886 bill included the doing away with any nominated Dublin members. Instead, there were to be two categories of Irish representatives, both elected, one based upon a household suffrage and the other on a propertied franchise, while areas such as defence, foreign policy, trade regulation, currency, and the Post Office were to be excluded from the control of the new Dublin assembly. One important final aspect of the bill was that the Irish legislature would pay Westminster an annual sum, approximately £4,500,000 million, to service the Irish share of the national debt and to contribute to defence expenditure. On 7 June Gladstone's Home Rule bill was defeated on its second Commons reading by 341 to 311 votes; a defeat Gladstone recorded in his diary as 'a serious mischief'.[45] Every Liberal waverer followed Hartington. A total of 93 Liberals, including Hartington, Chamberlain, and Bright, voted alongside the Conservatives to throw out the bill. Gladstone promptly called an election, inviting the country to decide the destiny of Ireland. To resign, he told the cabinet, would be to abandon the great cause to which they were now committed.

While Gladstone was fracturing the Liberal party over his rush into Home Rule, both Salisbury and Churchill embraced the cause of Protestant Ulster Unionism. Since early 1885 Ulster Unionist opinion had been solidifying, its public rhetoric becoming more fevered. On 30 December 1885 Unionist leaders called for armed resistance to Home Rule and predicted a violent civil war should the Liberals yield to Parnell. In January 1886 Churchill took up Protestant feeling in Ulster and Lancashire. In London on 13 February, talking of Protestants rather than loyalists or Unionists, Churchill declared that England could not abandon the Protestants of Ireland. Home Rule, he asserted, meant the bitter and terrible oppression of Protestants by Catholics. The political temperature was raised further when

Salisbury, on 17 February, stated that Irish Protestants were threatened with 'absolute slavery' under Parnell.

Churchill's arrival in Belfast during February raised Ulster passions to hysterical levels. He recalled the dark tragedies of 1641, talked of Parnellite dictatorship, and declared that Ulster should remember its historical cry of 'no surrender'. Resistance to Home Rule, Churchill suggested, could go beyond constitutional action. Gladstone responded that no man in a responsible position had done a wickeder act than when Churchill advocated a breach of the law in Ulster. Forsaking his former flexibility, in February 1886 Churchill became Ulster's implacable champion. Unionist demonstrations culminated in Protestant riots in June 1886. A secret Unionist army was formed and rumours spread of some British army officers defecting, in the event of Home Rule, to fight alongside Ulster Protestants. In a public letter on 7 May Churchill coined the phrase 'Ulster will fight. Ulster will be right.' On 15 May Salisbury delivered a major staunchly Unionist speech to the National Union of Conservative Associations. This ruthlessly undercut any moderate ground upon which others, such as Hartington, might attempt to stand. As over reform in 1884, so with Home Rule in 1886, Gladstone and Salisbury polarised opinion and smothered centrist options. At the same time, Churchill's implacable Unionism made him, for all practical purposes, Conservative leader in the Commons.

The general election of July 1886 produced a decisive rejection of Home Rule, though no one party had an overall Commons majority. Gladstone called the election result 'a smash', but accepted it as 'the Will of God'. Chamberlain founded the National Radical Union. Hartington formed the Liberal Unionist Association which benefited from electoral pacts negotiated with Conservatives. Gladstone's Commons support shrank to 191 Liberal MPs; anti-Home Rule Liberals, or Liberal Unionists, won 78 seats. The Conservatives returned 316 MPs; Parnell retained 85 seats. On 20 July Gladstone's government resigned and five days later Salisbury formed his second Conservative government firmly committed to preservation of the Union. The Liberal party, meanwhile, remained irrevocably split. Having fought the election on an anti-Home Rule platform, Hartington, Chamberlain, and other Liberal Unionists prepared to support Salisbury's defence of the Union. Gladstone rallied his supporters round the single transcendent cry of self-government for Ireland. This schism shattered the Liberal party and ushered in a period of Conservative Unionist dominance.

From 1886 to 1905, with the exception of 1892–5, Conservatives continuously held office. From 1886 to 1892 Salisbury, as premier, relied on Liberal Unionist support. Indeed, in January 1887 the Liberal Unionist Goschen became Chancellor of the Exchequer in Salisbury's cabinet. In 1887 efforts by Chamberlain and Trevelyan to reunite their Unionist supporters with the Gladstonian Liberal party, through a series of 'round table' meetings, failed. In 1889 Chamberlain facilitated the merger of his supporters with Hartington's followers by renaming his organisation the National Liberal Union. After Hartington succeeded his father as eighth Duke of Devonshire, in 1891, and took his seat in the Lords, Chamberlain became Liberal Unionist leader in the Commons. At the 1892 general election 47 Liberal Unionist MPs were returned, and, following the failure of Gladstone's second Home Rule bill in 1893, they moved towards even closer collaboration with the Conservative party. In the election of 1895, 70 Liberal Unionist MPs were returned and both Chamberlain and the Duke of Devonshire joined Salisbury's Conservative government. Thus, within ten years of the Home Rule crisis, Liberal Unionists were, for most practical purposes, absorbed into the Conservative party, although a distinct organisation and political fund survived until 1912.

The year 1886 stands alongside 1846 as a moment of dramatic reconfiguration in British party politics. The extraordinary events of 1886, therefore, have long fascinated historians. In particular, historical examination has focused on the inscrutability of Gladstone's precise intentions. In the monumental 1938 study *Gladstone and the Irish Nation*, by J. L. Hammond, Gladstone's conversion to Home Rule is set in the context of his life-long search for justice for Ireland. The mature Gladstone's dedication to freedom, which raised him above the pettiness of his contemporaries, created a golden opportunity to resolve the

Irish question; which would have been a fitting memorial to his Liberal vision and moral grandeur. The development of Gladstone's thinking is, for Hammond, unproblematic and linear. Having sought a religious solution to the Irish question, by disestablishing the Irish Church in 1869, and an economic solution, through the Irish Land Acts of 1870 and 1881, Gladstone perceived, by the autumn of 1885, that Irish grievances could only be answered by a far-reaching political settlement – what Gladstone described to Rosebery in November 1885 as 'a mighty heave in the body politic'.[46] But the bigotry and narrow self-interest of opponents ensured the rejection of his Home Rule bill in 1886. For Donald Southgate, in his 1962 study of Whiggism, *The Passing of the Whigs, 1832–1886*, the Home Rule crisis proved the climactic moment when the powerful tensions between Whig traditions and Gladstone's radicalism finally tore apart the Victorian Liberal party. This set 1886 in the context of deeper, underlying forces and the inability of Liberals to continue to reconcile radical challenges to the rights of property with a Whig tradition based on the power of the landed class.

Then, in 1974, A. B. Cooke and John Vincent published their scintillating and provocative analysis *The Governing Passion: Cabinet Government and Party Politics, 1885–6*. This 'high politics' study set Gladstone's approach to Home Rule in the immediate and intimate context of parliamentary politics. Cooke and Vincent presented 1886 as a juncture of great political fluidity. In the uncertain aftermath of 1884, the strategic possibilities for the talented and ambitious were enormous. This brought the competing aspirations of leading figures to the fore. Gladstone's charisma, they argued, has obscured the degree to which his views were unexceptional and, until late in the day, unformed. Gladstone did not enter upon Home Rule in a state of incandescence. Rather, he sought to keep options open, eventually coming to see in Home Rule a way of preserving the Liberal party in his own image, while also purging it of those distasteful elements which subverted the Gladstonian politics of moral passion. In particular, it drove out Chamberlain and his radical brand of creeping municipal socialism. Hartington's going also removed Whiggish caution as a brake on the momentum of Gladstone's reforming zeal. Salisbury, meanwhile, also with options before him until early 1886, deliberately polarised opinion by playing to Unionist emotions. This staked out a broad ground upon which to marginalise Gladstone, stifle proto-socialist radicalism, and force penitent Liberal Unionists into the Tory fold. In the tactical intricacies of 1886 Cooke and Vincent found competing ambiguities, skilfully exploited by astute political minds, where Hammond had seen moral certainty plough-ing through narrow prejudice and historical error.

The historian D. A. Hamer, in *Liberal Politics in the Age of Gladstone and Rosebery* (1972), also took a more strategic view of Gladstone's commitment to Home Rule, seeing it as a charac-teristic response by Gladstone to the dangerous centrifugal forces of Liberal sectionalism. Home Rule provided a single great unifying issue binding the party together, just as Irish disestabl-ishment in 1868–9 and Beaconsfieldism in 1879–80 had done. More recently, in 1988, W. C. Lubenow's study *Parliamentary Politics and the Home Rule Crisis* helpfully puts 1886 Commons division voting under detailed statistical scrutiny. Such statistical analysis more easily disproves theories, showing what was *not* happening, than it readily explains why politicians acted as they did. But Lubenow shows that different social backgrounds had little to do with the policy preferences of MPs; 1886 was not a conflict of different economic interests, nor a conflict between social classes, nor a clash between urban and rural communities, nor the product of constituency influence over MPs. Home Rulers and Unionists both represented a variety of types of constituency, though region and organisation were factors. Nor was the Liberal schism a split between experienced moderates and radical newcomers to Westminster. Lubenow shows that, while the Conservative and Irish Nationalist parties were largely cohesive parliamentary groups, the Liberal party was far less so, with Liberal dissent usually assuming the form of radical re-bellions. The schism over Home Rule, however, was largely a centrist revolt, with some radicals following Chamberlain. It did not follow the normal dimensions of Liberal party voting. In other words, Home Rule fractured Liberal votes in a different and far more damaging way than differences over other issues. Home Rule was *not* simply the dramatic eruption of those internal Liberal tensions present over most policy.

Perhaps most importantly, H. C. G. Matthew's magisterial edition of *Gladstone's Diaries* now provides us with Gladstone's own record. Matthew argues that Home Rule did not involve for Gladstone, in his own mind, a sudden conversion. Rather, it represented the culmination of a long consideration of Ireland's troubles. From 1868 to 1886 it was Gladstone's consistent mission to pacify Ireland. Nor did Gladstone in 1885–6 experience any private crises, such as accompanied traumatic political junctures earlier in his career. Home Rule was a natural outcome of the Liberal desire for decentralisation, combining nationalism with efficient devolved government. Moreover, it promised to resolve an issue whose presence in British politics had, in various ways, corrupted the ideal of a liberal state. Obstructive Irish tactics in Westminster had forced the installation of closure motions curtailing Commons debate; a necessary, but undesirable, restraint on free rational debate; while Fenian violence, both in Ireland and through bombing campaigns on the English mainland, had required the introduction of security measures antithetical to liberal ideals of individual freedom. By 1885–6 Gladstone sought a resolution of the Irish question whereby land reform and Irish autonomy in Irish affairs would restore social order according to the norms of liberal civil society. T. A. Jenkins's important study *Gladstone, Whiggery and the Liberal Party, 1874–1886* (1988) also argues for Gladstone's consistent commitment to a Home Rule policy already formed by November 1885, played upon, but not deflected by, the strategic complexities of 1886.

It is now possible, therefore, to understand Gladstone's actions during 1885–6 in a way which balances his general ideological commitment to Home Rule with the tactical intricacies of the parliamentary situation during this critical period. If Liberal principles explain how Gladstone was able to embrace the idea of Home Rule, it was immediate political circumstances that determined the manner and moment when that conviction was acted upon. Clearly, by June 1885, Liberals were at a stalemate with regard to Irish policy. Chamberlain's Central Board scheme was a dead letter. The anticipation of increased Parnellite strength in the next parliament emphasised the need for a new, more far-reaching solution. Repeal of the Union was now insufficient. A large constructive measure was called for. This crisis, moreover, was seen by Gladstone as precisely one of those great problems in national life which required his continued presence at the forefront of politics. Retirement, in such circumstances, was unthinkable. By September 1885 Gladstone was privately convinced that Home Rule was both necessary and desirable. His Liberal beliefs reinforced the need for a large constitutional settlement restoring social order in Ireland and removing the cancer of the Irish question from the British body politic. On 1 November Gladstone privately learnt from Parnell, through Parnell's 'Proposed Constitution', what Irish Nationalists looked to from Home Rule. On 14 November, as we have seen, Gladstone sketched out his own Home Rule scheme. Though in detail it differed from Parnell's outline, it covered many of the same headings the Irish leader had used.

But political circumstances, Gladstone judged, did not recommend he make public his private views on Ireland. The Liberal party, he recognised, was not ready for Home Rule. A process of education would have to occur. Moreover, he believed it was, in the first instance, the responsibility of Salisbury's government to attempt a solution of the Irish difficulty. It was these considerations that governed Gladstone's public actions from November 1885 to January 1886. Gladstone prepared during August an election manifesto that avoided any commitment to Home Rule. Instead, it focused on reform of parliamentary procedure, land law, electoral registration, and local government. These were issues on which Liberals could agree. At the same time, Gladstone watched to see if the Salisbury cabinet, in negotiation with Parnell, would propose a Conservative settlement for Ireland. In 1829, 1846, and 1867, over Catholic Emancipation, Corn Law repeal, and parliamentary reform, Conservative governments had resolved issues which reformers had not been able to settle. But Salisbury was no Peel or Disraeli. Conservative inactivity belatedly gave way to a commitment to the Union. This, after the 'Harwarden Kite' on 17 December, revived the Liberal–Parnellite alliance. Though Gladstone did not collude in his son's revelation, neither was he alarmed by the sensational leak. It eclipsed Chamberlain's 'socialistic' radical programme. But it also, less happily, drove Hartington from the fold. Now the speed of events was accelerating. Gladstone could no longer sustain a public reticence and hope for the luxury of time with which to bring nervous Liberals along with him.

From January 1886 onward it was Gladstone who forced the pace; particularly once it was clear that Hartington and other Whigs were not willing to join him in office. If forcefully pressing ahead also meant Chamberlain jumped ship then this might be regarded as a benefit. Having formed his government on the basis that it was going merely to examine the question of Home Rule, Gladstone withdrew to the relative seclusion of Rosebery's Buckinghamshire house, Mentmore, to draft a Home Rule bill. Thoughts of allowing a period to educate the party and the country, through Commons statements and extra-parliamentary speaking campaigns, were pushed aside. The situation required 'action at a stroke'. The Canadian Government Act of 1867, granting self-government to British North America, provided an historical model for Irish legislation. From his reading of eighteenth-century Irish history during this period Gladstone deduced that Protestantism was not inimical to Irish nationalism. Parnell himself was a Protestant, albeit of a vehemently anti-English kind. This encouraged the premier to ignore the problem of Ulster Unionism. His righteous sense of mission was, by March 1886, also prompting him to ignore the problem of entrenched opposition in the House of Lords. Liberal Unionists were, he declared, dangerous 'separatists' in a two-fold sense. First, they were separatists from the Liberal party. Secondly, by opposing Home Rule, they were inflaming Nationalist desires for a more radical separation of Ireland from Great Britain. Englishmen faced, he told the Commons in April 1886, 'one of those golden moments of our history; one of those opportunities which may come and may go, but which rarely return. . .'.

Gladstone's sense of destiny was sincere and profound. Historians can debate to what extent it was self-induced. But many among subsequent generations of British politicians have looked back on 1886 as a lost golden opportunity. Gladstone preferred to talk of 'local autonomy' rather than Home Rule and perceived his policy as reconciliatory rather than separatist. It was sound Peelite practice to pursue legislative redress for proven and legitimate grievances. Did Gladstone offer up an answer to the Irish question in April 1886? If so, how was one to reconcile increasingly militant Ulster Unionists and entrenched English opposition to Irish self-government? Hartington denounced Gladstone's Home Rule bill for removing Irish representation from Westminster, while still subjecting the Irish people to taxation for Imperial purposes; taxation without representation. Hartington believed that Gladstone's scheme was, despite the premier's insistence, just a stepping-stone to the complete independence of Ireland from Britain. Many agreed with Hartington. Conservatives and Chamberlain attacked Gladstone for precipitating the break-up of the Empire.

What was clear was that in 1886 Gladstone split the Liberal party asunder. Also, the Irish question now became locked into the rigid alignments of Home Rule versus Unionism. The fluidity that had prevailed in late 1885 was gone. Parnell had succeeded in committing a major British political party to Irish self-government. But likewise the Parnellites were now firmly committed to a Liberal alliance. After 1886, as in 1829 and 1868, Ireland's future became the touchstone of British party connection.

Gladstone's Legacy

Gladstone always generated powerful and contradictory responses. For opponents he was an impulsive and reckless demagogue who, as 'an old man in a hurry', did irreparable damage to the fabric of British society. For supporters he personified a Liberal moral vision that inspired their historic struggle against injustice and vested self-interest. During his brief fourth premiership, from 1892 to 1894, Gladstone again sought Home Rule for Ireland. When this was defeated by the Lords, reform of the

Upper House was added to Irish Home Rule as one of the crucial questions of the day. His eventual retirement from politics in March 1894 left the Liberal party confused and demoralised. Liberal Imperialists, mainly younger Anglican or Wesleyan upper middle-class Liberals such as H.H. Asquith, R.B. Haldane, and Edward Grey, moved toward collectivist social reforms combined with an Imperialist foreign policy; while advocates of 'New Liberalism' merged collectivist reforms and social analysis couched in organic metaphors, as elaborated in the writings of J.A. Hobson and L.T. Hobhouse, with anti-Imperialist policies abroad. This 'New Liberalism' established connections with Fabian Socialists and the new Independent Labour Party. Elements of German philosophy were brought to bear on the social problems caused by economic recession. The problem of 'poverty' was discovered and a more extended role for the state proposed. All this was doctrinal territory far removed from the individualist, devolved minimal state espoused by Gladstone.

The sheer scale and complexity of Gladstone's achievement has defied consensus among historians. In his best-selling official three-volume *Life of Gladstone*, published in 1903, John Morley portrayed the power of Gladstone's personality in bringing a scrupulous, tenacious, idealistic, and missionary gaze, his piercing falcon's eye, on the great issues of his day. Gladstone 'had in his soul a vision high in the heavens of the flash of an uplifted sword and the gleam of the arm of the avenging angel'.[47] Morley chronicled Gladstone's march towards the luminous ends of freedom and justice, although, as a self-confessed agnostic, Morley's portrait was one in which secular ideals overshadowed religious conviction. In 1954 Phillip Magnus produced a widely-read biography of Gladstone in which religious faith was restored. But the relation between Gladstone's devotion to the will of God and his political behaviour remained problematic. How did Gladstone discern a virtuous path through the intricate ambiguities of practical action. During the 1960s and 1970s the work of historians of Victorian 'high politics', such as Maurice Cowling and John Vincent, plunged Gladstone's missionary charisma into the darker depths of political manoeuvre.

Transcendent issues became the product of immediate political circumstances; ambiguity the deliberate instrument of political advantage. This suggested an elusive relation between conviction, vision, and the tactical which was more complex than Morley and Magnus had suggested. As Gladstone himself confessed, at the close of his diary in December 1896, it was 'nearly impossible' to write honestly on 'interior matters'.

The publication of *Gladstone's Diaries*, between 1968 and 1995, has confirmed the close interconnection between Gladstone's turbulent emotions, religious struggles, and political exertions. His extraordinary energy, stamina, and diligence mark every page of his private journal. Through Matthew's invaluable introductions, Gladstone emerges as a man constantly balancing the conflicting demands of liberty and reverence, powerful nervous energies seeking an outlet in the resolution of historic injustices. Yet Gladstone's journal, as a single source, presents a portrait whose authenticity should not obscure the fact that this is Gladstone as he saw himself. It has no room for those contemporaries who saw Gladstone as an unpredictable old man acting upon a self-concocted sense of the public conscience. For some he was less the saviour of Liberalism than a sincere but deluded Samson pulling down around him the temple of the great Liberal party.

Recent work by historians such as J. Parry and T. A. Jenkins, rehabilitating the Whig tradition within Victorian Liberalism, throws just such critical light on Gladstone's achievement. Whiggism, through individuals such as Lord Hartington, continued through the 1880s to offer safe hands for progressive aspirations. Administrative competence and pragmatic common sense provided a balance to Gladstone's campaigns of moral passion. Rather than the embodiment of Liberal belief, Gladstone is presented as someone outside the mainstream of Liberal politics. The Whig current provided authoritative and well-regulated government, securing political and economic progress within the framework of a well-ordered civil society. 'Gladstone's behaviour in 1886 turned the Liberal party from a great party of government into a gaggle of outsiders.'[48] The elderly Gladstone's subsequent obsession with popular control, encapsulated in the

262

1892 electoral cry 'Trust the people', transformed, or rather debased, the Liberals into a party driven by sectionalism and populism. As Jenkins concludes: 'Gladstone . . . by prematurely forcing the issue of Irish Home Rule and staking his own political career on it, succeeded in creating an artificial division among the Liberals, and enabled the Conservatives, with their Liberal Unionist allies, to establish themselves as the "natural" majority party.'[49]

At the time and since, others have argued that Gladstone's preoccupation with Home Rule after 1886 prevented the development of a broader Liberal policy. Implicit in this argument is the view that Home Rule represented a pressing diversion which, once resolved, would allow the Liberal party to return to its natural course. Certainly concentration on Home Rule made it easy for Gladstone to play down calls for social reform from radicals urging tax on land values and the widening of death duties, as well as the old sectarian demands for Scottish Church disestablishment and temperance reform. The Newcastle Programme, compiled at the annual conference of the National Liberal Federation in October 1891, pulled many of these issues together. But, as always, Gladstone was insistent that justice must first be given to Ireland before attending to other questions. The Liberal commitment to Home Rule lost the Liberal party broad areas of support within society. The intelligentsia largely went against Gladstone and continued to be staunchly Unionist. Influential thinkers such as A. V. Dicey, Henry Sidgwick, Goldwin Smith, and Matthew Arnold denounced Gladstone's demagoguery. Respectable society in London, taking its cue from the Queen and Unionist peers, decried Gladstone's attack on the integrity of the United Kingdom. This outcry intensified when in 1891 Gladstone committed himself to Welsh Church disestablishment, having previously declared that 'Welsh nationality is as great a reality as English nationality.'[50] Electorally, Liberalism lost much of its support in English boroughs and counties. The urban and suburban middle classes deserted the Liberal cause. Irish Home Rule also lost the Liberals much support in Scotland. In the general election of 1900 Conservatives and Liberal Unionists won a majority of Scottish seats. Liberal electoral support shrank back into rural Scotland, Wales, and localised areas such as the West Riding of Yorkshire, the North-east of England, and parts of the East Midlands. After 1886 Liberalism did indeed become, in social, geographical, and electoral senses, marginal.

Another aspect of Gladstone's Home Rule crusade after 1886 was his increasing employment of the language of 'the masses' against 'the classes'. By 'the classes' Gladstone meant those metropolitan and provincial elites committed to Unionism. These selfish privileged elites, he maintained, were obstructing the will of the nation. This populist strain in Gladstone's rhetoric emphasised his long-standing belief in the moral integrity of the common man. The last thing Gladstone wished was to incite class warfare. Liberalism, he insisted, must continue to espouse high ideals beyond the narrow material interests of any particular social group. But it was subsequently relatively easy for others to recruit Gladstone's language to the cause of the working-class struggle against bourgeois self-interest and the exploitation of labour by capital.

Gladstone's immediate legacy to the Liberal party was, therefore, mixed. He had towered above his contemporaries, commanding an authority based upon his inspirational oratory, executive powers, remarkable stamina and profound moral vision. The wide-ranging reforms of 1868–74 comprised an unrivalled legislative achievement bringing greater meritocratic efficiency to many parts of Victorian society and government. His Reform Act of 1884 launched Britain on the path to a broader democracy. But he left the party divided and demoralised. As a weakened electoral force Liberalism found itself competing for progressive working-class opinion alongside the newly formed Independent Labour Party.

What remained was Gladstone's heroic stature as a moral force in public life. Whether self-deluding or penetratingly perceptive, his profound sense of moral vision, built upon personal religious conviction, defined his sense of being the imperfect instrument of a Providential Will. He was, he always maintained, a man in politics, not a politician. During the 1860s this moral vision galvanised the varied elements of mid-Victorian progressive opinion. It helped fuse those elements forming his great reforming government of 1868. For much of the next 18 years he presented his moral presence as the necessary condition for continued Liberal unity. This encouraged a view of the Liberal party as comprising two distinct antagonistic sections, Whig and radical, whose cooperation was dependent upon Gladstone's brokership. Arguably this was not a particularly helpful or always accurate portrayal of Liberal differences. Undeniably, it played down the ability of some Whigs, such as Hartington, should circumstances permit, to align radical aspirations with executive competence and moderate reform. Gladstone's unique authority was not as indispensable to Liberal unity as he believed. In 1886 it was precisely his powerful sense of mission that split the Liberal party apart, driving Whigs and Chamberlainite radicals into the arms of Conservative Unionism. By 1888 even loyal Gladstonians such as Rosebery were regretting the Grand Old Man's lack of proportion and feared he would politically outlive his time. 'He was still of course a tower of strength; and yet it was he who made an united Liberal party an impossibility.'[51]

8

THE RISE OF THE PARTY SYSTEM

In Gilbert and Sullivan's operetta *HMS Pinafore*, which opened
before enthusiastic London audiences in 1878, Sir Joseph Porter,
First Lord of the Admiralty, sings:

> I always voted at my party's call,
> And never thought of thinking for myself at all.

W. S. Gilbert's satirical lines touched a nerve of contemporary
sensibility. The supplanting of parliamentary government by a
more rigid party system appeared to be imposing on MPs the
increasingly powerful dictates of cabinet and electorate. In his
book *Popular Government*, published in 1885, a forum far removed
from the Savoy operas, Sir Henry Maine, anxious at the advance
of democracy, saw MPs being demoted from unfettered representatives to instructed delegates.[1] Two comparisons readily
illustrate the transition highlighted by Gilbert and Maine: first,
the contrast between those differing parliamentary processes
which produced the Reform Acts of 1867 and 1884; secondly,
a comparison of those two great crises of party dislocation, 1846
and 1886.

Both the 1867 and 1884 Reform Acts extended the vote and
enfranchised a broader section of the male population. But 1867
was largely the product of intense and complex parliamentary
struggle, skilfully exploited by Disraeli between March and July
1867. It was in the Commons that the details of reform were

decided, with Disraelian suppleness exploiting Liberal disarray. In 1884, by contrast, the reform issue was settled by a small group of party leaders, principally Gladstone and Salisbury, in conclave. Behind closed doors in Downing Street was where reform and redistribution were decided. After the fact, the Commons dutifully complied with the results of private negotiation; 1884 showed party leaders exercising an enhanced authority.

A comparison between 1846 and 1886 is also instructive. 1846 was the first great party crisis of Victoria's reign, Peel's conversion to Corn Law repeal splitting the Conservative party; 1886 was the last great party crisis of Victoria's reign, Gladstone's conversion to Irish Home rule shattering the Liberal party. The recurring *bête noir* of Ireland, first the Great Famine and secondly the demand for self-government, was the occasion of party dislocation. After 1846 the Conservatives suffered a prolonged period of opposition, as did Liberals after 1886. Those with an eye for symmetry will discern a pleasing design. But beyond such obvious echoes each crisis displays, in important ways, the different contexts in which dramatic party displacement occurred. After 1846 Peel deliberately avoided forming a Peelite party. Neither in Westminster nor in the constituencies was party rupture formalised. Attention focused on the paths chosen by individual MPs as they sought out congenial company. By 1852 a good number of Peelites had reverted to the Conservatives. A prominent few, such as Gladstone, began a long journey which, with hesitancies and diversions, eventually led to Palmerstonian Liberalism. What was noticeably absent was an extra-parliamentary organisation either reflecting or determining allegiances within Westminster. In July 1886, by contrast, following Gladstone's prompt call for a dissolution, leading Liberal Unionists immediately created separate party organisations. Chamberlain formed the National Radical Union and Hartington the Liberal Unionist Association. For both this was an urgent necessity. In 1886 a formalised Liberal rupture was quickly presented to the electorate, nominated candidates each pronouncing their respective party line. Electoral judgement, in turn, decided the balance of parties in parliament.

Such comparisons illustrate the erosion of parliamentary autonomy. In the context of mid-Victorian parliamentary government what happened within Westminster was what really mattered. By 1886 party leaders, with their tightening grip on parliamentary business, enjoyed the procedural resources of the 'closure' and 'guillotine' with which to control Commons debate, while after 1884 household suffrage formed the basis of a broadened male electorate. At the expense of parliament itself both party leaders and the electorate acquired, after 1884–6, greater authority. Parliamentary supremacy had given way to the sovereignty of national parties. When Hartington, as Duke of Devonshire, declared in 1893 that parliament, enjoying an absolute sovereignty, still directly governed the nation, he was whistling a tired Whig tune into the hostile wind of democratic party change.

The Emergence of Party Government, 1867–86

The Whig notion of the sufficiency of parliament gradually, between 1852 and 1886, gave way to national parties as the source of authority upon which cabinets governed. This transition weaves through the narrative of earlier chapters. By broadening the electorate and stimulating extra-parliamentary organisation the 1867 Reform Act was a major impetus to change. The number of votes cast in subsequent general elections rose rapidly. In 1874, for the first time, both the Liberal and Conservative parties each received over a million votes. Numbers required organisation. In *Elections and Party Management* H. J. Hanham describes 1867 as 'undoubtedly the first decisive event in what has been called the "transition to democracy"'.[2] Thereafter aspects of parliamentary government existed uneasily alongside the emergent realities of party government. By 1886 parliamentary government had gone. As the historian J. A. Froude dryly observed in 1874, it was becoming an assumption that the nation was wiser than its leaders.[3] Parties and their leadership, whether in office or in opposition, incontestably exercised that sovereignty formerly belonging to parliament itself.

If 1867 marks a significant legislative challenge to parliamentary government, it was the concurrent political practice of three non-Whigs, Palmerston, Gladstone, and Disraeli, that further loosened the fabric of Whig constitutionalism. After 1855 Palmerston delivered with great effect extra-parliamentary speeches to popular audiences. By the 1860s Gladstone was doing likewise. For both men popular endorsement offset parliamentary weaknesses. Such occasions gave concrete form to a national opinion distinct from the judgement of the Commons. By implication such opinion was more authentic. Palmerston and Gladstone created an alternative court of appeal to which hostile parliamentary verdicts might be submitted. Electors themselves, gratified by the mutual flattery, embraced their new role. A growing provincial press, militant Nonconformity, and organised labour supported such relations. In 1868, two specific decisions by Disraeli over Irish disestablishment reinforced the idea of greater electoral authority. First, Disraeli declared the parliament elected in 1865 incapable of deciding on a question in 1868 not put before voters on the hustings. Secondly, the newly-enfranchised electorate having decided on Irish disestablishment in November 1868, Disraeli resigned as prime minister before parliament met. Gladstone reluctantly in 1874, and Disraeli again in 1880, followed this precedent. Implicit in Disraeli's actions was the embryonic concept of an electoral mandate as the basis of the cabinet's power to govern.

In the post-1867 world, politicians encountered, decried, and exploited changes in structure, practice, and style that hastened the demise of parliamentary government. Changes in structure had much to do with organisation. At the constituency level, party organisation became more intense and increasingly professional. Battles over the electoral register became more sophisticated. Professional full-time party agents began to replace part-time amateur agents, usually local solicitors. Local party-sponsored clubs became features of all popular constituencies, while formal constituency associations, based upon individual membership, organised the work of party activists. After 1867 the incidence of split-voting (electors with two votes splitting their votes between different parties) sharply decreased. Older forms of community were replaced by new partisan political factors. This was a process given additional momentum by the Ballot Act of 1872, transforming the vote from a public trust to a private right.

The boisterous carnival atmosphere of traditional constituency contests, embracing non-electors in public demonstrations of allegiance, became a thing of the past. Nomination and polling were now spheres increasingly dominated by formal organisation, the printed word, and private choice, rather than traditional symbols, community-wide affiliations, and public ceremony. The old electoral culture was tamed. Although the introduction of the ballot had a less dramatic effect on party returns than opponents had feared, the impact was most strongly felt in those rural areas where many enfranchised tenants farmed for absentee landlords, that is in Ireland and Wales. In 1874 Liberals gained seats in Wales against the general trend, while after 1874 Liberal support in Ireland was lost to Home Rulers. The Corrupt Practices Act of 1883 abolished the old system of paid canvassers and imposed expenditure limits on election campaigns. As a result it became more important to marshall and organise volunteer support on a large scale. Old electoral rituals with their carnival flavour passed away as formal party organisation tightened its grip on the dynamics of local political competition.

First the Conservatives and then the Liberals brought local associations under central control. In 1867 the National Union of Conservative and Constitutional Associations was established. By 1870 the Conservative Central Office was set up. In the early 1870s, under the temperamental and prickly Gorst, stationed in Central Office in Smith Square, Westminster, the National Union monitored the selection of candidates and the use of campaign funds. It provided speakers for public meetings, posters for hoardings, and leaflets for letter boxes. By 1877 a total of 791 local clubs and associations had affiliated themselves with the National Union. The National Union, in turn, became increasingly dependent on Central Office; except for the period

1882–4 when Randolph Churchill, as Chairman with Gorst's support, used it as a personal power base, encouraging the National Union to assert its independence. This brief Churchillian flirtation came to an abrupt end, however, in 1884. Very quickly thereafter the National Union reverted to its former reliance on Central Office as the control of the party leadership was restored. In 1885 the loyal and tactful R. W. E. Middleton, known familiarly as 'the Skipper', became principal party agent and in 1886 honorary secretary of the National Union. Working closely with Salisbury, the 'Middleton machine', through a network of professional agents, did much to bolster Conservative electoral dominance during the late 1880s and 1890s. Middleton's great triumph came in the 1895 general election when Conservatives gained a total of 341 Commons seats, the Liberals under Lord Rosebery won a mere 177 seats.

After 1883 the Primrose League came to rival the National Union in rural areas as an institutional focus for popular Conservative support. Formed on the suggestion of Drummond Wolff, a member of Churchill's Fourth Party, the League was committed to promoting Tory principles. It proved extraordinarily popular among Conservative voters and also staunchly loyal to the party leadership. While energetically disseminating Central Office material, local groups organised a full calendar of social events, fêtes, dances, and evening entertainments, establishing the presence of the League in the community. That women could be full members of the League gave many aristocratic and middle-class ladies a formal role in fostering grassroots Conservatism.

In the Liberal party after 1867 party organisation always coexisted uneasily alongside Gladstone's single-issue moral crusades, which sought to bind Liberals together through a shared 'virtuous passion' rather than through bureaucracy. The Liberal Registration Association, based in Parliament Street, Westminster, had been founded in the 1860s by Palmerston, mainly to control Liberal nominations and defuse the threat from radical candidates. Under W. P. Adam, Liberal Chief Whip from 1873 to 1880, it became the Liberal Central Association with, in 1877, Thomas Roberts as secretary. In the 1840s Roberts had orga-

271

nised the electoral registration office of the Anti-Corn Law League, and since 1861 he had worked for the Liberal Registration Association. But the existence of pressure groups committed to a single question, such as the National Education League and the United Kingdom Alliance, complicated the task of integrating popular Liberal support into a centralised party organisation.

At the local level, most notably in Birmingham, party organisation by an energetic committee could effectively marshall popular support. Chamberlain's 'caucus system' had emerged from collaboration between the local Reform League and Liberal Association during 1866–7 over parliamentary reform. The Birmingham caucus provided Chamberlain, as mayor of the city from 1873 to 1876, with a platform for entering national politics. It also enabled Chamberlain to establish the National Liberal Federation, with the formidable and resourceful Francis Schnadhorst as secretary, in 1877 on the remains of the National Education League. Chamberlain hoped, with Schnadhorst, to merge the party machine and popular radicalism under his own auspices. Schnadhorst described the Birmingham Liberal Association as 'an honest attempt to put the management of the party (by means of a thoroughly representative committee) where it should rest – in the hands of the people themselves'.[4]

The Birmingham Liberal Association, with two-thirds of its membership estimated to be working-class, spawned other associations in large urban areas, such organisations attending the inauguration of the NLF in May 1877 at Birmingham. But Chamberlain's control of radicalism and the dominance of the NLF in constituency affairs fell far short of what he hoped for. In May 1886 the NLF and its local affiliate associations overwhelmingly endorsed Irish Home Rule. Both Chamberlain and Jesse Collings promptly resigned. In September 1886 the NLF moved its headquarters to London, next to the Liberal Central Association, and Schnadhorst became secretary of both. Thus in 1886 Liberal organisation, at the very moment of party schism, achieved a centralised control closer to that of the efficient Conservative machine overseen by Middleton.

While the creation of national party bureaucracies, embracing mass membership, brought centralised organisation to the constituencies, the practice of politicians after 1867 further eroded the autonomy of parliament. 1868 provided Gladstone with a style of leadership, the single overriding moral cause galvanising Liberal support, which he replicated in 1876–7 over Bulgarian atrocities, in 1879–80 decrying Beaconsfieldism, and in 1886 calling for Irish Home Rule. Each occasion put forward a simple single test of orthodoxy – a test to which, in 1886, Hartington and Chamberlain refused to submit. The accompaniment to Gladstone's moral crusades was the virtuous passion excited by his extensive popular-speaking campaigns. In 1866 Lowe criticised Gladstone for undertaking an unseemly form of ministerial agitation over parliamentary reform. By 1876–7 Gladstone's Bulgarian campaign was forging a new relationship between the governing classes and the recently enfranchised: what Colin Matthew has described as 'a popular front of moral outrage'. The moral compact Gladstone created between his leadership and his popular audiences asserted an authority superior to the judgement of the Commons. The high pitch of activity during his Midlothian campaigns of 1879–80 saw Gladstone create extraordinary levels of popular fervour. The historian W. E. H. Lecky, lamenting the passing of parliamentary government in *Democracy and Liberty*, derided the trend for politicians to be found 'declaiming on platforms about the iniquity of privilege, [and] extolling the matchless wisdom and nobility of the masses'.[5] But the moral stature with which Gladstone imbued the respectable working man suggested an authority superior to the parliamentary endorsement of the governing classes.

The nature of the Liberal party itself after 1859 also applied hostile pressures on the structure of parliamentary government. The assimilation of radicalism into the rich mix of the Liberal parliamentary party brought with it populist presumptions. As noted in Chapter 3, after 1859 radicalism became respectable, losing some of its urban coarseness and acquiring a sleeker gloss. The subsequent careers of Dilke (before scandal discredited him in 1886) and Trevelyan illustrate the point. After 1867 popular pressure groups, such as the Liberation Society and the United

Kingdom Alliance, became part of the fabric of Liberal politics. Militant Nonconformity provided the moral conscience of Liberal activism, as evident in the agitation against the Bulgarian atrocities during 1876–7. These forces, focusing upon the moral zeal of Gladstone's leadership after 1866, saw religious issues return to the forefront of political attention. As Disraeli foresaw in 1868 it was religious issues that gave much of the colour to the character and form of newly-enfranchised constituencies. During the 1820s and 1830s religious questions had, as Palmerston and the elder Derby well remembered, polarised politics and prevented centrist coalitions. It was ecclesiastical issues that had kept Whigs and liberal Tories apart. Again, during the 1860s, religious issues, as championed by Gladstone, undercut the middle ground. During the 1870s Hartington and the young Derby bemoaned the religious ardour which obstructed calm rational moderation. The rise of Tractarianism and ritualism within the Anglican Church, as well as Papal declarations and ultramontanism in the Catholic church, revitalised Protestant campaigns during the 1860s. The anti-Catholic riots inspired by the Irish evangelical W. Murphy in Lancashire in 1868 and the anti-convent crusade of Ultra-Tory Charles Newdegate MP displayed the inflammatory passions excited by sectarian issues. All this brought populist excitement into more intimate contact with parliamentary deliberation.

As before, in 1885 the tough and aggressive Chamberlain embraced an innovative populist approach to Westminster politics hostile to traditional practices. Between September and December 1885, following the introduction of household suffrage to the counties, Chamberlain embarked on an extensive speaking campaign extolling his 'Unauthorised Programme'. The act of seeking electoral support on the basis of a programme was itself innovatory. The 'Unauthorised Programme' called for free education, graduated taxation, and allotments for rural labourers ('three acres and a cow'). With characteristic zeal Chamberlain sought to commit as many Liberal candidates as possible to this package of reforms, forsaking the conventional expression of a broad commitment to general principles. Chamberlain's campaign failed. He was marginalised by the revelation of the 'Hawarden Kite'. Many Liberals decried his programme as 'socialistic'. With a personality compounded of bluster and insecurity Chamberlain himself was dogged by social suspicions.

None the less, Chamberlain demonstrated the emergent power of popular programmatic politics. He provided an example others were subsequently to follow. In 1891 the NLF gave sanction to an official 'Newcastle Programme' embracing the issues of Irish Home Rule, Welsh disestablishment, London local government, free education, electoral registration reform, allotments for rural labourers, and reform of land laws. In the 1892 general election the 'Newcastle Programme' became Liberal party policy. Equally importantly, in 1885 Chamberlain began using the language of political rights. As noted in Chapter 1, for most mid-Victorians the idea of political rights was an alien continental concept, rights only having meaning in a legal context. But at Birmingham in January 1885 Chamberlain declared every man's 'right to be a part of the land of his birth'. More boldly, in Warrington in September 1885, he pronounced:

> now we have a government of the people by the people, we will go on and make it the government for the people in which all shall cooperate in order to secure to every man his natural rights – his right to existence, and to a fair enjoyment of it.[6]

By 1885 Chamberlain had conjoined democratic politics with popular rights.

The Conservative party after 1867 also cultivated popular support in a way which eroded the supremacy of the Commons. In 1872 Disraeli formulated Conservative policy in two major extra-parliamentary speeches, at Manchester and Crystal Palace; though the style of Disraeli's oratory, in sharp contrast to Gladstone's, always remained better suited to the tastes of the Commons. Disraeli elaborated upon his life-long themes of elevating 'the condition of the people', upholding the Empire, and maintaining the monarchy, aristocracy, and Church. Social reform would secure the health and unity of the nation. The Empire, combining, as he had earlier described it, the durability of Rome with the adventure of Carthage, provided a common object of shared pride, prosperity, and endeavour. A Providential duty placed on the shoulders of a great power an Empire belonging to the nation as a whole. This was an exercise in public relations, rather than innovative policy, comprising an invitation to popular participation rather than mass arousal. But it also represented a direct Conservative appeal to the nation rather than just Westminster, as the embodiment of those Conservative instincts exhausted by Liberal fervour.

Lord Randolph Churchill, during 1882–4, used the NUCCA to proclaim a vision of Tory Democracy, supposedly drawing on Disraeli's legacy, to excite Conservative supporters in the country. For his own immediate purposes Churchill took a delight, exuberant or vulgar according to taste, in portraying Conservative policy as subject to popular approval. Churchill's shock tactics, his invective and populist style, forced Northcote's hand. For example, Churchill obliged Northcote, against his own wishes, to oppose Gladstone's ministry over the Bradlaugh affair. Churchill's purpose was to discredit Northcote, ensure Salisbury's overall leadership of the party, and assert his own claim as Salisbury's lieutenant in the Commons. In June 1885 Northcote was removed to the Lords. In July 1886 Churchill was appointed leader of the Commons and Chancellor of the Exchequer in Salisbury's cabinet. Only Churchill's over-reaching arrogance and belief in his own indispensability, bringing on his resignation from office in December 1886, kept him from success as an exemplar of the new-style politics of popular self-advertisement.

Most importantly however, Salisbury, as sole Conservative leader after 1885, was to formulate, as a weapon against Gladstone, constitutional views deeply antithetical to traditional perspectives of parliamentary government. In particular, Salisbury conceived of the House of Lords as possessing a right to veto any Commons legislation not directly endorsed by an electoral mandate. This partly echoed Disraeli's argument against the authority of the Commons to legislate on Irish disestablishment in 1868, the issue not having been presented on the hustings. To this argument Salisbury's formidable intellect added the responsibility of the Lords, in such circumstances, to reject the decision of the Lower House. The broader context for Salisbury's views was a profound fear of impending social disintegration as democracy brought on class warfare; 1867, he believed, had made resistance to mass politics useless – a surrender compounded by the Ballot Act in 1872. All that remained to genuine Conservatives was the attempt to discipline the forces of democratic change. By the 1880s Salisbury saw the Commons, dependent on a mass electorate, as simply an accomplice to the agents of social fragmentation. Radicals extorted violent extreme measures from spineless Whigs as the price of their allegiance. Small shifts of extremist votes made and unmade Commons majorities and determined government policy, rendering parliament's claim to represent the bulk of national opinion an illusion. Thus the national interest became the helpless victim of internal Liberal politics. As a result, Salisbury believed, patriotism waned, class antagonism intensified, and attacks on all forms of property increased. Such pessimism demanded that the constitutional supremacy of the Commons be checked.

Salisbury saw two means of effective resistance available to Conservatives seeking to discipline an unfettered democracy. First, a well-organised party in the constituencies, which could ensure the due representation of Conservative opinions, those supporting patriotic policies, national unity, and traditional values. This was realised by Salisbury after 1885 through the 'Middleton machine'. Secondly, a vigilant House of Lords prepared to veto dangerous Commons legislation. In the 1880s this meant Gladstonian Home Rule, with its concomitant attacks on Empire and the aristocracy. Central to Salisbury's views was the denial of the Commons' claim to sovereignty. During the constitutional crisis of 1910, over the power of the Lords to block Lloyd George's radical 1909 budget, the Conservative peer Lord Selborne gave renewed expression to Salisbury's doctrine. Selborne, Salisbury's son-in-law, believed the Commons to be in the grip of the cabinet and the caucus. 'There is no more a House of Commons than a House of Lords. There is nothing but the cabinet, subject to a continuous but slight check of the Crown, and the violent but occasional check of the electors'.[7] Given that the Commons only expressed the views of party managers and professional politicians, it was necessary for the peerage to represent the real opinions and interests of the people. The sovereignty of the Commons had become merely a means of realising the tyranny of the party machine.

While Gladstone's Liberalism, Chamberlain's radicalism, Churchill's antics, and Salisbury's Conservatism, in very different ways, debunked the sufficiency of parliament, Irish Nationalists also, during the 1870s and 1880s, undermined parliament's claims to autonomy. Not simply was this part of the well-publicised obstructive tactics adopted by Irish MPs after 1877, designed to incapacitate the Commons. Home Rule MPs were required to take a pledge prior to nomination, committing them to Irish self-government. Parnell's Home Rule party also exploited its association with violent revolutionary agitation in Ireland, particularly after Parnell became President of the Land League in 1879. The independent authority of parliament and the rights of landlords were challenged. Revolutionary separatists and agrarian agitators, as well as constitutional politicians, swelled the ranks of Home Rule supporters. Home Rule MPs presented themselves as the instructed delegates of Irish nationalist opinion, although this did not prevent Parnell also playing the parliamentary game, as in 1885–6, when it suited his purposes. None the less, Irish Nationalist MPs of the 1880s had little time or regard for the notions of Burke (an Irishman of a far earlier generation) that MPs should be representatives not delegates. In the election of 1885 Parnellites won 85 out of 103 Irish seats. Their claim to embody Irish opinion Gladstone, for one, found incontestable. The ferment of the Irish electoral campaigns of 1885–6, in turn, gave shape to fierce sectarian mythologies, Catholic and Protestant, Nationalist and Unionist, which defined popular Irish passions for decades to follow.

But, as noted earlier, while powerful forces were demolishing the mid-Victorian constitution between 1867 and 1886, features of parliamentary government endured alongside new assumptions and practices. First of all, the Whigs themselves survived as an important part of the Liberal leadership, continuing to provide safe hands for progressive aspirations. Religious tolerance and belief in the rule of law and administrative expertise continued to frame their commitment to the reconciliation of progress, property, intelligence and order. It would be wrong to bury Whiggism too soon. Gladstone's ministerial appointments reflected his own belief in the inheritors of landed wealth as the natural leaders of society. In his first government, as initially formed, 8 out of 14 cabinet members were landed Whigs, even with Russell, Halifax, Sir George Grey, and Somerset declining to join the ministry. Between 1835 and 1885, of the 80 or so ministers who served in Liberal cabinets, roughly 50 of them were part of the kinship of leading Whig families.

During 1878–9 Hartington began to show how Whig leadership might still accommodate radical, or rather Chamberlainite, aims. Hartington showed himself willing to respond to new political necessities by undertaking popular speaking, offering public audiences a more detached style in contrast to Gladstonian passion. Moreover, the depiction of the Liberal party as simply comprised of two antagonistic blocs, one Whig the other radical, which at different times suited the purposes of Gladstone and radicals like Chamberlain, belied a more complex reality – a reality in which the Whig ability to embrace and lead a spectrum of progressive views should not be discounted.

But it was the Midlothian juggernaut that crushed Whig hopes in 1879 of maintaining an enlightened aristocracy firmly at the head of Liberal aims. Gladstone's 1880 cabinet contained its share of Whigs and broad acres, Granville, Hartington, Argyll, and Spencer. But the calamity of 1886 drove the Whigs *en masse* towards the Conservative Unionist fold. In private letters and journals Whigs recorded their growing distaste for Gladstone's impassioned harangues, outdoor speaking, and the novel requirements of party obligation. In 1887 the former Peelite Lord Selborne described Gladstone as 'a Christian statesman' turned 'revolutionary demagogue'.[8] 'Every day', Kimberley recorded, 'it becomes more apparent that political power is being transferred from parliament to the platform – a momentous change.' In 1883 a plaintive Kimberley observed of outdoor speeches: 'I always feel a wish to avoid them altogether, but they are one of the duties in public life with which unfortunately one cannot dispense, and I am sorry to say that in this country "going to the stump" has become a recognised part of the business of politics and will become more and more indispensable, every year, as the democracy gains in strength.'[9] Derby caught the mood in characteristic tones in his journal in January 1887: 'I do not think democratic politics will have many attractions for cultivated men in the next generation.'[10] Mass politics was not a suitable occupation for gentlemen.

But while the Whigs remained a part of Liberal government between 1867 and 1886, aspects of parliamentary government survived. The Commons continued to be critically important. Arguably it was Gladstone's ill-tempered incapacity as Commons leader, as much as any other single factor such as sectarian animosities, that brought down his first government. After 1867 party discipline in division votes increased, but it was not absolute. Solid party voting in the Commons increased compared with pre-1867 sessions; but there were still divisions, monitored by the party Whips, which revealed either moderates voting with the other party, or extreme, usually radical, MPs voting against Whigs and Conservatives combined. In the early 1880s radical attempts to cut government expenditure and amend Liberal legislation, the Agricultural Holdings and Corrupt Practices bills of 1883 for example, frequently occurred. Management of the Commons remained necessary to political survival. Moreover, as Hugh Berrington has shown, tighter party discipline in the Commons should not be seen as simply a process of front benches and constituencies browbeating MPs into compliance.[11] While Conservative dissidents came to accept the claims of party loyalty it was also the case that the Liberal party became more radical as a result of the schism of 1886. Home Rule radicals found the party coming to them, so that Liberal extremists became absorbed into the main body of the Gladstonian Home Rule party.

Opposition leaders after 1867 retained earlier attitudes. More often than not they chose to await the disintegration of the government, rather than forcing hostile motions or hoping for an electoral reaction at a dissolution. The idea that it was the duty of an opposition to oppose all government legislation did not arrive until after 1886. From 1870 to 1873 Disraeli exercised restraint, hoping Gladstone would soon become a prisoner of the radicals and be repudiated by the Whigs. Resorting to the elder Derby's strategy of 'killing with kindness' he supported the government over their controversial 1870 Education bill. In March 1873 he declined to accept office, thereby prolonging the agonies of Liberal fragmentation. Similarly, between 1874 and 1880, the Whig duumvirate of Hartington and Granville looked to Conservative disintegration as their best hope. During 1877–8, when war with Russia seemed likely, they avoided unpatriotic opposition, believing Disraeli's cabinet would fall apart of its own volition. The resignations of Derby and Carnarvon in early 1878 seemed to confirm their expectations. After 1880 Northcote resumed the traditional Conservative opposition strategy of looking towards Liberal collapse. In April 1880 Northcote noted in his journal:

> I think it likely enough that a conservative cave may be formed on the Liberal side . . . and that if we manage our opposition discreetly, we may often join hands with them, and perhaps ultimately bring some of them to take part in a Conservative cabinet.[12]

It was Churchill's biting ridicule, as the Conservative's *enfant terrible*, that savagely discredited Northcote's strategy. Nevertheless, between 1867 and 1886, aspects of parliamentary government existed uneasily alongside an emergent party system.

The Ascendancy of the Party System after 1886

The Reform legislation and Home Rule crisis of 1884–6 were a watershed. By 1886 party government was established and the mid-Victorian constitution dead. The Liberal commentator A. V. Dicey privately observed in 1894 that 'I have not the remotest doubt that under the present condition of things sham parliamentary government means a very vicious form of government by party.'[13] The transition from parliamentary to party government, begun in the 1860s, culminated in the last great party crisis of Victoria's reign. The sheer bitterness of political divisions over Home Rule, which split families and shattered old friendships, cemented the new alignments of fierce party feeling. After 1886 national parties, enjoying mass membership and centralised bureaucracy, came to exercise the power to make and unmake governments. The House of Commons surrendered authority to the cabinet on one hand and found its power transferred to the electorate on the other. After 1886 governments increasingly possessed office by virtue of electoral verdicts registered at general elections. In 1895 one backbench MP complained

> The House has no voice in the selection of the Government, only the invidious and practically useless option of objecting. Once in, the party heads, not elected, but co-opted by predecessors similarly co-opted, are masters of the situation. On any sign of independent action in their party, they can put the pistol of Dissolution to their heads and say, 'your vote or your life; if you do not come to heel, we will blow your parliamentary brains out', and so bring mutineers to their senses.[14]

The 1892 election ended Salisbury's second ministry. The election of 1895, a defeat for Lord Rosebery (Gladstone's successor as Liberal leader), affirmed Salisbury's return to office at the head of his third ministry. The life of governments became aligned with the calling of general elections.

Cabinets governed after 1886 through an electoral mandate, rather than from Commons support independent of any recall to the nation's voters. In 1884 Lord Fife described the 'mandat imperatif' as 'one of the most dangerous continental perversions of our parliamentary system'. But by April 1886 Hartington was telling the Commons that, although the principle of a mandate had no constitutional existence, it was becoming a moral constraint on parliament, with the constituencies becoming the source of power. In 1901 the *Daily News* accused Salisbury of being 'the first to introduce into English politics that essentially Jacobinical phrase', the mandate.[15] But such Canute-like laments could not force back new realities. Increasingly governments became bound by party programmes presented at general elections. Lowell noted that prior to the 1890s the notion that parliament only possessed a delegated authority, thereby being morally restrained from dealing with questions not laid before voters at the preceding general election, was widely regarded as a dangerous political heresy.[16] After the 1890s it became orthodoxy.

This, in turn, required disciplined parliamentary parties within Westminster displaying ideological homogeneity. MPs were expected to speak and vote as a bloc. After 1886 party conformity in Commons divisions overseen by Whips sharply increased, dissidence dropping to negligible levels. In the parliament of 1880–5 eleven amendments to government legislation were carried in divisions in which Whips acted as tellers, as one measure of party dissidence. Between 1887 and 1892 only three such amendments against government legislation were carried. Between 1893 and 1895 only one amendment was successful, likewise only one amendment to government legislation was carried against the party Whips between 1896 and 1900. At the same time as party dissent sharply declined, more MPs voted more often in divisions. In the 1860s a typical MP voted in about 25% of all Commons divisions. After 1867 this figure rose to about 35%. By 1893–1904 the figure rose to 40%, and in 1905–14, to 48%.[17] The advocates of party government claimed that this ensured strong and stable government standing on declared policy and electoral supremacy. Sovereignty irrevocably passed from parliament to party.

From 1880 onwards the very nature of general elections becomes more recognisably modern. In 1880, 67 constituencies were uncontested. In 1885 a mere 39. Elections did, indeed, become general. Breaking with mid-Victorian convention, party leaders commonly spoke in constituencies other than their own. This was another precedent set by Gladstone in his barnstorming Midlothian campaigns. Few candidates could hope for a successful contest by the 1880s without the support of an agent, a permanent association, or a formal organisational network. Central Office and the Liberal Association provided party candidates with suitable material for their hustings speeches, ensuring they propounded the official party line. In 1885 Conservative Central Office produced the first *Constitutional Yearbook*, a ready guide supplying speakers and pamphleteers with suitable statistics and information. In 1887 the first *Liberal Yearbook* appeared, providing data for local Liberal Associations and their members. Electors, in turn, became used to voting for parties as much as for individual candidates, their vote being seen as part of a plebiscitary verdict passed on the incumbent administration. The modern party system disciplined not only MPs, but also voters.

Following the 1880s popular movements, unconnected with party politics, became rarer. Formal organisation and the growing dominance of print over older, more spontaneous symbolic and oral forms of political expression tamed popular activism. The excitement created by the Tichborne claimant during the 1870s, for example, generated a form of popular social protest not readily aligned with political parties.[18] In subsequent decades such localised popular protest became increasingly assimilated within the formal embrace of national parties. After 1886, following its move to London, the National Liberal Federation became a truly national association. It was no longer in the pocket of Chamberlain in Birmingham, with rival regional Federations in London, Manchester, and the Home Counties. Conservative loyalties, after 1883, were reinforced by the rapidly expanding activities of the Primrose League. Centralised bureaucracies more and more efficiently directed their mass membership towards support for party candidates.

Such developments had a profound social impact both within and outside Westminster. Within Westminster after 1886 fewer old county families provided local MPs. During the eighteenth century parliamentary families, usually from among the gentry, who supplied MPs over a number of generations, dominated the Commons. Individuals, carrying the same name, represented their locality over long periods. After 1832 and 1867 their number began to decline. After 1884–6 their presence in the Commons dropped dramatically. One recent analysis has calculated that in 1870, 39% of MPs came from such traditional parliamentary families. By 1890 they comprised only 21% of MPs, their presence nearly halved. In 1914 they constituted only 13% of the Commons.[19] For example, in Lincolnshire two local gentry families, the Welbys and the Tollemaches, had historically represented the borough of Grantham, and did so continuously during the period 1832–68. Then in 1874 the last Tollemache representing Grantham retired and in 1885 a Welby candidate was defeated. Thereafter no members of either family represented Grantham in the Commons. After 1886 traditional parliamentary families gave way to members of a new plutocracy: bankers, stockbrokers, investors, and other members of the professions, such as lawyers, whose wealth commanded increasing prestige. Indeed, after 1884–6 the landed classes as a whole became a minority within the Commons. As W. C. Lubenow has observed 'the reforms of 1884–5 did what those of 1832 and 1867 did not do; they broke the numerical hold of the landed elite in the House of Commons'.[20] It is striking that in 1886 nearly half the Commons, 48% of MPs, were entering parliament for the first time. The face of the Commons, both figuratively and literally, was rapidly changing.

Social transformation within the Commons mirrored wider social change. The shift of middle-class and propertied interests towards Conservatism, evident since the 1860s, was cemented by the events of 1884–6. The bulk of the new plutocracy, which displaced the landed interest in the Commons, was Conservative and Unionist in sentiment. The Edwardian Conservative party welcomed into its inner councils professional and business wealth supplementing the traditional landed backgrounds of the party hierarchy. Indeed, 1886 not only split the Liberal party, but also prompted a fundamental realignment within the governing classes as a whole. Wealth and status, in all forms, became overwhelmingly Unionist in opinion during the 1890s. In 1905, when the Conservatives resigned from office, practically the whole of the British peerage moved into opposition. The flight of the Whigs and other Unionists from Gladstone in the 1880s helped shape the Conservatives as the exclusive party of wealth and property. In the Lords in 1887 only 43 peers supported

Gladstone over Home Rule. They were a small minority given lustre by the presence of loyal Gladstonians such as Granville, Kimberley, Spencer, Ripon, and Rosebery; a front bench without a following. By 1897 their number had dwindled to 25, out of an Upper House of 565 peers. In subsequent confrontations between Lords and Commons it was easy for critics to characterise the clash as one between property (the Lords) and the popular will (the Commons).

While 1886 propelled forward the party realignment of the governing classes, the working classes were also politically reorientated following 1886. In part this was due to economic restructuring as the growing division of labour and the increasing scale of industrial manufacturing cut the links between skilled labourers and Liberalism. The reforms of 1884–5, which dramatically increased the county electorate, gave vigorous life to rural radicalism. The emergence of proletarian socialism, usually dated from the Great Dock Strike of 1889, revealed the beginnings of an organised workers' movement seeking independent representation. The Liberal party's preoccupation with Irish Home Rule hastened the process. At a Bradford conference in January 1893 the Independent Labour Party (ILP) was formed, the evangelical Scottish miner and union organiser Keir Hardie having become an Independent Labour MP in 1892. The sight of Hardie's cloth cap, amid the top hats of the Commons, symbolised the arrival of proletarian politics in parliament. Alongside the Social Democratic Federation, formed by H. M. Hyndman in 1881, the ILP formed constituency branches and put forward its own parliamentary candidates. The mainly middle-class Fabian Society, founded in 1884 and led by Annie Besant, George Bernard Shaw, and Sidney and Beatrice Webb, provided an intellectual utilitarian thrust to socialist ideas through meetings, debates, and pamphlet literature. In 1899 the Trades Union Congress called together a conference of trade unions, cooperative societies, and socialist societies. From this the Labour Representation Committee was subsequently formed in February 1900, to ensure greater labour representation in parliament. This brought the various strands of proletarian and socialist politics together.

These developments had two major effects on British politics after 1886. First, party politics became increasingly about class. Secondly, collectivist ideas began to redefine notions of the State and the role of government. By the 1890s class was subsuming other social categories in British society. Work, education, housing, entertainment, sport, and pronunciation were all being increasingly defined in class terms. Older social attitudes, based upon region and religion for example, were eroded. Regional culture came under intense pressure. As the creation of national wealth shifted away from industrial manufacturing towards international finance, so London increasingly became the hub of national economic life. This reinforced the status of London as the centre of fashionable and artistic life. The arrival of mass consumerism also blurred regional variations. The expansion of public schools created a more homogeneous upper-class culture divorced from its local roots. The establishment of the speech of the Home Counties as 'standard' English marginalised local dialects. Characteristics of the urban workplace which had mitigated class differences, such as the survival of workshop autonomy, the rigidity of skill distinctions, and the social proximity of employee and employer, became less prevalent. Equally, by the 1890s religion, within an increasingly pluralistic society, was less a collective institutional force than a matter of private faith. A greater reticence about religion permeated professional and public life. As regional and religious influences weakened so class became more prominent. Political debate became couched in terms of class.

After 1886 collectivism, influenced by German philosophy, also transformed the language of political argument. For mid-Victorian Whigs, in the context of parliamentary government, politics, as institutionalised in the State, was separate from society. The role of politics was to balance and integrate those dynamic forces of economic and moral change driving on social progress. The State, through parliamentary government, provided a supportive framework for social progress, upholding the rights of property, the rule of law, and sound national finance. For mid-Victorian Liberals, influenced by theorists such as John Stuart Mill and Matthew Arnold, the virtuous and diligent individual, triumphing over adversity and seizing the opportunities offered by progress, was central to their view of society. Politics was a public duty incumbent on respectable, financially self-sufficient, male members of the community. Collectivists, after the 1880s, merged notions of the State and society, portraying the State as 'organic' to the wider community. Radicals of the 1890s were less concerned with reforming institutions, unlike their predecessors of the 1850s, than with changing social structures. Even voices such as that of the political theorist Herbert Spencer in 1884, arguing, against the collectivist tide, for the cause of rugged individualism, denounced the sovereignty of parliament as a great political superstition. The ultimate location of power, sovereignty, was now embedded in society itself.

At the same time many Liberals were rejecting the mid-Victorian definition of liberty as the absence of constraint; feeling such a negative description to be inadequate in dealing with growing social evils such as urban poverty. A positive definition of liberty, as equality of opportunity, allowed New Liberals to advocate a far more active role for government. The ethical basis of New Liberal arguments for greater state activity contrasted with the more utilitarian arguments of the Fabian socialists. Some, such as the theorist Graham Wallas, adopted a 'mechanical' approach to social-democratic reform and the amelioration of injustices and inequality; while thinkers such as D. G. Ritchie in *Principles of State Intervention* (1891), suggested a 'moral' approach in which the very nature of the individual as citizen be reformulated. But the single result of all such new avenues of thought was that the conception of the State itself was considerably broadened and its ability to regulate society extended. Again, economic change gave momentum to such new ideas, as the scale of economic organisation expanded. Local and voluntary provision no longer appeared able to provide an adequate infrastructure for national economic life. The *laissez faire* individualism of the mid-Victorian period was giving way, by the 1890s, to the interventionist State.

Finally, the popularity of Empire in late-Victorian Britain and the force of jingoistic enthusiasms permeated political debate.

Imperialism acquired important new connotations as industrial competitors, such as Germany and the United States, began to challenge Britain's economic pre-eminence. Informal spheres of colonial interest gave way to formal political annexation, as evidenced in 'the scramble for Africa' during the 1880s and 1890s. Imperial dominion bolstered assumptions about the innate superiority of British institutions. Salisbury's Conservatism of the 1890s channelled imperial ardour into party support. Patriotic enthusiasm complemented the rise of Orangeism and militant Unionism as a basis for popular Conservative commitment. Chamberlain had rejected Irish Home Rule in 1886 on the grounds that it was a repudiation of Britain's Imperial role. The cause of the Empire was to seal Chamberlain's merger with the Conservatives in the 1890s; while Queen Victoria's Diamond Jubilee in 1897 provided the occasion for unparalleled celebrations of Imperial exuberance. Around a less reclusive monarch a panoply of public ceremony and invented tradition gave popular expression to patriotic feeling. National rejoicing momentarily eclipsed domestic divisions, relative economic decline and the forces of disunion within the United Kingdom.

The emergence of class politics, the secularisation of public life, the rise of socialism, collectivist redefinitions of the State, 'organic' views of society, and Imperial ardour all reinforced the supremacy of parties in the late-Victorian constitution. Political sentiment became solidified around the partisanship of party. In December 1886 Chamberlain warned Churchill that 'the party tie is the strongest sentiment in this country – stronger than patriotism or even self-interest'.[21] This was an ironic source for such comment. During his career Chamberlain helped to shatter two great parties, the Liberals in 1886 and the Conservatives in 1903. But Chamberlain recognised, none the less, that national popular parties now possessed the power to install or bring down governments. The partisan alignments that emerged from the Home Rule crisis of 1886 formed the basis of Britain's much-vaunted modern party system.

It would be misleading to see this system as based on a direct contest between two rival parties. The titanic struggle between Gladstone and Disraeli in the late 1870s had suggested a simple bi-polar alignment, but even this cloaked more complex political realities. Only occasionally since 1886 has British politics operated as a simple *two*-party system.[22] Rather, what has distinguished party government since 1886, from mid-Victorian parliamentary government, is that the preferences of an increasingly democratic electorate have decided who should govern the nation. Centralised and bureaucratic national parties, with a mass membership, have registered electoral preference.

In his novel *Falconet*, left unfinished on his desk when he died in 1881, Disraeli declared that political institutions were now 'all challenged, and statesmen, conscious of what is at hand, are changing nations into armies'. Disraeli sensed what was in the air. In the dawning age of mass politics the serried partisan ranks of the party faithful were to form the organised might of the modern political will. Popular mass support fell in behind the command of the party leadership and their general staff of party managers, with MPs demoted to junior officers as the division fodder of parliamentary battles. Voting behaviour in British elections of the twentieth century has exhibited two marked characteristics. First, that voters choose between national parties rather than local candidates. Secondly, that to a significant degree the choice between parties is determined by the voter's social class. This has meant that national parties, not the Commons, are the autonomous elements within the constitution. Since 1886 popular sovereignty, expressed through the partisanship of national parties, has formed the basis of constitutional thinking and debate.

NOTES

INTRODUCTION

1. James FitzJames Stephen, *Horae Sabbaticae*, 2 vols (1892) ii, p. 201.
2. Walter Bagehot, *The English Constitution*, Introduction by R. H. S. Crossman (1963) p. 65. Bagehot's study first appeared as a series of articles in the *Fortnightly Review* before being published as a book in 1867. Bagehot produced a second edition, taking account of the 1867 Reform Act, in 1872.
3. Gladstone at Greenwich, *The Times*, 29 January 1874, p. 5.
4. Leslie Stephen 'The Value of Political Machinery', *Fortnightly Review*, 24 (1875) p. 849.
5. A. L. Lowell, *The Government of England*, 2 vols (1908) i, p. 447.
6. Bagehot, *English Constitution*, p. 151.
7. W. H. Lecky, *Democracy and Liberty*, 2 vols (1896) i, p. 21.

1 PARLIAMENTARY GOVERNMENT

1. 'Earl Grey on Parliamentary Government', *Edinburgh Review*, 219 (July 1858) p. 272.
2. Third Earl Grey, *Parliamentary Government Considered with Reference to Reform of Parliament* (1858) p. 11.
3. 'Grey on Parliamentary Government', *Edinburgh Review*, 219, p. 272. The term 'parliamentary government' was first used in this sense by the legal jurist J. J. Park in *Dogmas of the Constitution* (1832).
4. R. Quinault, 'Westminster and the Victorian Constitution', *Transactions of the Royal Historical Society*, 6th series, 11 (1992) p. 79.
5. Walter Bagehot, *The English Constitution* (1963) p. 158. See also T. A. Jenkins, *Parliament, Party and Politics in Victorian Britain* (1996) pp. 28–58.

6. Stanley journal, 14 March 1853, *Disraeli, Derby and the Conservative Party: Political Journals of Lord Stanley, 1848–69*, ed. J. Vincent (Brighton, 1978) p. 103.

7. Derby to Lord Blandford, 26 January 1854, Derby Mss. 182/2.

8. *The Times*, 4 February 1859, p. 9; E.J. Evans, *The Forging of the Modern State* (1983) p. 326; Stanley journal, 13 May 1861, *Disraeli, Derby and the Conservative Party*, p. 170; E.M. Whitty, *St Stephen's in the Fifties: The Session 1852–3, a Political Retrospect*, ed. J. McCarthy (1906) p. 2.

9. Trelawny diary, 25 April 1860, *The Parliamentary Diaries of Sir John Trelawny, 1858–1865*, ed. T.A. Jenkins (Royal Historical Society, Camden Fourth series, 1990) vol. 40, p. 116.

10. Gladstone memo, 'Party as it was and as it is', Gladstone Mss. 44745, fol. 198. The distinction between 'voluntary subordination' and 'unconditional obedience' was drawn by T.E. Kebbel in *Fraser's Magazine*, 68 (1863) p. 240.

11. See Jonathan Parry, *The Rise and Fall of Liberal Government in Victorian Britain* (1993) p. 99.

12. Stanley journal, 9 February and July 1853, *Disraeli, Derby and the Conservative Party*, pp. 96 and 111.

13. [W.E. Gladstone], 'The Declining Efficiency of Parliament', *Quarterly Review*, 99 (1856) p. 551. On the frequency of whipped Commons votes see two articles by Gary Cox, 'The Origin of Whip Votes in the House of Commons', *Parliamentary History*, 11 (1992) pp. 278–85; and 'The Development of Collective Responsibility in the United Kingdom', *Parliamentary History*, 13 (1994) pp. 32–47.

14. William White, *The Inner Life of the House of Commons*, ed. J. McCarthy, 2 vols (1897) i, p. 27.

15. John Hogan, 'Party Management in the House of Lords', *Parliamentary History*, 10:1 (1991) p. 125; Stanley journal, 28 February 1854, *Disraeli, Derby and the Conservative Party*, p. 122.

16. See Norman Gash, *Aristocracy and People: Britain, 1815–1865* (1979); Olive Anderson, *A Liberal State at War* (1967) p. 168; J.B. Conacher, 'Party Politics in the Age of Palmerston', in *1859: Entering an Age of Crisis* (Indiana, 1959) p. 163; R. Blake, *Disraeli* (1966) p. 272.

17. See P.M. Gurowich, 'The Continuation of War by Other Means: Party and Politics, 1855–1865', *Historical Journal*, 27:3 (1984) pp. 603–31; and Angus Hawkins, *Parliament, Party and the Art of Politics in Britain, 1855–59* (1987) pp. 12–13.

18. Cox, *The Efficient Secret: The Cabinet and the Development of Political Parties in Victorian England* (1987) p. 64.
19. See the important article by Hugh Berrington, 'Partisanship and Dissidence in the Nineteenth-Century House of Commons', *Parliamentary Affairs*, 21:4 (1968) pp. 338–74.
20. Thomas Erskine May, *The Constitutional History of England since the Accession of George III, 1760–1860*, 3 vols (5th edn, 1875) ii, pp. 236–7.
21. F. W. S. Craig, *British Parliamentary Election Results, 1832–1885* (1977) p. 624.
22. Robert Stewart, *The Foundation of the Conservative Party, 1830–1867* (1978) p. 146.
23. George Meredith, *Beauchamp's Career* (World Classics edition, 1988) p. 254.
24. Gary Cox, *The Efficient Secret*, pp. 103–5. Between 1818 and 1831 the average incidence of such split voting was 22 per cent.
25. Meredith, *Beauchamp's Career*, p. 156.
26. J. Hamburger, 'The Whig Conscience', in *The Conscience of the Victorian State*, ed. P. Marsh (1979) p. 27.
27. Abraham Kriegel (ed.), *The Holland House Diaries* (1977) p. 348.
28. Gary Cox, 'The Development of Collective Responsibility in the United Kingdom', *Parliamentary History*, 13 (1994) pp. 32–47.
29. Russell, 1 March 1831, *Hansard*, 3rd series, ii, 1086–7.
30. Walter Bagehot, 'Parliamentary Reform', in *Bagehot's Historical Essays*, ed. N. St John Stevas (1971) p. 304.
31. 'Parliamentary Government', *Edinburgh Review* (1858) p. 285.
32. Stanley journal, 24 March 1853, *Disraeli, Derby and the Conservative Party*, p. 104.
33. According to *Dod's Parliamentary Companion for 1852* (1852).
34. Russell to Graham, 2 November 1852, Graham Mss., cit. Hawkins, *Parliament, Party and the Art of Politics*, p. 14.
35. Angus Hawkins ' "Parliamentary Government" and Victorian Political Parties, c.1830–c.1880', *English Historical Review*, 104 (1989) p. 654.
36. Lord Mahon and Edward Cardwell (eds), *The Memoirs of Sir Robert Peel*, 2 vols (1856–7) ii, p. 58.
37. C. S. Parker, *Sir Robert Peel from his Private Papers*, 3 vols (1899) ii, p. 299.
38. Disraeli to Manners, 17 December 1845, cit. Blake, *Disraeli*, p. 223; and Disraeli, 22 January 1846, cit. Blake, *Disraeli*, p. 227.
39. Stanley journal, 4 July 1850, *Disraeli, Derby and the Conservative Party*, p. 26.

40. Peel to Hardinge, 24 September 1846, cit. Parker, *Peel*, iii, p. 474.

41. Peel to Prince Albert, 11 August 1847, cit. Donald Read, *Peel and the Victorians* (1987) p. 256.

42. G. H. L. LeMay, *The Victorian Constitution: Conventions, Usages and Contingencies* (1979) p. 64.

43. Stanley to Disraeli, 22 August 1854, Hughenden Mss. B/XX/S/ 609.

44. Derby to Disraeli, 6 January 1849, cit. W. F. Monypenny and G. E. Buckle, *The Life of Benjamin Disraeli*, 6 vols (1910–20) iii, pp. 127–8.

45. Gladstone memo (n.d), 'Party as it was and as it is', Gladstone Mss. 44745, fol.203.

46. Stanley journal, 21 July 1850, *Disraeli, Derby and the Conservative Party*, p. 28.

47. John Derry, *Charles, Earl Grey, Aristocratic Reformer* (1992) p. 172.

48. J. Morley, *The Life of Richard Cobden*, 2 vols (1879) ii, p. 54.

49. Hume, 12 May 1848, *Hansard*, 3rd series, XCVIII, 905. For the constitutionalist temper of radicalism after 1848 see Miles Taylor, *The Decline of British Radicalism, 1847–1860* (1995).

50. Morley, *Cobden*, ii, pp. 349–50.

51. See Taylor, *Decline of British Radicalism*, pp. 19–60.

2   Mid-Victorian Parties, 1852–9

1. Derby to Disraeli, 14 November 1853, Derby Mss. 182/1.

2. *Dod's Parliamentary Companion* for 1852. For the difficulties of defining party allegiance in 1852 see J. B. Conacher, *Peelites and the Party System* (1972) pp. 115–20. The Conservative leadership, in December 1852, estimated party numbers in the Commons as follows: approximately 300 Conservatives, 35–40 Peelites, about 170 Whigs, 60 Irish Brigade, and 80 radicals. Stanley journal, 17 December 1852, *Disraeli, Derby and the Conservative Party: Political Journals of Lord Stanley, 1848–69*, ed. J. Vincent (Brighton, 1978) p. 90.

3. Ian Newbould, 'Sir Robert Peel and the Conservative Party: A Study in Failure?', *English Historical Review*, XCVIII (1983) pp. 529–57. See also T. A. Jenkins, *Parliament, Party and Politics in Victorian Britain* (1996) pp. 28–58.

4. E. M. Whitty, *St Stephen's in the Fifties: The Session 1852–3, A Political Retrospect*, ed. J. McCarthy (1906) p. 40.

5. Prince Albert memo, 21 February 1855, *The Letters of Queen Victoria*, 1st series, 3 vols (1907) A. C. Benson and Lord Esher (eds), iii, p. 137; John Morley, *Life of Gladstone*, 3 vols (1903) i, p. 540.

6. Broughton diary, 25 December 1852, Broughton Mss. 43757, fol. 83.

7. Parkes to Ellice, 30 December 1852, Ellice Mss. 15041, fol. 64.

8. Greville diary, 24 December 1852, *The Greville Memoirs*, ed. H. Reeve, 8 vols (1888) vii, p. 24.

9. See H. C. G. Matthew, 'Disraeli, Gladstone and the Politics of Mid-Victorian Budgets', *Historical Journal*, 22:3 (1979) pp. 615–43.

10. Palmerston to Lansdowne, 8 December 1853, Palmerston Mss. GC/LA/III.

11. Derby to Liddell, 4 January 1853, Derby Mss. 182/1.

12. Derby to Walpole, 30 January 1853, Derby Mss. 182/1; Stanley journal, 20 December 1852 and 17 February 1853, *Disraeli, Derby and the Conservative Party*, pp. 92 and 99.

13. Stanley journal, 25 January 1854, *Disraeli, Derby and the Conservative Party*, p. 117.

14. Stanley journal, 22 January 1855, *Disraeli, Derby and the Conservative Party*, p. 127.

15. R. Blake, *Disraeli* (1966) p. 363.

16. Greville Diary, 7 and 19 February 1855, *Greville Memoirs*, vii, pp. 243 and 247.

17. Russell to Minto, 22 July 1855, Minto Mss. 11775 fol. 102.

18. Clarendon to Granville, 16 September 1855, cit. H. Maxwell, *The Life of the Fourth Earl of Clarendon*, 2 vols (1913) ii, p. 92.

19. Bright to Ellice, 4 February 1857, Ellice Mss. 15006, fol.76.

20. Greville Diary, 3 April 1856, *Greville Memoirs*, viii, p. 41.

21. Robert Lowe, 'The Past Session and the New Parliament', *Edinburgh Review*, 204 (April 1857) p. 562.

22. Stanley journal, 22 March 1865, *Disraeli, Derby and the Conservative Party*, p. 230.

23. Duchess of Argyll (ed.), *Duke of Argyll: Autobiography and Memoirs*, 2 vols (1906) ii, p. 73.

24. Milner Gibson, 3 March 1857, *Hansard*, 3rd series, cxliv, 1745–52; Disraeli, 3 March 1857, *Hansard*, 3rd series, cxliv, 1834–40; Lowe, 'The Past Session', *Edinburgh Review* (April 1857) p. 562.

25. Palmerston to Granville, 24 and 25 March 1857, cit. H. C. F. Bell, *Lord Palmerston*, 2 vols (1936) ii, p. 170.

26. Clark to the Dean of Bristol, n.d. (? April 1857), Russell Mss. PRO 30/22/13/C, fol. 19; Dallas to Cass, 26 May 1857, cit. G. M. Dallas, *Letters from London*, ed. J. Dallas, 2 vols (1870) i. p. 262.

27. Granville to Canning, 24 October 1857, cit. Lord E. Fitzmaurice, *The Life of the Second Earl Granville*, 2 vols (1905) i, p. 262.

28. Trelawny diary, 5 July 1858 and 18 February 1859, cit. *Trelawny Diaries*, pp. 54 and 65.

29. Gladstone to Robertson Gladstone, 18 March 1858, cit. David Steele, 'Gladstone and Palmerston, 1855–65', in *Gladstone, Politics and Religion*, ed. P. J. Jagger (1985) p. 124.

30. Graham to Ellice, 7 January 1859, Ellice Mss. 15019, fol. 46.

31. Trelawny diary, 6 July 1858, cit. *Trelawny Diaries*, p. 55.

32. Gladstone to Aberdeen, 20 September 1868, Aberdeen Mss. 43071.

33. Bulwer Lytton to Gladstone, 1 February 1859, Lytton Mss. D/EK/028/2; Graham to Aberdeen, 12 December 1858, Aberdeen Mss. 43192, fol. 276.

34. Lytton, 22 March 1859, *Hansard*, 3rd series, CLIII, 542–9. Lytton's taunt prompted the Liberal Whip Hayter to walk out of the chamber amid much laughter.

35. Robert Blake, *The Conservative Party from Peel to Churchill* (1970) p. 46.

36. Stanley journal, 17 June 1861, *Disraeli, Derby and the Conservative Party*, p. 173.

37. Russell to Clarendon, 12 May 1859, Clarendon Mss. C104, fol. 44.

38. Greville diary, 9 June 1859, *Greville Memoirs*, viii, p. 257.

39. Stanley journal, July 1853, *Disraeli, Derby and the Conservative Party*, p. 111.

40. Gladstone to Heathcote, 16 June 1859, cit. J. Morley, *Life of Gladstone*, 3 vols (1906) i, pp. 627–8.

3 PALMERSTON AND LIBERALISM, 1859–65

1. Lord E. Fitzmaurice *The Life of the Second Earl Granville*, 2 vols (1905) i, p. 487.

2. Palmerston to Bruce, 26 November 1860, cit. E. D. Steele, *Palmerston and Liberalism, 1855–1865* (1991) p. 94.

3. Palmerston to Brand, 14 August 1863, cit. Steele, *Palmerston and Liberalism*, p. 6.

4. *The Times*, 19 October 1865, p. 9.
5. Palmerston, 7 May 1860, *Hansard*, 3rd series, CLVIII, 77, cit. Steele, *Palmerston and Liberalism*, p. 25.
6. Stanley journal, 18 March 1865, *Disraeli, Derby and the Conservative Party: Political Journals of Lord Stanley, 1848–69*, ed. J. Vincent (Brighton, 1978) p. 229.
7. Wodehouse journal, 9 March 1864, Kimberley Mss e2790; Cobden to Lindsay, 7 April 1857, cit. J. Morley, *Life of Cobden*, 2 vols (1879) ii, p. 662; Bright to Cobden, 2 November 1856, cit. Steele, *Palmerston and Liberalism*, p. 120.
8. *The Times*, 21 October 1865, p. 8.
9. Stanley journal, 17 August 1852, *Disraeli, Derby and the Conservative Party*, p. 80.
10. W. White, *The Inner Life of the House of Commons*, 2 vols (1897) i, p. 2; Palmerston to the Queen, 26 July 1861, *Queen Victoria's Letters*, ed. A. C. Benson and Lord Esher, 3 vols (1907) iii, p. 570; Trelawny diary, 7 June 1860, *Trelawny Diaries*, p. 128.
11. Acton to Simpson, 30 April 1862, cit. Angus Hawkins, *Parliament, Party and the Art of Politics in Britain, 1855–59* (1987) p. 278; Broughton diary, 25 June 1859, Broughton Mss. 43762, fol. 19.
12. *The Times*, 29 April 1863, cit. Steele, *Palmerston and Liberalism*, p. 126.
13. Gladstone memo, 20–25 May 1860, cit. *Prime Ministers' Papers: W. E. Gladstone, III, Autobiographical Memoranda, 1845–1866* (1978) p. 228.
14. See *Dod's Parliamentary Companion* for years 1852 and 1861.
15. Statistics drawn from T. A. Jenkins, *The Liberal Ascendancy, 1830–1886* (1994) pp. 104–5.
16. See Eugenio Biagini, *Liberty, Retrenchment and Reform: Popular Liberalism in the Age of Gladstone, 1860–1880* (1992) *passim*.
17. Wodehouse to Raikes Currie, 13 July 1861, cit. *Liberal by Principle: The Politics of John Wodehouse, 1st Earl of Kimberley, 1843–1902*, ed. John Powell, (1996) p. 56.
18. Stanley journal, 23 January 1862, *Disraeli, Derby and the Conservative Party*, p. 182.
19. Trelawny diary, 11 July 1860, *Trelawny Diaries*, p. 135.
20. Gladstone memo, 30 May 1860, cit. *Gladstone, III: Autobiographical Memoranda*, p. 236.
21. Derby to Jolliffe, 4 March 1857, Hylton Mss. 18/2, cit. Hawkins, *Parliament, Party and the Art of Politics*, p. 62.
22. Jenkins, *Liberal Ascendancy*, p. 90.

23. See J. Morley, *Life of Gladstone*, 3 vols (1903) ii, pp. 42–53. Comments on 'bourgeois triumphalism' were made by the *Saturday Review*, 10 August 1861, pp. 131–2.

24. Derby to Pakington, 28 May 1860 Derby Mss. 188/2. See also Angus Hawkins, 'Lord Derby', *Lords of Parliament, Studies, 1714–1914* (1995) p. 155.

25. Malmesbury to Derby, 6 February 1860, cit. Lord Malmesbury, *Memoirs of an Ex-Minister*, 2 vols (1884) ii, p. 215.

26. Stanley journal, 17 February 1861, *Disraeli, Derby and the Conservative Party*, p. 167.

27. Derby to M'Ghee, 21 February 1855, Derby Mss. 183/1.

28. Wodehouse journal, 26 January 1864, Kimberley Mss e2790; Derby, 4 February 1864, *Hansard*, 3rd series, CLXXXIII, 28.

29. Wodehouse journal, 4 August 1862, Kimberley Mss e2790; Stanley journal, 23 June 1864, *Disraeli, Derby and the Conservative Party*, p. 219.

30. *Ibid.*, 14 February 1865, p. 228.

31. *Ibid.*, 11 April 1864, p. 213.

32. H. C. G. Matthew, *Gladstone, 1809–1874* (1986) p. 139.

33. Trelawny diary, 11 May 1864, *Trelawny Diaries*, p. 278.

34. Stanley journal, 11 May 1864, *Disraeli, Derby and the Conservative Party*, p. 215.

35. *Ibid.*, 26 May 1864, p. 217.

36. Jenkins, *Liberal Ascendancy*, p. 103.

37. Jonathan Parry, *The Rise and Fall of Liberal Government in Victorian Britain* (1993) p. 194.

38. Palmerston to Brand, 3 August 1865, cit. Jenkins, *Liberal Ascendancy*, p. 101.

39. Keith Robbins, *John Bright* (1979) p. 175.

40. Shaftesbury diary, 25 October 1865, cit. E. Hodder, *Life and Work of the Earl of Shaftesbury* (1887) p. 604; Greville *Memoirs*, viii, p. 297.

41. Morley, *Gladstone*, ii, pp. 151–2.

42. Parry, *Rise and Fall of Liberal Government*, p. 192.

43. Derby to Disraeli, 24 July 1865, cit. R. Stewart, *The Foundation of the Conservative Party, 1830–1867* (1978) p. 352.

44. Disraeli to Lonsdale, 20 October 1865, cit. W. F. Monypenny and G. E. Buckle, *Life of Benjamin Disraeli*, 6 vols (1910–20) iv, p. 424.

45. A. P. Martin, *Life and Letters of Robert Lowe, Viscount Sherbrooke*, 2 vols (1893) ii, p. 243.

46. Algernon West, *Recollections*, 2 vols (1899) i, p. 306.

4 'A Leap in the Dark', 1866–8

1. Thomas Erskine May, *The Constitutional History of England since the Accession of George III, 1760–1860*, 3 vols (5th edn, 1875) iii, p. 75.
2. T. E. Kebbel (ed.), *Selected Speeches of the Earl of Beaconsfield*, 2 vols (1882) ii, pp. 470–89.
3. G. M. Trevelyan, *Life of John Bright* (1913) p. 354.
4. Disraeli to Derby, 6 August 1865, cit. W. F. Monypenny and G. E. Buckle, *The Life of Benjamin Disraeli*, 6 vols (1910–20) iv, p. 417 and *ibid.*, p. 431.
5. A. E. Gathorne Hardy, *Cranbrook: A Memoir*, 2 vols (1910) i, p. 188.
6. Malmesbury diary, 27 June 1866, *Memoirs of an Ex-Minister*, 2 vols (1994) ii, p. 357.
7. Stanley journal, 10 June and 23–6 July 1866, *Disraeli, Derby and the Conservative Party: Political Journal of Lord Stanley, 1849–69*, ed. J. Vincent (Brighton, 1978) pp. 260–1.
8. See T. A. Jenkins, *The Liberal Ascendancy, 1830–1886* (1994) p. 103.
9. Maurice Cowling, *1867: Disraeli, Gladstone and Revolution* (1967) p. 42.
10. Derby to Pakington, 4 December 1866, Derby Mss. 193/1.
11. R. Stewart, *The Foundation of the Conservative Party, 1830–1867* (1978) p. 366.
12. J. Morley, *Life of Gladstone*, 3 vols (1903) ii, p. 214.
13. F. B. Smith, *The Making of the Second Reform Bill* (1966) p. 148.
14. Stanley journal, 10 March 1867, *Disraeli, Derby and the Conservative Party*, p. 294.
15. Gladstone diary, 12 April 1867, *Gladstone Diaries*, ed. H. C. G. Matthew, vi, p. 513.
16. Stanley journal, 13 April 1867, *Disraeli, Derby and the Conservative Party*, p. 301.
17. See Maurice Cowling, *1867, Disraeli, Gladstone and Revolution* (1967) pp. 166–216.
18. Stanley journal, 6 May 1867, *Disraeli, Derby and the Conservative Party*, p. 307.
19. W. D. Jones, *Lord Derby and Victorian Conservatism* (1956) p. 317.
20. Cranborne, 'The Conservative Surrender', *Quarterly Review* (October 1867), cit. Paul Smith (ed.), *Lord Salisbury on Politics* (1972) p. 267.
21. H. Maxwell, *The Life of the Fourth Earl of Clarendon*, 2 vols (1913) ii, p. 334.

22. Stewart, *Foundation of the Conservative Party*, p. 367.
23. E. J. Evans, *The Forging of the Modern State: Early Industrial Britain, 1783–1870* (1983) p. 351.
24. *Ibid.*, pp. 351–3.
25. Hartington to Granville, 13 September 1868, cit. J. Parry, *Democracy and Religion: Gladstone and the Liberal Party, 1867–1875* (1986) p. 118.
26. John Walton, *The Second Reform Act* (1987) p. 49.
27. Bright at Edinburgh, *The Times*, 6 November 1868, p. 5.
28. Argyll to Dufferin, 18 August 1873, cit. Parry, *Democracy and Religion*, p. 119.
29. Layard to Gregory, 6 February 1873, cit. Parry, *Democracy and Religion*, p. 121.
30. Cranborne, 'The Conservative Surrender', *Quarterly Review* (October 1867) cit. Smith (ed.), *Salisbury on Politics*, pp. 260 and 274.

5   GLADSTONE AND LIBERALISM, 1868–74

1. W. E. Gladstone, *A Chapter of Autobiography* (1868) p. 58.
2. J. Morley, *Life of Gladstone*, 3 vols (1906) ii, p. 252; Gladstone diary, 29 December 1868, *Gladstone Diaries*, vi, p. 654.
3. See H. C. G. Matthew, *Gladstone, 1809–1874* (1986) pp. 142–8.
4. Disraeli at Aylesbury, *The Times*, 15 November 1861, p. 7.
5. Gladstone to wife, 12 October 1845, cit. Matthew, *Gladstone, 1809–1874*, p. 65.
6. Stanley journal, 24 July 1864, *Disraeli, Derby and the Conservative Party: Political Journals of Lord Stanley, 1849–69*, ed. J. Vincent (Brighton, 1978) p. 144.
7. Gladstone memo, n.d., cit. *Gladstone 1: Autobiographica*, p. 136.
8. See J. Parry, *Democracy and Religion: Gladstone and the Liberal Party, 1867–1875* (1986) p. 272.
9. Stanley journal, 6 March 1863, *Disraeli, Derby and the Conservative Party*, p. 197.
10. Trelawny diary, 16 February 1869, T. A. Jenkins (ed.), *The Parliamentary Diaries of Sir John Trelawny, 1868–73*, Royal Historical Society Camden Fifth Series, 3 (1994) p. 345.
11. T. A. Jenkins, *The Liberal Ascendancy, 1830–1886* (1994) pp. 126–7.
12. Morley, *Gladstone*, ii, p. 273.
13. Kimberley journal, 21 February 1870, Ethel Drus (ed.), *A Journal*

of Events during the Gladstone Ministry, 1868–74 by John, First Earl of Kimberley, Camden, series 21 (1958) p. 12.

14. See E. D. Steele, *Irish Land and British Politics* (1974).
15. Trelawny diary, 15 February 1870, *Diaries of Trelawny*, p. 375.
16. Derby journal, 17 February 1870, *The Diaries of the 15th Earl of Derby, 1869–1878*, Camden Fifth series, vol. 4 (1994) p. 50.
17. Trelawny diary, 23 February and 15 March 1870, *Diaries of Trelawny*, pp. 377 and 382.
18. Matthew, *Gladstone, 1809–1874*, p. 208.
19. Kimberley journal, 25 February 1871, Drus (ed.), *Kimberley Journal 1868–74*, p. 21.
20. Derby journal, 19 July 1870, *Diaries of Derby, 1869–1878*, p. 66.
21. See J. Parry, *The Rise and Fall of Liberal Government in Victorian Britain* (1993) p. 269.
22. Derby journal, 29 May 1870, *Diaries of Derby*, p. 60.
23. J. Winter, *Robert Lowe* (1976) p. 248.
24. Glyn to Gladstone, 27 May 1871, cit. Jenkins, *Liberal Ascendancy*, p. 139.
25. Stanley journal, 16 July 1869, *Disraeli, Derby and the Conservative Party*, p. 341.
26. Trelawny diary, 24 February 1871, *Diaries of Trelawny*, p. 420.
27. Derby journal, 2 July 1870, *Diaries of Derby*, p. 65.
28. Trelawny diary, 19 February 1872, *Diaries of Trelawny*, p. 448.
29. Derby journal, 29 April 1871, *Diaries of Derby*, pp. 78–9
30. Morley, *Gladstone*, ii, p. 369.
31. Grey to Denison, 22 November 1871, cit. Parry, *Democracy and Religion*, p. 323.
32. Derby journal, 6 September 1871 and 13 February 1872, *Diaries of Derby*, pp. 89 and 99.
33. Fortescue to Brereton, n.d. 1871, cit. Parry, *Democracy and Religion*, p. 324.
34. Trelawny diary, 14 March 1872, *Diaries of Trelawny*, p. 453.
35. Derby journal, 25 January 1872, *Derby Diaries*, p. 97.
36. Kimberley journal, 18 March 1873, Drus (ed.), *Kimberley Journal 1868–74*, p. 37.
37. Gladstone to Hartington, 16 January 1873, Gladstone Mss. 44144, fol. 25; Gladstone note, n.d., Gladstone Mss. 44640, fol. 199.
38. See Parry, *Democracy and Religion*, pp. 353–68.
39. Disraeli to Corry, 22 February 1873, Hughenden Mss. B/XX/D/200; Gathorne Hardy diary, 2 March 1873, N. Johnson (ed.),

Diary of Cranbrook (1981) p. 172; Gladstone to Ripon, 4 March 1873, *Gladstone Diaries*, viii, p. 296.

40. Gladstone note, n.d., *Gladstone Diaries*, viii, p. 299.
41. Trelawny diary, 11 March 1873, *Diaries of Trelawny*, p. 479.
42. Gladstone diary, 31 December 1872, *Gladstone Diaries*, viii, p. 265.
43. Gathorne Hardy diary, 4 March 1873, *Diary of Cranbrook*, p. 173; Northcote to Disraeli, 14 March 1873, Iddesleigh Mss. 50016, fol. 144.
44. Derby diary, 16 March 1873, *Diaries of Derby*, p. 132.
45. Richard Shannon, *The Age of Disraeli, 1868–1881: The Rise of Tory Democracy* (1992) p. 153.
46. Kimberley journal, 18 March 1873, Drus (ed.), *Kimberley Journal, 1868–74*, p. 37.
47. Trelawny diary, 15 May 1873, *Diaries of Trelawny*, p. 486.
48. Fortescue diary, 15 June 1873, cit. Jenkins, *Liberal Ascendancy*, p. 139.
49. Gladstone diary, 31 December 1873, *Gladstone Diaries*, viii, p. 433.
50. Disraeli to Grey de Wilton, 3 October 1873, W. F. Monypenny and G. E. Buckle, *The Life of Benjamin Disraeli*, 6 vols (1910–20) v, p. 262. Disraeli first used the phrase in his novel *Coningsby*.
51. Disraeli at Glasgow, *The Times*, 20 November 1873, p. 10.
52. Trelawny diary, 23 July 1873, *Diaries of Trelawny*, p. 499.
53. Gladstone to Bright, 14 August 1873, Morley, *Gladstone*, ii, p. 479.
54. Spofforth to Disraeli, 8 February 1874, cit. Shannon, *Age of Disraeli*, p. 178.
55. See Jenkins, *Liberal Ascendancy*, p. 146.
56. Parry, *Democracy and Religion*, p. 402.
57. Maurice Cowling, *1867: Disraeli, Gladstone and Revolution* (1967) p. 101.
58. Gladstone to Granville, 12 March 1874, Agatha Ramm (ed.), *The Political Correspondence of Gladstone and Lord Granville, 1868–1876*, Camden Society, 81–2 (1952) ii, p. 449.
59. Halifax to Northbrook, 12 August 1874, cit. Parry, *Democracy and Religion*, p. 422.
60. Gladstone to Granville, 27 January 1875, Ramm, *Gladstone–Granville Correspondence*, ii, p. 468.
61. A. G. Gardiner, *The Life of Sir William Harcourt*, 2 vols (1923) i, p. 270.
62. H. Reeve, 'Plain Whig Principles', *Edinburgh Review* (January 1880) p. 279.

6 DISRAELI AND CONSERVATISM, 1874–80

1. Derby journal, 26 August 1871, *Diaries of Derby*, p. 88.
2. Derby journal, 30 May 1870, *Diaries of Derby*, p. 61.
3. Gathorne Hardy diary, 3 February 1872, Johnson, *Gathorne Hardy Diary*.
4. Sir A. Hardinge, *Life of Fourth Earl of Carnarvon*, 3 vols (1925) iii, p. 46.
5. Derby journal, 1 January 1870, *Diaries of Derby*, p. 45.
6. W. F. Monypenny and G. E. Buckle, *The Life of Benjamin Disraeli*, 6 vols (1910–20) v, pp. 190–1.
7. T. E. Kebbel, *Selected Speeches of the Earl of Beaconsfield* (1882) ii, pp. 470–89.
8. Gorst to Noel, 22 September 1870, cit. Richard Shannon, *The Age of Disraeli, 1868–1881: The Rise of Tory Democracy* (1992) p. 120. See also E. J. Feuchtwanger, *Disraeli, Democracy and the Tory Party* (1968) pp. 105–31.
9. Derby journal, 25 March 1873, *Diaries of Derby*, p. 133.
10. Derby journal, 26 November 1877, *Diaries of Derby*, p. 457.
11. Disraeli, 14 July 1874, *Hansard*, CCXXI, 78–80.
12. Monypenny and Buckle, *Disraeli*, v, p. 327.
13. Gorst to Disraeli, 16 December 1874, cit. Shannon, *Age of Disraeli*, p. 205.
14. R. Blake, *Disraeli* (1966) p. 550. Paul Smith, *Disraelian Conservatism and Social Reform* (1967) remains essential reading on this topic.
15. *Ibid.*, p. 555.
16. Shannon, *Age of Disraeli*, p. 214.
17. *Ibid.*, pp. 214–15.
18. Disraeli at the Mansion House, *The Times*, 5 August 1875, p. 8.
19. Derby journal, 19 November 1874, *Diaries of Derby*, p. 182.
20. See T. A. Jenkins, *Gladstone, Whiggery and the Liberal Party, 1874–1886* (1988) p. 54.
21. Derby journal, 17 August 1875, *Diaries of Derby*, p. 238.
22. See P. R. Ghosh, 'Style and Substance in Disraelian Social Reform c.1860–80', in P. J. Waller (ed.), *Politics and Social Change in Modern Britain* (1987) pp. 59–90.
23. Derby journal, 17 December 1875, *Diaries of Derby*, p. 259.
24. Derby journal, 23 June, 6 November 1875 and 25 January 1876, *Diaries of Derby*, pp. 226, 250 and 273.

25. Marvin Swartz, *The Politics of British Foreign Policy in the Era of Disraeli and Gladstone* (1985) pp. 6–30.
26. Derby journal, 25 October 1877, *Diaries of Derby*, p. 448.
27. Derby journal, 24 October 1876, *Diaries of Derby*, p. 337.
28. John Vincent, *Disraeli* (1990) pp. 27–37.
29. Derby journal, 13 August 1876, *Diaries of Derby*, p. 319.
30. Derby journal, 29 November 1875, *Diaries of Derby*, p. 257.
31. Swartz, *Politics of British Foreign Policy*, pp. 31–50.
32. Derby journal, 29 August 1875, *Diaries of Derby*, p. 240.
33. See Vincent, *Disraeli*, pp. 86–7.
34. Richard Shannon, *Gladstone and the Bulgarian Agitation, 1876* (1963) p. 45.
35. Derby journal, 1 July 1876, *Diaries of Derby*, p. 306.
36. Derby journal, 10 August 1876, *Diaries of Derby*, p. 318.
37. Shannon, *Gladstone and the Bulgarian Agitation*, pp. 49–88.
38. E. Hodder, *Life and Work of the Earl of Shaftesbury* (1887) iii, p. 375.
39. Derby journal, 2 September 1876, *Diaries of Derby*, p. 323.
40. Gladstone to Granville, 29 August 1876, Agatha Ramm (ed.), *The Political Correspondence of Gladstone and Lord Granville, 1876–1886*, 2 vols (1962) i, p. 3.
41. Derby journal, 14 September 1876, *Diaries of Derby*, p. 326.
42. Derby journal, 30 June 1877, *Diaries of Derby*, p. 413.
43. Blake, *Disraeli*, p. 638 and Swartz, *Politics of British Foreign Policy*, p. 79.
44. Derby journal, 11 February 1878, *Diaries of Derby*, p. 505.
45. Shannon, *Age of Disraeli*, p. 348.
46. Jenkins, *Gladstone, Whiggery and the Liberal Party*, p. 128.
47. Monypenny and Buckle, *Disraeli*, vi, p. 524.
48. Blake, *Disraeli*, p. 717.
49. *Ibid.*, pp. 721–2.
50. H. C. G. Matthew, *Gladstone, 1875–1898*, p. 259.
51. Stanley journal, 1851, *Disraeli, Derby and the Conservative Party: Political Journals of Lord Stanley, 1848–69*, ed. J. Vincent (Brighton, 1978) p. 31.
52. Stanley journal, 23 January 1854, *ibid.*, p. 116.
53. P. R. Ghosh, 'Disraelian Conservatism: A Financial Approach', *English Historical Review*, 99 (1984) pp. 268–96.
54. Paul Smith, 'Disraeli's Politics', *Transactions of the Royal Historical Society*, 37 (1987) pp. 65–86; and Vincent, *Disraeli* (1990).

55. Stanley journal, 1857, *Disraeli, Derby and the Conservative Party*, p. 33; and Disraeli to Mrs Brydges Williams, 9 December 1862, Monypenny and Buckle, *Disraeli*, iv p. 331.

56. Stanley journal, 9 February 1853, *ibid.*, p. 96.

7 THE CRISIS OF LIBERALISM, 1880–6

1. T. A. Jenkins, *Gladstone, Whiggery and the Liberal Party, 1874–1886*, pp. 102–40.

2. Brand diary, 12 August 1875, cit. Jenkins, *Gladstone, Whiggery and the Liberal Party*, p. 54.

3. Gladstone to Granville, 7 October 1876, Agatha Ramm (ed.), *Gladstone–Granville Correspondence, 1876–1886* (1952) i, pp. 13–14.

4. Gladstone to Granville, 19 November 1876, *ibid.*, i, pp. 22–3.

5. Gladstone diary, 27 April 1899, *Gladstone Diaries*, ix, p. 214.

6. Hartington to Lady Waldegrave, 1 January 1878, cit. Jenkins, *Gladstone, Whiggery and the Liberal Party*, p. 68; *Leeds Mercury*, 11 February 1878, *ibid.*, p. 70.

7. Chamberlain to Harcourt, 4 November 1879, cit. Jenkins, *ibid.*, p. 98.

8. H. J. Hanham, *Elections and Party Management: Politics in the time of Disraeli and Gladstone* (1959) pp. 137–8.

9. Mundella to Leader, 5 and 23 June 1877, cit. Jenkins, *Gladstone, Whiggery and the Liberal Party*, p. 14.

10. Parry, *The Rise and Fall of Liberal Government in Victorian Britain* (1993) pp. 274–6.

11. Jenkins, *Gladstone, Whiggery and the Liberal Party*, p. 93.

12. *Ibid.*, pp. 98–100 and 109–12.

13. Gladstone diary, 28 December 1879, *Gladstone Diaries*, ix, p. 471.

14. See Parry, *Rise and Fall of Liberal Government*, p. 277.

15. Gladstone diary, 24 November 1879, *Gladstone Diaries*, ix, p. 461.

16. Christopher Harvie, 'Gladstonianism, the Provinces, and Popular Political Culture, 1860–1906', in R. Bellamy (ed.), *Victorian Liberalism* (1990) p. 158.

17. Gladstone diary, 4 and 8 December 1879, *Gladstone Diaries*, ix, pp. 464–5. See also H. C. G. Matthew, *Gladstone, 1875–1898*, pp. 41–60.

18. Jenkins, *Gladstone, Whiggery and the Liberal Party*, pp. 110–1.

19. *Ibid.*, p. 144.

20. Derby diary, 24 February 1883, cit. Jenkins, *Gladstone, Whiggery and the Liberal Party*, p. 142; Andrew Jones, *The Politics of Reform 1884* (1972) p. 13.

21. *Ibid.*, p. 194.

22. Gladstone diary, 20 May 1880, *Gladstone Diaries*, ix, p. 526.

23. Jenkins, *Gladstone, Whiggery and the Liberal Party*, p. 169.

24. T. A. Jenkins, *Parliament, Party and Politics in Victorian Britain* (1996) p. 169.

25. Gladstone to Granville, 11 November 1882, *Gladstone–Granville Correspondence, 1876–1886*, i, p. 451.

26. Parry, *Rise and Fall of Liberal Government*, pp. 242–3.

27. Derby diary, 27 November 1884, cit. Jenkins, *Gladstone, Whiggery and the Liberal Party*, p. 189.

28. Hartington to Spencer, 18 October 1883, cit. Jones, *Politics of Reform*, p. 24.

29. Brett to Wolseley, 9 January 1885, cit. Jones, *Politics of Reform*, p. 52; Gladstone to Granville, 3 January 1884, *Gladstone–Granville Correspondence, 1876–1886*, ii, p. 143.

30. Jones, *Politics of Reform*, p. 125.

31. Elliot Diary, 18 November 1884, cit. Jones, *Politics of Reform*, p. 196.

32. Derby to Granville, 5 January 1885, cit. Jenkins, *Gladstone, Whiggery and the Liberal Party*, p. 198.

33. Richard Shannon, *The Crisis of Imperialism, 1865–1914* (1976) p. 185.

34. J. L. Garvin, *Life of Joseph Chamberlain*, 6 vols (1932) i, p. 548.

35. T. A. Jenkins, *Liberal Ascendancy 1830–1886* (1994) p. 188.

36. A. B. Cooke and John Vincent, *The Governing Passion: Cabinet Government and Party Politics in Britain, 1885–86* (1974) p. 254.

37. Derby journal, 12 August 1876, *Diaries of Derby*, p. 318.

38. R. F. Foster, *Lord Randolph Churchill: A Political Life* (1981) p. 77.

39. *Ibid.*, p. 232.

40. Hamilton diary, 21 July 1885, W. R. Bahlman (ed.), *The Diary of Sir Edward Walter Hamilton 1885–1906* (1993) p. 1.

41. Gladstone diary, 9 October 1885, *Gladstone Diaries*, xi, p. 411. See also Matthew, *Gladstone, 1875–1898*, pp. 211–58.

42. Foster, *Churchill*, p. 238.

43. Matthew, *Gladstone, 1875–1898*, p. 240.

44. *Ibid.*, p. 248.

45. Gladstone diary, 7 June 1886, *Gladstone Diaries*, xi, p. 566.

46. Matthew, *Gladstone, 1875–1898*, p. 211.
47. John Morley, *Recollections*, 2 vols (1917) ii, p. 93.
48. Parry, *Rise and Fall of Liberal Government*, p. 306.
49. Jenkins, *Gladstone, Whiggery and the Liberal Party*, p. 292.
50. Parry, *Rise and Fall of Liberal Government*, p. 306.
51. Hamilton diary, 23 September 1888, Bahlman, *Diary of Sir Edward Hamilton, 1885–1906*, p. 81.

8 THE RISE OF THE PARTY SYSTEM

1. Sir Henry Maine, *Popular Government* (1885) p. 94.
2. H. J. Hanham, *Elections and Party Management: Politics in the Time of Disraeli and Gladstone* (1959) p. xxvi.
3. J. A. Froude, 'Party Politics', *Short Studies on Great Subjects*, 3 vols (1894) iii, p. 437.
4. *The Times*, 23 August 1878, p. 8.
5. W. H. Lecky, *Democracy and Liberty*, 2 vols (1896) i, p. 30.
6. John Robertson, *Chamberlain: A Study* (1905) pp. 23 and 26.
7. Selborne to Palmer, 10 January 1912, cit. D. G. Boyce (ed.), *The Crisis of British Unionism* (1987) p. 79. See also C. C. Weston, *The House of Lords and Ideological Politics* (1995).
8. Boyce, *Crisis of British Unionism*, p. 11.
9. Kimberley journal, 6 April 1887, Kimberley Mss. e2793; and Kimberley to Ripon, 3 October 1883, cit. J. Powell (ed.), *Liberal by Principle: The Politics of John Wodehouse, 1st Earl of Kimberley, 1843–1902* (1996) p. 167.
10. Derby journal, 14 January 1887, John Vincent (ed.), *The Later Derby Diaries: Home Rule, Liberal Unionism, and Aristocratic Life in Late Victorian England* (1981) p. 76.
11. Hugh Berrington, 'Partisanship and Dissidence in the Nineteenth-Century House of Commons', *Parliamentary Affairs*, 21:4 (1968) pp. 338–74.
12. A. Lang, *Sir Stafford Northcote, First Earl of Iddesleigh*, 2 vols (1890) ii, p. 150.
13. Dicey to Strachey, 29 January 1894, cit. G. R. Searle, *Country Before Party: Coalition and the Idea of 'National Government' in Modern Britain, 1885–1987* (1995) p. 23.
14. R. Wallace, in *Nineteenth Century*, 37 (1895), cit. H. J. Hanham, *The Nineteenth Century Constitution* (1969) p. 147.
15. *The Daily News*, 27 March 1901.

16. A. L. Lowell, *The Government of England*, 2 vols (1908) i, p. 440.
17. Gary Cox, *The Efficient Secret: The Cabinet and the Development of Political Parties in Victorian England* (1987) pp. 54 and 64.
18. During sensational trials from 1871 to 1874 one Arthur Orton, claiming to be heir to the rich Tichborne estates, became a *cause célèbre*. The most extensive protest movement of the 1860s and 1870s took up the populist call for 'fair play', in support of the claimant. See Rohan McWilliam, 'Radicalism and Popular Culture: The Tichborne Case and the Politics of "Fair Play", 1867–1886', in Eugenio Biagini and Alastair Reid (eds), *Currents of Radicalism* (1991) pp. 44–64.
19. E. A. Wasson, 'The House of Commons, 1660–1945: Parliamentary Families and the Political Elite', *English Historical Review*, 106 (1991) pp. 635–51.
20. W. C. Lubenow, *Parliamentary Politics and the Home Rule Crisis: The British House of Commons in 1886* (1988) p. 57.
21. Chamberlain to Churchill, 26 December 1886, cit. Searle, *Country Before Party*, p. 1.
22. See Searle, *Country Before Party*; and Alan Beattie, 'The Two-Party System: Room for Scepticism', in S. E. Finer (ed.), *Adversary Politics and Electoral Reform* (1975).

BIBLIOGRAPHY

1. Morley diary, 12–14 July 1892, *Gladstone Diaries*, xiii, p. 431.
2. J. Parry, *The Rise and Fall of Liberal Government in Victorian Britain* (1993) p. 306.
3. Derby journal, 30 January 1876, *Diaries of Derby*, p. 276.

ANNOTATED BIBLIOGRAPHY

Victorian party politics has been well served by historians. Much valuable primary material, journals, letters, and memoranda have been published. Most notably H. C. G. Matthew's monumental edition of *Gladstone's Diaries*, now in thirteen volumes plus an index, chronicles a remarkable career spanning over sixty years. This Bibliography identifies that literature of most immediate relevance to the themes discussed in previous chapters, but a general comment on recent views of the shape of Victorian politics may be helpful, in part to indicate where the narrative and analysis of this study confirms or diverges from some other recent perspectives. In particular, two general trends in recent writing can be seen: first, the argument for continuity where earlier historians saw disjunction, a perception generally affirmed in this study; secondly, a tendency to place both the formation and the demise of Liberalism earlier than previously portrayed by some, a perspective from which this study dissents.

Two strong strands of continuity in Victorian politics have recently been identified by historians. First, a continuity in popular radicalism bridging the age of Chartism, the 1830s and 1840s, with the rise of popular Liberalism during the 1860s and 1870s. A second strand is the continuing vitality of Whiggism through the 1870s and 1880s, again carrying forward traditions of the 1830s and 1840s. In *Currents of Radicalism* (1991), edited by Eugenio Biagini and Alastair Reid, it is argued that those who originally called themselves Chartists later became Liberal and then Labour activists. The call for open government, the rule of law, freedom from intervention both at home and abroad, and for individual liberty in the context of a community-centred democracy, remained central to popular radicalism both before and after 1848 – a conventional watershed in radical history supposedly marked by the demise of Chartism. Popular slogans such as 'anti-corruption' and 'fair play' continued to be directed against the enemies of 'the people', namely the landed aristocracy and the

Established Church. This view of the essential continuity of popular radicalism is elaborated further by Biagini in his *Liberty, Retrenchment and Reform: Popular Liberalism in the Age of Gladstone, 1860–1880* (1992).

Implicit in the approach of Biagini and others has been a rejection of more materialistic explanations of radicalism: the view, at its most crude, that economic conditions determined political consciousness along primarily class lines. Instead, attention has focused on the way in which language itself shaped consciousness. Rather than material conditions, it was radical rhetoric, with its roots in the polemic of earlier periods, that defined purposes and actions. This 'linguistic turn' draws on a seminal article by Gareth Stedman Jones, 'Rethinking Chartism', in *Languages of Class: Studies in English Working Class History, 1832–1982* (1983). The important work of Patrick Joyce, particularly *Visions of the People: Industrial England and the Question of Class, 1840–1914* (1991), has also asserted the primacy of linguistic reality to demonstrate that historical populist perceptions of the struggle for political entitlements, rather than class-consciousness, more accurately describes the aspirations of working men for much of this period. Thus radicalism could unite those whose material circumstances differed considerably. It was a struggle between 'the people' and the vested interests of the aristocracy, rather than a Marxian conflict between proletariat and bourgeoisie, that drove forward popular radicalism. The continuity of radicalism, its historical populist nature, and the importance of language in defining the purposes of political activism, have informed much of the foregoing narrative. Not until the 1880s do we see class-consciousness become a determining reality in party politics as, for example, the Liberal party became less a moral coalition than a class alliance.

The continued vitality of the Whig tradition has been helpfully explored by J. P. Parry, *Democracy and Religion: Gladstone and the Liberal Party, 1867–1875* (1986), and T. A. Jenkins, *Gladstone, Whiggery and the Liberal Party, 1874–1886* (1988). Parry laid out the ethical dimension of Whig ideology as the basis of a high-minded commitment to an administrative tradition protecting the rule of law, the sanctity of property, and the virtuous prosperity of the newly-enfranchised. Jenkins, warning against reading events of the 1870s backwards from the 1880s, argued that Gladstone's autocratic leadership and the Whig's defection in 1886 were not the inevitable and only path along which the Liberal party could have passed. Hartington and Granville did not see themselves solely as sectional leaders, but as a credible possible leadership for a broad spectrum of Liberal opinion. As well as revealing the vitality and relevance of Whiggism to the Liberal party of the 1870s and 1880s, this perspective emphasises how Gladstone differed in important ways from many within the party he led. Both the style and missionary zeal of mature Gladstonianism were often unpalatable to more sober-minded Whigs. Even the devoted acolyte and faithful biographer John Morley could come away from a dinner-table conversation with Gladstone about Scottish disestablishment, in July 1892, feeling there was something 'horrible and gruesome about it'.[1] Did Gladstone rescue or hijack the Liberal party? The answer, of course, is that he did both. By shaping Liberalism in his own image the charismatic Gladstone inspired a powerful popular movement and spearheaded fundamental and far-reaching reforms. He squared the political circle by bringing together an extraordinary range of progressive aspirations in an appeal at once both rational and impassioned. But by the mid-1880s he had also submerged other important aspects of the Liberal tradition. It remains important to remember that Gladstone guided his party along just one of the routes that Victorian Liberalism might have travelled.

The second trend in recent historical literature noted above is the shifting of Liberal genesis and demise to earlier in the period. Most important in this respect is J. P. Parry's *The Rise and Fall of Liberal Government in Victorian Britain* (1993). In this erudite work Parry places the beginning of Liberal government in the 1830s. The end of Liberal government comes in 1886 when Gladstone's behaviour turns the Liberals 'from a great party of government into a gaggle of outsiders'.[2] In between, Parry argues, Liberalism provided government by a propertied, rational, and civilised elite, ensuring economic and equitable administration and encouraging industrious and moral citizenship. This subtle analysis has much to offer students of the period. But where Parry sees Liberals, the present study more often prefers to see Whigs. Whigs did combine with radicals and Irish repealers in the Lichfield House Compact of 1835; but such alliance building was at the heart of those shifting party dynamics integral to parliamentary government. The concept of parliamentary government itself is presented in this study as a Whig belief, adopted by others, rather than a Liberal precept as argued by Parry. In the preceding narrative the formation of the Liberal party dates from 1859 rather than 1835 and the ministries of Lord Melbourne. Similarly, 1886 sees the passing of the vestiges of Whig parliamentary government, but it was not the death of Liberal government. The Liberal party, albeit significantly transformed, returned to power in 1906 and under Asquith saw through major and far-reaching reforms. Indeed, in the 1906 general election Liberals took 400 seats, while Conservative ranks were slashed to a mere 157 MPs. After 1903 it was Conservatism that was in crisis, desperately seeking responses to class, imperial, economic, and socialist challenges.

This book attempts to place the narrative of Victorian party politics in a constitutional context, exploring the changing *function* of parties, electors, and constituency organisation. Constitutional history has not been fashionable since the 1950s. But familiarity with the *structure* of politics and the *function* of elements within it is necessary to understanding the significance of events. This book is complemented, in this respect, by T. A. Jenkins's recent *Parliament, Party and Politics in Victorian Britain* (1996). Jenkins affirms many of the points made here, charting the triumph of 'partisan politics' by 1886. It is worth remembering, however, that the rehabilitation of constitutional history cannot be divorced from the interplay of contingent political forces. The structure was never rigid. The rules of the game, conceived as unwritten protocols or precedents, were constantly being transformed by the actual practice of politicians themselves. Party leaders were both referees and players. Here were created, for example, the intricate relations between 'high politics' and popular activism; the comfortable world of Pall Mall clubs and country houses, on the one hand, encountering the boisterous often rowdy arena of public meetings and electioneering on the other. Constitutional history should not be the stale recital of procedural inevitabilities. Moreover, politics, then as now, was an untidy practical activity. As different issues bore down on political discussion, so contingent interrelations between them arose, even between issues which, in substance, were distinct from each other. The responses to foreign crises, for example, were filtered through the lens of domestic preoccupations. Equally, the ambiguities of free choice played upon those courses considered, but not pursued. As in chess so in politics; the moves of an opponent anticipated, forestalled and never played can be as important as those actually made; while the impact of the unforeseen counters the historical temptation to over-rationalise. As Derby observed in his diary in January 1876:

> . . . when we reflect at all on the motives of others, we are apt to over-refine, and ascribe to deep-laid policy what is, as often as not, the result of mere laziness or blunder.[3]

The fascination of political history partly lies in unravelling the circumstantial and inadvertent from the thoughtful and deliberate.

A task in which undue cynicism can be as sentimental a pose as naive idealism.

For general works on this period students should turn to Norman Gash, *Aristocracy and People: Britain 1815–1865* (London, 1979); E. J. Evans, *The Forging of the Modern State: Early Industrial Britain, 1783–1870* (London, 1983); the stimulating overview by Michael Bentley, *Politics without Democracy, 1815–1914* (2nd edn, London, 1996); Martin Pugh, *The Making of Modern British Politics, 1867–1939* (2nd edn, London, 1993); Richard Shannon, *The Crisis of Imperialism, 1865–1914* (London, 1974); and Brian Harrison, *The Transformation of British Politics, 1860–1995* (Oxford, 1996). On the Liberal party there is J. P. Parry, *The Rise and Fall of Liberal Government in Victorian Britain* (New Haven, CT, 1993); Michael Bentley, *The Climax of Liberal Politics: British Liberalism in Theory and Practice, 1868–1918* (London, 1987); and T. A. Jenkins, *The Liberal Ascendancy, 1830–1886* (London, 1994). For the Conservatives there is Robert Blake, *The Conservative Party from Peel to Thatcher* (London, 1985); and Bruce Coleman, *Conservatism and the Conservative Party in Nineteenth-Century Britain* (London, 1988). Two helpful short introductions to radicalism are Paul Adelman, *Victorian Radicalism: The Middle Class Experience, 1830–1914* (London, 1984); and Edward Royle, *Radical Politics 1790–1900: Religion and Unbelief* (London, 1971). For religion and politics during this period see Owen Chadwick, *The Victorian Church*, 2 vols (London, 1966–70), and G. I. T. Machin's two studies, *Politics and the Churches in Great Britain, 1832 to 1868* (Oxford, 1977) and *Politics and the Churches in Great Britain, 1869 to 1921* (Oxford, 1987). Social change is analysed by Jose Harris, *Private Lives, Public Spirit: Britain, 1870–1914* (Oxford, 1993), and older interpretations are challenged by Patrick Joyce in *Visions of the People: Industrial England and the Question of Class, 1840–1914* (Oxford, 1991). See also John Belchem, *Class, Party and the Political System in Britain, 1867–1914* (London, 1990). R. Foster, *Modern Ireland, 1600–1972* (London, 1988), and Theodore Hoppen, *Ireland since 1800: Conflict and Conformity* (London, 1989), are essential reading on Ireland, to be supplemented by Theodore Hoppen, *Elections, Politics and Society in Ireland, 1832–1885* (Oxford, 1984). Kenneth Bourne, *The Foreign Policy of Victorian England, 1830–1902* (Oxford, 1970) remains the best survey of diplomatic relations. Useful collections of essays are R. Robson (ed.), *Ideas and Institutions of Victorian Britain* (London, 1967); Michael Bentley and John Stevenson (eds), *High and Low Politics in Modern Britain* (Oxford, 1983); Bruce Kinzer (ed.), *The Gladstonian Turn of Mind* (Toronto, 1985); and Peter Jagger (ed.), *Gladstone, Politics and Religion* (London, 1985).

As well as Walter Bagehot's contemporary *The English Constitution*, ed. with an intro. by R. H. S. Crossman (London, 1963), important recent guides to Victorian constitutionalism are T. A. Jenkins, *Parliament, Party and Politics in Victorian Britain* (Manchester, 1996); G. H. Le May, *The Victorian Constitution* (London, 1979); Gary Cox, *The Efficient Secret: The Cabinet and the Development of Political Parties in Victorian England* (Cambridge, 1987); and the documents and commentary in H. J. Hanham, *The Nineteenth-Century Constitution* (Cambridge, 1969). The landmark study *Elections and Party Management: Politics in the Time of Disraeli and Gladstone* (London, 1959) by H. J. Hanham remains seminal. This present book develops some of the arguments put forward in my ' "Parliamentary Government" and Victorian Political Parties, *c*.1830–*c*.1880', *English Historical Review*, CIV (1989) pp. 638–69. The article by Hugh Berrington, 'Partisanship and Dissidence in the Nineteenth-Century House of Commons', *Parliamentary Affairs*, XXI (1968) pp. 338–74, contains many important observations.

For mid-Victorian politics see Robert Stewart, *The Foundation of the Conservative Party, 1830–1867* (London, 1978); J. B. Conacher, *The Aberdeen Coalition, 1852–1855* (Cambridge, 1968); and Angus Hawkins' *Parliament, Party and the Art of Politics in Britain, 1855–59* (London, 1987). Two helpful studies of mid-Victorian radicalism have recently appeared, Miles Taylor, *The Decline of British Radicalism, 1847–1860* (Oxford, 1995); and G. R. Searle, *Entrepreneurial Politics in Mid-Victorian Britain* (Oxford, 1993). Other significant work is in article form, H. C. G. Matthew, 'Disraeli, Gladstone and the Politics of Mid-Victorian Budgets', *Historical Journal*, 22:3 (1979) pp. 615–43; P. M. Gurowich, 'The Continuation of War by Other Means: Party and Politics, 1855–1865', *Historical Journal*, 27:3 (1984) pp. 603–31; and John Vincent, 'The Parliamentary Dimension of the Crimean War', *Transactions of the Royal Historical Society*, 31 (1981) pp. 31–49. Angus Hawkins, 'Lord Derby', in R. W. Davis (ed.), *Lords of Parliament: Studies, 1714–1914* (Stanford, 1995) pp. 134–62, examines the unduly neglected 14th Earl of Derby.

The brilliant analysis in John Vincent, *The Formation of the Liberal Party, 1857–1868* (London, 1966) is a necessary starting point for understanding mid-Victorian Liberalism. For Palmerston's place in party politics see E. D. Steele, *Palmerston and Liberalism, 1855–1865* (Cambridge, 1991). The biography by H. C. F. Bell, *Lord Palmerston*, 2 vols (London, 1936) repays attention. An informative backbench viewpoint emerges from T. A. Jenkins (ed.), *The Parliamentary Diaries of Sir John Trelawny, 1858–1865*, Royal Historical Society, Camden Fourth

Series, 40 (1990), and an intelligent Conservative perspective in John Vincent (ed.), *Disraeli, Derby and the Conservative Party: The Political Journals of Lord Stanley, 1849–69* (Brighton, 1978). On the 1867 Reform Act two contrasting studies hold the ground unchallenged, F. B. Smith, *The Making of the Second Reform Act* (Cambridge, 1966); and Maurice Cowling, *1867: Disraeli, Gladstone and Revolution* (Cambridge, 1967); the latter an astute 'high political study'.

Gladstonian Liberalism has produced much excellent recent scholarship, in part stimulated by the completion of the *Gladstone Diaries* (Oxford, 1968–94) edited by H. C. G. Matthew. Most important are J. P. Parry, *Democracy and Religion: Gladstone and the Liberal Party, 1867–75* (Cambridge, 1986); Eugenio Biagini, *Liberty, Retrenchment and Reform: Popular Liberalism in the Age of Gladstone, 1860–1880* (Cambridge, 1992); and the still pertinent Richard Shannon, *Gladstone and the Bulgarian Agitation* (Brighton, 1975). For biographical treatments of Gladstone during this period see H. C. G. Matthew, *Gladstone, 1809–1874* (Oxford, 1986); and *Gladstone 1875–1898* (Oxford, 1995) – a compilation of his masterful introductions for the diaries – and the shorter study by Agatha Ramm, *William Ewart Gladstone* (Cardiff, 1989). Rich documentary editions for Gladstone's first government are Agatha Ramm (ed.), *The Political Correspondence of Mr. Gladstone and Lord Granville, 1868–1876*, Royal Historical Society, Camden Third Series, 81–2 (1952); Ethel Drus (ed.), *A Journal of Events during the Gladstone Ministry, 1868–74, by John, First Earl of Kimberley*, Royal Historical Society, Camden Series, 21 (1958); and the backbench observations in T. A. Jenkins (ed.), *The Parliamentary Diaries of Sir John Trelawny, 1868–73*, Royal Historical Society, Camden Fifth Series, 3 (1994) pp. 329–504.

For Disraelian Conservatism see Richard Shannon, *The Age of Disraeli, 1868–1881: The Rise of Tory Democracy* (London, 1992), Paul Smith, *Disraelian Conservatism and Social Reform* (Cambridge, 1967) and E. J. Feuchtwanger, *Disraeli, Democracy and the Tory Party* (Oxford, 1968). Conservative foreign policy is discussed in Richard Millman, *Britain and the Eastern Question, 1875–1878)* (Oxford, 1979) and Marvin Swartz, *The Politics of British Foreign Policy in the Era of Disraeli and Gladstone* (London, 1985). Robert Blake's biography *Disraeli* (London, 1966) remains a classic, but needs to be read in the light of Paul Smith, *Disraeli: A Brief Life* (Cambridge, 1996). Other short studies of Disraeli that have much to say are John Vincent, *Disraeli* (London, 1990); T. A. Jenkins, *Disraeli and Victorian Conservatism* (London, 1996); and Ian Machin, *Disraeli* (London, 1995). Two Conservative diaries provide valuable insights, John Vincent (ed.), *A Selection from the Diaries of the*

15th Earl of Derby between 1869 and 1878, Royal Historical Society, Camden Fifth Series, 4 (1994); and Nancy Johnson (ed.), *The Diary of Gathorne Hardy, Later Lord Cranbrook, 1866–1892: Political Selections* (Oxford, 1981).

The dynamics of Liberal politics at different levels by the late 1870s are examined by D. A. Hamer, *The Politics of Electoral Pressure* (Brighton, 1977); the same author's *Liberal Politics in the Age of Gladstone and Rosebery* (Oxford, 1972); and T. A. Jenkins, *Gladstone, Whiggery and the Liberal Party, 1874–86* (Oxford, 1988). Andrew Jones, *The Politics of Reform, 1884* (Cambridge, 1972) is rich in insight and sharp in judgement; while A. B. Cooke and John Vincent, *The Governing Passion: Cabinet Government and Party Politics, 1885–6* (Brighton, 1974) is a dazzling analysis with implications reaching beyond its focus on the Home Rule crisis. Also essential for this period is W. C. Lubenow, *Parliamentary Politics and the Home Rule Crisis: The British House of Commons in 1886* (Oxford, 1988). *The Political Correspondence of Mr Gladstone and Lord Granville, 1876–1886*, Agatha Ramm (ed.), 2 vols (Oxford, 1962) is an important documentary source. There are two helpful biographies of Chamberlain, by Richard Jay, *Joseph Chamberlain* (Oxford, 1981) and Peter Marsh, *Joseph Chamberlain: An Entrepreneur in Politics* (1994).

Late-Victorian Conservatism is well-served by Roy Foster's scintillating biography *Lord Randolph Churchill: A Political Life* (Oxford, 1981); Peter Marsh, *The Discipline of Popular Government: Lord Salisbury's Domestic Statecraft, 1881–1902* (Brighton, 1978); and Paul Smith (ed.), *Lord Salisbury on Politics: A Selection from his Articles in the Quarterly Review, 1860–1883* (Cambridge, 1972). Essential reading is the analysis in E. H. H. Green, *The Crisis of Conservatism: The Politics, Economics and Ideology of the British Conservative Party, 1880–1914* (London, 1995).

INDEX

Index

and Palmerston, 56, 57, 58, 60,
  61, 62, 66; death
  of, 107–8; second
  ministry, 92, 93, 94–5
and parliamentary
  reform, 110–11, 113, 114,
  117–18, 119–20, 122,
  124–5
  Reform Act (1867), 126–7,
  128, 129–30, 132, 184
on Peel, 32–3
and the radicals, 36
reform (1870s), 186–95
refusal to form a government
  (1873), 167–8
and religion, 97, 145–6, 147,
  176, 182, 188–9
and the traditions of the past, 6
Sybil, 192
Dissent see Nonconformity
Duncombe, Thomas
  (1796–1861), 88
Dunkellin, Lord (1827–67), 109,
  118

Edinburgh Review, 9, 10, 14, 25–6,
  29, 37, 62, 174–5, 177
on the Midlothian
  campaign, 224
education, elementary education
  reform, 141, 145, 154–6,
  162, 169–70, 191
Egyptian crisis, 231–2
Elcho, Lord (1818–1914), 109,
  117, 118, 124, 129
election manifestos, 138–9
elections
  by-elections
  1871, 161
  1873–4, 170
and voting behaviour, 134, 290

elections, general
  1857, 62–4, 135
  1859, 73–5
  1865, 105–6, 121–2
  1868, 112, 134, 136, 144, 147–9
  1874, 172–5, 178, 184, 268
  1880, 209–10, 217, 222
  1885, 248
  1886, 253
  1892, 282
  1895, 271, 282
  1900, 263–4
  mid-Victorian, 22–4
  and party government, 283–4
  and the secret ballot, 141, 163
electoral mandate, 282–3
electoral register, and the Reform
  Act (1867), 133
Ellenborough, Lord
  (1790–1871), 67
Ellice, Edward (1781–1863), 72
Elliot, Sir Henry (1817–1907),
  199, 200, 203
Engels, Friedrich (1820–95), 136,
  241
English Constitution, The
  (Bagehot), 1
Erskine May, Sir Thomas see
  May, Sir Thomas Erskine

Fabian Society, 286, 288
factory legislation, 189, 193–4
Fawcett, Henry (1833–84), 85,
  105, 166, 169
Fife, Lord, 282
Foreign Secretaryship, 18
Forster, W. E. (1818–86), 149–50,
  154, 155, 170, 176, 177, 226,
  228
  as Irish Chief Secretary, 228,
  230

323